D1123675

History Alive!®
The Ancient World

Chief Executive Officer: Bert Bower
Chief Operating Officer: Amy Larson
Director of Curriculum: Liz Russell
Managing Editor: Laura Alavosus
Editorial Project Manager: Nancy Rogier
Project Editor: Pat Sills
Copyeditor: Susan Arnold
Editorial Associates: Anna Embree, Sarah Sudano
Production Manager: Lynn Sanchez
Art Director: John F. Kelly
Senior Graphic Designer: Christy Uyeno
Graphic Designers: Sarah Wildfang, Don Taka, Victoria Philp
Photo Edit Manager: Margee Robinson
Photo Editor: Diane Austin
Production Project Manager: Eric Houts
Art Editor: Mary Swab
Audio Director: Katy Haun

TCi™

Teachers' Curriculum Institute
PO Box 1327
Rancho Cordova, CA 95741

Customer Service: 800-497-6138
www.teachtci.com

ISBN 978-1-58371-901-5
9 10 11 12 13 14 15 -WC- 21 20 19 18 17 16

Manufactured by Webcrafters, Inc., Madison, WI
United States of America, June, 2016, Job# 126217

SUSTAINABLE
FORESTRY
INITIATIVE
Certified Sourcing
www.sfiprogram.org
SFI-00617

Program Director
Bert Bower

Program Author
Wendy Frey

Creative Development Manager
Kelly Shafsky

Contributing Writers
John Bergez
Mark Falstein
Diane Hart
Marisa A. Howard
Amy Joseph

Curriculum Developers
Joyce Bartky
April Bennett
Nicole Boylan
Terry Coburn
Julie Cremin
Erin Fry
Amy George
Anne Maloney
Steve Seely
Nathan Wellborne

Reading Specialist
Kate Kinsella, Ed.D
Reading and TESOL Specialist
San Francisco State University

Teacher Consultants
Melissa Aubuchon
Indian Trail Middle School
Plainfield, Illinois

Anthony Braxton
Cruickshank Middle School
Merced, California

Amy George
Weston Middle School
Weston, Massachusetts

Randi Gibson
Stanford Middle School
Long Beach, California

Lisa Macurak
New Windsor Middle School
New Windsor, Maryland

Sherry Owens
Lubbock Independent School
District
Lubbock, Texas

Scholars
Dr. Anthony Bulloch
University of California, Berkeley

Dr. Mark W. Chavalas
University of Wisconsin, La Crosse

Dr. Eun Mi Cho
California State University Sacramento

Dr. Steve Farmer
Palo Alto, California

Dr. Bruce Grelle
California State University Chico

Dr. David N. Keightley
University of California, Berkeley

Dr. Brij Khare
California State University San Bernardino

Dr. Gary Miles
University of California, Santa Cruz

Dr. Daniel Veidlinger
California State University Chico

Dr. Jed Wyrick
California State University Chico

Dr. Joel Zimbelman
California State University Chico

Assessment Consultants

Denny Chandler
*Curriculum and Assessment
Specialist*
Cold Spring, Kentucky

Julie Weiss
*Curriculum and Assessment
Specialist*
Elliot, Maine

Music Consultant

Melanie Pinkert
Music Faculty
Montgomery College, Maryland

Cartographer

Mapping Specialists
Madison, Wisconsin

Internet Consultant

Amy George
Weston, Massachusetts

Diverse Needs Consultants

Erin Fry
Glendora, California

Colleen Guccione
Naperville, Illinois

Cathy Hix
Swanson Middle School
Arlington, Virginia

UNIT 1

Early Humans and the Rise of Civilization

UNIT 2

Ancient Egypt and the Middle East

UNIT 3

Ancient India

UNIT 4

Ancient China

UNIT 5

Ancient Greece

UNIT 6

Ancient Rome

Maps

Diagrams and Tables

Selected Primary Source Quotations

Unit 1

Early Humans and the Rise of Civilization

The sun sets over the African savannah. Scientists have found many remains of early hominids in Africa.

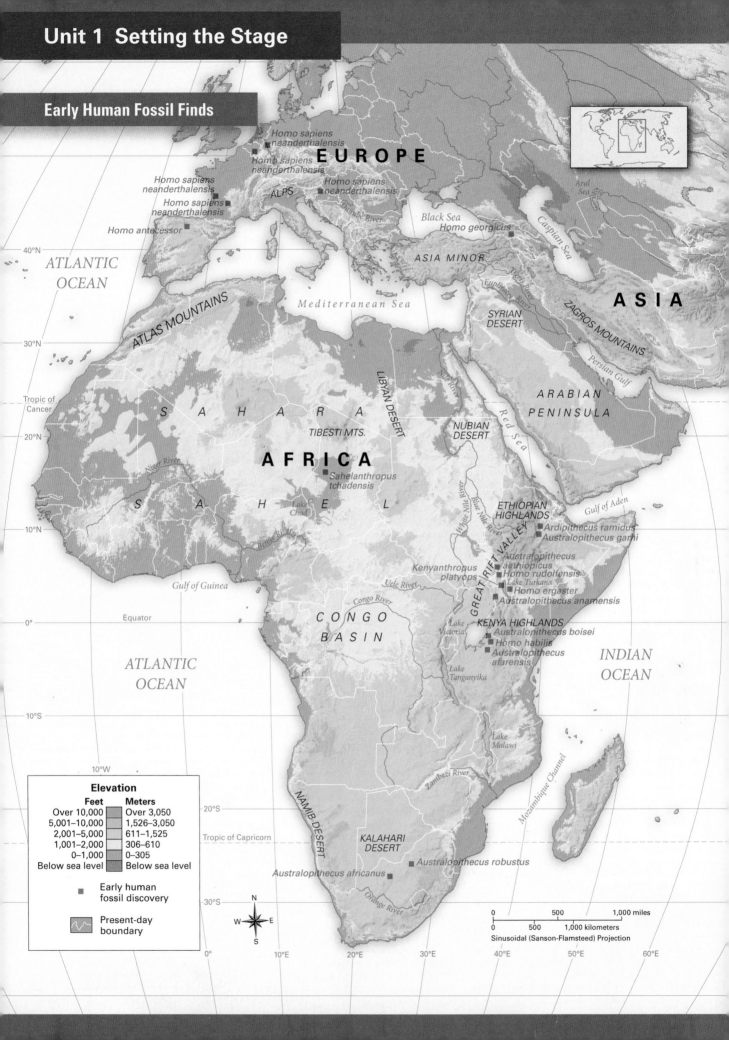

EUROPE

Homo sapiens neanderthalensis

Homo sapiens neanderthalensis

Homo sapiens neanderthalensis

Homo sapiens neanderthalensis

ALPS

Homo sapiens neanderthalensis

Homo antecessor

Danube River

Black Sea

Homo georgicus

Aral Sea

Caspian Sea

ASIA MINOR

ASIA

40°N

ATLANTIC OCEAN

Mediterranean Sea

ATLAS MOUNTAINS

SYRIAN DESERT

ZAGROS MOUNTAINS

30°N

Euphrates River

Tigris River

ARABIAN PENINSULA

Persian Gulf

Tropic of Cancer

S A H A R A

LIBYAN DESERT

Nile River

NUBIAN DESERT

Red Sea

20°N

TIBESTI MTS.

AFRICA

Sahelanthropus tchadensis

S   A   H   E   L

Niger River

Lake Chad

ETHIOPIAN HIGHLANDS

Gulf of Aden

Ardipithecus ramidus

Australopithecus garhi

10°N

Benue River

White Nile River

Blue Nile River

Australopithecus aethiopicus

Kenyanthropus platyops

Homo rudolfensis

Lake Turkana

Homo ergaster

Australopithecus anamensis

Uele River

GREAT RIFT VALLEY

Gulf of Guinea

Congo River

CONGO BASIN

KENYA HIGHLANDS

Australopithecus boisei

Homo habilis

Australopithecus afarensis

INDIAN OCEAN

Equator

0°

Lake Victoria

ATLANTIC OCEAN

Lake Tanganyika

10°S

Lake Malawi

10°W

Zambezi River

NAMIB DESERT

Mozambique Channel

Elevation

Feet	Meters
Over 10,000	Over 3,050
5,001–10,000	1,526–3,050
2,001–5,000	611–1,525
1,001–2,000	306–610
0–1,000	0–305
Below sea level	Below sea level

20°S

Tropic of Capricorn

KALAHARI DESERT

Australopithecus robustus

■ Early human fossil discovery

Australopithecus africanus

Present-day boundary

Orange River

30°S

N W E S

0   500   1,000 miles

0   500   1,000 kilometers

Sinusoidal (Sanson-Flamsteed) Projection

0°   10°E   20°E   30°E   40°E   50°E   60°E

Early Humans and the Rise of Civilization

Our study of the ancient world begins with a look at the roots of human life and the beginnings of civilization. Many scientists believe that the earliest ancestors of humans first appeared in eastern Africa. Scientists have studied fossils and bones left by these early humans. This evidence has led scientists to believe that five major groups of early humans developed over millions of years. The places where the remains of these groups were discovered are shown on the map on the opposite page.

From these beginnings, humans spread to other parts of the world. Over time, these early people learned to grow crops. The first human settlements grew in regions where people found the resources they needed to survive.

One of these regions, in North Africa, is mostly desert. Through the desert flows the Nile River—the longest river in the world. The Nile had an enormous impact on the development of civilization. The Nile River begins in East Africa. The river flows north and empties into the Mediterranean Sea. Along the way, the Nile picks up lots of rich, dark soil. Each year, the river overflows its banks, flooding the land around it. Beginning in ancient times, the floodwaters left behind soil that was perfect for growing crops. This factor greatly influenced early human settlement in the Nile River valley.

Another region in which ancient people settled was in an area of land stretching from the Persian Gulf to the Mediterranean Sea. This region is known as the Fertile Crescent because of its rich (fertile) soil and its curved (crescent) shape when drawn on a map.

Ancient people living in the Fertile Crescent were able to grow plenty of wheat and barley. No longer needing to move constantly in search of food, people could settle down and build communities. Permanent shelters and a dependable food supply allowed people to advance in important ways. They learned to make stone and metal tools; to raise animals such as cows, sheep, and pigs; and to develop a system of writing. In time, settlements began trading with nearby groups. An exchange of people, goods, and ideas blossomed. The first civilizations had begun.

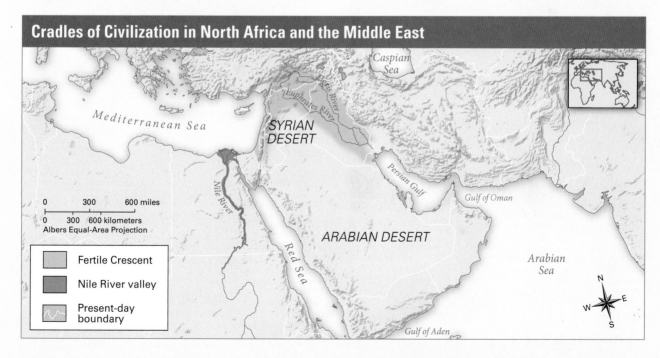

Cradles of Civilization in North Africa and the Middle East

Caspian Sea

Euphrates River

Tigris River

Mediterranean Sea

SYRIAN DESERT

Persian Gulf

Gulf of Oman

0 300 600 miles

0 300 600 kilometers
Albers Equal-Area Projection

Nile River

Red Sea

ARABIAN DESERT

Arabian Sea

Gulf of Aden

- Fertile Crescent
- Nile River valley
- Present-day boundary

Chapter 1

Investigating the Past

How do social scientists interpret the past?

1.1 Introduction

Welcome to the world of ancient history. Studying history involves investigating what happened in the past and why. Ancient history concerns the distant past, from the earliest humans through the first great civilizations.

How can we learn about events that happened so long ago? People who study history are a lot like detectives conducting an investigation. They ask questions, study the evidence for clues, and form hypotheses (educated guesses).

This scientist examines an ancient painting that was found in a cave in California.

Our investigation of the ancient past starts near the very beginning of human history. What was life like long, long ago?

One amazing clue about life long ago was discovered at Lascaux (lah-SKOH), France, by four teenagers. On September 12, 1940, the boys found a cave. Covering the walls and ceiling of the cave were paintings of animals. The paintings seemed very old. Who had created them? What did they mean?

How would you solve a mystery like this one? The clues are centuries old, and the witnesses are long gone. You might need the help of an expert detective, but who would that be?

In this chapter, you'll meet three kinds of experts who study the past. Then you'll look at some fascinating examples of cave art to see what this evidence can teach us about life long ago.

◀ Prehistoric paintings of bulls were found in a cave in Lascaux, France.

archaeologist an expert who studies the past by examining objects that people have left behind

historian an expert who studies and records the past

geographer an expert who studies and creates maps of Earth's natural and human-made features

artifact an object made or used by people in the past

prehistoric before written history

Archaeologists look for artifacts to learn about the past.

1.2 Detectives Who Study the Past

Scholars who study human society are called social scientists. Many social scientists can help us study the past. Among these "history detectives" are **archaeologists, historians,** and **geographers**.

Archaeologists: Digging Up the Past
Archaeologists study the past by examining objects that people have left behind. These **artifacts** are anything made or used by humans, such as clothing, tools, weapons, and coins. When archaeologists discover a place that has artifacts, they ask questions like these: Who lived in this place? When did they live here? What were they like? Then archaeologists study the artifacts for clues.

Historians: Recording the Past
Historians are the recorders of the past. Human beings have been around for such a long time that historians tend to focus mostly on the last few thousand years, when people began leaving written records. Historians want to answer this question: What happened in the past? To find out, they study all kinds of artifacts and documents. They read diaries and letters. Besides asking what happened in the past, historians try to understand why events happened the way they did.

Geographers: Mapping the Past
Geographers study the natural **features** of Earth, such as water, landforms, plants, and animals. Geographers also look at human-made features, such as towns, roads, bridges, and dams. These scientists help us answer such questions as: Where did people live? How did they use their **environment** to survive? Geographers often create maps to show what they have learned.

Social scientists who study **prehistoric** history face a unique challenge—a lack of evidence from this period. In fact, huge gaps of time have no evidence at all. Therefore, scientists may come up with different answers or theories about how humans came to be.

1.3 Cave Art: Treasures of the Past

Cave paintings like those at Lascaux, France, provide clues about what life was like in prehistoric times, before writing was invented. Caves with paintings thousands of years old have been found all over the world. Some paintings show what kinds of animals roamed the Earth and what methods people used to hunt them. Often, the paintings offer hints about people's beliefs.

Many of the rooms decorated with paintings are deep inside the caves. Scientists guess that cave artists used torches to work in these dark places. Some paintings are very large in size and taller than a person's height. Some paintings are found on high ceilings. Scientists guess that prehistoric artists built scaffolding, or planks raised above the floor, to reach the highest places.

Caves have also provided clues in the form of artifacts. Scientists have found bits of rope, lamps for burning animal fat, and tools for painting and engraving. Cave paintings and artifacts are amazing treasures that can help answer many questions about how humans lived in ancient times. But, as you will see, these treasures also raise new questions for scientists to puzzle over.

Cave painters developed a variety of methods for applying paint to the walls of a cave. This museum exhibit shows one such technique.

1.4 Cave Painting of a Human

The painting below was found inside the cave at Lascaux, France. It was painted between 11,000 and 18,000 years ago.

The painting shows a scene from a hunt. The man is about to be gored (pierced by the horn of an animal). The animal, a woolly mammoth or a bison (a kind of buffalo), is wounded. There is a spear in its side, and the animal's insides spill to the ground. The man lies in front of the wounded animal. He wears a mask that looks like a bird. Next to the man is a long stick with a bird on top. The stick is probably a spear thrower, a kind of handle used to hurl a spear.

Paintings of humans are rare in cave art. Notice the simple drawing of the man, like a stick figure. The animal is much more realistic.

Many social scientists think that this painting was created as part of a hunting **ritual**. The artist may have been asking for a successful hunt. It is also possible that the painting is a record of an actual event, or it may simply be a decoration.

This hunting scene may show items used in special ceremonies. Notice the man's bird mask and the bird on top of the stick.

1.5   Cave Painting of Animals

This image is a copy of one found at Lascaux. The real painting lies in a part of the cave that has been closed to protect the art.

The painting was created about 17,000 years ago. It shows many prehistoric animals, such as bulls, bison, and horses.

The painters used the cave's uneven walls as part of their composition. At the lower left, a ledge juts out from the wall. The artists painted the horses to look as though they were running along it.

Scientists have many ideas about why animal paintings were created. One idea is that the artists were trying to capture the "magical powers" of certain animals. Another idea is that the painters believed in the spirit world and were creating art to honor or influence their gods. Some scientists speculate that caves were places of worship and that paintings were used in rituals or ceremonies.

Look at the bull in the center of this painting. Do you see how the neck stretches out, as though the bull were running away?

1.6   Cave Painting of Shapes and Handprints

This painting is in a cave in Argentina, South America. It shows a circular shape, a sticklike animal, and several handprints.

Paintings of shapes and handprints are fairly common in cave art. Their meaning, though, is a bit of a mystery. Many scientists believe that handprints were a way for artists to sign their paintings. Some scientists think that **geometric** shapes had special meanings in rituals.

Researchers tried singing inside one painted cave in France. They discovered that the sound was loudest in the painted areas. Their guess is that those areas were used for special gatherings.

The handprints seen in this cave painting are very small. Prehistoric people were probably smaller in size than people are today.

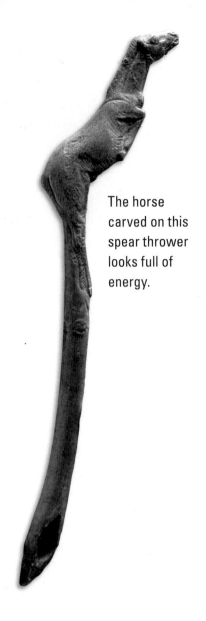

The horse carved on this spear thrower looks full of energy.

1.7 Spear Thrower

This prehistoric spear thrower was found in France. Made from a reindeer antler bone, it measures 10 inches long. It was probably made about 18,000 years ago.

The spear thrower has a leaping horse carved into the top. The artist engraved, or carved, hundreds of tiny dashes to show details in the horse's head. The artist must have cared a great deal about decorating this important hunting tool.

Some scientists believe that the artist carved the horse for decoration. But the carving may have been a good-luck charm to protect the hunter or make him or her more successful. It may have had some relation to the hunter's name. Or it may have been a way of identifying the clan that the hunter belonged to.

1.8 Clay Sculptures

These clay sculptures of two bison were found in a low room, deep inside a cave in France. They were made about 10,000 to 14,000 years ago. They measure 23 inches in length. The artist sculpted them from gold-colored clay. Carved lines show details such as the animals' faces, coat markings, and the fringe of fur below their powerful necks.

Scientists have two main ideas about why these sculptures were created. One idea is that the sculptures were a sign that the cave belonged to a certain clan. The other idea is that the sculptures were used in an important ceremony held deep inside the cave. Perhaps it was a coming-of-age ceremony to show that a person had passed from childhood to adulthood. One clue that supports this idea is that footprints of young people have been found near the sculptures.

These clay sculptures may offer clues about the people who made them and their reasons for creating them.

1.9 Cave Art Tools

The prehistoric materials and tools you see here include two piles of colored, rock-hard minerals and a grindstone used for grinding the minerals. There are also a sculptor's pick and an engraving tool.

Scientists study tools like these and try to guess how they were used. For example, scientists believe that cave artists made paints by grinding colored minerals into powder. They probably mixed the powder with animal fat or vegetable oil to create various colors.

Cave artists used tools made of sharpened stones to grind minerals for paints and to sculpt and engrave objects and cave walls.

You've already seen how prehistoric artists engraved some of their art. For painting, they may have used brushes made of moss, fur, or human hair. They may even have blown paint through hollow bird bones to create softer **textures,** such as shaggy winter coats on horses.

Chapter Summary

In this chapter, you've learned how social scientists investigate the past by using clues they find to form hypotheses.

Detectives Who Study the Past Social scientists might be archaeologists who examine artifacts that people have made and left behind, historians who study the written records that people began to leave in the last few thousand years, or geographers who look at the natural and human-made features of Earth.

Cave Art Caves have provided clues to the past for social scientists. Cave paintings and sculptures thousands of year old have been found all over the world. Artifacts also have been discovered in caves. The art and artifacts provide information about how people lived long ago.

Cave Art Tools Cave artists used sharp stones to grind colored minerals into powder. They mixed the powder with animal fat to create paint. They may have used moss, fur, hollow reeds, or their own hair as paintbrushes.

Chapter 2

Early Hominids

What capabilities helped hominids survive?

2.1 Introduction

Prehistoric humans left clues about their lives in cave paintings. Scientists call these prehistoric humans hominids. In this chapter, you will learn about five important groups of hominids.

Three kinds of "history detectives" that study the past are archaeologists, historians, and geographers. The study of hominids involves a fourth type, paleo-anthropologists. Paleoanthropologists specialize in studying the development and culture of the earliest hominids. (*Paleo* means "ancient.")

In 1974, an American paleoanthropologist named Donald Johanson made an exciting discovery. While searching for artifacts under a hot African sun, he found a partial **skeleton**. The bones included a piece of skull, a jawbone, a rib, and leg bones.

After careful study, Johanson determined that the bones had come from a female hominid who had lived more than 3 million years ago. She is one of the earliest hominids ever discovered. Johanson nicknamed her "Lucy," from the Beatles' song "Lucy in the Sky with Diamonds," which was playing at his celebration party.

What have scientists found out about Lucy and other hominids? How were these hominids like us? How were they different? What abilities did each of the five hominid groups have? Let's find out.

Scientist Donald Johanson displays the partial skeleton, nicknamed Lucy, that he discovered in Africa in 1974.

◀ Humans living 2 million years ago made tools from stone and bone.

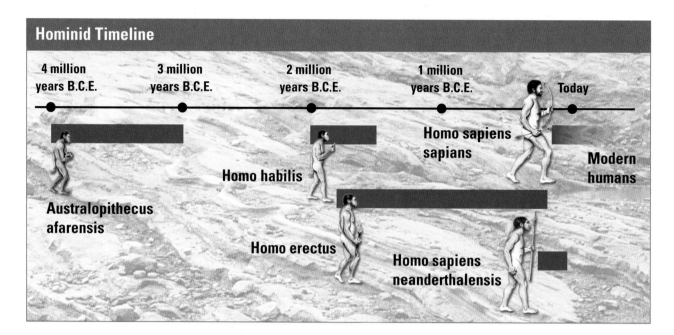

Hominid Timeline

4 million years B.C.E.

3 million years B.C.E.

2 million years B.C.E.

1 million years B.C.E.

Today

Homo sapiens sapians

Modern humans

Homo habilis

Australopithecus afarensis

Homo erectus

Homo sapiens neanderthalensis

Paleoanthropologists have studied the remains and artifacts of five groups of hominids to learn about them.

Australopithecus afarensis

2.2 *Australopithecus Afarensis*: Lucy and Her Relatives

Scientists usually give Latin names to groups of living things. (Latin was the language of the ancient Romans who ruled a great empire for a thousand years, starting about 500 B.C.E.) An **anthropologist** in Africa called the earliest known group of **hominids** *Australopithecus* (aws-tray-loh-PIH-thuh-kuhs), meaning "southern ape." Donald Johanson called Lucy's group *Australopithecus afarensis*. The second part of this name refers to the Afar Triangle, the part of Africa where Lucy was found.

Through their studies of Lucy, scientists have learned a lot about early hominids. By assembling her bones, they know something about what she looked like. Lucy was short compared with humans today—between 3 and 4 feet tall. She had a mix of ape and human features. Her arms were long, but her hands and feet were similar to a modern human's. She had a large head, and her forehead and jaw stuck out from her face.

The remains of other hominids like Lucy have been found in the same area. Scientists guess that Lucy's relatives lived in Africa, about 3 to 4 million years ago.

How are hominids like Lucy related to later hominids and to us? Anthropologists often disagree about the answer to this question. One reason may be that anthropologists have so few clues to work with. Bones as old as Lucy's are very hard to find. Even so, most anthropologists agree that Lucy and her relatives were very early forms of humans.

One discovery about Lucy was especially exciting. By studying her skeleton, scientists found out that she was a biped. That means she had the **capability** to walk on two feet. This gave Lucy and her relatives many advantages compared with animals such as gorillas and chimpanzees. With their hands free, the hominids could gather and carry food more easily. They could also use their hands to defend themselves and their children.

This biped **trait** was one key way in which Lucy resembled us. But in other ways, hominids like Lucy were quite different from modern humans. Lucy's brain was only about one-third the size of ours. Scientists have not found any remains of tools from Lucy's time. The study of Lucy's remains indicate that these early hominids likely could not speak.

anthropologist a scientist who studies human development and culture

hominid an early ancestor of humans

capability ability or skill

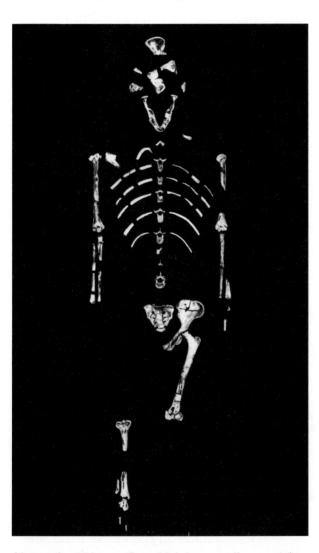 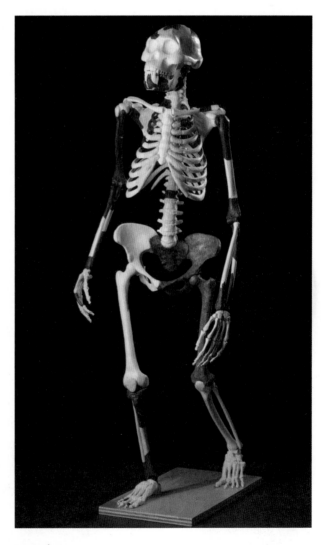

Above, the 47 bones Donald Johanson discovered are arranged as the skeleton would have looked. The image at right is a model of Lucy's skeleton with the bones assembled in an upright position.

2.3 *Homo Habilis:* Handy Man

A second group of hominids was discovered by the husband-and-wife team of Louis and Mary Leakey. When the Leakeys were searching for evidence of early hominids in Africa, they discovered some hominid bones. The bones were scattered among artifacts that looked like tools. The Leakeys named their discovery *Homo habilis* (HA-buh-lis), or "Handy Man," in honor of this hominid group's ability to make tools.

Handy Man lived a little closer to our time than Lucy did, about 1.5 to 2 million years ago. Like Lucy, this group combined ape and human features. They also walked on two feet. But they were taller than Lucy. Their features were slightly more human-like, and their brains were twice the size of hers.

Scientists have discovered Handy Man remains only in Africa. Sometimes, the bones of more than one Handy Man were found together. It is likely that these hominids lived in groups. This would have helped them survive. They could have worked together to protect themselves against animal attacks. They also could have collected food over larger areas of land.

Homo habilis

The tools found by the Leakeys were an important clue about this hominid group. Their larger brains and their ability to use tools were key differences between the Handy Man group and hominids like Lucy. These traits show that Handy Man was more advanced and more like modern humans than Lucy was.

Handy Man's tools were very simple. These hominids used animal bones as digging sticks and rocks as chopping tools. They also made sharp pieces of stone for cutting.

Making a tool, even a simple one, takes thought and effort. First, the hominids had to think about what kind of tool was needed. Then, they had to plan how to make it. Finally, they had to craft the tool themselves and try using it. Handy Man may even have passed these early skills on to others.

The ability to make tools helped Handy Man live better and longer than Lucy and early hominids like her. The use of cutting tools allowed these later hominids to tear the meat from dead animals. Crushing tools may have helped them crack animal bones, to eat the marrow inside. Handy Man hominids may even have dug or made traps for small animals.

Homo habilis may have used simple stone tools to skin animals. Scientists believe that this group ate meat as well as fruits and vegetables.

2.4 *Homo Erectus:* Upright Man

A third type of hominid was discovered in 1891 by a Dutchman named Eugene Dubois (doo-BWAH). While he and his team were searching for artifacts on the island of Java, off the southern coast of Asia, they found a new type of hominid skull.

In time, Dubois' team discovered the bones of many more hominids. As scientists assembled the bones, they observed that these hominids stood up straight. Dubois named this hominid group *Homo erectus* (UH-rek-tuhs), or "Upright Man." (At this time, Lucy and Handy Man had not yet been discovered.)

Upright Man lived on Earth longer than any other hominid group, from 1.8 million to 200,000 B.C.E. Scientists believe that they were the first hominids to **migrate** out of Africa. Their remains have been found in both Asia and Europe.

It is no wonder that scientists have found the bones of Upright Man in many places. This group of hominids was well-suited for traveling. They were taller and thinner than earlier hominids—some even reaching the height of modern humans. Their bones were very strong. And they were good walkers and runners.

The facial features of Upright Man looked more like those of modern humans than the faces of earlier hominids. Upright Man hominids had foreheads that were round and smooth. But they still had a large ridge above the eyes, a thicker skull, and a jaw that stuck out.

Like Handy Man, hominids in the Upright Man group were toolmakers. But their larger brains enabled them to invent more complex tools, including strong hand axes made of stone.

One of Upright Man's greatest advantages was the ability to use fire. Anthropologists have found burned animal bones in the same places as Upright Man remains. This is a clue that Upright Man may have used fire to cook animal meat.

Scientists aren't sure whether these hominids were hunters or merely gatherers, finding dead animals to eat. But studies of their tools and teeth show that they ate more meat than earlier hominids did. They feasted on red deer, elephant, rhinoceros, goat, boar, and oysters.

The remains of an ancient campsite found in France have offered additional clues about how Upright Man lived. Scientists guess that this group built oval huts by covering posts with tree branches. The group kept a fire burning in the center of the hut. It is likely that group members sat and slept on animal skins.

migrate to move from one geographic region to another

Homo erectus

Homo erectus was the first hominid to use fire for warmth and cooking. These hominids may have tried to carry a glowing ember with them, as they moved from place to place.

They may have decorated their bodies with yellow-colored mud called ocher.

Scientists believe that Upright Man groups moved from place to place, building shelters with tools, and using fire to keep warm. These capabilities helped them travel farther and survive for longer periods than earlier hominids could. The ability to construct shelters allowed Upright Man to adapt to colder climates and live in areas without caves or other natural shelters. The ability to control fire helped them survive the cold, cook animal meat, and protect themselves from predators.

2.5 *Homo Sapiens Neanderthalensis:* Neanderthal Man

In 1856, some mine workers in Germany's Neander Valley found a skeleton. It had thick bones and a ridge above the eyes, but was also very humanlike. Today, most scientists consider this fourth group of hominids to be a distinct type of *Homo sapiens* ("Wise Man"), the large-brained group that modern humans belong to. Scientists call this group *Homo sapiens neanderthalensis,* or Neanderthal (nee-AN-der-tahl) Man.

Neanderthals lived after Upright Man, from 200,000 to 28,000 years ago. Neanderthals lived in Africa, Europe, and parts of western Asia.

The appearance of the skeleton found in Germany led scientists to believe that Neanderthals walked hunched over, with their hands dragging on the ground. As it turned out, the skeleton was of an older man who had a bone disease. In reality, Neanderthals walked upright. They were shorter and stockier than modern humans, but they were also much stronger.

Most important, Neanderthals had large brains. They used their **intelligence** to become skilled toolmakers. More than 60 types of Neanderthal tools have been found. These tools required much more planning, skill, and knowledge than the tools made by earlier hominids. Neanderthals created knives, scrapers, and spear points. They learned how to make sharp, thin blades by breaking off the top of a rock and then chipping two or three sharp flakes from the original piece.

The ability to make better tools improved Neanderthals' chances for survival. But their ability to work together helped even more. Neanderthals lived and traveled in groups. And they were the first early hominids to hunt in an organized group.

Scientists believe that Neanderthals may have had a sense of **community**. When members of a group died, their bodies were laid in burial mounds, along with hunting tools and flowers. This is a clue that Neanderthals cared about one another and had a sense of ritual.

When on a hunt, Neanderthals worked together to surround and trap an animal. Then they would close in and kill it with spears. Evidence suggests that if some hunters were injured, other group members would help them.

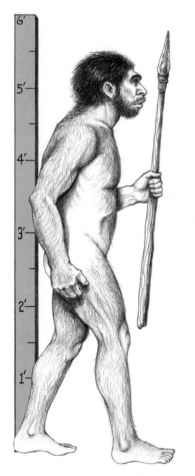

Homo sapiens neanderthalensis

Paleoanthropologists have found some Neanderthal bones showing signs of serious breaks that had healed. These clues lead them to think that Neanderthals helped members of their group who were hurt or sick.

Scientists interpret these indications that Neanderthals cared for each other to mean that Neanderthals lived as a community. This capability would have given them benefits in surviving. For example, they would have been able to learn from the experience and the wisdom of older members of the group.

How exactly are Neanderthals related to the early modern humans? Scientists aren't sure. Judging from the remains that have been found of both groups, Neanderthals existed side by side with early modern humans for about 10,000 years. No one knows the reason why Neanderthal populations disappeared. All we know for certain is that only one type of *Homo sapiens* survived to become early modern humans.

Evidence suggests that *Homo sapiens neanderthalensis* lived in communities and cared for each other.

Once *Homo sapiens sapiens* had food and shelter, they had time to create art that expressed their feelings about the world. They may have built scaffolding to help place art in high places.

2.6 *Homo Sapiens Sapiens:* Doubly Wise Man

In 1879, an eight-year-old Spanish girl named Maria was off exploring a cave with her father when she made an amazing discovery. She found a cave room filled with ancient paintings of deer, bison, wild horses, and boars. They were the first prehistoric cave paintings ever discovered.

The people who created these ancient cave paintings were the earliest members of our own group, *Homo sapiens sapiens* (SAY-pee-enz), or "Doubly Wise Man." Homo sapiens sapiens first appeared about 150,000 years ago. Most scientists believe that they originated in Africa. From there, they spread to Europe, Asia, and Australia. Eventually, they migrated to North and South America, probably traveling across land bridges, which were later covered by water.

The first modern humans looked more like us than the Neanderthals did. They had high, rounded skulls, large brains, small teeth, and slender bones. But their bodies were not as well adapted to the cold as those of Neanderthals. Early modern humans may have survived because of their ability to create better tools, shelter, and clothing.

As toolmakers, early modern humans were even more skilled than Neanderthals. They attached thin blades to bone, antler, and stone to create a wide variety of tools. They made tools used for engraving and sculpting. They fashioned needles for sewing animal skins together. They also built shelters of earth and stone.

These prehistoric humans were also better hunters than earlier hominids. They made hooks and spears to catch fish. Most important, they invented the spear thrower and the bow and arrow. Armed with these weapons, they could hunt from a distance, making hunting much safer.

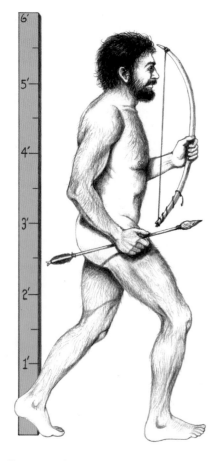

Homo sapiens sapiens

Through their artwork, early modern humans left behind a fascinating record of their lives. They left paintings on the walls of their caves. Artists also carved and shaped images out of clay, bone, flint (a hard mineral), and ivory. They even created musical instruments.

Prehistoric artists created a variety of images. Some images came from the world around them, like the animals they hunted. Some images came from their imaginations, such as mythical creatures. These early artists also made patterns using shapes. Paleoanthropologists think the artists may have signed their work with handprints.

Why did early modern humans create art? Many scientists believe that they painted to express themselves. Some think that pictures were used to teach children. Others think that images had religious purposes.

One thing is certain. These early humans did not merely exist in their world. They had many feelings about it and created images to communicate those feelings. They had the ability to express thoughts to others through pictures and symbols. Some scientists believe that these abilities were able to **contribute** to the development of complex language, one of the capabilities that makes us fully human.

Chapter Summary

In this chapter, you learned about the capabilities of five hominid groups.

"Lucy" and Her Relatives A scientist found the bones of a hominid who lived more than 3 million years ago in Africa. He nicknamed the bones Lucy. Lucy belonged to the group *Australopithecus afarensis.* She had the capability to walk on two feet.

Handy Man and Upright Man The group *Homo habilis,* or Handy Man, was taller than Lucy and had the capability to make simple stone tools. The group *Homo erectus,* or Upright Man, were the first hominids to migrate out of Africa into Asia and Europe. They stood up straight and had the capability to make tools, fire, and shelters to protect them from the cold.

Neanderthal Man and Doubly Wise Man The group scientists called *Homo sapiens neanderthalensis,* or Neanderthal Man, had large brains, made complex tools, and lived in communities. *Homo sapiens sapiens,* or Doubly Wise Man, made more complex tools, were skilled hunters, and created artwork.

Chapter 3

From Hunters and Gatherers to Farmers

How did the development of agriculture change daily life in the Neolithic Age?

3.1 Introduction

Scientists have identified and studied five important groups of hominids. Like the hominids before them, early modern humans hunted and gathered their food. In this chapter, you'll read about how early people learned, over thousands of years, to produce food by farming.

Humans discovered farming toward the end of the Stone Age. This period gets its name from the stone tools prehistoric people made and used. Historians divide the Stone Age into two periods. The first is the Paleolithic Age, or Old Stone Age. During this period, people got food by roaming from place to place to hunt wild animals and gather nuts, berries, and seeds from the plants they found.

By about 8000 B.C.E., some people had learned how to raise animals and crops for food. This knowledge **enabled** these people, for the first time, to live in one place. The Neolithic Age, or New Stone Age, had begun.

This gradual shift from hunter-gatherers (food collectors) to farmers (food producers) is one of the most important advances in human development. People built permanent shelters. They settled in larger communities. Together, they produced what they needed. People developed new skills and made a variety of things that improved the quality of their lives. Over time, they also began to exchange goods with people in other communities for the things they lacked in their own villages. In this chapter, you will explore the many ways in which the development of farming changed human life.

◄ Gradually, over thousands of years, hunter-gatherers became farmers.

The Granger Collection, New York

This prehistoric cave painting in northern Africa shows people herding animals. This ability marked a major change in how people lived.

Paleolithic Age the first period of the Stone Age, called the Old Stone Age, from about 2 million years ago to around 8000 B.C.E.

Neolithic Age the later part of the Stone Age, called the New Stone Age, lasted from around 8000 B.C.E. to 3000 B.C.E.

Fertile Crescent an arc-shaped region in Southwest Asia, with rich soil

Catal Hoyuk a Neolithic town discovered in central Turkey

Most people in the Neolithic Age settled in fertile areas near sources of water.

3.2 From Old Stone Age to New Stone Age

The Old Stone Age, or **Paleolithic Age,** began about 2 million years ago, with the first toolmaking hominids, and lasted until about 8000 B.C.E. It was during this time period that early modern humans developed. Like the hominids before them, early humans were hunter-gatherers. They wandered from place to place, hunting animals and gathering plants for food. Often, they took shelter in caves. Prehistoric cave painters left clues about their way of life.

The New Stone Age, or **Neolithic Age,** began when people started to farm and produce their own food. The discovery of farming did not happen all at once. Over thousands of years, people gradually learned to raise animals and plant crops. They eventually began to rely on these farms for their food. Now, rather than having to roam long distances in search of things to eat, people could settle down in one place.

The Neolithic Age began around 8000 B.C.E. and lasted until about 3000 B.C.E., when people learned to make tools out of metal instead of stone. During this time, farming developed in many places throughout the world, including parts of Europe, Africa, Asia, and the Americas.

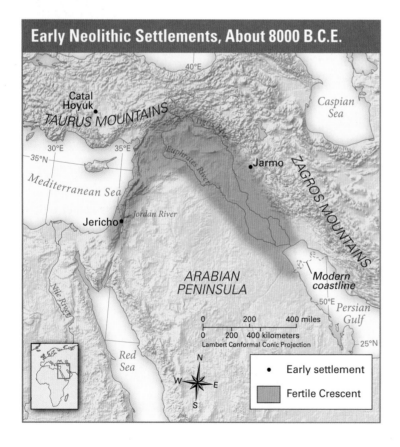

Early Neolithic Settlements, About 8000 B.C.E.

Many Neolithic settlements were located in the **Fertile Crescent,** east of the Mediterranean Sea, where the land was fertile (good for growing crops). Here, people built towns such as Jericho (JER-ih-koh), **Catal Hoyuk** (CHAHT-ul hoo-YOOK), and Jarmo (see map).

People in settlements like these lived very different lives from earlier hunter-gatherers. They could now concern themselves with other matters such as building permanent shelters and forming larger communities. They could make better tools and clothing. And they could swap items they had with other communities to get the things they lacked. As you will see, these changes made life safer, more comfortable, and more interesting.

3.3 Creating a Stable Food Supply

In this Neolithic painting, herdsmen work with cattle.

During the Paleolithic Age, people obtained food by hunting animals and gathering plants. They did not have a stable, or dependable, food supply. Wild plants and animals grew scarce when people stayed in one area for too long. And hunting was dangerous. Hunters were often injured or killed.

Gradually, people found ways to lessen their dependence on hunting and gathering. Instead of gathering wild plants, people discovered that they could plant seeds and harvest crops. Over time, farmers learned which seeds produced the most crops in the areas where they lived.

Early farmers also learned how to **domesticate** animals, to raise and use them for people's needs. They raised sheep, goats, and cattle for the meat. Goats and cattle also provided milk. Mules helped carry heavy loads and pull plows.

These two developments—the growing of crops and the domestication of animals—are called **agriculture**. The Neolithic Age began with the invention of agriculture. For the first time, people had some control over their food supply. Let's explore why this change was one of the most important advances in all of history.

domesticate to train a wild animal to be useful to humans

agriculture the business of farming; growing crops and raising animals

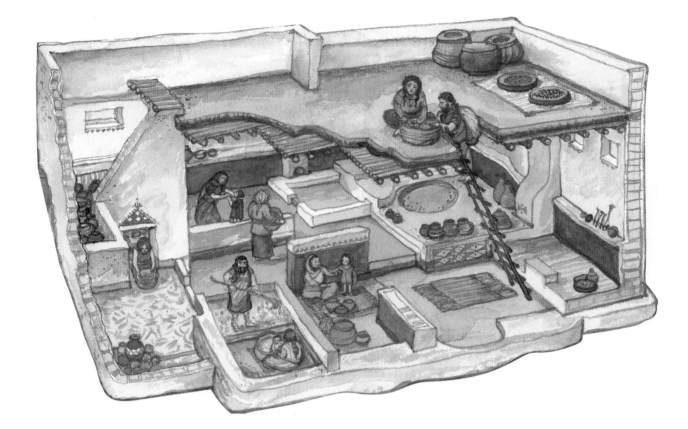

Neolithic houses made of packed mud helped people stay warm in winter and cool in summer.

nomad one who moves from place to place with no permanent home

3.4 Making Permanent Shelters

The first great change agriculture brought about was the use of permanent shelters. During the Paleolithic Age, people had lived in caves or rough, tentlike structures. These were **temporary** shelters because hunter-gatherers were **nomads**. They had to move often, to follow the wild animal herds or to find new plants to eat. As people settled down to farm during the Neolithic Age, they built shelters that were more permanent.

In many areas, people used mud bricks, packed together, to build houses that were round or **rectangular** in shape. Sometimes, people added stones and tree branches to the mud to strengthen the walls and roof. These houses had openings high in the walls. Historians believe that people may have climbed ladders to reach the openings and enter the house.

Inside were several rooms. Places to store food were built right into the floor. Pits for cooking were also dug into the floor, and lined with clay. People may have filled the pits with water, dropping in hot stones to make the water boil for cooking.

The development of permanent shelters was important in several ways. Houses gave people protection from harsh weather and wild animals. Houses made life more comfortable. People could cook food in new ways. The long-lasting shelters enabled people to settle together in larger communities.

3.5 Establishing Communities

The ability to raise food by farming allowed people to settle in permanent shelters. These structures, in turn, enabled people to form larger communities. In Paleolithic times, small bands of perhaps 20 to 60 people wandered from place to place in search of food. As people began growing food, they settled down near their farms. As a result, towns and villages grew up, like those at Jericho (in present-day Israel) and Catal Hoyuk (Turkey).

Living in communities made it possible for people to organize themselves more **efficiently**. They could divide up the work of producing food and other things they needed. While some people grew crops, others built houses and made tools.

Village dwellers also learned to cooperate to do a task more quickly. For example, toolmakers could share the work of making stone axes and knife blades. By working together, they could make more tools in the same amount of time.

With many of their basic needs now met, people had more time and energy for other activities. They could invent new ways of making their lives more comfortable and much safer. Larger communities could defend themselves more easily against their enemies. The Neolithic town of Jericho, for example, was protected by strong stone walls. All of these changes in farming villages led to growing populations.

Neolithic villages were the first real communities. People were able to cooperate as they worked and defended their homes.

The Granger Collection, New York

People in Neolithic communities had the time and the tools to create works of art.

3.6 Developing New Jobs

Having a stable food supply allowed people to develop new kinds of jobs. In Paleolithic times, people's main job was finding enough food to survive. With farms providing steadier supplies of food, Neolithic people could develop more specialized skills.

A good example is the town of Catal Hoyuk, which dates back to about 6000 B.C.E. Historians believe that the townspeople of Catal Hoyuk worked in a variety of jobs. Besides farmers, there were weavers, basket makers, toolmakers, and traders.

Focusing on one job at a time gave people the opportunity to improve the ways they worked. In Catal Hoyuk, farmers learned how to grow more than 14 kinds of food plants. Clothing makers developed a way to spin and weave. They wove natural fibers such as wool and linen into comfortable cloth. In some regions, people mined flint so that stoneworkers could create sharper tools.

Neolithic people didn't merely want to survive. They wanted to make themselves, and their surroundings, more beautiful. They decorated their pottery and baskets with geometric shapes. Stoneworkers learned to polish stones to make shiny jewelry and mirrors. House builders added special rooms to honor the gods and goddesses they believed in.

One effect of the development of different jobs was to inspire workers to improve their skills. This led to newer and better ways of doing things. And different jobs added much greater variety to community life.

3.7 Beginning to Trade

Another **major** change introduced in Neolithic times was the growth of **trade**. Paleolithic hunter-gatherers rarely traded with other groups. They were mostly concerned with the animals, plants, and other **resources** they found nearby. As people settled in towns and villages, trade became a more common activity.

Usually, people trade to get resources they do not have in their own area. As Neolithic people became more skilled in their crafts, they wanted materials that would improve the strength and beauty of the things they made. Getting those resources became the job of traders.

Traders often traveled hundreds of miles in search of these materials. They crossed mountains on foot, rode donkeys across deserts, and sailed the Mediterranean Sea on ships.

What kinds of things were traders looking for? Popular items included flint and obsidian. Obsidian is a black glass found at volcanic mountains. Craftspeople used it to make knife blades, arrowheads, and mirrors. People also traded for "beauty products" like shell ornaments and a red ore called *hematite*. Women rubbed hematite on their lips and cheeks to make them redder.

The growth of trade allowed people to make use of more resources. It also brought them into contact with people from distant places. These contacts helped spread ideas and knowledge throughout the ancient world.

> **trade** the business of buying and selling or exchanging items
>
> **resource** something that can be used to fulfill a need

This hand ax is made from obsidian. Neolithic traders in the Mediterranean region prized this resource. It was found mostly in the area that is now Turkey.

Chapter Summary

In this chapter, you learned how the development of farming changed people's lives between the Paleolithic Age and the Neolithic Age.

A Stable Food Supply During the Paleolithic Age, people lived as nomads, obtaining their food by hunting animals and gathering plants. Gradually, people discovered they could grow crops and domesticate animals. These two developments are called agriculture. Agriculture marked the beginning of the Neolithic Age.

Shelters and Communities As people began to farm, they built permanent shelters and formed communities. Towns and villages grew up near farms.

Jobs and Trade Living in communities allowed people to improve how they lived and worked. They created new jobs and traded for the resources they needed.

Chapter 4

The Rise of Sumerian City-States

How did geographic challenges lead to the rise of city-states in Mesopotamia?

4.1 Introduction

Early people who lived in the Fertile Crescent began farming and living in small villages. In this chapter, you'll see how small Neolithic villages grew into large, **complex** cities.

These villages were located in a land of rolling hills and low plains called Mesopotamia (meh-suh-puh-TAY-mee-uh). This land is in modern-day Iraq. *Mesopotamia* is a Greek word that means the "land between the rivers." The two main rivers of the Fertile Crescent are the Tigris (TIE-gruhs) River and the Euphrates (yuh-FRAY-teez) River. Cities first appeared in the southern part of this land.

The earliest cities in this area date back to about 3500 B.C.E. These first cities were like small, independent countries. They each had their own ruler, as well as their own farmland which provided food. Suppose that you were visiting one of these early cities. You would see a walled settlement surrounded by farmland used to supply food for the city. You would see strong city walls built of sunbaked bricks. Moats, or ditches filled with water, would surround these walls and help keep out enemies. During an attack, people living outside the city walls would flee inside for protection.

As you gazed at the city, you might wonder how it came to be built. Why didn't people in Mesopotamia go on living in small villages, as their ancestors had done for thousands of years? Why did large city-states grow in the "land between the rivers"? In this chapter, you'll find out.

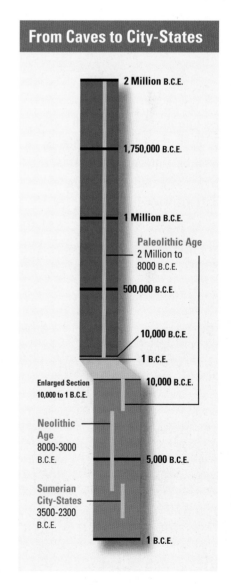

From Caves to City-States

2 Million B.C.E.

1,750,000 B.C.E.

1 Million B.C.E.

Paleolithic Age
2 Million to
8000 B.C.E.

500,000 B.C.E.

10,000 B.C.E.

1 B.C.E.

Enlarged Section
10,000 to 1 B.C.E.

10,000 B.C.E.

Neolithic
Age
8000-3000
B.C.E.

5,000 B.C.E.

Sumerian
City-States
3500-2300
B.C.E.

1 B.C.E.

◀ These ruins in the Syrian Desert reveal an ancient Sumerian walled city.

Mesopotamia in ancient times, the geographic area located between the Tigris and Euphrates rivers

Tigris River one of the two largest rivers in Southwest Asia that flow from the mountains in Turkey to the Persian Gulf

Euphrates River one of the two largest rivers in Southwest Asia that flow from mountains in Turkey to the Persian Gulf

Geographic features such as the climate, the Zagros Mountains, and the Tigris and Euphrates rivers affected where people settled in Mesopotamia.

4.2 Mesopotamia: A Difficult Environment

It was not easy to live in the part of the Fertile Crescent called **Mesopotamia**. The northern part was hilly and received rain. The southern part had low plains, or flat land. The sun beat down fiercely on the plains between the **Tigris River** and the **Euphrates River**. There was little rain. The Mesopotamians were farmers, and their farms needed water. The rivers brought water to the plains in flood season, but for most of the year the soil was hard and dry.

On the plains, building **materials** were difficult to find. There were plenty of reeds (weeds that grow near rivers). But there were few trees to provide wood. Even stones were scarce. And there were few natural barriers to keep out enemies.

Mesopotamians faced four major problems as they tried to survive in this environment:

- food shortages in the hills
- an uncontrolled water supply on the plains
- difficulties in building and **maintaining** systems that provided water across village boundaries
- attacks by neighboring communities

Over time, Mesopotamians found solutions to these four problems. Let's explore how their solutions led to the building of some of the first cities in the world.

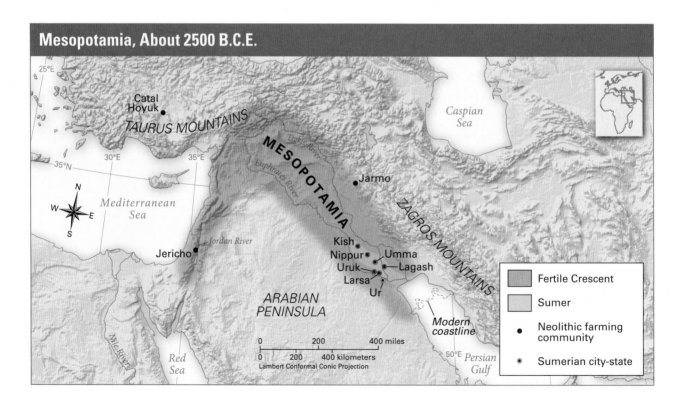

Mesopotamia, About 2500 B.C.E.

4.3 Food Shortages in the Hills

In Neolithic times, people in some areas of the world began farming. One of the areas that had good conditions for growing crops was the rolling foothills of the Zagros (ZAH-grihs) Mountains in northern Mesopotamia.

Mild weather and plentiful rains made the foothills a good place to farm. The wooded hills provided timber for building shelters. There were plenty of stones in the hills for toolmaking. Over several thousand years, these good conditions allowed the number of people in Mesopotamia to grow dramatically.

Then problems arose. Some historians believe that by 5000 B.C.E., farmers in the Zagros foothills did not have enough land to grow food for the increasing population. As a result, villages began to suffer from food shortages.

Below the foothills and to the south, the Euphrates and Tigris rivers ran through flat plains. The plains covered a large area of land, and few people lived there. During most of the year, the land was very hard and dry. And the plains lacked trees and stones for making shelters and tools.

Yet, the plains held promise, too. In the spring, both of the rivers flooded, bringing precious water to the land. Perhaps farms could be successful there.

Driven by the need to grow food, people moved out of the foothills and onto the plains. This region became known as **Sumer** (SOO-mer), and its people, the Sumerians.

The Zagros foothills were an ideal place to farm.

Sumer an area in southern Mesopotamia, where cities first appeared

The Euphrates is the longest river in Southwest Asia.

4.4 An Uncontrolled Water Supply in the River Valley

The farmers who moved to Sumer faced many challenges. One of the biggest problems was the uncontrolled water supply.

During the spring, rain and melted snow from the mountains flowed into the Tigris and Euphrates rivers, causing them to flood across the plains. But no one could be sure exactly when the floods would come. If it happened after farmers planted their crops, the young plants would be washed away.

For much of the rest of the year, the sunbaked soil was dry and hard as stone. Hot, strong winds blew thick **layers** of dust across the ground.

Faced with such dramatic seasonal changes, farmers had to constantly struggle to raise crops. They had either too little or too much water. To grow food, they needed a way to control the water so they would have a reliable water supply all year round.

Therefore, Sumerian farmers began to create **irrigation** systems for their fields. They built **levees** along the sides of the river to prevent flooding. When the land was dry, the farmers poked holes in the levees. The water flowed through the holes and into the thirsty fields.

Over time, the Sumerians learned other ways to control the supply of water. They dug canals to shape the paths the water took. They also constructed dams along the river to block the water and force it to collect in pools they had built. These pools, or reservoirs, stored the water for later use.

irrigation a means of supplying land with water

levee a wall of earth built to prevent a river from flooding its banks

4.5 Building and Maintaining a Complex Irrigation System

Irrigation systems provided enough water for Sumerian farmers to grow plenty of food. But a new problem arose: how to maintain the irrigation system across village boundaries.

The irrigation system passed through a number of villages as it carried water from the river to the fields. The system needed constant care and repair. Canals became clogged with **silt,** so farmers had to clean them regularly. One clogged canal could disrupt the entire system.

Since villages were connected for miles around by these canals, farmers could no longer live apart, or in small groups. They had to work together for the common good.

Gradually, villages came to depend on one another to build and maintain this complex irrigation system. People who lived in different villages may have worked together to clear the silt from the canals to keep them open. Workers may have scooped water from one reservoir into another to ensure that water levels were balanced. As the Sumerians worked together, they began to create larger communities. Between 3500 and 3000 B.C.E., villages grew into towns. Some towns in Sumer became cities with populations as large as several thousand people.

silt fine particles of rock

The Euphrates River still irrigates fields in Iraq today.

4.6 Attacks by Neighboring Communities

As Sumerian cities grew, they fought over the right to use more water. Sometimes, people in cities located upriver (closer to where the river begins) built new canals or blocked other cities' canals. In this way, they kept water from reaching the cities that were downriver (farther from where the river begins). **Disputes** over water became so intense that they often led to bloodshed.

The Sumerians looked for ways to protect their cities from neighboring communities. The plains provided no natural barriers. There were no mountain ranges or rushing rivers to keep out enemies. The Sumerians began to build strong walls around their cities. They constructed the walls out of mud bricks that were baked in the sun until hard. The Sumerians also dug moats outside city walls to help prevent enemies from entering their cities. Most people lived in houses within the walled cities, but the farms lay outside. In case of attack, farmers fled the fields for safety inside the city walls.

A stele (STEE-lee) is an upright slab of stone inscribed with letters and pictures to depict important events. This part of the Stele of the Vultures, which was found in Iraq, shows an attacking army.

The walled cities of Sumer were like independent countries. Historians call them **city-states**. By about 3000 B.C.E., most Sumerians lived in city-states.

4.7 From Small Farming Villages to Large City-States

As you've seen, beginning around 3500 B.C.E., the Sumerians progressed from living in small farming villages to building large, walled cities. How and why did this happen? The answer lies not only in the problems the Sumerians faced, but also in their solutions. A basic challenge for any group of people is how to provide food for itself. Food shortages had forced settlers in Mesopotamia to move from the foothills down to the river valley. There, farmers faced the problem of having either too much water or too little.

city-state an early city that was like a small, independent country with its own laws and government

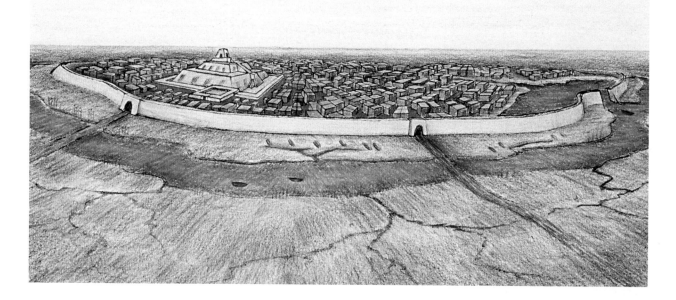

To control the water supply, Sumerians built a complex irrigation system. The system crossed village boundaries, so the Sumerians had to cooperate with one another. This led them to live in larger communities—the first cities.

These city-states were like independent countries. Often, they fought with one another. To defend themselves, the Sumerians built walls and dug moats around their cities. By 3000 B.C.E., the solutions to the challenges faced by the Sumerians had transformed Sumerian farming villages into walled city-states.

A Sumerian city-state was like a tiny country. Its surrounding walls helped protect the city against enemies.

Chapter Summary

In this chapter, you have learned how geographic challenges led to the rise of city-states in Mesopotamia.

Food Shortages in the Hills A shortage of food forced people to move from the foothills of the Zagros Mountains to the plains between the Tigris and Euphrates rivers. This plains area became Sumer.

Controlling the Water Supply on the Plains Farmers in Sumer faced times of flooding and drought. They built irrigation systems to create a steady water supply. Maintaining these complex systems required cooperation among villages.

From Farming Villages to City-States As villages grew into towns and cities, some became large city-states with protective walls around them.

Detecting the Past:
Clues from Archaeology

Suppose that you are standing in the desert, southwest of the present-day city of Baghdad in Iraq. In the distance to the east, you see the Euphrates River. To the west are miles of desert. You then notice that scattered on the ground are small mounds of dirt. What could have made these mounds?

British archaeologist Leonard Woolley worked like a real-life detective to reveal the secrets of the ancient city of Ur.

Leonard Woolley asked that same question in 1922 when he began excavating the ancient city of Ur in Mesopotamia. Woolley was a British archaeologist who had been trained to work much like a detective. His excavations and discoveries in Mesopotamia, between 1922 and 1934, tell a real-life detective story.

For an archaeologist working in the early 1900s, Woolley's approach was unusually careful and scientific. Many archaeologists of that time viewed research as an adventure, not as a science. They often dug up sites to search for treasure, more than to gain knowledge. They made little effort to preserve the sites or to prevent them from being damaged. These archaeologists often handed over artifacts to museums and private collectors in exchange for fame and money.

Woolley, on the other hand, wrote that his goal was "to get history, not to fill museum cases, . . . and [that] history could not be got unless both we and our men were duly trained." Therefore, he excavated using a basic plan. In this way, he preserved each clue that might help him understand life at Ur.

By the time he arrived at Ur, Woolley had already studied what others before him had found there. He knew where an ancient temple had once stood, who had built it, and when the construction had begun and ended. But, most important, Woolley knew that the city in which the temple had stood was called Ur, and its people, the Sumerians.

Woolley and His Team Begin

In general, archaeologists work in three stages. Woolley had just completed the first stage—Learn and Plan. He was now ready to begin the second stage—Dig and Discover. "The first thing that I did," he wrote in 1922, "was to dig trial trenches . . . [to] give us some idea of the layout of the city."

The ziggurat, or temple area, of Ur rises from the ruins of the ancient city. Woolley carried out excavations of Ur from 1922 to 1934.

Woolley dug deep trenches to discover how many generations of people had lived at Ur. He and his team examined each stratum, or layer of earth, from the top to the bottom of the trench.

When Woolley went down into the first trench, he found mud-brick buildings at the shallowest, or most recent, layer. Slowly, he uncovered layer after layer, moving back in time. At one point, the remains of the brick buildings disappeared. Next, he found reed huts.

Excited by these early discoveries, the team continued to dig in and around Ur. Each object, no matter how small, was considered important. As the team uncovered each layer of a trench, workers sifted the dirt. Others kept records of where objects were found. These artifacts were labeled and packed carefully in boxes.

More Discoveries

During the first four seasons, team members reached the bottom of the ziggurat, or temple area. They also explored other places. Slowly, one discovery at a time, a picture of Sumerian farming life came together. The evidence showed that the Sumerians used stone hoes to raise grain. They used grinding stones to grind the grain into flour, which they used to make bread.

In addition to these discoveries, the team found plaster made with cow dung, which the Sumerians used to build their houses. Also found was a statue of a pig, indicating to the team that the Sumerians had other farm animals.

This is one of the deep pits Woolley and his team dug at Ur. Woolley is one of the figures at the very bottom. His staff is standing along the steps and around the edge at the top. Shown below is a gameboard discovered by Woolley and his team.

The team of workers uncovered fish bones and the sinkers that were used to drop fishing nets to the river bottom. They discovered a clay model of a boat, similar to one that Iraqis were still using in Woolley's time. This indicated that the Sumerians ate fish and made nets to catch them. Finally, the team found parts of a weaving loom, showing that the people of Ur knew how to make cloth.

Woolley's Most Famous Discovery

In their fifth season, Woolley and his team started to excavate their most famous discovery—a graveyard. They uncovered more than 1,850 burial sites. Most of the burials dated from about 2600 to 2500 B.C.E. The burial techniques were simple. Bodies were wrapped in reed mats or put in clay coffins in small pits. This discovery made headlines all over the world. It was the first time that so many artifacts, including jewelry and weapons, had been found in Mesopotamia.

But the biggest discovery was yet to come. Woolley and his team uncovered graves that contained great riches—the Royal Tombs of Ur. These tombs sometimes had more than one room and contained many bodies surrounded by valuable objects. What Woolley found here would lead him to ask intriguing questions and to find startling answers.

What did the tombs reveal? Woolley was able to identify the bodies buried in two of the graves. Near the bodies, writing was found on clay cylinder seals: "Mesdalamdug lugal," or king, and "Puabi nin," or queen. These burials had been grander. The bodies were discovered in rooms in deep holes. The chambers were built of stone and had domed ceilings. The remains of jewelry, musical instruments, chariots, games, tools and weapons, and cups and jugs led the archaeologists to reach an interesting conclusion: the Sumerians must have believed in an afterlife. These were objects the deceased would need in the afterlife.

The team also uncovered ramps that led down into the tombs. All along the ramp and around the tomb were many other bodies. Woolley wondered why all these bodies were there. They were lined up as if the people had all gone to sleep. There were broken cups by their sides. He reached a surprising conclusion. It was likely that these people had deliberately taken poison. They likely expected to go with their king or queen into the next life.

What Happened After the Expedition?

Back home, Woolley and the team would complete the final stage of their work—Preserve, Reconstruct, and Interpret. They had already packed and shipped artifacts back to museums. There, scientists would study, and preserve or reconstruct them, if necessary.

What exactly would expensive jewelry from 4,500 years ago look like? One such puzzle was Queen Puabi's headdress and jewelry. When the items were uncovered, they were lying on the ground in pieces. They were made of gold, with lapis lazuli and carnelian beads as decoration.

First, the team photographed the jewelry and recorded exactly where each piece had been found in relation to the others. Then, the workers put them in boxes. Back in the lab, archaeologists pieced together the headdress. Team members also reassembled the queen's necklaces and large hoop earrings.

Woolley's Legacy

The final step in an expedition is figuring out how to fit all the clues together. Woolley finished his work at Ur in 1934. For the rest of his life, he wrote about what he had discovered at the site and what he had learned.

Here are Woolley's major contributions toward our understanding of Sumerian life: The Sumerians were farmers and fishermen. They dug canals and irrigated their fields. They raised animals. They ground grain to make bread. They made cloth. They even took time to make statues of animals. They lived in plastered reed huts and, later, in mud-brick buildings.

In addition, Woolley discovered clues that told him that the Sumerians believed in an afterlife and were willing to die for their king or queen. They used a writing system, called cuneiform, to identify kings, conduct business, and describe Sumerian life. They also created works of art and music.

Leonard Woolley set the stage for careful and scientific theories about Mesopotamia that later archaeologists would further investigate and build on. In the 1960s and 1970s, the Iraqi government used Woolley's research to reconstruct the Ur ziggurat. Woolley would likely have appreciated that. He truly believed that present and future generations would better understand who they were by knowing who had come before.

Woolley's most important find was the grave of Queen Puabi. His team found the remains of her body. The top picture shows the gold headdress she was wearing, just as it was when discovered in her grave. The bottom picture shows the reconstructed headdress.

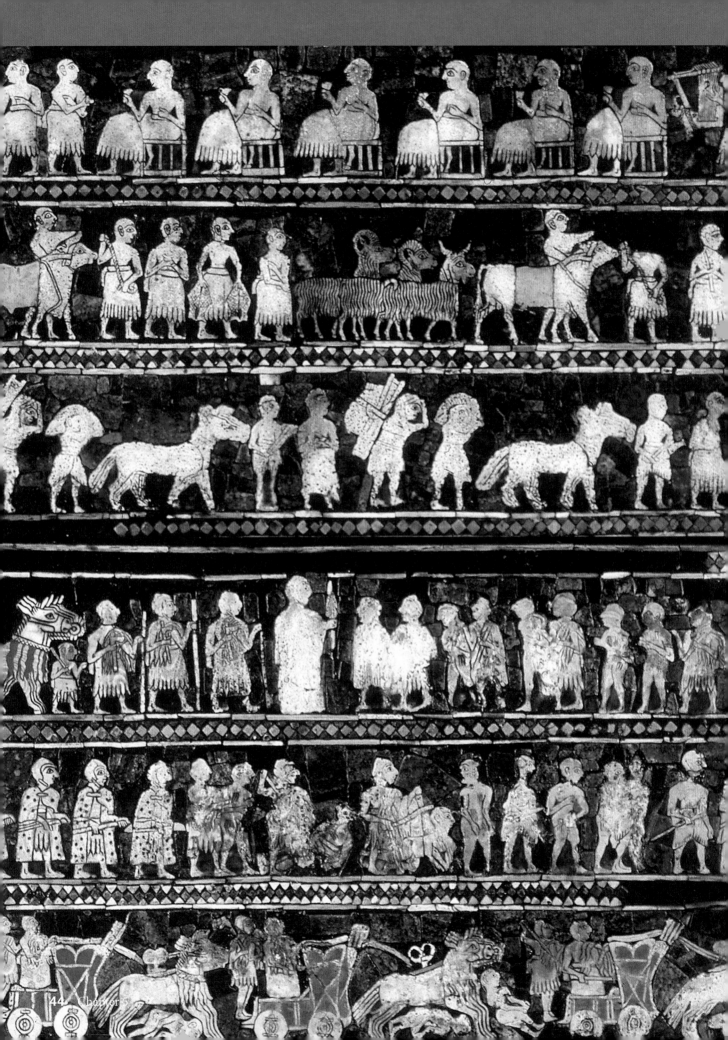

Chapter 5

Ancient Sumer

Why do historians classify ancient Sumer as a civilization?

5.1 Introduction

The rise of Sumerian city-states began around 3500 B.C.E. In this chapter, you'll take a closer look at life in Sumer. Like an archaeologist, you'll consider evidence to try to answer this question about the distant past: Why do historians classify ancient Sumer as a civilization? A civilization is a society that has developed arts and sciences and organization.

Until about 150 years ago, archaeologists had no idea that the Sumerian people had lived at all. Then, in the mid-19th century, archaeologists began finding artifacts in the area of the Fertile Crescent that we call Mesopotamia. They uncovered tablets, pottery, and the ruins of cities. They were surprised to find writing in a language they had never seen before.

By studying artifacts, archaeologists have been able to learn a lot about Sumer. One artifact is the Standard of Ur (uhr). It was found where the ancient city of Ur once stood. You can see the standard on the opposite page. It is made of wood and decorated with pieces of shell and lapis lazuli, a semiprecious blue stone. The standard shows the Sumerians in times of peace and war. Artifacts like this one can tell us a great deal about daily life in ancient Sumer.

We now know that the Sumerians had a complex society. Some of the things they invented, like the plow and writing, are still in use today. But which characteristics of Sumer society cause historians to classify it as a civilization? Let's take a closer look at ancient Sumer.

The Sumerian artifacts above include a necklace of lapis lazuli and marble pearls, a limestone figure of a cow, and a stone bowl with a bull carved in relief.

◀ The Standard of Ur depicts scenes of war and peace in ancient Sumer.

5.2 Characteristics of Civilization

civilization a society marked by developed arts, sciences, government, and social structure

social structure the way a civilization is organized

technology the use of tools and other inventions for practical purposes

Sumer was a challenging place to live. It had hot summers, little rain, and rivers that flooded the plains in the spring. Yet the Sumerians were able to overcome these **challenges**. They built complex irrigation systems and large cities. By 3000 B.C.E., most Sumerians lived in powerful city-states like Ur, Lagash (LAY-gash), and Uruk (UH-ruhk). But what did the Sumerians do to **create** a **civilization**?

To answer this question, we need to examine what *civilization* means. What characteristics make a society into a civilization? Historians name several such characteristics, including these:

- a *stable food supply*, to ensure that the people of a society have the food they need to survive
- a *social structure* with different social levels and jobs
- a *system of government*, to ensure that life in the society is orderly
- a *religious system*, which involves both a set of beliefs and forms of worship
- a *highly developed way of life* that includes the arts, such as painting, architecture, music, and literature
- *advances in* **technology**
- a *highly developed written language*

Did Sumer have these characteristics? Let's find out what the evidence can tell us.

Which characteristics of a civilization do these artifacts represent?

5.3 Stable Food Supply

Civilizations need a stable food supply. A complex society can thrive only if its members have the food they need to survive.

The Sumerians invented two key things to help them create a stable food supply. One of these inventions was their complex irrigation systems. The Sumerians built **networks** of canals, dams, and reservoirs to provide their crops with a regular supply of water.

Their second invention was the plow. A plow is a tool used for tilling, or turning, the soil to prepare it for planting. Before the plow was invented, farmers used animal horns or pointed sticks to poke holes in the earth. Then they would plant seeds in the holes. This was a very slow way to farm. Farmers needed a faster way to prepare the land for planting.

The Sumerians made the first plow out of wood. One end of the plow was bent for cutting into the ground to turn the soil. Farmers themselves pushed and pulled the plow along the ground, or they used animals such as oxen to pull it.

The Sumerians invented the plow. Today, some people in Iraq, the present-day location of Sumer, still use plows to farm the land.

Ancient Sumer **47**

This man and child are standing in the ruins of the ancient city of Uruk, located in present-day Iraq.

merchant a person who makes money by selling goods

artisan a craftsperson

5.4 Social Structure

Civilizations have a complex organization, or social structure. A social structure includes different jobs and social levels. People at higher levels have greater status than others.

Archaeologists have found evidence that several classes of people lived in Sumer. At the top level were priests, landowners, and government officials. These people had the largest and most luxurious homes, near the center of the city. Their houses were two stories high. Evidence suggests that these mud houses had whitewashed walls.

At the middle level were **merchants** and **artisans**. Among the artisans were skilled metalworkers. They worked with such metals as gold, silver, tin, lead, copper, and bronze. Out of these materials, they made swords and arrowheads for the army. They made tools, like plows and hoes, for farmers. They also made **luxury** items, such as mirrors and jewelry, for the upper class.

The middle class also included farmers and fishers. They lived in small, mud-brick houses at the edge of the city. Farmers often worked to build or repair the irrigation systems. In times of war, they were forced to serve in the army.

At the bottom level of the social structure were slaves. They lived in their owners' homes and had no property of their own.

5.5 Government

All civilizations have a system of government to direct people's behavior and make life orderly. Sumerian city-states were ruled by kings. The Sumerians believed that their gods chose these kings. This belief made kings very powerful. It also helped to reinforce the social order, because obeying the will of the gods was one of the Sumerians' strongest beliefs.

Sumerian kings enforced the laws and collected taxes. They built temples and made sure irrigation systems were maintained.

A king also led his city-state's army. All the city-states needed armies because of constant fighting over land boundaries and the use of water. Leading the army was one of the king's most important jobs.

A Sumerian army included both **professional** soldiers and temporary citizen-soldiers. Some were foot soldiers. Others drove chariots, which were wheeled vehicles pulled by horses.

Kings appointed officials to help with certain duties. Governors ruled the outlying towns. Scribes helped record laws. The Sumerians were the first people to develop a system of written laws.

One special group of officials patrolled the canals. They looked for damage and made sure that farmers did not take water illegally.

scribe a person who writes

From his palace walls, a Sumerian king looks out over the city-state he rules.

5.6 Religion

All civilizations have some kind of religious system. A religious system includes both a set of beliefs, usually in a god or gods, and forms of worship.

In Sumer, religious beliefs influenced every part of daily life. The Sumerians tried to please their gods in all things, from growing crops to settling disputes. Religion bound the people together in a common way of life.

The ancient Sumerians expressed their religious beliefs by constructing temples and religious towers called **ziggurats** (ZIHG-guh-rats). It was the king's duty to build and maintain these ziggurats. The towers were platforms made of mud bricks, with shrines on the highest tier. Ziggurats were so large that they could be seen from 20 miles away. Some were as high as 8 stories and as wide as 200 feet.

The Sumerians believed that their gods lived in the ziggurats, most likely in the special shrines at the top. Attached to the outside walls of each ziggurat was a long staircase that the gods could use to climb down to Earth. Kings and priests stood inside the towers to ask for the gods' blessings.

Sumerian statues also expressed religious beliefs. Many of these statues were detailed and lifelike. They showed people worshipping the gods, often with eyes gazing upward. The Sumerians believed that the gods were pleased when people showed these signs of devotion, or love and obedience.

ziggurat an ancient Mesopotamian temple tower with outside staircases and a shrine at the top

This is a reconstruction of the ziggurat that once rose over the ancient city of Ur.

The Sumerians had many kinds of religious ceremonies. Often, musicians played at these ceremonies. Some ceremonies may have involved human sacrifice, the ritual killing of a person as an offering to the gods.

5.7 The Arts

All civilizations have a highly developed **culture,** including the arts. Arts include creative forms of expression such as painting, architecture, and music.

There were many kinds of artists and artisans in ancient Sumer. Metalworkers made objects, like weapons and cups. They made decorative items, such as mirrors and jewelry, too. Architects designed temples and ziggurats.

Music was another important art in Sumer. The Sumerians believed that music brought joy to gods and people alike. Musicians sang and played instruments during temple ceremonies. They wrote love songs and entertained guests at feasts.

Sumerian musicians played a variety of instruments, including drums and pipes. One favorite was a small harp called a *lyre*. Lyres were wooden instruments made of a sound box and strings. A wooden bar held the strings in place at the top. Lyre makers often decorated their instruments with precious stones and with carvings made of horn. These decorations show how much the Sumerians valued music.

culture a characteristic of civilization that includes the beliefs and behaviors of a society or a group of people

This fancy lyre has the head of a bull decorating its sound box. A musician would strum the strings to play musical notes.

This is a model of a wheeled chariot used in the Sumerian army. Chariots were pulled by horses or donkeys while soldiers stood behind the shields.

5.8 Technology

All civilizations create new forms of technology. The Sumerians made several technological advances.

The most important Sumerian invention was the wheel. The earliest examples of the wheel date back to 3500 B.C.E. Sumerian potters, or pottery makers, first used wheels as a surface for shaping clay into pots. Potters' wheels spun, flat side up, on an axle. The Sumerians discovered that a wheel that was flipped onto its edge could be rolled forward. They used this discovery to create wheeled carts for farmers, and chariots for the army. They built the wheels by clamping pieces of wood together.

It would be hard to discover a more powerful invention than the wheel. Before the wheel, people had to drag their goods on flat-bottomed carts called *sledges*. The sledges often got stuck in mud, and they couldn't support heavy loads. Wheeled carts made it much easier to move goods over long distances. Oxen could pull three times more weight on wheeled carts than on sledges.

Another technological advance was the arch. Sumerian arches were inverted (upside-down) U- or V-shaped structures built above doorways. To build arches, the Sumerians stacked bricks, made of clay and straw, to rise from the walls in steps until they met in the center.

Arches added strength and beauty to Sumerian buildings. They became a common feature of temple entrances and upper-class homes. Some historians say that the arch is the Sumerians' greatest architectural achievement.

5.9 Writing

A final characteristic of civilizations is a highly developed written language. The Sumerians created a written language called **cuneiform**. This name comes from the Latin word for "wedge." The Sumerians used a wedge-shaped stylus (a sharp, pointed tool) to etch their writing in clay tablets.

Shown here is cuneiform writing etched in a clay tablet.

Sumerians developed cuneiform around 2400 B.C.E. The earliest examples of cuneiform show that it was used to record information about the goods people exchanged with one another. At first, cuneiform writing may have contained as many as 2,000 symbols to stand for ideas and sounds. Over time, this number was reduced to about 700.

Cuneiform was based on an earlier, simpler form of writing that used **pictographs**. Pictographs are symbols that stand for real objects, such as a snake or water. Scribes used a sharpened reed to draw the symbols on wet clay. When the clay dried, the marks became a permanent record.

cuneiform writing that uses wedge-shaped characters

pictograph a symbol that stands for an object

Chapter Summary

In this chapter, you have learned about the characteristics of Sumer society that made it a civilization.

Stable Food Supply Ancient Sumerians invented an irrigation system and the plow to help them create a stable food supply.

Social Structure, Government, and Religion Ancient Sumer had a complex social structure with different jobs and social levels. The government was led by kings. Religious beliefs influenced every part of daily life.

Arts, Technology, and Writing Ancient Sumerians had a highly developed culture that included the creative arts of painting, architecture, and music. The Sumerians' most important technological invention was the wheel. They also created a written language called cuneiform that was based on pictographs.

Chapter 6

Exploring Four Empires of Mesopotamia

What were the most important achievements of the Mesopotamian empires?

6.1 Introduction

Ancient Sumer flourished in Mesopotamia between 3500 and 2300 B.C.E. In this chapter, you will discover what happened to the Sumerians and who ruled Mesopotamia after them.

The city-states of ancient Sumer were like small independent countries. They often fought over land and water rights. They never united into one group. Their lack of unity left them open to attacks by stronger groups.

About 2300 B.C.E., the Akkadians (uh-KAY-dee-unz) conquered Sumer. This group made the Sumerian city-states a part of an empire. An empire is a large territory where groups of people are ruled by a single leader or government. Groups like the Akkadians first conquer and then rule other lands.

In this chapter, you will learn about four empires that rose up in Mesopotamia between 2300 and 539 B.C.E. They were the Akkadian Empire, the Babylonian (bah-buh-LOH-nyuhn) Empire, the Assyrian (uh-SIR-ee-un) Empire, and the Neo-Babylonian Empire.

This timeline shows four empires that ruled Mesopotamia during a period of almost 1800 years.

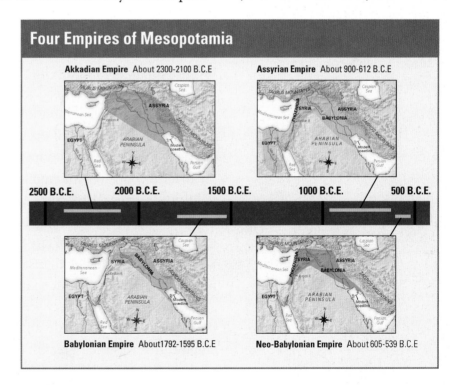

Four Empires of Mesopotamia

Akkadian Empire About 2300-2100 B.C.E

Assyrian Empire About 900-612 B.C.E

2500 B.C.E.   2000 B.C.E.   1500 B.C.E.   1000 B.C.E.   500 B.C.E.

Babylonian Empire About 1792-1595 B.C.E

Neo-Babylonian Empire About 605-539 B.C.E

◄ This Assyrian carving depicts soldiers marching off to battle.

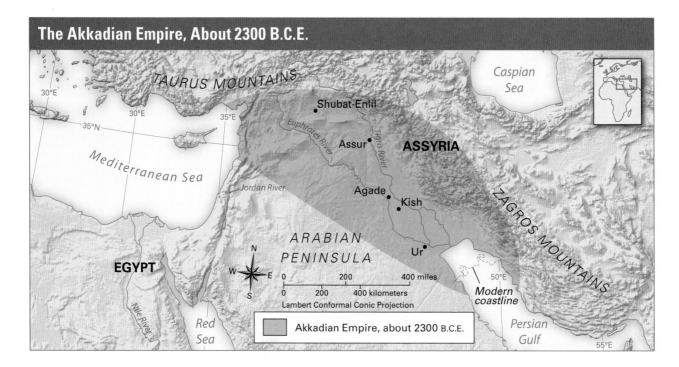

The Akkadian military conquered the independent city-states of Sumer and united them under King Sargon.

empire a large territory in which several groups of people are ruled by a single leader or government

6.2 The Akkadian Empire

For 1,200 years, Sumer was a land of independent city-states. Then, around 2300 B.C.E., the Akkadians conquered the land. The Akkadians came from northern Mesopotamia. They were led by a great king named Sargon. Sargon became the first ruler of the Akkadian Empire.

Sargon was both a strong king and a skilled general. He built his **empire** through effective military **strategies**. First, he **assembled** a large army. Then, he taught his soldiers to fight in tight formations. Soldiers carrying shields stood at the front of the formation. Behind this line stood soldiers carrying spears. The spear carriers extended their weapons between the shields.

Sargon used his military skills to win territory for his empire. After defeating the king of the city-state of Uruk, Sargon had gained control of all of Mesopotamia, including Sumer.

To keep control of his empire, Sargon used very clever political strategies. He destroyed the walls of many cities to make it harder for people to rebel. He also demanded the loyalty of the governors of city-states. If they were disloyal, Sargon replaced them with his own men. And he became the first king to decree that his sons rule after his death.

Sargon lived to be a very great age. His name soon passed into legend. He and the Akkadians had created the world's first empire. This was their greatest achievement.

6.3 Life Under Akkadian Rule

Sargon ruled his empire for 56 years. During that time, he made the city of Agade (uh-GAH-duh), in northern Mesopotamia, the empire's **capital**. He built up the city with **tributes** collected from the people he conquered. Agade became a cultural center, with many beautiful temples and palaces. It was one of the richest and most powerful cities in the world.

The Akkadians may have ruled Sumer, but the Sumerian culture lived on. The Akkadians farmed using the Sumerians' irrigation **techniques**. To record information, they used Sumer's system of cuneiform writing. They even worshipped the same gods and goddesses, although they called them by different names. Religion stayed central to the social order, and kings continued to rule in the name of the gods.

The Akkadians had their own cultural achievements. Over time, their language replaced the Sumerian language. In art, they became especially well known for their skillful three-dimensional sculptures. Artisans also carved relief sculptures on stones. These carved stones are called *steles*. The Victory Stele is a famous example. It was created to celebrate a military victory by Sargon's grandson, King Naram-Sin. The stele shows Naram-Sin leading his victorious army up a mountain slope. Some of his enemies are crushed underfoot. Others die, flee, or beg for mercy.

Sargon had hoped that his empire would last for a thousand years. But later kings found it difficult to rule such a large territory. The empire grew weak. After about 200 years, the Akkadian Empire fell to new **invaders** from the north.

capital a city that is the center of government

tribute wealth sent from one country or ruler to another as a sign that the other is superior

On the Victory Stele, King Naram-Sin is shown as taller than the other men. He wears a horned crown to make him look like a god.

King Hammurabi united Mesopotamia and made the city-state of Babylon the capital of the Babylonian Empire.

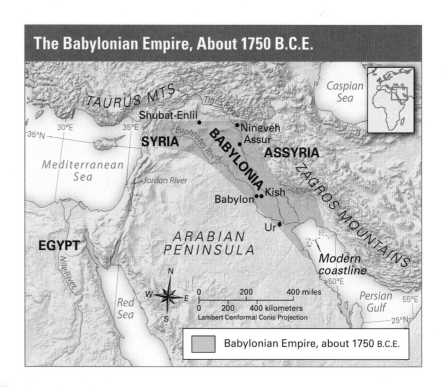

The Babylonian Empire, About 1750 B.C.E.

Babylonian Empire, about 1750 B.C.E.

code of laws a collection of written laws and rules

Hammurabi's code was carved on a stele so that all people would know their rights and responsibilities.

6.4 Hammurabi and the Babylonian Empire

For a time after the fall of the Akkadians, Sumer was once again a group of city-states. The next ruler to unite all of Mesopotamia was a king named Hammurabi (hah-muh-RAH-bee).

Hammurabi was the king of Babylon (BAH-buh-luhn), a small city-state in central Mesopotamia. After conquering the rest of Mesopotamia, Hammurabi made Babylon the capital of his empire. The region under his rule became known as the Babylonian Empire, or Babylonia.

Hammurabi is best known for his **code of laws,** which he wrote from 1792 to 1750 B.C.E. Hammurabi used the code of laws to **unify** his empire and to preserve order. He based the laws not merely on his own authority, but on the word of the gods. Hammurabi claimed that the gods had told him to create laws that applied to everyone in the empire. Laws that were based on the gods' will could never be changed. The code of laws was written on a stele and placed in a temple for everyone to see.

Hammurabi's code was detailed. It covered many situations, such as trade, payment for work, marriage, and divorce. The code spelled out punishments for crimes, such as stealing or causing injury. For example, if a poorly built house were to collapse and kill its owner, then the builder could be put to death. If the owner's son rather than the owner were killed in the collapse, the builder's son could be put to death.

Laws like this one seem harsh to us now. Yet Hammurabi's code was an important achievement. Although the laws and punishments did not treat all people equally, the code was the first set of laws to apply to everyone.

6.5 Life in the Babylonian Empire

Babylonia thrived under Hammurabi. He worked to unite the people of his empire. He made the Babylonian god, Marduk (MAHR-dook), supreme over other gods. He built roads and created a postal service.

Agriculture and trade flourished. Hammurabi was careful to maintain irrigation systems properly so that land remained fertile and provided plenty of food. Because the city of Babylon was on the banks of the Euphrates River, it became an important center of trade. Babylonians traded with people all along the Persian Gulf. They traded grain and woven cloth for wood, gold, silver, precious gems, and livestock (animals).

Trade helped the empire's **economy**. Many types of artisans used materials brought back from distant lands. The arts also flourished. Writers wrote historical poems, some of which survive to this day.

Most important, Babylonian society was unusually fair for its time. The laws treated the various classes differently, but even slaves had some rights. Slaves could work elsewhere and keep their wages. They could own property. If they saved enough money, they could even buy their freedom.

Women also had more rights than they did in most ancient societies. Even though their fathers chose their husbands, women could own property. They could also keep money of their own.

Hammurabi was proud of his achievements. He once wrote:

I rooted out the enemy above and below.
I made an end of war.
I promoted the welfare of the land. . . .
I have governed them [the people] in peace.
I have sheltered them in my strength.

This woman is weaving cloth on a simple loom. One end of the loom is tied around a tree or post, and the other end is tied around her back.

economy the way a region or country uses resources to produce and sell or trade goods and services to meet people's needs and wants

At its peak, the Assyrian Empire extended from Egypt to the Persian Gulf. This vast territory was difficult to control and defend.

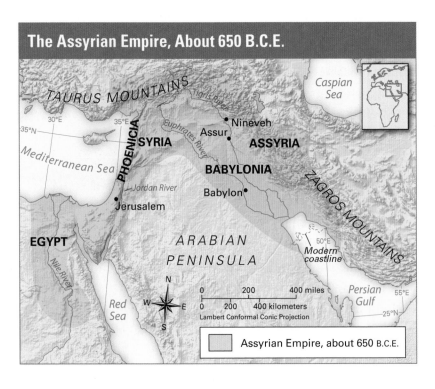

The Assyrian Empire, About 650 B.C.E.

This carving shows an army using a battering ram to break through the walls of a city.

siege a military blockade and attack on a city to force it to surrender

6.6 The Assyrian Empire

The line of kings begun by Hammurabi did not continue to rule Babylonia for long. Over the next several hundred years, a number of groups ruled parts of what had been the Babylonian Empire. The next great empire in Mesopotamia was created by a warlike people called the Assyrians.

Assyria lay to the north of Babylon. The Assyrians had lived in Mesopotamia for a long time. They had briefly established their own empire before Hammurabi conquered them. They rose to power again toward 900 B.C.E., when a series of rulers of Assyria began preparing for war. With a newly trained army, the Assyrians began to expand their territory.

The Assyrians were feared for their military might and their cruelty. Their greatest achievements were their new weapons and their war strategies. They perfected the use of horses and iron weapons in battle. They also became greatly skilled at **siege** warfare. In a siege, army soldiers camp outside a city and repeatedly attack it until the city falls. The Assyrians developed new ways of attacking cities. They were the first to use battering rams. These long, heavy beams on wheels were used for breaking down walls. The Assyrians also built moveable towers that were rolled up to a city's walls. Soldiers used the towers to climb over the walls.

The Assyrians were often ruthless. They might force entire populations to leave areas they had recently conquered. The Assyrians spread tales of their cruelty far and wide. Creating fear among their enemies was part of the Assyrian military strategy.

6.7 Life Under Assyrian Rule

The Assyrian Empire was ruled by powerful kings. Religion, however, remained very important in the social and political order. Even kings were obliged to obey the gods.

The Assyrians believed that their kings were special beings. To honor them, the Assyrians built beautiful palaces. The great palace in the capital city of Nineveh (NIH-nuh-vuh) had many rooms. Some palaces were built on tall mounds, to raise them higher than the surrounding buildings. Huge sculptures of winged bulls or lions, with human faces, stood at the entrances.

This winged bull with five legs stood guard before the palace of an Assyrian king.

Like other societies in Mesopotamia, the Assyrians dug canals to irrigate their land and keep it fertile for farming. They also built some of the first aqueducts. Aqueducts were pipes or channels used to carry water. A system of canals and aqueducts brought drinking water to Nineveh from 30 miles away.

Assyrian artisans were known for their two-dimensional sculptures called *bas-reliefs*. Many of their most famous bas-reliefs were on palace walls. They were amazingly realistic. Often they showed the king hunting, fighting in battle, or enjoying family life. The Assyrians used ivory to decorate thrones, beds, chairs, and doors.

The Assyrian Empire lasted about 300 years. At its height, it stretched from Egypt to the Persian Gulf. But its weakness lay in being too vast a territory to control. The army was stretched thin, and the Assyrians could not fight off neighbors who rose up against them. In 612 B.C.E., Nineveh was plundered by a combined army of Babylonians, Scythians, and a group called the Medes. The Assyrians' power was broken forever.

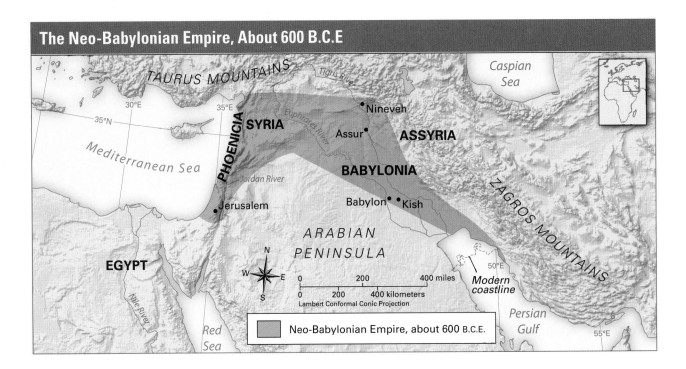

The Neo-Babylonian Empire, about 600 B.C.E.

Compare the area, above, of the Neo-Babylonian Empire with the area of the Babylonian Empire that existed about 1,000 years earlier.

6.8 The Neo-Babylonian Empire

After the fall of Nineveh, the Babylonians once again took control of Mesopotamia. They established a new empire, the Neo-Babylonian Empire. *Neo* means "new."

The new empire's most famous king was Nebuchadrezzar II (neh-byuh-kuh-DREH-zehr). A ruthless military leader, he reigned from 605 to 562 B.C.E.

Nebuchadrezzar expanded his empire whenever he could. He drove the Egyptians out of Syria. He also conquered part of Canaan (present-day Israel), the home of the Israelites, or Jews. When the Israelites rebelled, he took most of them captive and brought them to Babylonia. Many of them were never able to return to their homeland.

As a military leader, Nebuchadrezzar knew that it was important to keep the capital city of Babylon safe. He had an inner wall and an outer wall built around the city. These walls were so thick that two chariots could pass each other on top of them. Towers, for archers to stand on, were placed on the walls. Finally, a moat was dug around the outer wall and filled with water. During peacetime, people used bridges to cross the moat and enter the city. In times of war, the bridges were dismantled.

The Ishtar Gate was one of the entrances into Babylon. Each gate was dedicated to a Babylonian god or goddess. Ishtar was the goddess of war and love.

6.9 Life in the Neo-Babylonian Empire

Nebuchadrezzar worked hard to restore the splendor that Babylon had enjoyed under Hammurabi. From 605 to 562 B.C.E., he rebuilt the city's ziggurat. This huge structure was several stories high. The Babylonians called it the "House of the Platform of Heaven and Earth."

Nebuchadrezzar decorated his palace with lush gardens. The gardens were planted on rooftops and tall terraces so the greenery would cascade down the walls. A watering system kept the plantings fresh and green. These Hanging Gardens of Babylon became famous. This human-made display was viewed as one of the great wonders of the ancient world.

The Babylonians were also skilled in mathematics and astronomy. They created the first sundial, a device that uses the sun to tell time. They made discoveries that led to our present-day system of a 60-minute hour and a 7-day week.

The Neo-Babylonian Empire lasted only 75 years. Then, in 539 B.C.E., a new conqueror named Cyrus (SIE-ruhs) swept into Babylon from the east. He was the leader of the Persian Empire.

The Persians came from the land we now call Iran. For about 200 years, they ruled the most powerful empire in the world. Then the Persians were conquered by a man named Alexander the Great.

The Hanging Gardens of Babylon were one of the great wonders of the ancient world. The sight of so many trees and bushes rising above the desert landscape was astonishing.

Chapter Summary

In this chapter, you read about the most important achievements of the four empires that once ruled Mesopotamia.

The Akkadian Empire King Sargon created the world's first empire. The Akkadians developed their own language. Artists carved beautiful relief sculptures on stones.

The Babylonian Empire King Hammurabi created a code of laws that applied to everyone in the empire. Babylonian agriculture and trade thrived under his rule.

The Assyrian Empire The Assyrians honored their powerful kings with beautiful palaces and huge sculptures. They built some of the earliest aqueducts.

The Neo-Babylonian Empire King Nebuchadrezzar restored the splendor of King Hammurabi's time. His Hanging Gardens of Babylon became famous.

Early Humans and the Rise of Civilization

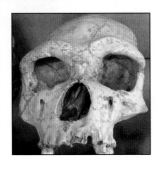

About 1.8 million B.C.E.–200,000 B.C.E.
Homo Erectus, **Upright Man**
Homo erectus hominids in the Paleolithic Age discover how to use fire.

About 230,000–30,000 B.C.E.
Homo Sapiens Neanderthalensis, **Neanderthal Man**
Homo sapiens neanderthalensis hominids make tools and live in groups.

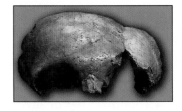

2,000,000 B.C.E.	1,500,000 B.C.E.	1,000,000 B.C.E.	500,000 B.C.E.

About 150,000 B.C.E.–Today
Homo Sapiens Sapiens, **Doubly Wise Man**
Homo sapiens sapiens create complex tools and art.

About 8000–3000 B.C.E.
Neolithic Age
People learn how to domesticate animals and grow crops for food.

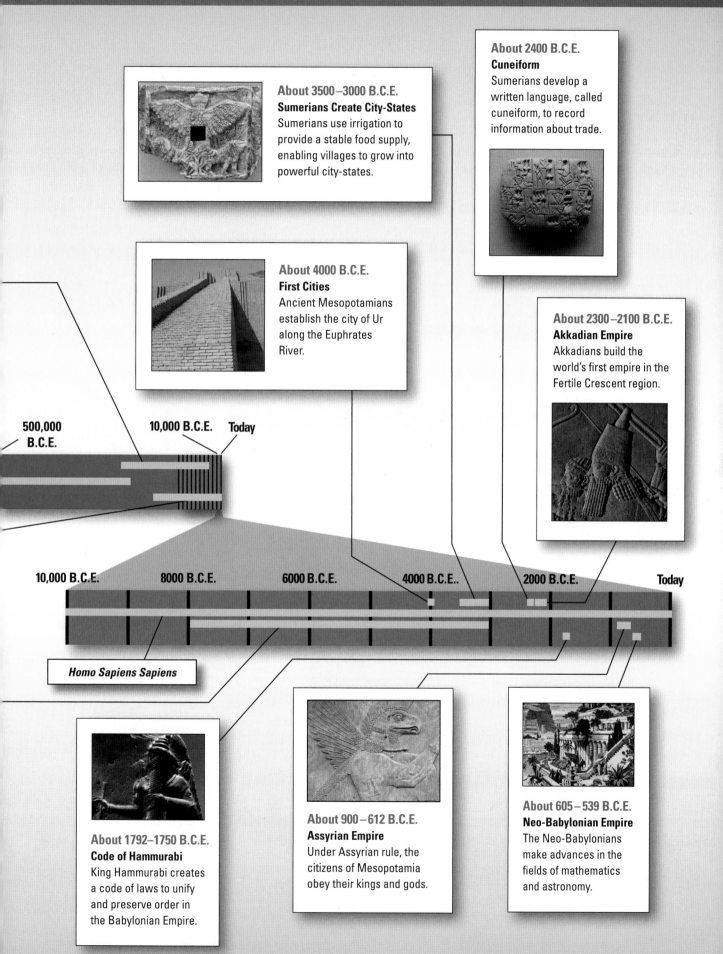

About 3500–3000 B.C.E.
Sumerians Create City-States
Sumerians use irrigation to provide a stable food supply, enabling villages to grow into powerful city-states.

About 2400 B.C.E.
Cuneiform
Sumerians develop a written language, called cuneiform, to record information about trade.

About 4000 B.C.E.
First Cities
Ancient Mesopotamians establish the city of Ur along the Euphrates River.

About 2300–2100 B.C.E.
Akkadian Empire
Akkadians build the world's first empire in the Fertile Crescent region.

500,000 B.C.E.

10,000 B.C.E.   Today

10,000 B.C.E.   8000 B.C.E.   6000 B.C.E.   4000 B.C.E.   2000 B.C.E.   Today

Homo Sapiens Sapiens

About 1792–1750 B.C.E.
Code of Hammurabi
King Hammurabi creates a code of laws to unify and preserve order in the Babylonian Empire.

About 900–612 B.C.E.
Assyrian Empire
Under Assyrian rule, the citizens of Mesopotamia obey their kings and gods.

About 605–539 B.C.E.
Neo-Babylonian Empire
The Neo-Babylonians make advances in the fields of mathematics and astronomy.

Ancient Egypt and the Middle East

Ancient Egyptians built massive pyramids as tombs for their rulers. This tomb near Giza is guarded by the Great Sphinx.

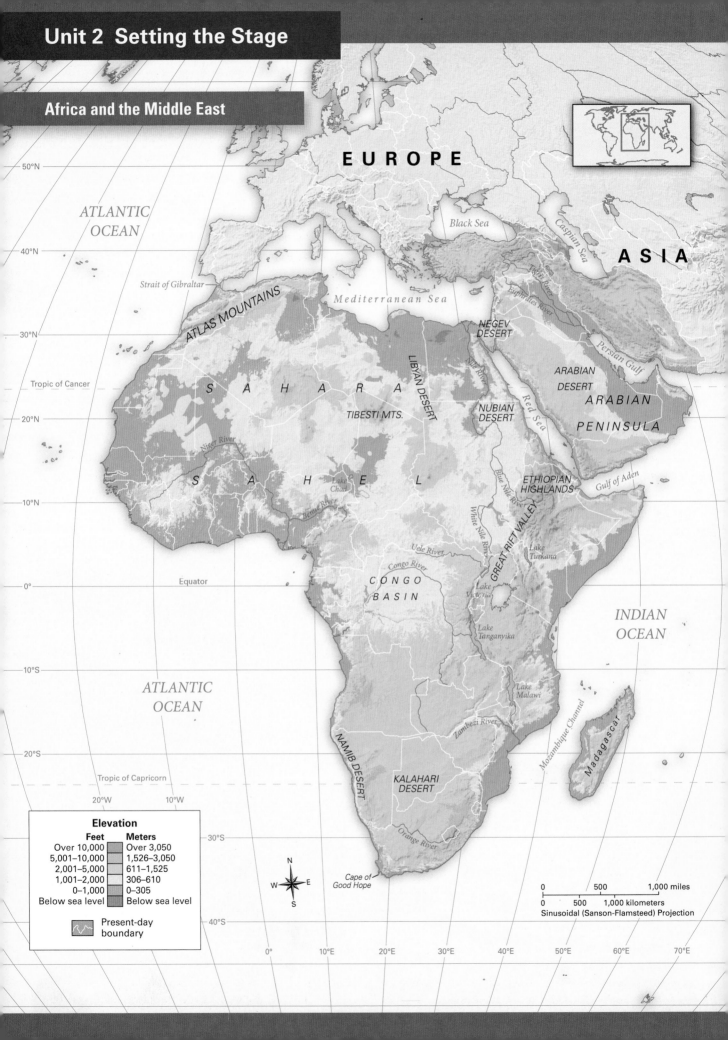

EUROPE

ASIA

ATLANTIC
OCEAN

Black Sea

Caspian Sea

Strait of Gibraltar

Mediterranean Sea

ATLAS MOUNTAINS

NEGEV
DESERT

LIBYAN DESERT

Tigris River

Euphrates River

Persian Gulf

Tropic of Cancer

S   A   H   A   R   A

ARABIAN
DESERT

ARABIAN
PENINSULA

Nile River

NUBIAN
DESERT

Red Sea

TIBESTI MTS.

Niger River

S   A   H   E   L

*Lake
Chad*

Benue River

ETHIOPIAN
HIGHLANDS

Gulf of Aden

Blue Nile River

Uele River

White Nile River

GREAT RIFT VALLEY

Congo River

CONGO
BASIN

*Lake
Turkana*

Equator

*Lake
Victoria*

INDIAN
OCEAN

*Lake
Tanganyika*

ATLANTIC
OCEAN

*Lake
Malawi*

Mozambique Channel

Zambezi River

Madagascar

NAMIB DESERT

Tropic of Capricorn

KALAHARI
DESERT

20°W   10°W

Orange River

Elevation

Feet	Meters
Over 10,000	Over 3,050
5,001–10,000	1,526–3,050
2,001–5,000	611–1,525
1,001–2,000	306–610
0–1,000	0–305
Below sea level	Below sea level

Present-day
boundary

Cape of
Good Hope

N
W   E
S

0	500	1,000 miles

0	500	1,000 kilometers

Sinusoidal (Sanson-Flamsteed) Projection

0°   10°E   20°E   30°E   40°E   50°E   60°E   70°E

50°N

40°N

30°N

20°N

10°N

0°

10°S

20°S

30°S

40°S

Ancient Egypt and the Middle East

Can you use one word to describe the geographic setting of an entire region? If that region is North Africa and the Middle East, you can. That one word would be *desert*. Locate both the northern part of Africa and the Arabian Peninsula on the map on the opposite page. Then look at the smaller vegetation map below on this page. The vegetation for most of the region is desert or desert scrub. Few plants grow in the desert. Small trees, bushes, and other plants that have adapted to a dry climate make up desert scrub.

Look again at the vegetation map. Notice the narrow band of broadleaf evergreen forest that extends through Egypt. How can trees that remain green all year grow in such a dry area? The answer is the Nile River. This vegetation zone follows the path of the Nile River in Egypt.

The Nile River has long been an essential source of life-giving water in a dry land. For thousands of years, the Nile flooded the land along its banks, leaving deposits of rich soil in the Nile River valley. The ancient Egyptians grew plentiful harvests of wheat and barley there. These harvests made it possible for the Egyptians to develop one of the world's greatest ancient civilizations.

Two other ancient civilizations developed in this region. Located south of Egypt was the ancient civilization of Kush. Kush developed close ties with Egypt. Northeast of Egypt is an area that borders the Mediterranean Sea. This is the land of ancient Canaan, where the Israelites settled. These people, sometimes called Hebrews, were the ancestors of the Jews. They gave the world one of its major religions—Judaism, and founded the Kingdom of Israel in Canaan.

The mostly dry and hot geographic setting of North Africa and the Middle East was home to three civilizations you will learn about in this unit. First, you will learn more about geography and its effect on where and how these civilizations grew. Then, you will explore each civilization, beginning with the ancient Egyptians.

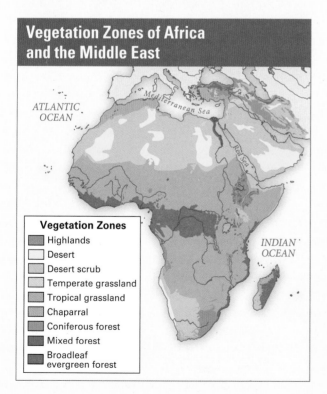

Vegetation Zones of Africa and the Middle East

Vegetation Zones
- Highlands
- Desert
- Desert scrub
- Temperate grassland
- Tropical grassland
- Chaparral
- Coniferous forest
- Mixed forest
- Broadleaf evergreen forest

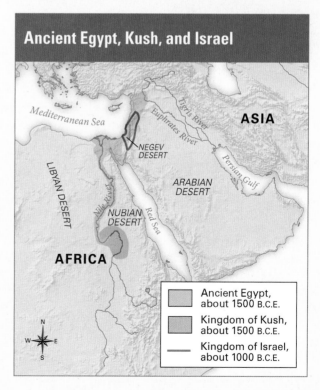

Ancient Egypt, Kush, and Israel

- Ancient Egypt, about 1500 B.C.E.
- Kingdom of Kush, about 1500 B.C.E.
- Kingdom of Israel, about 1000 B.C.E.

Chapter 7

Geography and the Early Settlement of Egypt, Kush, and Canaan

How did geography affect early settlement in Egypt, Kush, and Canaan?

7.1 Introduction

In this chapter, you will explore how geography affected three civilizations that arose in northern Africa and southwestern Asia. These were the civilizations of the ancient Egyptian, Kushite (KUH-shite), and Israelite peoples.

The Egyptians settled along the Nile River, in the northeast corner of Africa. Their civilization lasted from around 3100 B.C.E. to 350 C.E. The Kushites settled to the south of Egypt, along the southern part of the Nile River. Their civilization began around 2000 B.C.E. and lasted until 350 C.E. The Israelites, later called Jews, settled northeast of Egypt, along the coast of the Mediterranean Sea, in about 1800 B.C.E. Although the Jews were forced from their homeland in 70 C.E., their civilization continues to flourish today.

Environmental **factors** greatly affected where people settled. Three important factors were water, topography (the shape and elevation of the surface features of the land), and vegetation (plant life). These three factors were determined by each area's **physical geography**. Physical geography includes mountains, rivers, valleys, deserts, climate, and the fertility of the soil.

In this chapter, you will learn why water, topography, and vegetation were important to early human settlement. You will explore the physical geography of the lands of the ancient Egyptians, Kushites, and Israelites. You'll find out how environmental factors in these places affected people's choices of where to live.

This satellite photograph shows the Nile River and its delta at the Mediterranean Sea. The Red Sea is seen at right.

◀ The Nile River provided people with fresh water and fertile land.

topography the shape and elevation of surface features, such as mountains or deserts, of a place or region

vegetation the plants of a place or region

7.2 Environmental Factors and Early Human Settlement

In ancient times, environmental factors influenced people's choices of where to settle. Three important environmental factors were water, **topography,** and **vegetation.**

Water   The most important environmental factor in early human settlement was water. Physical features like rivers, lakes, and inland seas were good sources of fresh water.

Water was important for many reasons. People needed fresh drinking water to live. They also bathed and washed things in fresh water. Bathing and washing helped prevent disease.

Water was a source of food. People caught fish from rivers, lakes, and seas. They hunted water birds and other animals that gathered near water.

In addition, farmers needed water to grow their crops. For this reason, farmers often settled near rivers. A river's natural flooding could help irrigate their farms. Farmers could also dig canals or trenches to direct river water to their crops. For example, farmers in Mesopotamia dug canals for this purpose.

Water was also used for transportation. Cities and towns often used rivers as "highways." People traveled in boats to visit relatives and trade goods. Towns near the sea could trade goods with countries far away.

Topography   A second environmental factor was topography. Topography refers to the shape and elevation of the land. It includes features like mountains, hills, plains, valleys, and deserts.

The topography of an area was important for early human settlement. Farmers preferred to settle in flat, open areas such as plains and valleys. Large, flat spaces gave farmers room to plant crops. Also, the rich soil in coastal plains and river valleys was excellent for growing these crops.

Mountains were less friendly to human settlement. Steep mountains were hard to cross. Their jagged peaks, cold temperatures, and rocky land made farming difficult.

Deserts also discouraged settlement. They were hot and dry. They contained very little water for farming. Sandstorms occurred when strong winds carried dense clouds of sand that could block out the sun. The intense heat, lack of water, and sandstorms made travel and living in the desert difficult.

Vegetation   A third environmental factor was vegetation, or plant life. There are many kinds of vegetation, such as trees, bushes, flowers, grass, and reeds. The crops people grow are also a type of vegetation.

Many **aspects** of physical geography affect vegetation. A climate with mild weather and regular rain is good for plant life. Fresh water supports the growth of vegetation. The areas around rivers and lakes are usually green and lush. Mountains are often covered with thick groves of trees. Dry and hot deserts have very little vegetation.

The vegetation in an area influenced early human settlement in several ways. Most important, plants were a source of food. People could eat the wild plants available and also the crops they planted. Vegetation had other uses as well. People learned to make many useful products out of plants, including baskets, tools, medicine, rope, and even paper. Trees provided shade from the hot sun. And plants and flowers added natural beauty to a place.

Wherever people settled in the ancient world, water, topography, and vegetation were important factors. Let's look at how these environmental factors influenced the early settlements of the Egyptians, Kushites, and Israelites.

Identify three environmental factors in this photograph. Why might they be important to the people living here?

Nile River the longest river in the world, flowing through eastern Africa to a delta in northeastern Egypt

Egypt a nation in northeast Africa, first settled around 3100 B.C.E.

Kush a society along the Nile River, south of Egypt, from about 2000 B.C.E. to 350 B.C.E.

Mediterranean Sea a body of water north of Africa

7.3 Environmental Factors and the Early Settlement of Egypt and Kush

The Egyptians and Kushites both settled near the **Nile River**. The Egyptians lived along the northern part of the river. The Kushites lived to the south.

Why did settlements in these areas cluster around the Nile River? Let's look at the physical features of **Egypt** and **Kush** to see how environmental factors favored settlement near the Nile.

Physical Features of Egypt and Kush   The most important physical feature in ancient Egypt and Kush was the Nile River. Flowing north from east Africa, the Nile created a long, fertile valley that ended in a marshy delta where the river emptied into the **Mediterranean Sea**.

The Nile River valley was bordered by the Libyan Desert to the west and the Nubian Desert to the east. These sandy deserts were extremely hot and dry. Most people avoided these areas, although the deserts did play one important role in the settlement of Egypt and Kush. They formed a natural barrier that helped protect people living in the Nile River valley. The deserts did not support large settlements, and few invaders wanted to risk crossing these harsh places.

On the north, Egypt was bordered by the Mediterranean Sea. Settlers could not drink its sparkling salt water, but the sea was rich in fish and other kinds of seafood. It was also a waterway that linked ancient Egypt to other civilizations.

To the east of Egypt and Kush was a long channel of very salty water called the Red Sea. The climate in this area was hot and dry. Much of the land near the Red Sea was desert.

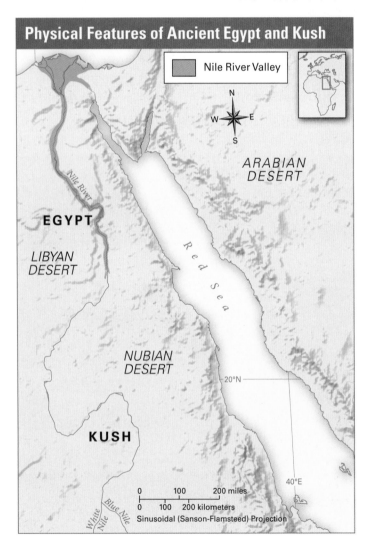

Physical Features of Ancient Egypt and Kush

Nile River Valley

This map shows bodies of water that encouraged settlement and travel in parts of ancient Egypt and Kush. It also shows deserts, which made life and travel hard.

Environmental Factors and Human Settlement in Egypt and Kush

Environmental factors in ancient Egypt and Kush greatly favored settlement near the Nile River. Most important, the Nile was a source of fresh water in an area that was mostly desert.

The lack of water in the deserts made them unfit for farming. But in the Nile River valley, the river provided natural irrigation and fertilization. Every summer, the river overflowed its banks. The floodwaters soaked the dry ground for several weeks. As the water level decreased, a thin layer of silt (very fine particles of rock) was left behind. This soil was perfect for farming.

Also, where there was fresh water, people were more likely to find fish to catch and animals to hunt. The abundant wildlife in the Nile region included fish, ducks, geese, hippos, crocodiles, giraffes, and ostriches.

The topography of the river valley also encouraged human settlement. In the south, parts of the Nile ran through narrow valleys between steep hills. But there were also wide, flat areas of land around deep bends in the river. These flat areas were good for farming. In the north, wide plains were watered by the Nile's annual flooding.

Vegetation was rare in the dry deserts, but it was plentiful in the Nile River valley. Useful plants included reeds and a tough water plant called papyrus. People wove reeds into baskets, and roofs for their huts. Papyrus was used to make rope and paper. And the rich farmland was good for growing crops like wheat and barley.

Africa's Nile River is the longest river in the world. It is more than 4,100 miles long and flows from south to north, emptying into the Mediterranean Sea.

Deserts are natural barriers against invaders. Would you spend days crossing this hot, dry desert to fight those who live on the other side?

Canaan a land northeast of Egypt, settled by the ancient Israelites, from about 1800 B.C.E. to 70 C.E.

Jordan River a river in southwestern Asia that flows from the Lebanon Mountains, south through the Sea of Galilee, into the Dead Sea

The physical features of Canaan affected where Israelites settled.

7.4 Environmental Factors and the Early Settlement of Canaan

The ancient Israelites settled in **Canaan** (KAY-nen), a **diverse** land along the coast of the Mediterranean Sea. Canaan's physical features and environmental factors made settlement easier in some parts of the region than in others.

Physical Features of Canaan   Canaan's physical features included plains and valleys, hills and mountains, deserts, and bodies of water.

In the west, coastal plains bordered the Mediterranean Sea. To the north, the Lebanon Mountains rose steeply from the coast. The southern part of this range gave way to the lower hills of Galilee.

The **Jordan River** flowed down from a mountain range through the middle of Canaan, heading south through the Sea of Galilee to the Dead Sea. The land around the narrow river valley included hills, grassy slopes, and mountains. To the east lay the hot, dry Syrian Desert. In southwestern Canaan was the Negev (NEH-gehv) Desert. Rain soaked this area during the winter months, supplying the Negev with more water than most deserts receive.

Physical Features of Ancient Canaan

Environmental Factors and Human Settlement in Canaan   In Canaan, as in Egypt and Kush, water was a key environmental factor. In very ancient times, the wet, fertile plains near the Mediterranean Sea were farmed. The Mediterranean also enabled traders from many lands to visit Canaan.

Other bodies of water also played a role in the settlement of Canaan. The Sea of Galilee was actually a freshwater lake. It had plentiful fish, and fertile land was nearby. Another large lake, the Dead Sea, was so salty that nothing grew in it, not even plants. The area near the Dead Sea was hot and dry, making it unsuitable for farming.

The main source of fresh water was the Jordan River. People living near the river hunted, fished, and farmed along its banks.

But unlike the Nile River, the Jordan River did not flood regularly, so its valley was not as fertile as the Nile's.

Canaan's varied topography greatly influenced patterns of settlement. Farmers found it easiest to live on the Mediterranean's coastal plains and near the Jordan River. In other areas, the hilly land and dry soil made growing crops difficult. As a result, many people, including the ancient Israelites, became herders rather than farmers. Herders tended flocks of sheep, goats, cattle, donkeys, and camels. Unlike farmers, herders were nomads, wandering from place to place in search of good land for their animals to graze.

People found it hardest to settle in the mountains and deserts. Mountainous land and dry desert land were both difficult to farm. Still, some people did live in these areas. Nomads sometimes herded cattle and camels in the Negev and Syrian deserts.

In general, Canaan's hot, dry climate discouraged abundant plant life. Vegetation was most plentiful near the Jordan River. Some areas had small forests. Others had only short, scrubby plants. Grasslands were common, though, and herders made good use of them to feed their animals.

While parts of the Jordan River valley were lush, the area was not as fertile as the Nile River valley.

Chapter Summary

In this chapter, you learned how three environmental factors influenced the early settlement of ancient Egypt, Kush, and Canaan.

Environmental Factors Three important environmental factors are water, topography, and vegetation. These factors greatly affected where ancient people settled.

Early Settlement of Egypt and Kush In Egypt and Kush, most people farmed in the fertile Nile River valley. The Nile River provided fresh water in an area that was mostly desert. The topography of the Nile River valley made the land good for farming. The valley also supported useful vegetation like reeds and papyrus.

Early Settlement of Canaan In Canaan, the Jordan River and the Sea of Galilee were important sources of fresh water. Much of the land, however, was too hot, dry, or hilly for farming. As a result, many people, including the ancient Israelites, were herders rather than farmers. Herders were nomads who moved from place to place to find grasslands where their animals could graze.

Chapter 8

The Ancient Egyptian Pharaohs

What did the pharaohs of ancient Egypt accomplish, and how did they do it?

8.1 Introduction

In this chapter, you will visit ancient Egypt. You will meet four leaders, called pharaohs.

In 1922, archaeologists discovered the tomb of a pharaoh known as King Tutankhaten (too-tan-KAH-tin), or King Tut. Inside a small burial chamber, they found three coffins nested inside each other. The smallest coffin was made of solid gold. It held the king's mummy. (A mummy is a body that has been preserved after death to keep it from decaying.) On the mummy's head was a magnificent golden mask. Jewelry and good luck charms lay on the mummy and in the wrappings that protected it. Other rooms of the tomb were filled with statues, weapons, furniture, and even a chariot.

The treasures in King Tut's tomb provided an amazing glimpse into ancient Egypt. Other pharaohs also left behind fabulous riches and artwork. Many of these pharaohs had great monuments built to celebrate their lives and their accomplishments. Like King Tut's tomb, these artifacts have much to teach us about this ancient civilization.

In this chapter, you will learn about three important **periods** in ancient Egyptian history. Then you will meet four pharaohs who ruled during these periods, learn what they **accomplished,** and explore some of the monuments they left behind.

This view of the inside of King Tut's tomb, discovered in 1922, shows the pharaoh's coffin and some of the chamber's detailed wall paintings.

◀ This is King Tutankhaten's funeral or death mask.

pharaoh a ruler of ancient
Egypt

8.2 Ancient Egypt and Its Rulers

Ancient Egypt enjoyed three long periods of stability and unity
under the rule of **pharaohs**. Historians call these periods the
Old Kingdom, the Middle Kingdom, and the New Kingdom.

The Old Kingdom lasted from about 2700 to 2200 B.C.E.
During this time, early pharaohs set up a strong central government. They also had great pyramids built as tombs for themselves. Some historians call this time the Age of the Pyramids.

The Middle Kingdom (about 2000 to 1800 B.C.E.) is sometimes called the Period of Reunification because it followed years
of chaos and disunity. During this era, Egyptians enjoyed many
great achievements in literature, art, and architecture.

The New Kingdom (about 1600 to 1100 B.C.E.) is often called
Egypt's Golden Age. During
this time of peace and stability,
ancient Egypt's power reached its
height. Pharaohs increased trade
and had huge monuments built.

As in Mesopotamia, religion
played a central role in Egypt's
social and political order.
Pharaohs were believed to be
gods. They owned all the land
and were responsible for their
people's well-being. They were
kings, generals, and religious
leaders, all combined.

After they died, pharaohs
were thought to enter an afterlife that would never end. Their
tombs were built to last. Many
objects were buried with the pharaoh for use in the next world.

The pharaohs built other
monuments to glorify their
power and success. The map
shows the locations of some of
the greatest monuments. Let's
find out more about these
structures and the pharaohs
who ordered their creation.

This map shows some of the sites
of great monuments built during
Egypt's three periods of stability
under the pharaohs.

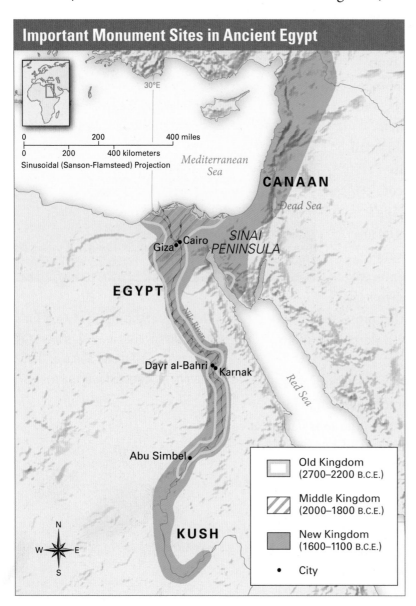

Important Monument Sites in Ancient Egypt

0   200   400 miles
0   200   400 kilometers
Sinusoidal (Sanson-Flamsteed) Projection

30°E

Mediterranean Sea

CANAAN

Dead Sea

SINAI PENINSULA

Giza•• Cairo

EGYPT

Nile River

Dayr al-Bahri • • Karnak

Red Sea

Abu Simbel •

KUSH

☐ Old Kingdom
(2700–2200 B.C.E.)

▨ Middle Kingdom
(2000–1800 B.C.E.)

■ New Kingdom
(1600–1100 B.C.E.)

• City

N
W ✦ E
S

As soon as Khufu became pharaoh, he began construction on the Great Pyramid.

8.3   Pharaoh Khufu: The Pyramid Builder

The pharaoh Khufu (KOO-foo) ruled from about 2551 to 2528 B.C.E., during the Old Kingdom period. Today, he is best known as the builder of a famous pyramid.

Not much is known about Khufu. Some stories describe him as a cruel, harsh ruler. Others say that he was powerful but kind.

We do know that Khufu helped establish the pharaoh as a central **authority**. For example, he kept strict control over Egypt's food supply. He oversaw the harvest and the storage of extra grain. He also controlled a large network of government officials who carried out his laws. Khufu emphasized his supreme power by declaring himself a god.

Khufu and other Old Kingdom pharaohs had magnificent pyramids built as tombs for themselves and their families. Khufu was responsible for the building of the Great Pyramid at Giza. It is one of the wonders of the ancient world.

The Great Pyramid sat at the center of a huge complex of temples, statues, monuments, and smaller tombs. It was made of more than 2 million stone blocks, perfectly fitted together. Inside, tunnels led to several burial chambers. The king's chamber had six roofs to hold up the weight of the stone layers above it.

Building the Great Pyramid was an amazing feat. No one knows exactly how the Egyptians did it. The pyramid took about 20 years to complete. Khufu had strict control of the building project. He organized and fed thousands of workers. The finished pyramid was a stunning monument to Egyptian engineering.

This three-inch-high ivory statue of Khufu was discovered during the excavation of a temple in 1903. It is displayed in the Egyptian Museum in Cairo.

8.4 Pharaoh Senusret I: Patron of the Arts

The pharaoh Senusret I (SEHN-oos-ret) ruled from about 1971 to 1926 B.C.E., during the Middle Kingdom. He was a strong leader who ruled a stable, unified Egypt. Art, literature, and architecture flourished during his **reign**.

The arts thrived under Senusret's rule. The pharaoh controlled mines filled with gold, copper, and gems such as purple amethyst. Artisans fashioned these materials into beautiful pieces of jewelry. Bracelets and necklaces were often highly detailed. They were also decorated with stones like turquoise.

Some of the greatest works in Egyptian literature were written during Senusret's reign. "The Story of Sinuhe" tells of a young official named Sinuhe who overhears a plot to kill the pharaoh.

This statue of Senusret shows him clutching an ankh in each hand. The ankh was the Egyptian symbol of immortality, or eternal life.

Fearing for his own life, Sinuhe flees Egypt. He thrives in his new land, but he grows very homesick. When a new pharaoh calls him home, Sinuhe returns joyfully to Egypt.

Senusret's greatest accomplishments were in religious architecture. He had many temples, shrines, and religious monuments built and improved.

Perhaps Senusret's finest architectural achievement was the White Chapel. (A chapel is a small temple.) It was made of alabaster, a hard white stone. Some historians think that the chapel was originally covered in a thin layer of gold.

Beautiful artwork decorated the chapel's pillars. Carved scenes showed the pharaoh with various gods. Birds, animals, and Egyptian symbols were also depicted.

Senusret wanted his memory to live on through his monuments. But few of his buildings survived the passage of time. A later pharaoh took the White Chapel apart and used the pieces in a monument of his own. Archaeologists later discovered the pieces and reconstructed the White Chapel.

8.5 Pharaoh Hatshepsut: Promoter of Egyptian Trade

During the New Kingdom, the pharaoh **Hatshepsut** (haht-SHEP-soot) ruled Egypt from about 1473 to 1458 B.C.E. Hatshepsut was Egypt's first female pharaoh. Under her rule, Egyptian art and architecture flourished. Hatshepsut was also known for encouraging trade.

One of her greatest accomplishments was her rise to power. Never before had a woman pharaoh ruled Egypt. At first, she shared power with her male relatives. However, she soon took over as sole ruler.

Hatshepsut strengthened her position in several ways. She filled her government with loyal advisers. She demanded the same respect shown to male rulers. Sometimes, she dressed in men's clothing. She even put on the fake beard worn by male pharaohs. Artists were often instructed to portray her as a man. She also spread stories that her father was a god.

As pharaoh, Hatshepsut promoted trade with other countries. Her biggest trade expedition was to the African kingdom of Punt, at the southern end of the Red Sea. Over 200 men in five ships brought gifts and trade goods to Punt.

Hatshepsut left behind a stunning monument to her reign—a great temple at Dayr al-Bahri (deer ahl-BAH-ray). The main part of the temple was built into a cliff above the Nile River. At the entrance were two tall, thin monuments called *obelisks*. The entrance was also graced by 200 sphinx statues. The sphinx is a mythical creature with the body of a lion and the head of a man.

Scenes from Hatshepsut's reign decorated the temple walls. Detailed carvings portrayed the great voyage to Punt. The carvings showed the valuable things that the pharaoh's traders had brought back to Egypt.

Hatshepsut actively encouraged trade. During her reign, trade helped spread Egyptian influence along the Nile and in nearby lands in the Middle East (western Asia).

Hatshepsut the first woman pharaoh of ancient Egypt

This painting shows Ramses II in battle. He was a brilliant military leader who became a captain in his father's army at the age of ten.

Ramses II an ancient Egyptian pharaoh, known as "Ramses the Great"; skilled as a military leader; and responsible for building many monuments, including the temple at Abu Simbel

treaty a written agreement by which two or more states agree to peaceful relations

8.6 Pharaoh Ramses II: Military Leader and Master Builder

The pharaoh **Ramses II** (RAM-seez) ruled from about 1290 to 1224 B.C.E., during the New Kingdom. Called Ramses the Great, he is one of the most famous pharaohs. He reigned for more than 60 years, longer than almost any other pharaoh. He is best known for his military leadership and for building numerous monuments.

Ramses used his power to excess. He had over 100 wives, and more than 100 children. Never shy about his importance, he had hundreds of statues of himself erected throughout Egypt. Some of them were over 60 feet high.

From a young age, Ramses was a fearless soldier. He fought alongside his father in various battles. At the age of ten, Ramses was made a captain in the Egyptian army.

Ramses tried to defend an Egyptian empire that extended north into Canaan. His most famous military campaigns were against the Hittite Empire in Anatolia (present-day Turkey). The Hittites constantly threatened Egypt's northern borders. In his best known battle, Ramses reached a standoff with the Hittites, even though he was greatly outnumbered.

Ramses was also a peacemaker. He and the Hittites signed the world's first peace **treaty**. This peace lasted until the Hittite Empire collapsed around 1190 B.C.E.

One of Ramses' greatest projects was the temple complex at Abu Simbel. The main temple was carved into the side of a cliff. The cliff was on a bank of the Nile River. A smaller temple honored his favorite wife, Nefertari.

Four giant statues of a seated Ramses framed the entrance to the main temple. The figures were carved right out of the rock face of the cliff. They are among the finest examples of the artistic skill of Egyptian sculptors.

The inside of the temple was also remarkable. Visitors passed through three large rooms, called halls, to reach the temple's main room. This room's altar contained statues of Ramses and three Egyptian gods. The temple was built so that, twice a year, the sun lined up with the entrance. Beams of sunlight would shine down the halls and light up the statues.

Ramses ordered more temples and monuments built than any other pharaoh in history. When he died, he was buried in the tomb that he had ordered workers to construct solely for him. His mummy is one of the best-preserved bodies ever found.

This is a view, from below, of one of the four 66-foot statues of Ramses II, seated at the entrance of the main temple at Abu Simbel.

Chapter Summary

In this chapter, you learned about the accomplishments of four of the pharaohs of ancient Egypt who ruled during three long periods of stability.

Ancient Egypt and Its Rulers Ancient Egypt enjoyed three periods of stability and unity under the rule of pharaohs. These periods were the Old Kingdom (Age of the Pyramids) from about 2700 to 2200 B.C.E; the Middle Kingdom, (Period of Reunification) from about 2000 to 1800 B.C.E.; and the New Kingdom, (Golden Age) from about 1600 to 1100 B.C.E.

Pharaoh Khufu During the Old Kingdom, Khufu set up a strong central government. He also had the Great Pyramid built at Giza. It was an amazing construction feat and one of the wonders of the ancient world.

Pharaoh Senusret During the Middle Kingdom, Senusret encouraged Egyptian art and literature. Artisans and architects created fine works, including White Chapel.

Pharaoh Hatshepsut Hatshepsut, Egypt's first female pharaoh, promoted Egyptian trade during the New Kingdom. She had a great temple built at Dayr al-Bahri.

Pharaoh Ramses II Ramses the Great was a superior military leader and builder of monuments during the New Kingdom. He signed the world's first peace treaty with the Hittites. He had the temple complex at Abu Simbel built.

Carter's archaeologists found three nested golden mummy-shaped coffins in King Tut's stone sarcophagus. Inside the third coffin was King Tut's mummy.

The Egyptian Mummy Project

King Tutankhaten—whose remains are one of the most famous Egyptian mummies—died in 1323 B.C.E. He was 18 or 19 years old. For a long time, archaeologists wondered how the young pharaoh had died. In January 2005, for the first time in 80 years, a team of scientists took "King Tut" from his tomb. They used new technologies to reexamine the mummy, searching for answers to age-old questions about the lives and deaths of ancient Egyptians.

The team of scientists removed the stone lid from King Tut's sarcophagus, or stone coffin. They lifted the wooden box containing the mummy and carefully carried it outside. A van holding a CT (or CAT) scanner was waiting near the tomb. This scanner is a large, specialized X-ray machine that uses a computer to show three-dimensional images of a body.

Inside the van, the scientists pulled back layers of cloth surrounding the king. Still in its box, the mummy was placed in the CT scanner for about 15 minutes. The machine took around 1,700 images. Scanning King Tut was the first act of the members of the Egyptian Mummy Project. Scientists from around the world took part in this five-year project to study and preserve the ancient mummies of Egypt.

Ancient Embalmers

The ancient Egyptians turned their dead into mummies to prevent decay and to preserve their bodies. The Egyptians believed that a person would need his or her body in the afterlife.

The process of making a mummy was complex. First, the embalmers took the internal organs out of the body. They dried the organs and the body with *natron*, a type of salt that they found in the desert. The organs were then wrapped in linen and stored in jars or placed back inside the body. Sometimes the body was stuffed and decorated with makeup, jewelry, and clothing. Finally, it was wrapped in long strips of linen and put in a coffin.

Two British scientists, named Richard Evershed and Stephen Buckley, studied 13 mummies that had been created over a 2,300-year period. They concluded that the ancient Egyptian embalmers used very advanced methods in their work.

Studying Mummies, Then and Now

In 1922, Englishman Howard Carter made one of the most important discoveries in Egyptian archaeology—he found the tomb of Tutankhaten in the Valley of the Kings. This was important because Tutankhaten's mummy was found exactly as the priests had left it more than 3,000 years earlier. In most other tombs, the mummies were missing. This kept archaeologists from studying the details about how ancient Egyptians were buried.

In Carter's time, the study of mummies was a simpler process than it is today. Back then, archaeologists would remove the bandages from a mummy to examine the remains. But after a time, scientists began to realize that their actions were causing damage to the bodies. Often, mummies fell apart when taken out of their wrappings. Today, it's sometimes hard to tell if damage to a mummy dates from a king's lifetime, the embalming process, or the way archaeologists treated mummies that were discovered in the 1920s.

Modern scientists use all sorts of technology to study mummies. One technique is to X-ray the body. As people age, their bones become thinner and weaker. By examining X-rays of bones, scientists can tell how old people are. In this way, archaeologists have discovered that ancient Egyptians lived short lives, at least by modern standards. Most rich Egyptians lived no longer than about 35 years. For poor Egyptians, life was even shorter. Most did not live much beyond about 25 years.

Since 1926, the year Carter returned King Tut to his tomb, the young pharaoh's remains have been X-rayed twice. The first time was in 1968. Those X-rays showed a bone fragment inside the king's skull. The finding prompted the idea that King Tut might have died as a result of a blow to the head.

In 2007, King Tut was transferred from the wooden box in which Carter's team had placed him to a climate-controlled glass box. The head of Egypt's Supreme Council of Antiquities, Dr. Zahi Hawass (center), supervised the move.

Scientists from the Egyptian Mummy Project used a CT scan to create three-dimensional images of King Tut's mummy.

Was Tutankhaten murdered? Scientists from the Egyptian Mummy Project set out to answer that question. This time, rather than rely on a one-dimensional X-ray, scientists used the CT scan. They created three-dimensional images that would show more information.

CT Scan Findings

Did the young pharaoh die from a blow to the head? Definitely not, say the nine doctors who studied the CT images.

Scientists believe that the bone fragment discovered in the king's head, in 1968, occurred after his death. It is likely that this damage was caused by the team of archaeologist Howard Carter. Scientists reached this conclusion because they found no traces of embalming fluid in the wound.

Scientists have agreed that there is no evidence of head injury. But they also found a broken bone in the mummy's left leg. Some experts thought that the broken bone was a serious injury Tut suffered shortly before death. They wondered whether the break led to a life-threatening infection. From the CT scans, scientists concluded that Tut died from complications from a broken leg, made worse by disease, probably malaria.

Reconstructing King Tut's Face

Scientists also used the three-dimensional CT scans to create the first busts of the Egyptian king. A bust is a three-dimensional sculpture of a head. Three separate teams—from France, the United States, and Egypt—created busts of King Tut.

The National Geographic Society chose a French team to create the first bust. A CT–scan–based skull model was made for forensic anthropologist Jean-Noël Vignal. Vignal often works with police to reconstruct the heads of victims of violent crimes. Using the CT images, Vignal created a rough plastic skull.

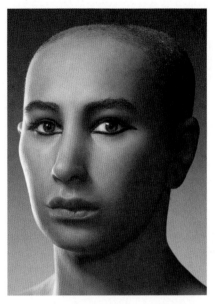

This bust of King Tut was created by a French team. Sculptor Daynès used hair, makeup, and glass eyes to make the bust extremely lifelike.

Vignal gave the plastic skull to sculptor Elisabeth Daynès. Using Vignal's data and two wooden sculptures of Tutankhaten for reference, she created a lifelike clay face. She then created a plaster mold with a silicone "skin," and covered it with a flesh color based on an average shade for modern Egyptians. Next, Daynès added hair, makeup, and glass eyes. The bust was meant to show what Tut had looked like on the day of his death. It is the most lifelike image ever seen of the long-dead ruler.

The National Geographic Society then asked a group of experts from the United States to make a second bust. This time the experts weren't told who their famous subject was.

Susan Antón, an associate professor of anthropology at New York University, and Bradley Adams, of New York City's Chief Medical Examiner's office, both studied the CT scans. At first, Antón thought that the unusual-looking skull was that of a female. But after further study, she determined that her subject was an 18- to 19-year-old male, most likely of North African origin. Forensic artist Michael Anderson, of Yale University's Peabody Museum, used the CT scans and Antón's data to create his own bust of the mystery subject's head.

Finally, Egypt's Supreme Council of Antiquities selected an Egyptian team to make a third bust. Like the French team, the Egyptians knew who their famous subject was. The Egyptian team used the same CT scan data to build a plastic skull model. They added clay features inspired by ancient portraits of Tut.

Archaeologists have not been able to solve all the mysteries of King Tut's death, but they did solve some. First they asked key questions, and then they used the latest technology to gather information. In what other ways might archaeologists use CT scans? What questions do *you* have about ancient mummies?

Chapter 9

Daily Life in Ancient Egypt

How did social class affect daily life in ancient Egypt?

9.1 Introduction

In this chapter, you will meet members of Egyptian society. You'll learn what Egyptian life was like during the New Kingdom (about 1600 to 1100 B.C.E.).

Each year, when the Nile River flooded its banks, all of Egypt celebrated the Opet Festival. Work in the fields stopped while people at all levels of Egyptian society joined in a great festival honoring the pharaoh and his patron, the god Amon-Re (AH-muhn-RAY).

Almost everyone in Egyptian society took part in the Opet Festival. Priests decorated the god's statue with jewelry. They put the statue in a shrine and placed the shrine on a ceremonial boat called a barque. The beautifully decorated boat was made by artisans, or craftspeople. High-ranking government officials competed for the honor of carrying the barque on poles through town. Members at the lower levels of society, such as farmers, lined the streets to watch the procession. Scribes made a written record of the celebration.

The Opet Festival brought all these groups together. But in everyday life, they belonged to very different social classes. These classes made up a social pyramid, with the pharaoh at the top and peasants at the bottom. In between were government officials, priests, scribes, and artisans. The daily lives of the Egyptian people were distinct for each class.

In this chapter, you will learn about the various classes that made up Egypt's social pyramid. Then you'll explore how social rank determined advantages and disadvantages, work responsibilities, and the quality of daily life for the members in each class.

Skilled artisans created this sculpture of the Egyptian sun god Amon-Re.

◀ Festivals brought together ancient Egyptians of every social class.

9.2 Ancient Egypt's Social Pyramid

Egyptian society was structured like a pyramid. At the very top of this **social pyramid** was the pharaoh, Egypt's **supreme** ruler. Egyptian religion strengthened the pharaoh's authority. Pharaohs were believed to be gods, and their word was law.

Next in importance were several layers of **social classes**. The classes near the top of the pyramid had fewer people and enjoyed higher **status**. The classes nearer the bottom had greater numbers of people but lower status.

Egypt's Social Classes   Below the pharaoh were the next two highest classes in the social pyramid—government officials and priests. They were the most powerful groups in Egypt.

Government officials carried out the orders of the pharaoh. Most officials came from **noble** families. They were powerful and wealthy, and they enjoyed a high quality of life.

Priests were also a powerful group, because religion touched every part of people's daily lives. Priests were in charge of the temples and religious rituals. They also oversaw the important ceremonies surrounding death and burial.

Next on the social pyramid were scribes. Scribes held a respected position in society. They recorded information for government and religious leaders. It took many years of schooling to become a scribe.

Artisans **occupied** the next layer of the social pyramid. This group included craftspeople like carpenters, metalworkers, painters, sculptors, and stone carvers. Artisans were highly skilled, but they had little social status.

At the bottom of the social pyramid were the **peasants**. They were the largest social class. Peasants worked the land, providing the Egyptians with a steady food supply. When not farming, peasants worked on the pharaoh's massive building projects.

social pyramid a pyramid outline showing the positions of social classes according to their status in a society

social class a group in a society that is ranked by factors such as wealth, property, and rights

status importance

noble of high birth or rank

peasant a person who does farmwork for wealthy land-owners

pharaoh

government officials

priests

scribes

artisans

peasants

Ancient Egyptian society was organized like a pyramid. The groups near the top had the most power and status.

Egyptian women enjoyed more freedom and rights than most women in the ancient world. A few women even became pharaohs.

Life in Egypt's Social Classes Egypt's social pyramid was fairly **rigid**. Most people belonged to the same social class as their parents. There was little chance of moving to a higher class. Members of different classes may have had some things in common, but, in general, their lives were quite different.

Egyptians in all social classes cherished family life. Most Egyptians married within their social group. Children were highly valued.

Men and women had different **roles** within the family. Men were the heads of their households. They worked to support the family. Fathers often began to train their sons at a young age to take on their line of work. Women typically managed the home and raised the children. Upper-class women had servants or slaves to help them. Lower-class women did the work themselves.

Men were in charge of Egyptian society, but women enjoyed more freedom and rights than most women in the ancient world. They could own land and run businesses. They could also ask for divorces and represent themselves in legal matters. Some women in the middle and upper classes worked as doctors, government officials, or priestesses. Both women and men enjoyed a better quality of life the higher they were on the social pyramid.

The Egyptians believed that their class system created a stable, well-ordered society. Each group had its own role to play. Let's take a look at the duties and daily lives of the various social classes during the time of the New Kingdom.

9.3 Government Officials

Government officials belonged to the highest class on Egypt's social pyramid, after the pharaoh. Their job was to assist the pharaoh in his or her role as supreme ruler of Egypt.

Government officials were often members of the pharaoh's family or other upper-class families. Most of them inherited their positions from family members. However, trusted servants from the royal court sometimes rose to power.

This is a statue of Imhotep, who was an early and powerful vizier in ancient Egypt. Imhotep was famous for his role in designing and building great monuments.

Important Government Officials Three important officials were the vizier (vuh-ZEER), the chief treasurer, and the general of the armies. Each had his own duties.

The vizier had more power than anyone except the pharaoh. The vizier advised the pharaoh and carried out his commands. He appointed and supervised many of the other government officials.

The vizier also served as a kind of chief judge. Other judges would bring him their toughest cases. A vizier was expected to be fair and **neutral**, showing no special favor to either side in a dispute. One vizier gave this advice about being impartial, or not taking sides: "Regard one you know like one you don't know, one near you like one far from you." In works of art, viziers were often shown wearing white, the color of neutrality.

The chief treasurer oversaw the government's wealth. His main duty was to collect taxes. Egypt's economy was based on goods rather than money. People paid their taxes in grain, cows, cloth, and silver.

After the pharaoh, the top military commander in Egypt was the general of the armies. He advised the pharaoh in matters of war and national security, such as how to protect Egypt's borders from invaders. He also helped the pharaoh make alliances with other kingdoms.

Lives of Luxury High government officials led lives of luxury. Most were nobles who had great wealth, fine homes, and plenty of time to socialize.

The lavish banquets enjoyed by these wealthy Egyptians illustrate their grand lifestyle. Hosts took pride in the meal. Cooks might roast duck, goose, pigeon, quail, antelope, sheep, and goat.

Dishes were piled high with special delicacies that might include figs, dates, grapes, and coconuts. A variety of breads and cakes and honey completed the feast.

Guests at banquets dressed in fine linen clothing. Both men and women wore perfume. Women often wore ropes of beads as jewelry. They painted their nails, lined their eyes with makeup, and used lipstick.

At the start of a banquet, it was customary for guests to offer the host lengthy blessings, such as wealth, great happiness, a long life, and good health. The host often responded simply with "Welcome, welcome," or "Bread and beer," as a way of saying, "Come and eat!"

The feast began with men and women taking their seats on opposite sides of the room. Important guests were given chairs with high backs. Everyone else sat on stools or cushions. Servants, mostly women, waited on the guests. There were no forks or spoons, so people ate with their fingers.

While the guests ate, musicians, dancers, and acrobats provided entertainment. Musicians were usually women. They played flutes, harps, rattles, and lutes (a guitarlike instrument). Guests often clapped along with the music.

These women of high social class enjoy a banquet.

Priests shaved their heads as one of many steps in achieving religious purity.

9.4 Priests

Like government officials, priests were powerful and highly respected in society. A large network of priests served under the pharaoh, who was considered the highest-ranked priest of all.

The Duties of Priests   Priests had different jobs. The High Priest advised the pharaoh and oversaw all religious ceremonies. Temple priests were in charge of the temples scattered throughout Egypt. Other priests handled more common concerns and requests. They gave advice and performed healings.

Women were allowed to be priestesses in Egypt. They were generally regarded as equal to male priests. Their main duty was to oversee temples that were devoted to music and dancing.

Temple priests played an extremely important role in Egyptian religion. Every temple was home to one or more Egyptian gods. A temple priest's primary job was to take care of his temple's special god in a variety of ways.

A temple's god was thought to live in a statue. The statue was housed in a holy room called a sanctuary. Only a priest who had purified (cleansed) himself could enter the sanctuary. There were many steps a priest had to take to be purified. He had to avoid certain foods, such as fish, that were associated with the lower classes. He had to cleanse his body by bathing in holy pools, three or four times a day. He also had to shave off his body hair. And he had to wear clothes made of linen cloth, because animal products like leather and wool were considered unclean. Once he was purified, the priest could perform his sacred duties.

afterlife an existence after death

The Priests' Role in Burial Practices

Priests had a special role to play in burial practices. Egyptians believed in a life after death. They thought that in the **afterlife,** a person's body remained with his or her dead spirit. For this reason, the Egyptians used a method called embalming to preserve bodies from decay. Priests oversaw this sacred ritual.

The embalming process had many steps. First, the embalmers removed the body's organs, such as the brain, lungs, and liver. They used hooks to pull the brain out through the nostrils. Only the heart was left in the body. Egyptians believed that the gods used the heart to judge a dead person's soul.

Then, the organs were packed in jars to preserve them. The organs and body were dried out with a special salt called natron.

After about 70 days, the embalmers washed and oiled the body. Then they wrapped it in hundreds of yards of linen. The embalmers decorated the wrapped body, or mummy, with pieces of jewelry and protective charms. Often, they placed a mask over the head. Finally, they spread a black, gooey gum over the body and wrapped it a final time.

The mummy was then ready for burial. First, it was placed in a wooden box. The box was then stored inside a large stone coffin called a sarcophagus. Because the ancient Egyptians believed that the afterlife was much like life in this world, they buried other items along with the box or coffin. These included food and drink, furniture, statues, jewelry, gold, clothes, games, and mirrors.

Not all Egyptians could afford such complicated burials. But even poor Egyptians wrapped their dead in cloth and buried them with loaves of bread and other items they thought would be needed in the afterlife.

The Egyptian process of embalming a body produced a mummy, such as the one shown here.

This engraving shows students in a scribe school, working at their writing.

9.5 Scribes

In the social pyramid, scribes were one level below priests. Scribes were Egypt's official writers and record keepers. They were highly respected and well paid. Most scribes worked for the government. Others worked for priests or nobles.

Only men were allowed to be scribes. They came from all classes of society. Becoming a scribe was one of the few ways that men could rise above their parents' social class.

Scribe Schools Boys who wanted to become scribes had to attend scribe schools. The schools were run by priests. Most students came from artisan or merchant families. Very few boys came from the peasant class.

Schooling started around the age of five. Students typically spent 12 years or more learning **hieroglyphs,** the symbols used in the Egyptian system of writing. This writing system was quite complicated. Most students first mastered a simpler form of writing and then worked their way up to hieroglyphs.

Students had to memorize over 700 hieroglyphs. They spent as many as four years copying the signs, over and over. They practiced their writing on pieces of wood, flakes of stone, and even broken bits of pottery. As their skills improved, students were allowed to write on papyrus, a type of paper made from the papyrus plant.

Students in scribe schools did not have an easy life. Classes sometimes lasted from dawn until sunset. Teachers were strict and often treated their students harshly. Teachers punished students for being lazy or for not paying attention. Beatings were common. One stern schoolmaster wrote, "A youngster's ear is on his back; he only listens to the man who beats him."

hieroglyph a symbol used in hieroglyphics, a system of writing developed around 3000 B.C.E.

The Work of the Scribes   Ancient Egyptians kept all kinds of records, so scribes held a wide variety of jobs. They recorded accounts of the grain and food supply. They wrote down the results of the government census, which counted the people living in Egypt. Some scribes calculated and collected taxes. Legal scribes recorded court cases and helped enforce laws. Military scribes kept track of the army's soldiers and food supply, and the number of enemies killed in battle.

Every scribe used the same tools. For pens, a scribe used finely sharpened reeds. For paper, he used a sheet of papyrus laid on a writing tablet. The tablets were made of wood or stone. Each tablet contained two wells, one for black ink and one for red ink. A small container held water that was used to wet the ink.

A scribe carried his tools with him wherever he traveled. His tablet hung from a cord slung over his shoulder. Attached to the tablet were leather bags and cases that held his other tools.

Scribes also carried rolls of papyrus. This paper was a remarkable Egyptian invention. The Egyptians made paper by first cutting the inner part of the papyrus plant into strips. These strips were soaked in water for several days until they were soft. The soft strips were laid out in a crisscross pattern, and then pressed between two sheets of cloth until all the water was absorbed. Finally, the papyrus strips were pressed one more time to form a sheet of paper.

This relief shows two scribes. Only men were allowed to be scribes, although women were sometimes taught to read and write.

9.6 Artisans

Below the scribes on the social pyramid were the artisans. Egypt's artisans were highly skilled laborers who created some of the most beautiful art objects in the ancient world. Yet, unlike scribes, they rarely got respect from higher classes. Only the few who became masters at their craft were sometimes honored for their work.

Types of Artisans Artisans specialized in any one of a number of crafts. Workers in this class included carpenters, jewelers, leatherworkers, metalworkers, painters, potters, sculptors, and weavers. Artisans made many beautiful objects, including stunning jewelry and elegant furniture. Painters portrayed scenes of Egyptian daily life. Most artisans were men, but some women wove fabric, beaded clothing, and made perfume.

The most skilled artisans were the stone carvers. They produced the statues, engravings, and reliefs found in Egyptian temples, tombs, and monuments.

Stone carvers played an important role in tomb building. The belief in an afterlife inspired wealthy Egyptians to order elaborate tombs for themselves. Stone carvers helped equip the tombs with artworks to honor and preserve the dead. Artworks might include statues of the deceased, highly detailed wall engravings, and stone coffins.

Stone carving was demanding and time-consuming work. Carvers often worked with hard rock, such as granite. They used dolerite, another type of hard rock, to pound out an initial shape. Next, they refined the shape and carved in details, using stone tools and copper chisels. Then, they used quartz sand to smooth and polish the object. Painters often added color to the finished product.

Stone carvers were some of the most skilled workers in the artisan class.

The Daily Life and Work of Artisans

Artisans were a class toward the lower middle of society. They lived with their families in modest homes. Their houses were usually rectangular and barely 10 yards long. Three rooms stretched from front to back. The first room was used as a workroom or to house animals.

The living room came next. The final room was divided into a kitchen and a bedroom. The roof was sometimes used as another place to work or sleep.

Artisans typically worked side by side in big workshops. They usually worked for ten days at a stretch before taking time off. The workers depended entirely on their employers for food. In hard times, when food was in short supply, artisans often went hungry.

Pharaohs called upon hundreds of artisans at a time to work on royal projects. Artisans created the fine artwork that often covered temples, royal tombs, and other monuments. They worked in large groups to complete engravings, paintings, and hieroglyphics.

Despite artisans' skill and creativity, the upper classes often viewed them as little more than common laborers. Even the most talented artists were rarely allowed to sign their work. But some artists did receive recognition. Employers sometimes threw a banquet for their favorite artist. Occasionally, they honored an artist by letting him portray himself in a painting or an engraving.

This painting shows different types of artisans at work. Look carefully. What do you see?

9.7 Peasants

Peasants made up the lowest and largest class in Egypt's social pyramid. They were generally considered unskilled laborers. Yet Egyptian society depended on their work. Peasants grew the crops that supplied everyone with food. When not busy working the fields, peasants helped build monuments like the pyramids.

The Three Seasons of the Nile   Peasant life revolved around the Nile River. Its three seasons were the flooding season, the planting season, and the harvest season.

The flooding season lasted from June to September. During this time, the Nile overran its banks and fertilized the fields. Farmers had to wait for the waters to go down before they could work the fields. In the meantime, they labored on royal projects, such as building pyramids and temples.

This engraving shows a young peasant with his cow. Peasants worked hard to supply Egyptians with food.

In October, the planting season began, and farmers sowed their fields with seeds. The biggest crops were wheat and barley, which were used to make bread.

Peasants worked in pairs to sow the fields. The farmer softened the earth with a plow pulled by cattle. A second person, often the farmer's wife, followed behind to scatter the seeds. Throughout the season, farmers carefully irrigated the land.

The harvest season began in March. Usually the farmer's entire family helped with the harvest. The men cut down the plants with sickles (metal blades with short wooden handles). Then the women and children gathered the tall stalks of grain.

During harvest time, everyone worked from dawn to dusk. Peasants often sang songs to make the long hours of labor go more quickly. Sometimes, musicians played in the fields while the workers sang.

The Daily Lives of Peasants   Peasants had the fewest comforts of any of the social classes. They lived in plain houses made of mud bricks. Their furniture was sparse, often just woven mats.

The peasants' diet was also simple. A typical daily meal might be made up of onions, cucumbers, fish, and homemade bread.

Peas and lentils were also common. Unlike the upper classes, peasants rarely ate meat. In times of famine, they often had to boil tough papyrus plants for food.

Peasants spent most of their lives working, but they did have some time for fun. Men enjoyed a river game that involved knocking each other off papyrus rafts. Holidays were celebrated before planting and after the crops were harvested. Peasants also took part in festivals held to honor the Egyptian gods.

An important time of year for peasants was the end of the harvest season. As a reward for their hard work, they were allowed to gather up any leftover grain and keep it for food.

But farmers could also be punished for a poor harvest. They had to pay taxes in the form of crops. If a harvest came up too short to pay the required tax, a farmer might be brutally beaten.

This painting shows peasants cutting and gathering the wheat harvest.

Chapter Summary

In this chapter, you learned about Egypt's social pyramid. Their social class determined the daily life of ancient Egyptians.

Government Officials This was the highest social class after the pharaoh. Many officials were nobles who inherited their jobs, but some rose to power. Three key officials were the vizier, the chief treasurer, and the general of the armies.

Priests Priests were powerful and respected. They advised the pharaoh, oversaw religious ceremonies, took care of temple gods, and prepared bodies for the afterlife.

Scribes Scribes were Egypt's official writers and record keepers. They were well paid and respected. They trained for many years in special schools to learn hieroglyphs, Egypt's writing symbols. Boys from several social classes could become scribes.

Artisans These highly skilled laborers created beautiful objects but got little respect. Stone carvers were among the most skilled and important artisans.

Peasants This lowest and largest social class grew crops that supplied food and also helped build monuments such as the pyramids. Peasants' lives revolved around the three seasons of the Nile River.

Chapter 10

The Kingdom of Kush

In what ways did location influence the history of Kush?

10.1 Introduction

In this chapter, you will learn about the African kingdom of Kush. Kush was located on the Nile River, to the south of Egypt.

The civilization of Kush thrived from about 2000 B.C.E. to 350 C.E. Kush and Egypt had a close relationship throughout much of Kush's long history. Signs of their close ties can be found in pictures on the walls of some Egyptian tombs and temples.

A good example is the tomb of Hatshepsut, Egypt's first female pharaoh. Many painted scenes of Egyptian life decorate the walls. But on closer examination, not all the people in the paintings are Egyptian. Some people look a little different. They have darker skin and curly hair. These people are Kushites (KUH-shites). In some scenes, the Kushites appear to be bearing gifts. In others, they look as if they are armed with bows and arrows. As these images suggest, Egypt and Kush had a **complicated** relationship. Sometimes it was peaceful. Often it was not.

In this chapter, you will learn about the relationship between Egypt and Kush and the influence of each culture on the other. You will also discover how the location of Kush influenced its history and how Kush created its own **unique** civilization.

Kushites built pyramids and temples. The pyramids shown here are south of Egypt, in the present-day African country of Sudan.

◀ A part of a tomb wall shows Kushites bearing gifts for the pharaoh.

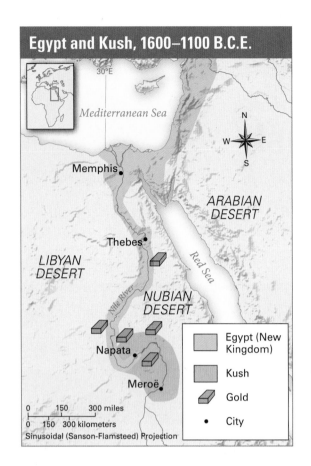

Egypt and Kush, 1600–1100 B.C.E.

Mediterranean Sea

30°E

Memphis

ARABIAN DESERT

Thebes

LIBYAN DESERT

Red Sea

Nile River

NUBIAN DESERT

Napata

Meroë

0   150   300 miles
0   150   300 kilometers
Sinusoidal (Sanson-Flamsteed) Projection

- Egypt (New Kingdom)
- Kush
- Gold
- City

Its location along the Nile River, to the south of ancient Egypt, affected the history of Kush.

Kushites had to bring gifts, such as exotic giraffes and monkeys, to Egypt's governor as tribute.

10.2 The Egyptianization of Kush

Aside from Egypt, Kush was the greatest ancient civilization in Africa. Like its neighbor to the north, Kush grew up around the fertile banks of the Nile River. Kush was known for its rich gold mines. In fact, another name for *Kush* is *Nubia,* which comes from *nub,* the Egyptian word for gold.

Kush's location and natural **resources** made it an important trading hub, or center. Kush linked central and southern Africa to Egypt. Pharaohs sent expeditions on ships south along the Nile to buy, or sometimes steal, goods. The Egyptians traded grain and linen for Kush's gold, ivory, leather, and timber. The Egyptians also bought slaves.

At times, Egypt raided Kush or took control of some of its lands. During the New Kingdom (about 1600–1100 B.C.E.), Egypt's power was at its height. Egypt conquered Kush. Kush was forced to pay tribute to Egypt in the form of gifts. The pharaoh appointed a governor to make sure the tribute was paid every year. The Kushites gave the governor gold, cattle, ivory, ebony, ostrich feathers, and slaves.

While under Egypt's control, Kushite society became Egyptianized, or more like Egypt. For example, Kushites spoke and wrote in Egyptian. They worshiped Egyptian gods and wore Egyptian-style clothes. Kush's archers fought in Egypt's army. Kush's royal princes were sent to Egypt to be educated.

Around 1100 B.C.E., Egypt's New Kingdom collapsed. Kush regained its independence. However, Egyptian culture persisted. About 900 B.C.E., a new line of Kushite kings was **established**. But even these kings continued to follow Egyptian traditions.

10.3 Kush Conquers Egypt

After the collapse of the New Kingdom, Egypt fell into political chaos. At least ten Egyptian kingdoms fought one another for power. The constant fighting made Egypt weak and unstable.

In the mid-700s B.C.E., Kush took advantage of Egypt's weakness. Kushite armies invaded Egypt. In about 730 B.C.E., the kings in northern Egypt surrendered to Piye, king of Kush.

After his conquest of Egypt, Piye declared himself pharaoh. One of his titles was "Uniter of the Two Lands." The kingdom of Kush now extended 1,500 miles. It reached from the Kushite city of **Meroë** (MER-oh-ee), located on the southern Nile River, to the Mediterranean Sea.

In Egypt, Piye and his family became the 25th **dynasty,** or line of rulers. Kushite pharaohs ruled over Egypt for nearly a century. Historians have traditionally called them the "black pharaohs."

The Kushite pharaohs did not want to destroy Egypt. Instead, they wanted to revive Egypt's past glory. They built magnificent new temples and pyramids in both Egypt and Kush. One of the most beautiful was the temple at Jebel Barkal. It was modeled after the temple built by Egyptian pharaoh Ramses II at Abu Simbel.

By the 670s B.C.E., Egypt was being attacked by the Assyrians. The Assyrians had created a powerful empire in Mesopotamia. In 671 B.C.E., an Assyrian king invaded Egypt. For many years, the Kushites tried to hold off the forces of the Assyrians. But the Assyrians used their advanced iron weaponry to drive the Kushites out of Egypt. By the mid 650s B.C.E., the last of the Kushite pharaohs had fled to Kush.

Meroë a city on the Nile River that became the center of Kushite culture and industry

dynasty a family or group that rules for several generations

This painting shows Egyptian royalty bowing and offering gifts to King Piye. Now, Egypt was forced to pay tribute to Kush.

10.4 The Kush Capital of Meroë

A new dynasty in Kush followed the Kushite pharaohs that had ruled Egypt. About 590 B.C.E., Egypt once more invaded Kush and was able to destroy its capital city, Napata (NAP-uh-tuh). The Kushites decided to make Meroë their new capital. Meroë was 300 miles south of Napata, safely out of Egypt's reach.

Meroë's location helped Kush remain an important center of trade. Traders used the Nile, the Red Sea, and overland routes to transport their goods. Most of these routes took traders through Kush. As a result, Kushites traded with many lands. Some of these lands were nearby, such as other African kingdoms and Arabia. But Kush also traded with such distant lands as Rome (on the peninsula of Italy), India, and possibly even China.

Meroë was a large and wealthy city. It became the center of a Kushite civilization that lasted for nearly 1,000 years. At its height, the city thrived as a great center of industry as well as culture. It became especially well known for producing iron. Because of their **superior** knowledge of iron technology, the Assyrians had triumphed over the Kushites in Egypt. The Kushites were now determined to equal the military might of the Assyrians.

Meroë had everything needed to produce iron. It had a rich supply of iron deposits. It also had plenty of forests, which provided the wood needed to make charcoal. The charcoal was used to heat the iron deposits. Once the hot iron separated from the rock, it was cooled in the Nile's waters.

Ironworkers in Kush made a variety of things. They crafted weapons such as spears, arrows, and swords. They also created tools to make farming faster and easier. These tools included axes, for quickly clearing forests, and hoes, for loosening soil.

Kushites used iron to make many useful objects. Here, we see Kushite ironworkers crafting spearheads.

kandake a powerful female leader who co-ruled Kush with her husband or sons

10.5 Kush Returns to Its African Roots

After its separation from Egypt, Kush returned to its African roots. Artwork, clothing, and buildings no longer imitated Egyptian styles. Kushites worshiped an African lion-god rather than Egyptian gods. The Kushite people wrote and spoke a native language called Meroitic (mer-uh-wid-ik), after Meroë, which had its own alphabet.

Kushite art and architecture flourished. Artisans made beautiful pottery, cloth, and gold and silver jewelry. Rulers built grand palaces, temples, and pyramids.

Kush also revived the African practice of female leadership. Powerful **kandakes,** or queen mothers, ruled Meroë. The kandakes usually co-ruled with their sons or husbands. Kandakes were considered goddesses and were very powerful.

One of the greatest kandakes was Queen Amanirenas. She defended Kush against the powerful Romans in 24 B.C.E. The Romans had taken over Egypt as they expanded their vast empire. They then demanded tribute from Kush. Kandake Amanirenas and her son, Prince Akinidad, led an attack that destroyed several Roman forts on Kush's borders. The war with Rome raged on.

After three years of fierce fighting, Rome signed a peace treaty with Kush. Kush no longer had to pay tribute to Rome.

Under Amanirenas, Kush had defeated the most powerful empire in the world. The kingdom of Kush survived for nearly 400 more years. In 350 C.E., Kush fell to invaders from the African country of Ethiopia.

Amanirenas and her son, Akinidad, watch a Roman fort burn. Amanirenas fought side by side with her soldiers, even losing an eye in battle.

Chapter Summary

In this chapter, you learned about the African kingdom of Kush. Kush had a complicated relationship with ancient Egypt, its neighbor to the north.

The Egyptianization of Kush Kush's location on the Nile River and its natural resources made it a trade center. During the New Kingdom period, Egypt conquered Kush and Kushites adopted Egyptian ways.

Kush Conquers Egypt Under the rule of King Piye, Kush conquered Egypt. Kushite pharaohs ruled Egypt for nearly a century, building new temples and pyramids in both Egypt and Kush. Then the Assyrians forced the Kushites to leave Egypt.

The Kush Capital of Meroë Meroë became the capital of Kush about 590 B.C.E. It was the center of Kushite industry, such as ironwork, and trade for 1,000 years.

Kush Returns to Its African Roots Kush returned to its African culture and revived the African practice of powerful women leaders, called kandakes. Kandake Amanirenas stopped Rome's attempt to take control of Kush.

Chapter 11

The Origins of Judaism

How did Judaism originate and develop?

11.1 Introduction

In this chapter, you will learn about a group of people who lived northeast of Egypt. These people were known as the Israelites, later called Jews.

Jewish civilization developed gradually after about 1800 B.C.E. and continues to flourish today. The people who became the Jews originally lived in Mesopotamia. Around 1950 B.C.E., they moved to Canaan. Canaan was located on a strip of land extending along the eastern coast of the Mediterranean Sea.

The Israelites, sometimes called Hebrews, were the ancestors of the Jewish people. Judaism is the religion of the Jewish people and is one of the world's most influential religious traditions.

The origins of Judaism and its basic teachings and laws are recorded in its most sacred text, the Torah. The word *Torah* means "teaching." The Torah consists of the first five books of the Hebrew Bible. This bible is also called the *Tanakh* (TAH-nahkh). In addition to the Torah, the Hebrew Bible includes two collections of texts known as the Prophets and the Writings. Christians use a version of the Hebrew Bible as their Old Testament.

In this chapter, you will find out about the origins, or beginnings, of Judaism. You will read about some of the early history of the Jewish people, as told in the Hebrew Bible. You will also meet four leaders of the ancient Israelites—Abraham, Moses, and kings David and Solomon (SAH-leh-mehn)—and learn about their contributions to the development of Judaism.

The Torah scroll contains the first five books of the Hebrew Bible.

◀ Moses and the Ten Commandments

Torah Judaism's most sacred text, consisting of the first five books of the Hebrew Bible

Israelite an early name for the Jewish people

Judaism the first religion to worship one God, developed among the ancient Israelites

tradition an inherited or customary pattern of thought, action, or behavior

Israel the Israelites' kingdom; divided about 930 B.C.E. into two kingdoms called Judah and Israel

11.2 What We Know About the Ancient Israelites

Historians rely on sources of information such as artifacts and writings, including the **Torah** and the other parts of the Hebrew Bible. From such sources, scholars have learned much about the ancient **Israelites** and the development of **Judaism**.

The Torah The Torah contains written records and teachings of the Jews, and 613 commandments that direct moral and religious conduct. As often happened in ancient times, accounts of the history of the Jewish people were handed down orally from generation to generation. Later on, these stories and **traditions** were written down.

Besides the Torah and the other parts of the Hebrew Bible, historians look at additional sources of information about events and ideas in early Jewish history. Historians often examine archaeological artifacts as well as written records to gain a better understanding of life in this time period.

Every Torah scroll is handwritten by a specially trained scribe on sheets of parchment made from animal skins.

The Early History of the Israelites

According to the Torah, the ancestor of the Israelites was a man named Abraham who lived near Ur in Mesopotamia. Around 1950 B.C.E., Abraham and his family migrated to Canaan, a region of land along the eastern coast of the Mediterranean Sea. Settling in Canaan, the Israelites herded flocks of sheep and goats.

About 1800 B.C.E., according to the first book of the Torah, a famine forced many Israelites to flee from Canaan to Egypt. For a while, the Israelites prospered in Egypt, but **eventually** they were enslaved. In time, one of their leaders, Moses, led the Israelites in their escape from Egypt.

For 40 years, says the Torah, the Israelites traveled in the wilderness, until they settled once again in Canaan. By 1000 B.C.E., the Israelites had set up the kingdom of **Israel** in Canaan. Israel was ruled by King David and then by his son, King Solomon. David united the Israelites into one kingdom. Solomon built a magnificent temple in the capital city. When Solomon died, in about 930 B.C.E., the kingdom of Israel separated into two kingdoms—Israel in the north and Judah in the south.

11.3 Important Jewish Leaders

The Hebrew Bible tells of the lives of early Jewish leaders. Four key leaders were Abraham, Moses, David, and Solomon.

Abraham   Abraham is called the "father of the Jews." One central idea of Judaism is the belief in a single God. According to the Torah, it was Abraham who introduced this belief to the Israelites, ancestors of the Jews. This was a new idea in the ancient world. At that time, most people worshiped many gods and goddesses.

According to the Torah, God first spoke to Abraham, telling him to move his family from Mesopotamia to Canaan. God also promised to make Abraham the father of a great nation and to bless this nation. Abraham did as he was told, and his descendants became known as the Jewish people.

The ancient Jewish leaders Abraham and Moses (at left), and David (at far right), were honored in these 13th century statues at the Chartres Cathedral in France. In this way, Christianity honored its Jewish origins.

Moses   The greatest leader of the Israelites was Moses. The Torah tells how he led his people out of **slavery** in Egypt. Moses told the Israelites that God would lead them to Canaan, the "promised land," in exchange for their faithful obedience.

Moses also gave Judaism its **fundamental** teachings. The Torah tells how God gave Moses ten important commandments, or laws, engraved on two stone tablets. These teachings became the **foundation** of Judaism. The books of the Torah are also called the Five Books of Moses.

Kings David and Solomon   After escaping from Egypt and traveling in the wilderness, the Israelites returned to Canaan. It was here that they created a united kingdom, called Israel, during the reigns of King David and his son, King Solomon.

King David established **Jerusalem** as a holy city and the capital of Israel. King Solomon built Jerusalem's great First Temple. To the Israelites, and later the Jews, the city of Jerusalem and its Temple became powerful **symbols** of their faith in God.

You will now learn more about each of these four important leaders. Let's find out what the Hebrew Bible tells about them.

slavery   the state of a person who is treated as the property of another

Jerusalem   the holiest city of the Jews; capital of the ancient kingdoms of Israel and then Judah

covenant an agreement or promise

11.4 The Life of Abraham: Father of the Jews

Some scholars believe that Abraham, originally named Abram (AY-brum), was born about 2000 B.C.E. in Ur in Mesopotamia. The people of Ur worshiped many gods. But Abram came to believe that there was one true God. This belief would set Judaism apart from other ancient religions. Abram's special relationship to God would become the foundation of the Jewish faith.

Abraham's Covenant with God According to the Torah, the faith that would become Judaism began with a sacred agreement, or **covenant,** between God and Abram. When Abram was about 50 years old, the Torah says that God visited him. God said to him, "Leave your own country and your father's house, and go to a country that I will show you." God promised to make Abram the father of a great nation of people.

Abram obeyed. Around 1950 B.C.E., he gathered his many relatives and went west into the land of Canaan.

This map shows the route that Abraham may have taken when God told him to leave his home in Ur and go to the land of Canaan.

The Torah says that when Abram was 99 years old, God spoke to him again: "I will make a covenant between myself and you." God promised to love and protect Abram's descendants, meaning Abram's children and the generations that would follow. In return, Abram agreed that he and his people would always devote themselves to God.

To mark their covenant, the Torah says, God gave Abram a new name, Abraham, which means "father of many." God also promised the land of Canaan to Abraham's people. For Jews, Canaan became the "promised land." According to the Torah, the covenant meant that Jews would set an example by their actions for how God wanted people to live.

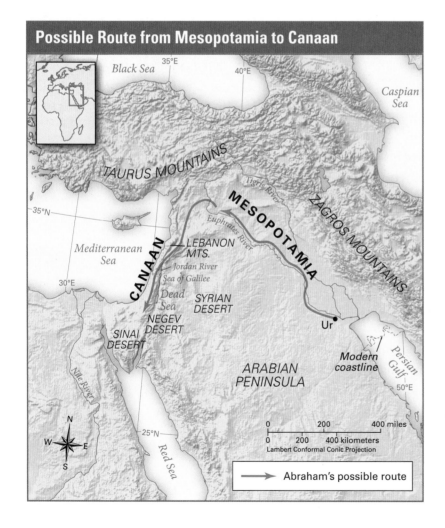

Possible Route from Mesopotamia to Canaan

Black Sea

Caspian Sea

TAURUS MOUNTAINS

Tigris River

ZAGROS MOUNTAINS

Euphrates River

MESOPOTAMIA

Mediterranean Sea

CANAAN

LEBANON MTS.

Jordan River

Sea of Galilee

Dead Sea

SYRIAN DESERT

NEGEV DESERT

SINAI DESERT

Nile River

Ur

Modern coastline

Persian Gulf

ARABIAN PENINSULA

Red Sea

N
W   E
S

0   200   400 miles
0   200   400 kilometers
Lambert Conformal Conic Projection

→ Abraham's possible route

According to the Hebrew Bible, God sent angels to Abraham (right) and Sarah (left) to tell them that they would have a son.

Abraham's Descendants   Many years earlier, before Abram left the city of Ur, he had married a beautiful woman named Sarai. She endured many hardships as she traveled with her husband to Canaan and Egypt. As the years passed, she did not have any children.

The Torah says that God promised that Abraham's wife would have a son. God gave Sarai a new name, Sarah, which means "princess." A year later, Sarah gave birth to Isaac. The Torah says that she was 90 and Abraham was 100 years old when their son was born. As Isaac's mother, Sarah was the ancestress of the Jewish people.

According to the Torah, the Jewish people are descended from Abraham and Sarah, through their son Isaac and his wife Rebekah. Rebekah gave birth to Jacob, whose name was later changed to Israel. The descendants of Jacob, Abraham's grandson, were the Israelites. They flourished as a nation made up of 12 tribes.

Abraham made many contributions to the development of Judaism. He introduced the belief in a single God. Because of his covenant with God, Jews believed that they should set an example of how to live. Their reward was the promised land. These beliefs became a central part of Judaism.

According to the Torah, Moses parted the waters of the Sea of Reeds. Jewish people believe that this miracle proved that God was watching over them.

11.5 The Life of Moses: Leader of the Israelites

Moses was a great leader of the Israelites. The Torah tells how Moses led the Israelites out of slavery in Egypt and gave them God's laws and teachings to live by.

The Exodus from Egypt By the time of Moses, in the 1300s B.C.E., a large group of Abraham's descendants were living in Egypt. There, the Torah says, the Israelites "increased in number and became very powerful." Fearful of their growing strength, the pharaoh forced them into slavery. According to the Torah, God told Moses, "I will send you to the pharaoh, and you shall free my people."

Moses went before the pharaoh, the Torah continues, and told him to let the Israelites go free. When the pharaoh refused, God punished Egypt with ten terrible plagues. Finally, the pharaoh gave in. Moses began to lead the Israelites out of Egypt.

According to the Torah, the pharaoh soon changed his mind. The Egyptian army chased after the Israelites and nearly caught up with them at the edge of the Sea of Reeds. But Moses raised his staff (walking stick), says the Torah, and the waters of the sea parted. The Israelites crossed safely to the other side. When the Egyptians tried to follow, the waters flooded over the army, drowning the soldiers. The Israelites escaped.

The Torah calls the flight from Egypt to freedom the **Exodus,** which means "departure." The Exodus became a central event in the history of the Jewish people.

Exodus the escape of the Israelites from slavery in Egypt to freedom

The Ten Commandments   As it is told in the Torah, after the Israelites left Egypt, they traveled through a wilderness for 40 years. During this time, God gave Moses the laws and teachings that became the foundation of Judaism. Some of these laws are called the **Ten Commandments**.

The Torah says that Moses received the Ten Commandments on Mount Sinai, the "Mountain of God." Alone, Moses had gone up the mountain to pray. He returned carrying two tablets of stone. Engraved on the tablets were the Ten Commandments.

Some of the commandments listed the Israelites' duties to God. For example, one commandment was, "You shall have no other gods besides me." This commandment reminded the Israelites of their promise to worship only one God. Another commandment told the Israelites to set aside one day a week, the Sabbath, for rest and worship.

Other commandments laid down basic moral teachings (ideas about the right way to live). For example, one said, "You shall honor your father and mother." Other commandments forbade stealing, lying, and murdering.

The Ten Commandments stated some of Judaism's basic teachings. The Torah says that by obeying God's commandments, the Jewish people would fulfill their part of the covenant with him. Their responsibility was to make God's moral teachings known to the world. In turn, God would protect them.

Moses made several key contributions to the development of Judaism. First, he led the Exodus out of Egypt. Jews have celebrated this event ever since to remember the journey from slavery to freedom and as proof that God watched over them. Second, Moses gave Judaism some of its most fundamental laws and teachings, which Jews and Christians call the Ten Commandments. Third, Moses forged the Israelites into a united Jewish people devoted to a single God.

Ten Commandments ten laws and teachings said to have been given to Moses by God

This map shows Moses' possible route in the Exodus from Egypt. Find where the Torah says he received the Ten Commandments.

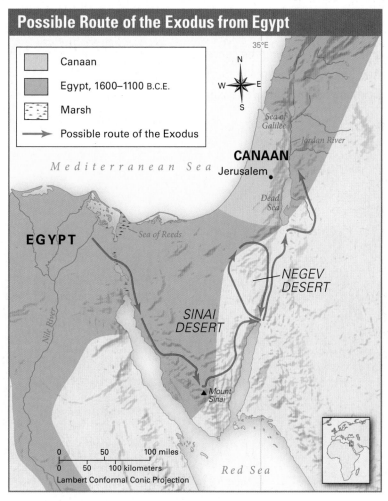

Possible Route of the Exodus from Egypt

Canaan

Egypt, 1600–1100 B.C.E.

Marsh

Possible route of the Exodus

Mediterranean Sea

CANAAN
Jerusalem

Sea of Galilee

Jordan River

Dead Sea

EGYPT

Sea of Reeds

NEGEV DESERT

SINAI DESERT

Nile River

▲ *Mount Sinai*

0   50   100 miles
0   50   100 kilometers
Lambert Conformal Conic Projection

Red Sea

35°E

N
W   E
S

11.6 The Lives of David and Solomon: Kings of Israel

After their travels in the wilderness, the Israelites settled once more in Canaan. The Hebrew Bible describes how they built a kingdom, called Israel, and the great First Temple during the reigns of two kings, David and Solomon.

David Expands the Kingdom of Israel In David's time, about 1000 B.C.E., the Israelites were at war with a rival people, the Philistines (FIH-lih-steenz). According to the Hebrew Bible, the Philistines promised to be the Israelites' slaves if an Israelite could beat their fiercest warrior, the giant Goliath (guh-LIE-uhth).

As it is told in the Hebrew Bible, David was not yet a grown man, but he was outraged at Goliath's mockery of God. Bravely, he stepped forward. His only weapon was a slingshot. With one mighty throw, he felled Goliath with a stone.

David's courage and faith were rewarded when he became king of the Israelites after the first king, Saul, fell in battle. According to the Hebrew Bible, God said, "The Israelite kingdom will remain with him and with his children and his children's children forever."

As king, David completed the defeat of the Philistines as well as other enemies. He united the Israelites into a single nation known as Israel. He created a strong central government. He gave the new kingdom its own army, courts, and officials. David himself served as the nation's chief priest. He was also a poet and a musician. Many of the Psalms in the Writings in the Hebrew Bible are attributed to David.

David chose Jerusalem as the capital city. Under his rule, this city became the center of Israel's political and religious life. David brought the Israelites' most sacred object, the Ark of the Covenant, to Jerusalem. The Ark was a wood and gold chest that held the tablets of the Ten Commandments. As the home of the Ark, Jerusalem became a holy city.

In this painting, Kind David leads a procession to bring the sacred Ark, holding the tablets of the Ten Commandments, into Jerusalem.

Solomon Builds the Great Temple of Jerusalem After David's death, his son, Solomon, became king about 965 B.C.E. Solomon built a magnificent temple in Jerusalem to house the Ark of the Covenant and to serve as the center of Jewish worship. According to the Hebrew Bible, he told God, "Thus all the peoples of the earth will know Your name."

Building the First Temple in Jerusalem was King Solomon's major achievement. He also strengthened the kingdom of Israel by making treaties with neighboring kingdoms. And he increased foreign trade and developed industries such as copper mining and metal working. Solomon was also a poet. The Book of Proverbs and Ecclesiastes in the Writings in the Hebrew Bible are attributed to him.

Kings David and Solomon made major contributions to Judaism. They laid the foundation for kings to govern the Jews for more than 400 years. David established Jerusalem as a holy city. Solomon built the great First Temple of Jerusalem. Because of the acts of David and Solomon, Jerusalem would always be the most holy city to the Jews, as well as a powerful symbol of their faith.

Solomon built the magnificent First Temple in Jerusalem. Today, the site of the Temple of Jerusalem is regarded by Jews as the holiest place in the world.

Chapter Summary

In this chapter, you read about the ancient Israelites and the origins of Judaism. You learned about four Jewish leaders who helped Judaism develop.

Ancient Israelites Historians study artifacts and writings such as the Hebrew Bible to learn about the ancient Israelites and the development of Judaism. The Torah has the first five books of the Hebrew Bible and commandments that direct Jewish life.

Abraham, Father of the Jews Abraham introduced the belief in one God. He made a covenant with God to go to Canaan, and in turn God made him the father of the Jews. The Jews believed they should act in a way that would fulfill God's covenant.

Moses, Leader of the Israelites Moses led the Israelites on an Exodus out of slavery in Egypt. At Mount Sinai, God gave Moses the Ten Commandments, basic laws and teachings of Judaism. Moses united the Jews into a people who worshiped one God.

Kings David and Solomon David defeated the Philistines, united the Israelites in a new nation called Israel, and made Jerusalem the capital and a holy city. Solomon, David's son, built the First Temple in Jerusalem, signed treaties, and increased trade. Both men were also poets with parts of the Hebrew Bible attributed to them.

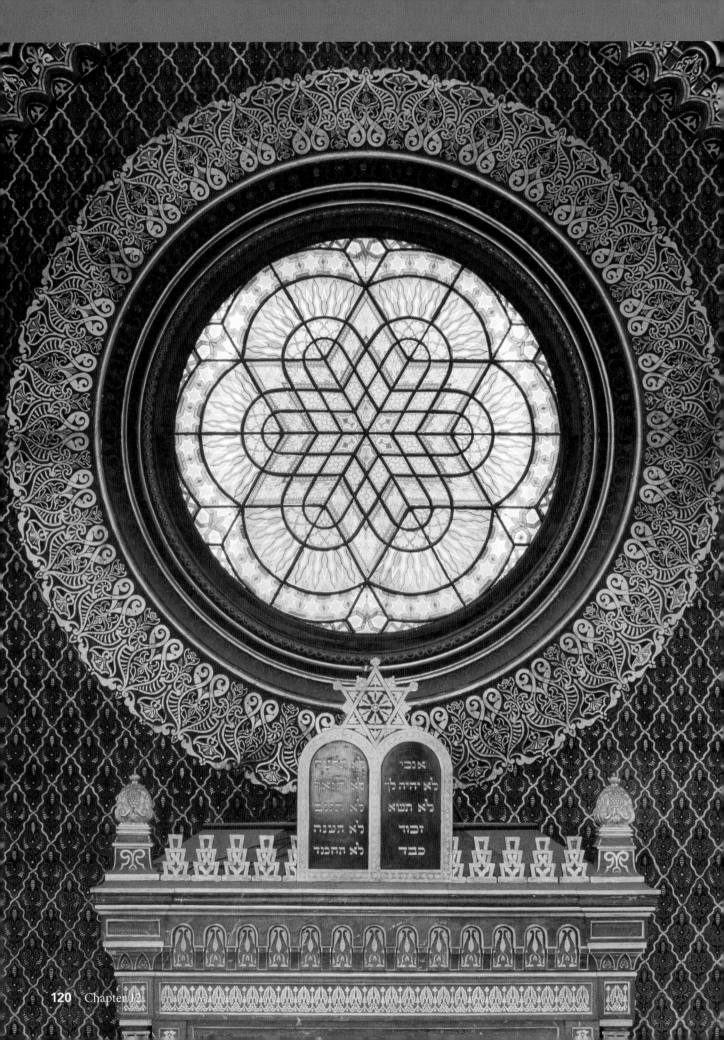

Chapter 12

Learning About World Religions: Judaism

What are the central teachings of Judaism, and why did they survive to modern day?

12.1 Introduction

In this chapter, you will learn about key Jewish teachings. You will also discover how Judaism was preserved after most Jews were driven from their homeland.

The kingdom of Israel split into the northern kingdom of Israel and the southern kingdom of Judah after the death of King Solomon in about 930 B.C.E. Weakened by this division, the people were less able to fight off invaders.

Israel was the first to fall. In 722 B.C.E., the Assyrians conquered the kingdom and took its leaders to Mesopotamia. The people of Israel were sent to many lands. In 597 B.C.E., another Mesopotamian power, Babylon, invaded Judah. Babylon's king, Nebuchadrezzar (neh-byuh-kuh-DREH-zehr), laid siege to the city of Jerusalem. The Jews, as they came to be known, fought until their food supplies ran out. With the Jews weakened by starvation, the Babylonians broke through the walls and **captured** the city. In 586 B.C.E., Nebuchadrezzar burned down Solomon's great Temple of Jerusalem and all the houses in the city. Most of the people of Judah were exiled as captives to Babylon.

The Babylonian Exile was the start of the Jewish Diaspora (die-AS-puh-ruh). The word *diaspora* means "a scattering over a wide area." This was the first exile of most of the Jewish people from their homeland.

Yet the Jews were able to keep Judaism alive. In this chapter, you will first learn about four important Jewish teachings. Then you will read about why the teachings of Judaism have **survived** to modern day.

This boy reads from the Torah during his bar mitzvah, a coming of age ceremony for Jewish children.

◀ A detail of a historic synagogue in Prague, in the Czech Republic

polytheism the belief that there are many gods

monotheism the belief that there is only one God

Talmud the collection of ancient Jewish writings, or commentaries, that interpret the laws and teachings of the Hebrew Bible, or *Tanakh*

12.2 The Central Teachings of Judaism

The religious and moral ideas of Judaism have had a lasting effect on Western civilization. Let's look at four central teachings of Judaism that remain very influential today.

Monotheism   Most people in ancient times believed in many gods. This belief is called **polytheism**. The Israelites, later called Jews, were different. They believed that there is only one God, a belief called **monotheism**. Judaism is the world's oldest monotheistic religion.

Judaism teaches that God is the **source** of morality (standards of right and wrong). These ideas of right and wrong had not always been known in ancient civilizations. Jews learn about and follow their religion by studying their sacred texts. Through study and prayer, many Jews feel that God is close to them in their daily lives.

Following Jewish Teachings   Following the teachings in the Hebrew Bible and the **Talmud** (TAHL-muhd) is central to Jewish life. The Torah **instructs** Jews about how to lead moral lives. For example, Jews are taught to "love your neighbor as yourself."

Among Judaism's oldest laws and teachings are the Ten Commandments. The commandments tell how to lead upright and honorable lives. For example, one commandment tells Jews to set aside a holy day, the Sabbath, every week. The Sabbath, a day of rest and prayer, is still practiced not only by Jews, but also by followers of other world religions, including Christianity and Islam. The commandments also lay down standards of right and wrong, such as "You shall not steal" and "You shall not murder."

Over time, Jewish religious leaders developed a larger set of laws and teachings. For example, there were rules about what foods to eat. Many religious practices began, such as the festival of Passover. These holy days celebrate the Exodus—the freeing of the enslaved Israelites from Egypt. Jews observe these rules and practices in different ways.

Jews around the world gather for Passover Seders (SAY-derz). They eat special foods as they read from Haggadahs (ha-GAH-dahz) to retell the story of the Exodus.

Equality and Social Justice   Beginning with the Ten Commandments, Judaism has always been concerned with a code of **ethics,** or moral values of right and wrong. Two important values that have influenced many societies are equality and social justice.

Unlike some other ancient civilizations, the Israelites did not view their leaders as gods. They believed that there is only one God, and even kings had to obey God's laws and teachings. Judaism teaches that God considers all people equal.

Belief in equality goes hand in hand with a concern for social justice. Many stories and sayings in the Hebrew Bible, or *Tanakh,* teach about treating everyone fairly. For example, one passage says, "You shall open wide your hand to your brother, to the needy and to the poor." Caring for the less fortunate people in society is a basic value in Judaism.

The Importance of Study   Studying the Hebrew Bible, and especially the Torah, is very important in Judaism. Jews also study interpretations of the Hebrew Bible made by scholars and rabbis, or religious teachers.

Jewish people today continue to read, study, and discuss the Torah as one way of understanding and practicing their religion.

In ancient times, those rabbis and scholars who were interpreting the basic teachings of the Torah made decisions that were passed down orally. In the 200s C.E., Jewish scholars began to write the Talmud, which contains this oral tradition along with academic analyses. The Talmud became a basic source of Jewish law. Later on, rabbis wrote their own studies of both the Hebrew Bible and the Talmud, continuing the tradition of interpreting the teachings of Judaism.

Throughout history, Jews have kept their reverence for study and learning. Many Jews learn about Jewish history, law, and traditions through reading and discussion. They also pass on their knowledge to other members of the faith.

exile to banish or expel from one's own country or home

Jewish Diaspora the scattering of the Jewish people outside their homeland, beginning about 586 B.C.E.

Many Jews were exiled from their homeland to Babylon at the start of the Jewish Diaspora.

12.3 Foreign Rule and the Jewish Diaspora

The invasion of Judah in 597 B.C.E. and the destruction of Jerusalem and its Temple in 586 B.C.E. threatened the survival of Judaism. Thousands of Jews were **exiled** in Babylon. By this time, the Israelites had become known as Jews. Members of the Israelite tribe of Judah called themselves "Judaeans," and their homeland, Judah. The name was later shortened to "Jews."

The **Jewish Diaspora** had begun. From this time on, the followers of Judaism were **dispersed,** or scattered, in many lands. Those who did return home found their land dominated by foreign rulers. It would not be easy to keep Judaism alive.

Rule by the Babylonians, Persians, and Greeks The Jewish captives lived in Babylon for about half a century. From then on, Jews outside their homeland prayed to return. During this exile in Babylon, men the Jews believed to be great prophets rose up to encourage the people to remain faithful to Judaism.

In 539 B.C.E., the Persians conquered the Babylonians. The Persian king, Cyrus, ended the Jews' exile. Many Jews returned to Judah, where Cyrus allowed them to rebuild the Temple in Jerusalem and to practice their religion. The rebuilt Temple became known as the Second Temple. Other Jews stayed in Babylon.

For nearly 400 years, Judah was ruled by foreigners. After the Persians came the Greeks. Often, the foreign rulers were harsh.

One Greek ruler, Antiochus (an-TIE-uh-kuhs), tried to force the Jews to worship idols of Greek gods in the Second Temple. In 168 B.C.E., the Jews rebelled and started a war that spanned more than 20 years. During that war, in the year 164 B.C.E., they drove the Greeks from Jerusalem and reclaimed and rededicated the Temple. Jews today celebrate Hanukkah (HAH-nuh-kuh) to honor this victory and the rededication of the Temple.

Jewish Diaspora, About 586–538 B.C.E.

ASIA MINOR

TAURUS MOUNTAINS

Caspian Sea

35°E

35°N

Ninevah

Assur

ASSYRIA

Euphrates River

Tigris River

ZAGROS MOUNTAINS

Mediterranean Sea

30°E

Jerusalem

Babylon

EGYPT

ARABIAN PENINSULA

Persian Gulf

Modern coastline

50°E

| 0 | 200 | 400 miles |
| 0 | 200 | 400 kilometers |

Lambert Conformal Conic Projection

Nile River

Red Sea

25°N

N W E S

☐ Neo-Babylonian Empire, about 600 B.C.E.

☐ Kingdom of Judah, 931–597 B.C.E.

→ Jews exiled to Babylon, 597–586 B.C.E.

→ Jews return to homeland under Persian rule, 538 B.C.E.

• City

Rule by the Romans

For about 80 years after the war with the Greeks, the Jews lived as an independent kingdom in Judah, now called Judea. Then, in 63 B.C.E., they fell under Roman rule.

The Romans were building a great empire, and they were quick to act against any sign of rebellion. More than 50,000 Jews were brutally executed under Roman rule. But the Romans did allow the Jews to practice their own religion and to govern some of their own affairs. In 22 B.C.E., the Romans appointed King Herod to rule all the Jews. Herod announced a big project to expand the Second Temple in Jerusalem, on an even grander scale than Solomon's Temple. The work took 46 years to complete.

In 66 C.E., the Jews rose up against the Romans. For three years, they managed to keep the Romans out of Jerusalem. Then, in 70 C.E., a Roman military leader named Titus led an army of 60,000 soldiers against the Jews. The Jews fought back fiercely, but they were hopelessly outnumbered. They watched in horror as the Romans destroyed the great Temple in Jerusalem. All that was known to remain of the Second Temple was its western wall. To this day, Jews consider the Western Wall their most sacred place.

In 135 C.E. the Romans put down another Jewish revolt. This Roman victory began the final exile of the Jewish people from their homeland. The Romans seized Jewish land and forbade the Jews from entering Jerusalem. Although some Jews always remained in the land of Israel, thousands were sent to other parts of the Roman Empire.

The Jews had lost their homeland and their holy city. Yet Judaism not only survived, it flourished. Next, you will learn how the Jews preserved their faith and way of life.

The Western Wall in Jerusalem was once a part of the network of walls that surrounded the Second Temple. This Temple was destroyed by the Romans. Today, Jews come from all over the world to pray at the wall.

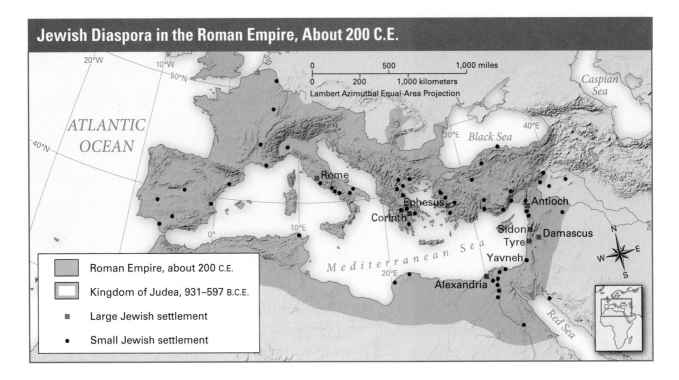

Roman Empire, about 200 C.E.

Kingdom of Judea, 931–597 B.C.E.

■ Large Jewish settlement

• Small Jewish settlement

After the Romans put down the Jewish revolts, they forced most Jews into exile in many parts of the Roman Empire.

12.4 Preserving the Teachings of Judaism

After losing control of their homeland, their holy city, and the great Temple that was the heart of their faith, the Jews faced a great struggle to preserve their religion. They were exiled throughout many gentile, or non-Jewish, lands. With creativity and dedication, they found ways to keep Judaism alive.

Rabbi Yohanan ben Zaccai   One rabbi who helped preserve Judaism was Yohanan ben Zaccai. When the revolt against Rome began in 66 C.E., ben Zaccai feared for the future of Judaism. He worried that if the rabbis died in the fighting and the Temple was destroyed, Judaism might not survive.

Ben Zaccai begged the Jews to surrender to save Judaism. When they refused, he decided to approach the Romans for help.

Ben Zaccai had himself smuggled out of Jerusalem in a coffin. He met with a Roman general named Vespasian (vuh-SPAY-zhee-ehn), and gained permission to open a Jewish school, with the help of other rabbis, in the town of **Yavneh** (YAHV-neh).

When Jerusalem fell, Yavneh became the center of Jewish learning. At their school, Ben Zaccai and the other rabbis taught new rabbis. Teachers came from many places to study at Yavneh. Then they returned to their communities to share what they had learned. In this way, the rabbis at Yavneh made sure that Jews still had leaders to guide them.

Yavneh an ancient city in Israel that became a center for Jewish learning

New Teachers and Practices   In addition to training other rabbis, the rabbis at Yavneh introduced new practices. These new ways ensured that the teachings of Judaism would be passed on.

The rabbis made the synagogue important. A synagogue is a house of worship. It is also a place to study, to meet, and to gather socially. Synagogues made Jewish communities stronger.

The rabbis also created a religious service for synagogues. Prayer and study of sacred texts became a new way to worship God without the Temple rituals. Today, Jews, Christians, and Muslims follow this model for services. In these ways, Yohanan ben Zaccai and other rabbis helped Judaism to adapt and flourish even after the destruction of its central holy site in Jerusalem.

These new practices helped Jews preserve their religion in communities around the world. Over the centuries, rabbis studied and commented on Judaism's sacred texts, and developed other new practices. Jews have faced prejudice and persecution, but they have kept their faith.

In 1948, a new Jewish state, Israel, was created in part of the lands once ruled by David and Solomon. Jews from many places settled in their ancient homeland. For other Jews around the world, Jewish traditions have enabled their religion to thrive.

In the tradition of Rabbi ben Zaccai's first school, scholars today continue to learn and to share their understanding in Torah study groups like this one.

Chapter Summary

In this chapter, you learned about how Judaism was preserved in the Diaspora.

The Central Teachings of Judaism   Earlier religions believed in polytheism. Judaism is the oldest monotheistic religion. The Hebrew Bible and the Talmud present a code of ethics with teachings that focus on social justice. Jews pass on learning to others.

Foreign Rule and the Jewish Diaspora   After Babylon destroyed Jerusalem in 586 B.C.E., most Jews were exiled to Babylon. When the Persians defeated Babylon in 539 B.C.E., many Jews returned to Judah under Persia's rule. Later, the Greeks and then the Romans ruled Judah, now Judea. The Jews fought the Romans in 66 C.E. and in 135 C.E. The Romans put down these revolts and exiled most of the Jews.

Preserving the Teachings of Judaism   During the Jewish Diaspora, Jews wanted to preserve their religion. Rabbi Yohanan ben Zaccai set up a center of Jewish learning in Yavneh. His rabbis taught other rabbis, who shared their knowledge at home. Ben Zaccai made synagogues a center of Jewish life and created a new religious service. These new practices preserved Judaism. In 1948, the Jewish state of Israel was created in lands once ruled by David and Solomon.

Ancient Egypt and the Middle East

About 2551–2528 B.C.E.
Reign of Khufu
Khufu builds the Great Pyramid and establishes the pharaoh as the central authority in Egypt.

About 3100 B.C.E.–350 C.E.
Ancient Egypt
Ancient Egyptian civilization flourishes along the Nile River.

About 1950 B.C.E.
Migration to Canaan
According to the Torah, Abraham, ancestor of the Israelites, moves his family from Ur in Mesopotamia to Canaan, where they become herders.

3000 B.C.E.   2500 B.C.E.   2000 B.C.E.   1500 B.C.E.

About 2000 B.C.E.–350 C.E.
Ancient Kush
The African kingdom of Kush thrives along the southern Nile River.

1473–1458 B.C.E.
Reign of Hatshepsut
During the reign of Hatshepsut, Egypt's first female pharaoh, art and architecture flourish, and trade is expanded.

About 965 B.C.E.
First Temple Built
King Solomon builds the First Temple of Jerusalem.

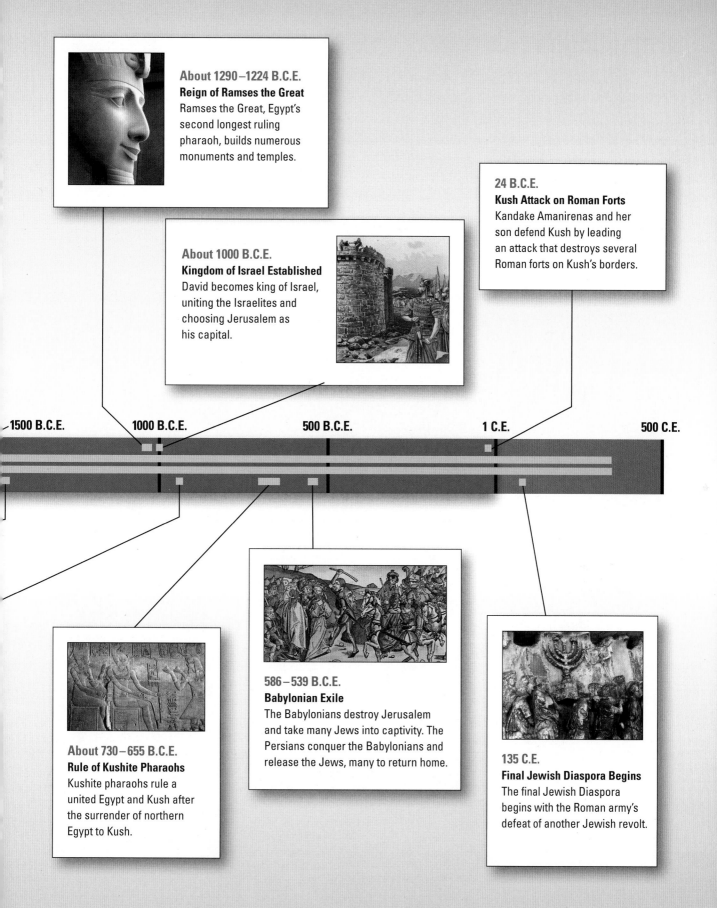

About 1290–1224 B.C.E.
Reign of Ramses the Great
Ramses the Great, Egypt's second longest ruling pharaoh, builds numerous monuments and temples.

About 1000 B.C.E.
Kingdom of Israel Established
David becomes king of Israel, uniting the Israelites and choosing Jerusalem as his capital.

24 B.C.E.
Kush Attack on Roman Forts
Kandake Amanirenas and her son defend Kush by leading an attack that destroys several Roman forts on Kush's borders.

1500 B.C.E.   1000 B.C.E.   500 B.C.E.   1 C.E.   500 C.E.

About 730–655 B.C.E.
Rule of Kushite Pharaohs
Kushite pharaohs rule a united Egypt and Kush after the surrender of northern Egypt to Kush.

586–539 B.C.E.
Babylonian Exile
The Babylonians destroy Jerusalem and take many Jews into captivity. The Persians conquer the Babylonians and release the Jews, many to return home.

135 C.E.
Final Jewish Diaspora Begins
The final Jewish Diaspora begins with the Roman army's defeat of another Jewish revolt.

Ancient Egypt and the Middle East **129**

Ancient India

The city of Varanasi dates back to ancient times. Varanasi is located on the banks of the Ganges River, a major river in India.

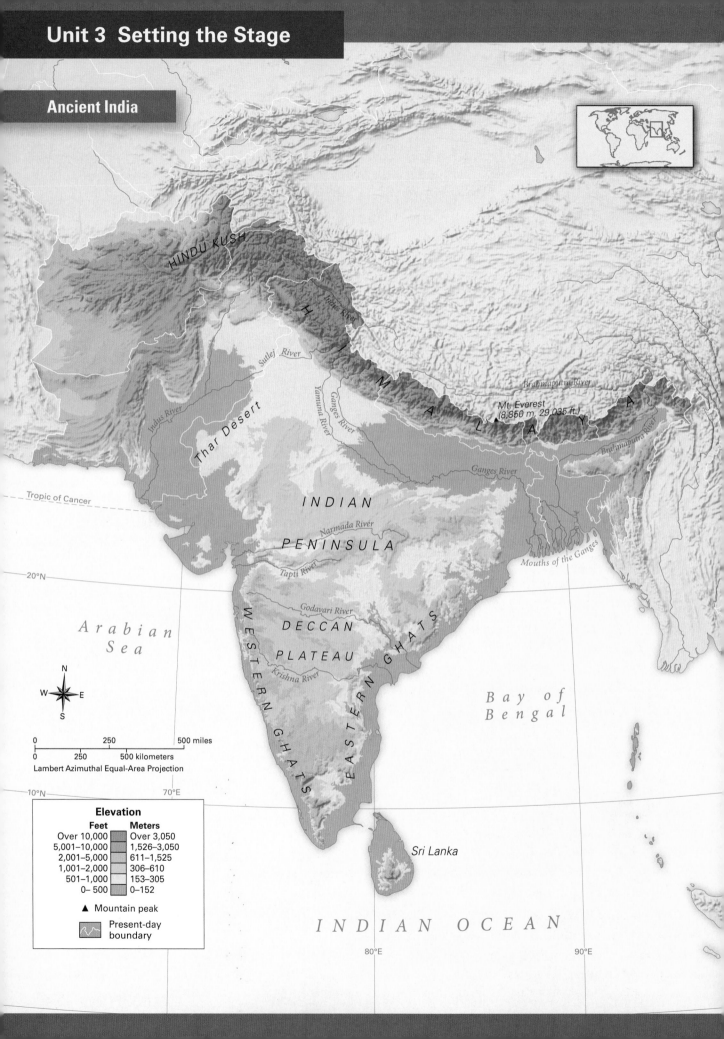

Ancient India

HINDU KUSH

H
I
M
A
L
A
Y
A

Indus River

Sutlej River

Yamuna River

Ganges River

Brahmaputra River

Mt. Everest
(8,850 m, 29,035 ft.)

Brahmaputra River

Ganges River

Thar Desert

Indus River

INDIAN

PENINSULA

Narmada River

Mouths of the Ganges

Tropic of Cancer

20°N

Tapti River

Godavari River

DECCAN

PLATEAU

Krishna River

WESTERN GHATS

EASTERN GHATS

A r a b i a n
S e a

N
W   E
S

B a y o f
B e n g a l

0   250   500 miles
0   250   500 kilometers
Lambert Azimuthal Equal-Area Projection

10°N   70°E

Sri Lanka

I N D I A N   O C E A N

80°E   90°E

Elevation

Feet		Meters
Over 10,000		Over 3,050
5,001–10,000		1,526–3,050
2,001–5,000		611–1,525
1,001–2,000		306–610
501–1,000		153–305
0– 500		0–152

▲ Mountain peak

Present-day
boundary

Ancient India

To the northeast of Africa lies the enormous continent of Asia. The south central part of Asia is known as the Indian subcontinent, which includes the country of India. Present-day India is a nation whose beginnings stretch back into the distant mists of time. When historians talk about ancient India, however, they are referring to the entire Indian subcontinent, not present-day India. Other present-day countries located on the Indian subcontinent include Bangladesh, Bhutan, Nepal, Pakistan, and the island nation of Sri Lanka.

The ancient civilization that developed on the Indian subcontinent was greatly influenced by the physical geography of the region. Look at the map on the opposite page. Notice the Himalayan mountain range. These towering peaks are the highest mountains in the world. They formed a natural barrier between ancient India and the rest of Asia. To the south, the Arabian Sea, the Indian Ocean, and the Bay of Bengal prevented contact with other people. This isolation meant that civilizations developed on the Indian subcontinent without outside influences and had their own unique cultures.

Look again at the map and find the Indus River. It begins high in the Himalayas and eventually empties into the Arabian Sea. Like other river valleys you have studied, the Indus River valley was the site of some early settlements, including Mohenjodaro and Harappa. Other rivers, like the Ganges and the Brahmaputra, also were home to early farming villages. These rivers provided the water and rich soil that allowed ancient cultures to grow and prosper.

In time, two ancient empires arose in India. As the maps below show, the Mauryan Empire was the first to develop, and the Gupta Empire was the second.

Two major religions have roots in ancient India. They are Hinduism and Buddhism. As you study this unit, you will learn about the development and beliefs of these two faiths. You will also study the achievements of the Mauryan and the Gupta empires.

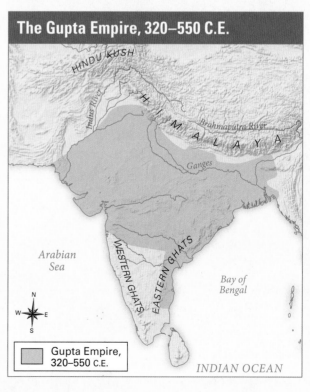

The Mauryan Empire, 269–232 B.C.E.

HINDU KUSH · Indus River · HIMALAYA · Brahmaputra River · Ganges · Arabian Sea · WESTERN GHATS · EASTERN GHATS · Bay of Bengal · N W E S · 0 · Mauryan Empire, 269–232 B.C.E. · INDIAN OCEAN

The Gupta Empire, 320–550 C.E.

HINDU KUSH · Indus River · HIMALAYA · Brahmaputra River · Ganges · Arabian Sea · WESTERN GHATS · EASTERN GHATS · Bay of Bengal · N W E S · 0 · Gupta Empire, 320–550 C.E. · INDIAN OCEAN

Chapter 13

Geography and the Early Settlement of India

How did geography affect early settlement in India?

13.1 Introduction

In this unit, you will learn about the civilization of ancient India. First, in this chapter, you will explore the geography of the area, including its rivers, mountains, plains, plateaus, deserts, and valleys. These physical features influenced where ancient India's civilization arose.

Early towns began to appear in India in about 2500 B.C.E. Over the next 2,000 years, a unique civilization developed in India.

According to an ancient Indian story, a river god and a river goddess once lived in the snow-covered Himalayas (him-uh-LAY-uhz), a mountain range extending through northern India. One day, the two decided to race down the mountains to the plains below. The river goddess sped straight down and won the race. But her joy soon turned to worry. Where was the river god?

The river god had slowed down to admire the snowcapped mountains and the rich brown earth in the valleys. In time, he flowed down to meet his goddess. The two rivers became one, joined forever on India's plains. The rivers made the land good for farming.

In this chapter, you will learn about India's rivers and other physical features. You'll explore eight key features and their effects on the settlement of ancient India.

This stone sculpture represents Ganga, the goddess of the Ganges River.

◀ Boatmen glide along on the Ganges River in northern India.

subcontinent a large landmass that is smaller than a continent

monsoon a strong wind that brings heavy rain to southern Asia in the summer

A typical southern town along the Brahmaputra River gets between 70 and 150 inches of rain a year. The heaviest rainfall, occurs during the southwest monsoon between June and October. Temperatures along the entire river may range from 45°F to 85°F.

13.2 Brahmaputra River

The land of India is a **subcontinent** of Asia. Looking at a map of Asia, you can see that India is attached to this continent. Many geographers call this part of Asia the Indian subcontinent. It is a large, triangular landmass that juts out from the southern part of Asia. Mountain ranges separate much of the Indian subcontinent from the rest of Asia.

Our exploration of India begins with the Brahmaputra (brah-muh-POO-truh) River. This river runs through the steep Himalayas, the mountains along the northern border of India. From there, the Brahmaputra winds through snowcapped mountains and narrow canyons. The water is clear and cold as it rushes over the sharp rocks.

The river becomes slower and deeper as it flows into its valley. Every summer, this part of the river receives added water from heavy **monsoon** rains. A monsoon is a strong wind that often brings huge amounts of rain. These rains can cause the river to overflow its banks. As the river recedes, the rich minerals that have been carried down from the Himalayas remain in the soil of the valley.

Eventually, the Brahmaputra River joins another river, the Ganges (GAN-jeez), on the plains. The land where the two rivers meet is very **fertile**.

13.3 Deccan Plateau

The Deccan (DEH-kuhn) Plateau is a triangle-shaped area that lies between two mountain ranges in southern India. A **plateau** is an **elevated,** or raised, area of land that is flatter than a mountain. The Deccan Plateau has several kinds of land. In the flatter parts, large granite rocks formed by volcanoes cover the land. These rocks are among the world's oldest, dating back more than six hundred million years. The hillier parts of the plateau have thin forests and low, scrubby bushes.

The plateau is fairly dry. There are a few rivers, but the monsoon rains provide most of the water. The soil on the plateau is black, yellow, or red. The black soil is rich in iron and good for growing cotton. The yellow and red soils lack key minerals. This makes it harder for farmers to grow plants in those areas.

A typical town in the Deccan Plateau receives about 30 inches of rain a year. The heaviest rainfall occurs between June and October, during the southwest monsoon. Temperatures on the plateau range from 65°F to 100°F.

> **plateau** a flat area of land that is elevated, or raised, above the land around it

13.4 Eastern and Western Ghats

The Eastern and Western Ghats (gahts) are long mountain chains near the coasts of India. The Eastern Ghats extend along India's east coast. The Western Ghats extend along the west coast. When seen from above, the Ghats form a large "V." The Deccan Plateau lies between these two mountain ranges.

The Western Ghats are higher than the Eastern Ghats. The Western Ghats have steep slopes; narrow valleys; thick, hardwood forests; and extremely heavy rains. The wet climate encourages the growth of tropical plants.

The Eastern Ghats are not as wet as the Western Ghats. Several rivers flow through these green mountains, which are dotted with hardwood trees. The rivers rarely flood, but they are unsafe for travel. They move rapidly, contain many rocks, and often plunge suddenly over cliffs.

Parts of the Ghats receive 100 or more inches of rain a year. Temperatures range from 60°F to 90°F.

13.5 Ganges River

The Ganges River flows across most of northern India. It starts in the Himalaya Mountains. The river makes its way south through ice, rocks, and magnificent mountains and valleys.

The river carries silt from the Himalayas to the northern plains. As the river passes through the plains, it leaves the rich sediment behind. As a result, the northern plains contain some of the most fertile farmland in the world.

Melted ice carried down from the Himalayas provides the Ganges River plains with a good supply of water. During the rainy season, the river can flood and destroy crops planted along its banks.

Towns along the Ganges River receive 25 to 60 inches of rain a year. Temperatures in the Ganges plains range from 55°F to 90°F.

13.6 Himalaya Mountains

The Himalaya Mountains are located along India's northern border. This mountain range is the highest in the world. Mount Everest, the world's tallest mountain, is part of the Himalayas. It reaches more than five and a half miles into the sky. The Himalayas form a natural border between the Indian subcontinent and most of the rest of Asia.

The Himalayas live up to their name, which means "home of snows." The highest peaks are always covered in snow and ice. Fierce storms can dump 10 feet of snow on the area at one time. Water from glaciers in the Himalaya Mountains feeds northern India's major rivers.

Underneath the Himalaya Mountains, the Earth is always moving. This movement causes Mount Everest to rise slightly every year. It also makes earthquakes and landslides common in the area.

The upper peaks of the Himalayas are always covered in snow and ice. The heaviest snowfall occurs between June and October, during the southwest monsoon. Temperatures on the highest peaks never rise above freezing (32°F) and can go as low as –76°F.

13.7 Hindu Kush Mountains

The Hindu Kush mountains form a rugged barrier between the Indus (IN-duhs) River valley and Afghanistan. This mountain range is not as tall as the Himalayas, but it is still one of the highest in the world. Some of its peaks are almost five miles high. Many parts of the mountain range are unlivable. Snow and ice permanently cover the steep slopes and peaks.

The Khyber (KIE-ber) Pass forms a gap about 30 miles long in the mountains on the Afghanistan-Pakistan border. The pass connects central Asia to the Indian subcontinent. For thousands of years, traders used the pass to enter the Indus River valley. Invaders also used the pass. But many died in the mountains' unforgiving landscape.

The Hindu Kush mountain range receives about 15 inches of rain and snow a year. Weather and seasons vary greatly across the range. Temperatures in the Hindu Kush vary from about 25°F to 75°F.

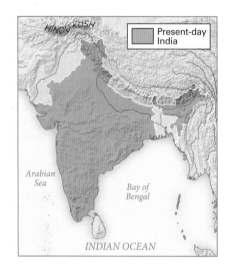

13.8 Indus River

The Indus River begins in the Himalaya Mountains. It gets water from snow melting in the Hindu Kush mountains and other mountain ranges. This runoff of melting snow and ice from the mountains keeps the river's water level high. Eventually, the river flows through present-day Pakistan and empties into the Arabian Sea.

The Indus River valley contains some of the best farmland in the world. Like the Ganges River, the Indus River carries silt from the mountains to the plains. The silt leaves the surrounding soil rich and fertile.

The Indus River has often been compared to Egypt's Nile River. Like the Nile, the Indus is an important source of water for the farmland that lies along its banks.

Towns along the Indus River receive from 5 to 20 inches of rain a year. The heaviest rains fall between June and October, during the southwest monsoon. Temperatures in the Indus River valley range from 65°F to 90°F.

The Thar Desert receives about 4 to 20 inches of rain a year. The heaviest rains fall between June and October, during the southwest monsoon. Temperatures in the desert range from 45°F to 120°F.

13.9 Thar Desert

The massive Thar (tahr) Desert in northern India is mostly sand and stone. Huge, rolling sand dunes stretch for hundreds of miles. The landscape is littered with rocks. There is very little plant life except for grass and low, hardy shrubs. Most of the time, the heat is unbearable.

Water is a very precious resource in the desert. Rain is rare, although the monsoons may occasionally bring a **brief** but **intense** storm. The dry conditions make dust storms common.

Many animals and birds make their home in the desert. There are more than forty-five kinds of lizards and snakes. Gazelles lope across the sand. Birds include quail, ducks, and geese.

13.10 Early Settlements in India

Like many ancient peoples, the first people in India most likely chose to settle near rivers. The rivers provided plenty of water. The fertile soil was ideal for farming. The rivers could also be used for travel and trade.

The first known settlements in ancient India were in the Indus River valley. There were farming communities in this valley as early as 6500 B.C.E. By 5000 B.C.E., people also lived near the Ganges River. By 2500 B.C.E., there were walled settlements in the Indus River valley.

The geography of India greatly influenced the location of early settlements on the subcontinent. Both the Indus and the Ganges rivers carried rich silt from the mountains to the plains. When the rivers flooded, the silt spread over the plains and made the soil in the river valleys fertile for farming. Over time, an ancient civilization developed and flourished in these settlements.

The Indus and Ganges river valleys attracted the earliest settlements in ancient India. Here people found fertile soil and enough water.

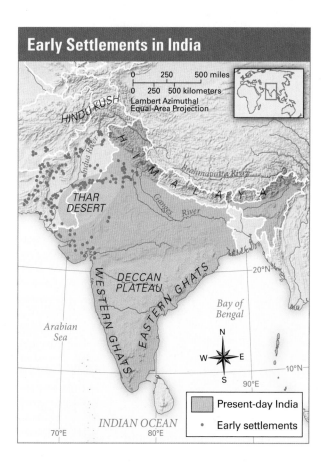

Early Settlements in India

Chapter Summary

In this chapter, you explored eight physical features of the Indian subcontinent and how they affected early settlement in India.

Major Rivers In northern India, the Brahmaputra, the Ganges, and the Indus rivers carry rich silt from the mountains to the plains. India's early settlers farmed and later built walled settlements in the river valleys. This was the start of civilization in India.

Deccan Plateau In some parts of this raised area between two mountain ranges in southern India, rich black soil is good for growing cotton.

Mountain Ranges The Eastern and Western Ghats are near India's coasts. Between them lies the Deccan Plateau. The Western Ghats are higher and wetter than the Eastern Ghats. The Himalayas along India's northern border are the highest mountains in the world. The Hindu Kush range runs through present-day Pakistan. It provides access through the Khyber Pass to the Indian subcontinent.

Thar Desert This vast desert in northern India has huge sand dunes, little plant life, and extreme heat. Dust storms are common. Animals, such as lizards, snakes, gazelles, and a variety of birds, live here.

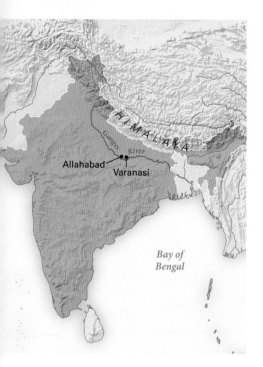

The Ganges begins in the Himalaya Mountains. It flows southeast for 1,560 miles until it joins with other rivers and empties into the Bay of Bengal.

Saving the Ganges

The Ganges is India's sacred river. In the Hindu religion, "Ganga," as the river is called, is considered a goddess. Yet the Ganges has become one of the most polluted rivers in the world. How did this happen? What are people doing to correct the problem?

It is Saturday in Allahabad, India. A large crowd of Hindu pilgrims descends the steps of a *ghat,* or ritual bathing area, to step into the waters of the Ganges. Devout Hindus believe that a dip in the river washes away their sins. About two million people take that dip every day. Children leap happily from the bottom step, as they would at a swimming pool. Mothers bathe their infants. People wash their hair, their clothes, even their mouths in the sacred river. One elderly man scoops up water in a pot. "I'll use this for drinking and cooking and get some more tonight," he says. "It's absolutely clean. Of course it is, it's Ganges water."

The Ganges begins where a number of small streams form from melting glaciers in the Himalaya Mountains. The river flows for 1,560 miles along its southeast course to the sea. It empties into the Bay of Bengal. Indian civilization developed along its banks. About four hundred million people—a third of India's population—still live along the river and its branches. The Ganges is their main source of water for drinking, cooking, and washing. Farmers depend on the river to grow rice, beans, sugarcane, potatoes, wheat, and other crops.

What that elderly man said about his pot of Ganges water may have been correct—once. Until the 1980s, the Ganges was a remarkably clean river. It is rich in dissolved oxygen. Disease-carrying bacteria did not live long in its waters. This was largely due to bacteria-eating viruses called *bacteriophages*. Unlike most river water, a pot of Ganges water would stay fresh for a long time. The river's self-purifying nature may be one reason why the Hindu people considered the Ganges a goddess.

Today, however, the situation is very different. The Ganges has become so polluted that it can no longer clean itself. Its waters are now unhealthful not only for drinking and bathing but for farming as well.

Ancient River, Modern Problems

The main source of pollution is untreated sewage. The Ganges flows past some of India's largest cities. In the last 60 years, India has struggled to develop a modern economy. While population and industry have grown enormously, sanitation has not kept pace. Fewer than half of India's people have modern plumbing.

Millions of gallons of sewage from more than 100 cities pour into the Ganges each day. Treatment plants can handle only a fraction of it. Much sewage does not reach the plants because many sewers are broken. Electricity sometimes goes out. Then the plants shut down, but the sewage keeps flowing. And many cities along the Ganges have no sewage treatment plants at all.

Sewage is not the only problem. Cows swim in the Ganges. People wash their laundry in it. Dead bodies and body parts drift in the water, because traditional Hindus do not bury their dead. They *cremate,* or burn, the bodies. Many Hindus ask to be cremated on the Ganges' banks. Their ashes are put in the river. But some bodies do not burn completely. And some people are too poor to buy firewood. They simply put the dead bodies of their loved ones into the river.

The pollution is very bad at Varanasi. This is a city downstream from Allahabad. To Hindus, Varanasi is the holiest of cities. Every year, millions of pilgrims bathe at its more than 75 ghats. As it enters Varanasi, the Ganges contains 120 times more disease-causing bacteria than is safe for bathing. Then it flows past 24 sewers. Four miles downstream, the bacterial count is *3,000 times* the safe level. Each day, more than 1,000 Indian children die of cholera, typhoid, or hepatitis. These are diseases caused by water-borne bacteria.

There are also the factories and farms. Leather tanning, cloth making, and fertilizer manufacturing use cancer-causing chemicals that end up in the Ganges. And when farmers spray their crops to kill insect pests, these poisons flow into the Ganges, too. The life-giving Ganga has become an agent of death.

Pollution in the Ganges comes from sewage and factory and farm chemicals. It also comes from litter and garbage that people put in the river.

Dr. Veer Bhadra Mishra (right) is both a Hindu priest and a water engineer. He has been working for many years to clean up the pollution in the Ganges.

A Hero of the Planet

Dr. Veer Bhadra Mishra is a Hindu priest. He is the head of Sankat Mochan, Varanasi's second-largest temple. Every morning, he takes his ritual dip in the Ganges. But more than most Hindus, he knows better than to drink the water. Mishra is a scientist, a water engineer who was once a university professor. He has made it his life's work to clean up "Mother Ganga."

"All our rivers have stories," Mishra says. "All our rivers are important. But there is nothing anywhere like the Ganga."

Mishra was born a priest. The leadership of his temple has passed from father to eldest son since the 16th century. He inherited the job when he was 14. But his mother urged him to attend college, too. No one in his family had ever been to school. Mishra believes it happened because the Ganges needed his help.

Mishra's education led him to understand that the Ganges was in trouble. But it seemed to him that nobody in India's government was interested in doing anything about the dangerous pollution. Even other Hindu priests seemed not to care about the problem.

So, in 1982, Mishra started the Sankat Mochan Foundation to help people living along the Ganges. The foundation set up a program called "Campaign for a Clean Ganga." Its goal is to educate people about the causes of pollution. It maintains a Web site, posting articles about environmental issues. India's news media may use the information for free.

Donations came from the United States and other nations. Other foundations, governments, and people also contributed. In 1999, Dr. Mishra won a *Time* magazine "Hero of the Planet" award. Three years later, the United Nations honored him.

The Indian government began to pay attention, too. In 1986, it launched the Ganga Action Plan, or GAP. The plan was to use sewage treatment plants to clean up the Ganges. The GAP was an expensive failure. There were not enough plants to handle the amount of sewage. There was not enough power to run the plants. By 2002, the Ganges was more polluted than ever.

Dr. Mishra did not give up. He had another plan that would use simpler technology. With a group of California scientists, he developed a system that did not need electricity. It used gravity to divert pollutants from the Ganges into ponds where they would be stored for 45 days. Helpful bacteria, algae, and sunlight would break the pollutants down into harmless substances.

Mishra wanted to try out this plan in Varanasi. He believed it would be cheaper and more effective than the government's plan. The Varanasi city council accepted the idea. But the state and national governments turned it down.

Mishra knew that it would take time to gain acceptance for his plan. In the meantime, he began to educate the people of his city. He wanted to change their age-old habits that harmed the river. His foundation met with priests and pilgrims. It organized citizens and children. Young workers cleaned up litter from the banks of the Ganges. But the problem was so huge that these efforts had little effect.

Scientists from other countries heard about Mishra's project. Steve Hamner, a scientist from Montana State University, traveled to India in 2003. He met with Dr. Mishra and other Indian scientists. Hamner and an Indian government lab made detailed studies of Ganges water. The pollution was measured in a scientific way. The Indian lab brought the findings to India's Supreme Court.

Today, Dr. Mishra, other scientists, and the government of India are experimenting with new ways to return the Ganges to its former unpolluted state.

This time the government listened. In 2007, India's prime minister met with Dr. Mishra. A year later, Mishra heard what he called "the best news in 20 years." The government was agreeing to support a pilot program of his plan in Varanasi. If it worked there, it could be put into effect all along the Ganges.

The Ganges' story is not over. Time will tell whether it is too late to restore India's sacred river. But Dr. Mishra seems to have no doubts. As he confidently puts it, "Mother Ganges will help me to save her."

Chapter 14

Unlocking the Secrets of Mohenjodaro

What can artifacts tell us about daily life in Mohenjodaro?

14.1 Introduction

The geography of the Indian subcontinent affected where early people lived. Early settlements in this region were in fertile river valleys. In this chapter, you will visit one of those settlements, the city of Mohenjodaro (moh-HEN-joh-dahr-oh).

Mohenjodaro was one of many settlements that were located in the Indus River valley. These settlements became known as the Indus valley civilization. It is also called the Harappan (huh-RAP-pen) civilization, after another city at that time, Harappa. The civilization flourished for about 800 years, from about 2700 B.C.E. to 1900 B.C.E.

The cities of Harappa and Mohenjodaro were the two great centers of the Indus valley civilization. Mohenjodaro means "place or hill of the dead." In 1922, archaeologists found the ruins of Mohenjodaro. Carefully, they excavated the city. They discovered that it had two main parts.

The first part was a raised area that was used as a citadel, or fortress. The citadel was surrounded by a wall. In times of danger or trouble, people may have gathered in this area for safety.

The second part of Mohenjodaro was below the citadel. The lower city had many houses and workshops. This is likely the area where most people lived their daily lives.

What was daily life like in Mohenjodaro? In this chapter, you will unlock some secrets of this ancient city. You'll explore its ruins and study its artifacts. What do these clues **reveal** about the city's people and their civilization?

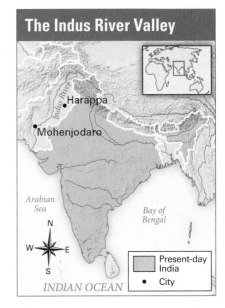

Two great centers of Indus valley civilization were the cities of Mohenjodaro and Harappa.

◀ The ruins of Mohenjodaro's walled citadel and lower city

Mohenjodaro one of the first major settlements in ancient India that became a center of the Indus valley civilization

citadel a fortress built to protect a city

Indus valley civilization an early civilization with an advanced culture, located in the Indus River valley on the Indian subcontinent

14.2 The Mystery of Mohenjodaro

Mohenjodaro was on the banks of the Indus River in present-day Pakistan. By studying the city's ruins, we see that the city was carefully planned. To the west, a **citadel** sat on a platform of mud and brick. Below the citadel, nine streets divided the lower city into blocks, like those of a modern city. The streets were lined with houses and workshops made of mud bricks.

Mohenjodaro was a large city. At one time, as many as 50,000 people may have lived there. Similar to other settlements of the **Indus valley civilization,** Mohenjodaro had an advanced culture. But one great mystery remains. What happened to this civilization?

No one knows for sure. After about 1900 B.C.E., the great cities of the Indus River valley disappeared. Some scientists believe that hostile invaders were to blame. According to this idea, fierce warriors swept in from central Asia and destroyed the local civilization. But with a lack of evidence to support it, this idea has been rejected in recent years by many scholars.

Other scientists think that natural events may have caused the decline of the Indus valley civilization. They point to floods and earthquakes that are known to have struck the region around 1900 B.C.E.

All that remains today of the Indus valley people are the buildings and artifacts they left behind. These clues can tell us a great deal about how they lived. Let's explore the ruins of Mohenjodaro and see what we can find out.

The photograph at right is a view of the Mohenjodaro ruins, as seen from the top of the citadel.

These stone weights were found in Mohenjodaro.

14.3 Weights and Scale

Inside the walls of Mohenjodaro's citadel, a scale and several kinds of stone weights were found near a large building. Some archaeologists believed that the design of this building suggested that it was used as a **granary**. Later studies, however, showed no evidence for this idea. Many archaeologists now agree that the building was probably a large public structure, but its specific **function** remains unknown. It may have been used as a store-house, a temple, or for some other purpose. Perhaps rulers and state officials met there.

The scale and weights found near the building are interesting artifacts. Similar to those found in other parts of the city, these objects suggest to archaeologists that ancient Indians used standard weights as they traded goods. Most of the small weights were cube shaped. They were made of a stone called chert. Chert could be chipped and ground to a certain weight but was hard enough to last. The weights were consistent and accurate. The smallest weights were found in jewelers' shops. Also found were marked rods. These suggest that the ancient Indians also had a uniform way to measure length.

granary a place to store grain

14.4 The Great Bath

The most dramatic feature of Mohenjodaro's citadel was the Great Bath. The Great Bath was a pool built of waterproofed brick. It was 39 feet long and 8 feet deep. Small dressing rooms circled the pool. One of the rooms contained a well that supplied the bath with water. Dirty water was removed through a **drain** that ran along one side of the bath.

It seems likely that the people of Mohenjodaro used the pool to bathe. On a hot, clear day, they might have enjoyed washing themselves in the bath's cooling waters. Some archaeologists think that the Great Bath might have been used for religious rituals. They point out that bathing rituals are important in India's major religion, Hinduism. Ancient Hindu temples often featured bathing pools.

These are the remains of the Great Bath at Mohenjodaro.

14.5 Statue and Beads

In the lower city, archaeologists found a stone statue, 7 inches high. It shows how men in Mohenjodaro might have looked and dressed. As you can see in the photograph, the figure has a short, tidy beard and a clean upper lip. His hair is tied back with a band. He is wearing a patterned robe draped over his left shoulder. His expression is calm and noble. Archaeologists wonder who the figure is. Some scientists think that he may have been both a priest and a king.

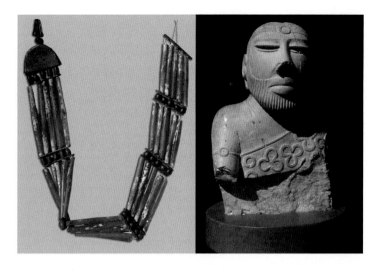

What do these artifacts reveal about the culture of the people who made them?

Beautiful stone beads, in many shapes and colors, have been found throughout Mohenjodaro. Women may have worn them in necklaces, bracelets, earrings, and rings. Bead makers also made beads of clay and baked them in hot ovens called kilns. These artisans then drilled holes in the beads for stringing into necklaces.

14.6 Seals

Small stone seals, found in large numbers throughout the ruins, are among the most mysterious of Mohenjodaro's artifacts. The seals are carved with pictographs, an ancient form of drawing that uses pictures to stand for objects, sounds, or ideas. More than four hundred pictographs have been discovered, but archaeologists know little of their meaning. Many seals show animals such as buffalo, bulls, tigers, elephants, rhinoceroses, fish, and crocodiles.

What do you think the images on these seals might represent?

No one knows how the seals were used, but scientists have made some educated guesses. Many of the seals have a small loop on the back. Perhaps people wore them as charms to keep away evil. The seals may also have been pressed into wax to make a kind of tag. Merchants might have placed the wax tags on their goods to show who owned them.

Parts of Mohenjodaro's sewer system can still be seen in the city's ruins.

14.7 Sewer System

A great achievement of Mohenjodaro was its advanced sewer system. A sewer system carries waste water away from houses. Mohenjodaro's complex system of drains, pipes, wells, and bathrooms set the city apart from other settlements of its time. Two thousand years would pass before the world would see another system like it, in ancient Rome.

A network of clay pipes connected Mohenjodaro's buildings and homes to the main sewer system. Dirty water and waste flowed in **channels** along the streets. This sewage then emptied into the Indus River. Archaeologists think that the sewer system made it possible for all residents of the city, rich or poor, to have had bathrooms in their homes.

Deep wells made of brick were located throughout the city. People stored water, including rainfall, in these wells.

14.8 Homes

Most of Mohenjodaro's people lived in the lower city, which was three times the size of the citadel. Rows of houses lined the streets. The houses had flat roofs and were two stories high. Like most of the city's buildings, they were made of mud bricks.

The houses faced narrow alleys. The backs of the houses opened onto courtyards where families could gather. The houses had narrow windows on the second floor. Screens for these windows were made of either a hard clay called terra-cotta or a see-through mineral called alabaster.

Homes had from one to a dozen rooms. Scientists believe that the poorer citizens may have lived in the smaller homes. The larger homes most likely belonged to the wealthy.

This narrow alley in the ruins of Mohenjodaro is lined with houses. Notice that there are no windows on the ground floor.

What game pieces can you identify in this picture?

14.9 Games

Evidence from Mohenjodaro suggests that the people who lived there enjoyed playing games. Many objects appear to be crafted for use as toys and parts of game sets. Archaeologists have uncovered dice, stone balls, grooved clay tracks, and stone game boards.

The game of chess may have originated in India. An ancient Indian book describes a war game played with dice and with pieces called pawns. Although modern chess is not played with dice, historians believe that the war game is an early form of chess. The small, carved game pieces found at Mohenjodaro may have been used to play this game.

The children of Mohenjodaro likely played simpler games. Some of the objects found by archaeologists look like children's toys. For example, children may have enjoyed rolling stone balls along clay mazes and tracks.

14.10 Clay Models

Archaeologists have found small clay models throughout Mohenjodaro. Most of these models are made of terra-cotta. In one model, shown here, two bulls are attached to a yoke, or wooden harness. The bulls are pulling a person in a two-wheeled cart. This model may be a form of ancient toy, but archaeologists believe that it also shows how people **transported** farm goods to the city's market. It is likely that on market day, farmers loaded their crops into carts. The crops may have included barley, cotton, dates, melons, peas, rice, sesame seeds, and wheat. Then the farmers hitched their bulls to the carts and headed to market, where they sold or traded their goods with other farmers.

Children in Mohenjodaro may have played with clay models like this one. Such artifacts provide clues on how Indus valley people might have transported crops to market.

Chapter Summary

In this chapter, you explored artifacts from the ruins of the two parts of the city of Mohenjodaro to learn about daily life in the Indus valley civilization.

The Mystery of Mohenjodaro Historians and archaeologists continue to investigate what happened to this remarkable civilization.

Weights and Scale The discovery of standard weights, a scale, and marked rods suggest that the ancient Indians had a uniform way to measure weight and length.

The Great Bath The remains of a brick pool, well, and drain system, lead archaeologists to believe that people may have bathed in and used the pool in religious rituals.

Statue, Beads, and Seals Other interesting artifacts include a small statue of a man, a variety of stone beads, and stone seals carved with pictographs.

Sewer System A sewer system carried waste away from the city's buildings and into the Indus River. Both rich and poor people likely had homes with indoor bathrooms.

Homes Most people lived in the lower city in rows of 2-story houses made of mud bricks. These homes had between one and a dozen rooms.

Games As the discovery of game pieces and toys suggests, the people had time to play. Adults may have played an early form of chess.

Clay Models Archaeologists have found clay models that may have been toys. Some models reveal information about ways of farming and transporting goods to market.

Chapter 15

Learning About World Religions: Hinduism

What are the origins and beliefs of Hinduism?

15.1 Introduction

In this chapter, you will learn about the origins and beliefs of Hinduism. Hinduism is the most influential set of religious beliefs in modern India.

The ancient traditions that gave rise to Hinduism have shaped Indian life in countless ways. This cultural heritage has **affected** how people worship, what jobs they do, and even what they eat. It has inspired great art and literature. And it has helped determine the status of people in Indian society.

One of the basic beliefs of Hinduism and some other Indian religions is dharma. Dharma refers to law, duty, and obligation. To follow one's dharma means to dedicate oneself to performing one's duties and to living by **specific** sets of rules.

The *Ramayana*, one of the most famous ancient literary texts, is sacred to many Hindus. It tells about life in ancient India and offers role models in dharma. For example, one of the central figures of the *Ramayana*, Rama, lives by the rules of dharma. When Rama is a young boy, he is a loyal son. When he grows up, he is a loving husband and a responsible ruler.

In this chapter, you will explore the origins of Hinduism. Then you will learn about dharma and a number of other Hindu beliefs: Brahman, deities, karma, and samsara.

This statue represents Rama, who is a role model as both a man and a ruler, in the way to live by the rules of dharma.

◀ A Brahmin, or Hindu priest, walks in the holy city of Varanasi.

Hinduism a religion that developed in India over many centuries; it traces its roots to older traditions, such as Vedic beliefs and Brahmanism

Vedas a collection of ancient writings viewed as sacred by many Hindus

Sanskrit an ancient Indian language

Brahmanism ancient ritual traditions in which Brahmins played a key role; it grew out of older Vedic religious beliefs and helped lead to Hinduism

15.2 The Origins of Hinduism

No single person founded **Hinduism**. It developed slowly, over a long period of time, growing out of centuries of older traditions.

In the second millennium B.C.E., nomadic people speaking Indo-European languages migrated into northern India. These nomads, sometimes called Aryans (AIR-ee-uhnz), brought to India their gods and rituals, some of which eventually became part of Hinduism. Other aspects of Hinduism drew on local traditions, which, over thousands of years, allowed a wide range of practices and beliefs to arise in different parts of India.

The oldest roots of Hinduism are found in Vedic religion, which is named for the earliest Indian texts. The **Vedas** (VAY-duhz) are a collection of sacred texts, including verses, hymns, prayers, and teachings composed in **Sanskrit** (SAN-skrit). (*Veda* is Sanskrit for "knowledge.") The earliest of the Vedas grew out of traditions brought into India by the Aryans. These traditions expanded over centuries in India, as the teachings of the Vedas were handed down orally from generation to generation, before India had a written form of Sanskrit.

The Vedas were composed in the ancient language of Sanskrit.

Vedic rituals and sacrifices honored a number of deities (gods and goddesses) associated with nature and social order. Over time, these rituals became more complex. A class of priests and religious scholars, called Brahmins (BRAH-minz), grew increasingly important. They were responsible for correctly **interpreting** the Vedas and performing the required rituals. Brahmins eventually became the dominant class in India. Later Vedic religion is often called **Brahmanism**. The word *Hinduism*, the term for the traditions that grew out of later Vedic religion or Brahmanism, came much later.

Modern-day Hinduism is a very complex religion. Many beliefs, forms of worship, and deities exist side by side, and often differ from place to place. The Vedas, to which Hinduism traces its early roots, remain sacred to many Hindus today. Along with later sacred texts, the Vedas lay out some of the basic beliefs of Hinduism. As you will see, these beliefs have influenced every aspect of life in India.

15.3 Hinduism and the Caste System

Brahmanism was more than a religion in ancient India. It was a way of life. It affected how Indians lived, what they believed, and even the way they organized their society. Many of those ideas live on in modern Hinduism.

Brahmanism taught that a well-organized society was divided into different social classes. Today, we call this practice of social organization, developed in India, the **caste** system. The Vedas describe four main social classes, or varnas:

caste a class, or group, in Hindu society

- Brahmins (priests and religious scholars)
- Kshatriyas (KSHA-tree-uhs) (rulers and warriors)
- Vaishyas (VIESH-yuhs) (herders and merchants)
- Shudras (SHOO-druhs) (servants, farmers, and laborers)

According to the Vedas, each class, or varna, had its own duties. For example, Brahmins had a duty to study and teach the Vedas. Warriors had a duty to become skilled with weapons. But the caste system meant that some people were favored much more than others. Brahmins held the highest place in society, while Shudras held the lowest.

Over the centuries, the caste system in India grew very complex. By medieval times, there were thousands of castes. The people in the lowest caste were known as Untouchables. Their descendants today often call themselves *Dalits*, from a word meaning "suppressed" or "crushed." This group had jobs or ways of life that involved activities that high-caste Indians considered lowly or "dirty," such as handling garbage and dead animals. Untouchables often had to live in their own villages or neighborhoods. They could not enter many temples or attend most schools. Other Hindus avoided touching, and in many cases, even looking at this group of people. Some of these rules separating the lowest caste remain today.

The caste system affected all aspects of people's lives. Indians were born into a certain caste, and they could not change it. They could only marry within their own caste. Today, caste discrimination is outlawed in India. But despite the laws, caste status continues to affect many parts of Indian life.

This way of organizing society is just one example of how ancient religion affected daily life in India. Let's look now at other aspects of Hinduism and how they helped shape Indian life and culture.

Even today, the highest caste in India is the Brahmins. Shown here is a gathering of Brahmin women in India.

15.4 Hindu Beliefs About Brahman

Brahman is the name of a supreme power, or a **divine** force, that some Hindus believe is greater than all other deities. To these Hindus, only Brahman exists forever. Everything else in the world changes, from the passing seasons to all living things that eventually die.

In many Indian traditions, including Hinduism, time moves forward in a circle, like a great wheel. The same events return, just as the sun rises each morning, and spring follows winter. Some Hindus see this **cycle** as the work of Brahman, who is constantly creating, destroying, and re-creating the universe. The cycle never ends.

According to Hindus following these traditions, everything in the world is a part of Brahman, including the human soul. Ancient Hindus called the soul *atman*. In certain traditions, Hindus view the soul as part of Brahman, just as a drop of water is part of the ocean. Through their souls, people are therefore connected to Brahman. In these traditions, the other deities worshipped in Hinduism are simply different forms of Brahman. Other Hindus have different beliefs about Hindu gods, such as Vishnu (VISH-noo) and Shiva (SHIH-vuh).

The Laxminarayan Temple, also called the Birla Temple, in Delhi, India, was built in 1622. The temple honors the Hindu god Vishnu.

To communicate with their deities, followers of the ancient Vedic religion and Brahmanism held their elaborate rites and sacrifices outdoors. In later Hindu times, as Indian civilization developed and cities grew, people began to build massive temples for worship. Today, many modern Hindu temples are modeled after the ancient principles used to design those early temples.

Many Hindu temples are magnificent in size and design. Their doors often face east, toward the rising sun. The buildings are covered with beautiful carvings and sculptures. These works of art usually show deities from Hindu sacred texts. The temple interiors usually contain a tower and a small shrine.

15.5 Hindu Beliefs About Deities

There are many deities in Hindu sacred texts and worship rituals. Over time, as we learned earlier, some Hindus came to believe that all the deities were different faces of a supreme force, Brahman. For these Hindus, each god represented a power or quality of Brahman.

Today, in some Hindu traditions, there are three important deities. They are Brahma (BRAH-mah) (not Brahman), Vishnu, and Shiva. Each deity controls one aspect of the universe. Brahma creates it, Vishnu preserves it, and Shiva destroys it. In other Indian traditions, another goddess named Devi (DAY-vee) embodies the female powers of the universe.

Hindu families light candles, lamps, and sparklers to celebrate Divali, the festival of lights.

Ancient Hindu sacred texts often describe heroic deities battling evil. One famous story is found in the *Ramayana*. It tells of Rama's fierce battle with Ravana, a demon (evil spirit). Such tales present in an entertaining way some of what later became Hindu beliefs. Many Hindu children have learned about their religion by listening to readings of the *Ramayana*, or in recent years, by seeing the stories dramatized on television.

Ancient literary texts like the *Ramayana*, which some Hindus view as sacred, have inspired many Hindu holidays and festivals. The Hindu New Year is celebrated at the Divali (dih-VAH-lee) festival. *Divali* means "row of lamps." The lamps are symbols of good (light) winning over evil (darkness). They are often said to represent Rama's triumph over the evil Ravana, and the start of the Hindu New Year.

An Indian groom (left) and bride (right) take part in preparations for a traditional Hindu wedding. Marriage is one form of dharma.

15.6 Hindu Beliefs About Dharma

Dharma is an important belief in Hinduism and other Indian traditions. Dharma stands for law, obligation, and duty. To follow one's dharma means to perform one's duties and to live in an honorable way.

As you have already read, according to the Vedas, each social class, or varna, had its own duties. These duties usually involved a certain type of work. Duties might include studying religious texts, herding animals, trading goods, or serving as a warrior. Therefore, each class was seen as having its own dharma. In fact, early Hindus called their system of social classes varna dharma, or "the way of one's kind." Early Hindus believed that when everyone followed the dharma of their varna, society would be in harmony.

dharma a belief found in Hinduism and other Indian traditions that a person has a duty or obligation to live an honorable life

Brahmins, for example, were ancient Hindu society's priests and religious scholars. Their duties included performing rituals and teaching the Vedas. This was quite an accomplishment, since ancient scholars had passed down this knowledge through word of mouth. To recite the Vedas orally, Brahmins had to memorize tens of thousands of verses!

In addition to following the dharma of their own varna, Hindus are expected to follow a common dharma, or set of values. This is often said to include the importance of marriage, sharing food with others, and caring for one's soul.

Another basic value is nonviolence. Many Hindus, as well as followers of other Indian traditions, have a respect for life that stems from their belief that all life forms have a soul. In Hindu traditions, reverence for life is symbolized by the cow. Hindus were taught not to kill them, perhaps because cows provided people with things they needed, such as milk and butter. Even in death, cows provided hides that could be made into clothing.

This Hindu man sits in prayer, or meditation.

15.7 Hindu Beliefs About Karma

The belief in dharma expresses much of what Hindus believe about the right way to live. **Karma** is another belief Hindus share with other Indian traditions. It explains the importance of living according to dharma.

In Hindu belief, the law of karma governs what happens to people's souls after death. From ancient times, many Indians believed that souls had many lives. When a person died, his or her soul was reborn in a new body. The type of body the reborn soul received depended on the soul's karma.

Karma was made up of all the good and evil that a person had done in past lives. If people lived good lives, they might be born into a higher social class in their next life. If they lived badly, they could expect to be reborn into a lower class. They might even be reborn as animals.

For Hindus, the law of karma meant that the universe was just, or fair. Souls were rewarded or punished for the good and evil they had done. Karma was also used to explain why people had a certain status in society. You may recall that in the caste system, people could not escape the social class of their birth. According to karma, this judgment was fair, because it was thought that people's social class reflected what they had done in their past lives.

karma a belief found in Hinduism and other Indian traditions that the good and evil done in a past life determines the nature of that person's next life

Hindus from all over the world travel to the Ganges River to bathe in its waters.

Over the centuries, many Indian scholars disapproved of the caste system. They thought that all people, including the Untouchables, should be treated equally. In the 20th century, the chief architect of India's first constitution, B. R. Ambedkar, sharply criticized the caste system. He, himself, came from the Untouchable caste. Today, Indian law makes caste discrimination illegal, but caste ideas continue to affect daily life. Other ancient ideas, like karma and rebirth, which are tied to views of caste, also remain central to Indian beliefs.

reincarnation the belief that a person's soul is reborn into a new body after death

pilgrimage a journey to a holy place

15.8 Hindu Beliefs About Samsara

As you have learned, Hindus and many other Indians believe in a continuous cycle of birth, death, and rebirth. They call this cycle *samsara*. As long as people are part of samsara, they will know pain and death. Samsara ends when the soul escapes from the cycle of rebirth, the time when some Hindus believe that they are united with Brahman, the supreme force in the universe.

It takes many lifetimes before a person can be released from samsara. People escape the cycle of rebirth, or **reincarnation,** by following their dharma. They behave correctly and perform their social duties. They worship faithfully according to prescribed rules. In these ways, they balance their karma with good actions.

The Indians of ancient times went on holy journeys called **pilgrimages**. People would travel to sacred places like the Ganges River. Such pilgrims believed that the difficulty of the journey would cleanse them of their sins.

Faithful Hindus still make pilgrimages today. Pilgrims travel for days over difficult land, including mountains. At each holy site and temple they encounter, they often lie facedown in worship. The Ganges River is still one of the most holy places in India. Like the ancient Indians, modern Hindus bathe in its waters as an act of devotion and purification.

A member of the Brahmin caste reads to his followers from sacred texts.

Chapter Summary

In this chapter, you learned about the major beliefs of Hinduism, which grew out of ancient religious traditions, such as the Vedic religion and Brahmanism.

Hinduism and the Caste System Brahmanism followed a social organization that was described in the Vedas. There were four main classes, or varnas. Each class had certain duties. This caste system became more complex over time.

Hindu Beliefs About Brahman and Other Deities Some Hindus believe that Brahman is a divine force and the greatest deity. They believe he exists forever, creating, destroying, and re-creating the universe in an endless cycle. Their many deities are different faces of Brahman. Some traditions worship three key deities who control aspects of the universe: Brahma creates, Vishnu preserves, and Shiva destroys. One text held sacred by some Hindus is the *Ramayana,* which contains stories about deities battling evil.

Dharma According to these beliefs, held by Hindus and other Indian traditions, people must live honorably, by performing duties. Each class has its own dharma, as well as a common set of values.

Karma According to these beliefs, shared by Hindus and other traditions, the good and evil done in a past life determine what happens to one's soul in the next life. Karma was used to explain why people were in particular castes.

Samsara Hindus and other Indians believe in this cycle of birth, death, and rebirth. The cycle ends after many lifetimes, when the soul is reunited with Brahman and is no longer reborn. Hindu beliefs continue to affect daily life in India. Hindus still worship in temples, make pilgrimages, and celebrate religious festivals.

Chapter 16

Learning About World Religions: Buddhism

What are the main beliefs and teachings of Buddhism?

16.1 Introduction

Hinduism, which developed in ancient India, is the oldest of the world's major religions. In this chapter, you will learn about Buddhism, another religion with roots in ancient India.

Buddhism is a religion based on the teachings of the Buddha (BOO-duh), which means "Awakened One." The Buddha was a man who lived in India from about 563 to 483 B.C.E. Before he became known as the Buddha, he was a young prince named Siddhartha Gautama (si-DAHR-tuh GOW-tuh-muh).

Prince Siddhartha grew up surrounded by wealth in the palaces of his father. At the age of 29, Siddhartha left his royal life to go in search of spiritual peace. During his journeys, he learned great truths that changed his life. By sharing these truths with others, he began the religion of Buddhism.

Buddhism was different from Hinduism in several ways. Whereas Hinduism was based on complicated rituals and beliefs in many gods, Buddhism was a way of life based on simple teachings. Unlike ancient Hinduism, Buddhism **embraced** all people regardless of their caste. It taught people how to reach enlightenment, or happiness that comes from the knowledge of deep truth. Buddhists believed that once they reached the level of enlightenment, they would escape from the cycle of rebirth.

In this chapter, you will learn about Buddhism through stories that are told about the Buddha's life. You will find out what Prince Siddhartha discovered during his life and how his teachings became the basis of Buddhism.

These young Buddhist monks stand in the large window of a Buddhist monastery in the nation of Myanmar, in Southeast Asia.

◀ A stone carving of Buddha, the founder of the Buddhist religion

This painting shows Siddhartha soon after his birth. At the far right, King Suddhodana holds his son. Queen Maya sits to the left of the king. Royal court members kneel below them.

Buddha a Sanskrit word meaning "enlightened;" the name given to the man who founded Buddhism

16.2 Prince Siddhartha's Birth

Prince Siddhartha was born about 563 B.C.E. in the present-day country of Nepal, near the Himalayas. His father, Suddhodana, was a powerful king. His mother was Queen Maya.

According to Buddhist tradition, before her son was born, the queen had a dream. In the dream, she was carried high over the Himalayas to a silver mountain and set on a silver couch. A white elephant with six tusks walked around her and then struck her in the right side.

The king and queen asked the Brahmins, or Hindu priests, to explain her dream. "You are carrying a child who will be a great man," they told the queen. The Brahmins declared that the prince's future held two possible paths. As a prince, he could rule the universe. But if he left his royal life to see the suffering in the world, he would become the **Buddha,** one who is enlightened.

The queen gave birth to Prince Siddhartha in a garden. Stories say that after the prince's birth, a soft, warm rain of heavenly flowers fell on the baby and his mother. According to Buddhist tradition, the infant prince already looked a few years old and could walk and talk. Siddhartha began his remarkable life by taking a few steps and declaring, "I am the leader of the world and the guide to the world."

16.3 The Prince's Royal Life

Prince Siddhartha's father wanted his son to be a great and powerful ruler. The king was worried about the **predictions** made by the Brahmins. If the prince saw the world's suffering, he might give up his royal duties to seek a spiritual path.

The king decided to protect his son from all of the horrors of the world. He raised the prince in a world of perfect wealth and beauty. He provided Siddhartha with only the finest gardens, houses, education, and food. Servants took care of the prince's every need, from washing his clothes to playing music for his amusement.

The prince enjoyed his life filled with lavish pleasures, yet he always felt curious about the world outside the palace walls. Some days, he would sit under a rose apple tree and think and wonder about the world beyond his reach.

At the age of 16, Prince Siddhartha married a beautiful young noblewoman. The wedding feast lasted seven days and seven nights. For 12 years, the couple lived together in perfect peace, enjoying the prince's many palaces. When Siddhartha turned 29, they had a son.

Prince Siddhartha enjoyed a life of luxury in his father's palaces. This painting shows his wedding ceremony, at left, and his skill at archery, at right.

Outside the palace, Siddhartha learned about three forms of suffering: aging, sickness, and death.

16.4 The Prince Discovers Three Forms of Suffering

After Siddhartha became a father himself, the king gave him more freedom to travel outside the royal palaces. According to Buddhist tradition, during his journeys, the prince discovered three forms of suffering.

On his first trip, the prince and his chariot driver saw a thin man who walked with the aid of a stick. "Why does that man look so terrible?" the prince asked. His driver replied that the man was old. He told the prince that everyone's body weakens as it ages.

On the second trip, the prince and his driver saw a man lying on the ground and crying out in pain. "What is the matter with that poor man?" the prince asked. The driver explained that the man was sick.

On the third trip, the prince saw a group of people walking slowly down the road. The group carried a figure wrapped in white cloth. "Death came for that man," Siddhartha's driver said quietly. "One day, it will come for you, too."

The prince was deeply troubled by his discovery of aging, sickness, and death. Unable to sit at home with his thoughts, he set out a fourth time. This time, he met a man who glowed with inner peace and calm. The man was an **ascetic** (uh-SEH-tik). An ascetic is someone who gives up worldly pleasures such as possessions, fine clothes, money, and even shelter.

"How can you sit there so peacefully when there is so much suffering in the world around you?" the prince asked the man. The ascetic replied, "To be free of suffering, one must give up the desires, pleasures, and comforts of the world. I find peace by helping others find peace."

ascetic a person who gives up worldly pleasures

When Siddhartha began his search for enlightenment, he gave up riches to live the simple life of an ascetic.

16.5 The Prince Becomes an Ascetic

Prince Siddhartha's experiences with suffering **transformed** him. Suddenly, his royal life seemed empty. He wanted to find the happiness and peace that the ascetic had found.

Siddhartha decided to give up his old life and search for **enlightenment**. Becoming enlightened would mean finding deep truth and freedom from suffering.

One night, the prince asked his driver to take him to the forest. At the edge of the dark woods, Siddhartha removed his royal robes, sandals, and jewels. He cut off his hair with a knife. He put on a simple robe and carried only a small bowl for **alms,** or gifts of food. Wishing his driver farewell, Siddhartha began his life as an ascetic.

Siddhartha met other ascetics as he wandered the forests and fields. Like him, they wanted to understand the nature of the world. They believed that they could reach enlightenment through meditation. While meditating, the ascetics sat quietly and focused their minds on spiritual questions. Siddhartha quickly became an expert at meditation.

The ascetics also **denied** themselves many basic needs. For example, they stayed up all night without sleeping. They sat in the hot sun without shelter. They held their breath for several minutes. They also fasted, or stopped eating, for many days at a time. They hoped to find spiritual truth through self-denial.

Siddhartha continued to follow the way of the ascetics for some time. He became terribly thin from lack of food. According to Buddhist tradition, he became so thin that he could touch his stomach and feel his backbone. Eventually, he became unhappy with this extreme way of living. And he had not yet found the key to enlightenment.

> **enlightenment** the state of gaining spiritual insight and finding universal truth; the goal of Buddhists
>
> **alms** goods or money given to the poor

During a night of deep meditation under the Bodhi tree, Siddhartha achieved enlightenment.

nirvana an ideal state of happiness and peace

Buddhism the religion founded by Siddhartha, which teaches that life brings suffering that one can escape by seeking nirvana through enlightenment

Four Noble Truths the four basic doctrines, or principles, of Buddhism

Eightfold Path a key idea of Buddhism whereby followers should live their lives according to these eight teachings

16.6 The Prince Becomes the Buddha

Siddhartha had learned that giving up bodily pleasures did not bring enlightenment. He decided to find a balance between the extremes of pleasure and pain. He would be neither a prince nor an ascetic. Instead, he would **seek** a "middle way" as a path to enlightenment.

The prince's new way of thinking caused the other ascetics to abandon him. But he was content to be alone. Although he had not yet found enlightenment, he believed that he was now on the right path.

A full moon rose on Siddhartha's 35th birthday. He bathed in the river and rested quietly in a grove of trees. When he awoke, he had a strong feeling that he would soon become enlightened. Then a grass cutter gave him eight handfuls of soft grass as a present. Siddhartha walked until he reached a tree that would become known as the Bodhi (BOH-dee), or Enlightenment, tree. He placed the grass at the foot of the tree and sat down. He vowed to meditate under the tree until he reached enlightenment.

According to Buddhist tradition, while Siddhartha was meditating, a wicked god named Mara tried to frighten him. Then Mara sent his three daughters—Discontent (unhappiness), Delight, and Desire—to try to tempt Siddhartha. But Siddhartha resisted them all. He then meditated through the rest of the night about the nature of reality and the way to reach **nirvana,** or true happiness and peace. During the night, his mind filled with the truths he had been seeking. He saw his past lives and the great cycle of rebirth. He saw the importance of karma. Eventually, he saw how to gain freedom from the continuous cycle, and therefore end all suffering.

By morning, the young prince had become the Buddha, the Awakened One. He had reached enlightenment.

The truths that the Buddha discovered under the Bodhi tree are the basic principles of **Buddhism**. They are often called the **Four Noble Truths**. The Buddha would spend the rest of his life sharing these truths with the people of India.

The Four Noble Truths

1. Suffering is present in all things, and nothing lasts forever.
2. Suffering is caused by cravings (desires and wants).
3. The way to end suffering is to give up all cravings.
4. The way to give up all cravings is to live life according to the **Eightfold Path**.

The Eightfold Path

The Buddha said that one could end suffering and find enlightenment by following these eight teachings.

1. Right understanding
Develop a deep understanding of the Four Noble Truths.

2. Right purpose
Live a life of selflessness (not selfishness), love, and nonviolence.

3. Right speech
Be careful and truthful in what you say. Do not lie or gossip.

4. Right action
Do not kill, steal, or lie. Be honest.

5. Right way to earn a living
Do not work at a job that causes harm to people or living creatures.

6. Right effort
Promote good actions and prevent evil actions.

7. Right mindfulness
Be aware of but not attached to your emotions, thoughts, and feelings.

8. Right concentration
Focus your mind with such practices as meditation.

16.7 The Buddha's Teachings

Behind Buddhism's Four Noble Truths is the idea that all things change. The Buddha saw that even when one finds pleasure, it does not last forever, and one suffers when it is lost. To end suffering, he taught, people should travel the Eightfold Path. This path follows the "middle way."

The Buddha could have selfishly escaped into enlightenment. Instead, he chose to teach others the path that he had found. In time, his followers spread his teachings throughout India and other parts of Asia.

Chapter Summary

In this chapter, you learned about the beliefs and teachings of Buddhism, a religion that developed in ancient India.

Siddhartha Gautama Buddhism is based on Siddhartha's teachings. Born a prince, he became an ascetic to find enlightenment. Later, he followed a middle way to reach nirvana. He became the Buddha and taught others how to seek enlightenment.

Buddha's Teachings Buddha shared his discovery of the Four Noble Truths about the state of suffering and the ways to end it. He believed that people could reach enlightenment by living according to the teachings of the Eightfold Path.

Chapter 17

The First Unification of India

How did Ashoka unify the Mauryan Empire and spread Buddhist values?

17.1 Introduction

In this chapter, you will learn about an Indian leader named King Ashoka (uh-SHOHKE-uh). He gave up wars of conquest and instead began to spread Buddhist values to unify India.

King Ashoka was a member of the Maurya (MOW-ree-yuh) family, the first leaders to unite the various kingdoms of India. The Mauryan Empire flourished from about 322 to 187 B.C.E. The Mauryas, including Ashoka, fought wars of conquest to build their empire. Then a great change came over Ashoka, and he turned to peaceful ways of keeping India united.

It is said that the change came about in this way. When King Ashoka was a young man, he was sitting on his horse one day, looking out over a bloody battlefield. Men and animals lay dying under the hot sun. Ashoka could hear the wounded groaning in pain. With growing **horror,** he thought of the thousands of people who had been killed or enslaved in his family's ongoing quest for land. In that moment, the king swore to give up the ways of violence.

Ashoka's promise led him to the Buddhist religion. Rather than rule by war, he chose to create an empire based on Buddhist values. He spread Buddhist beliefs through edicts, official orders or messages, carved on walls, rocks, and tall pillars.

In this chapter, you will read about how the Mauryan family unified India. Then you will see how King Ashoka used Buddhist values to rule his empire.

This fine stone sculpture of King Ashoka was created in the 12th century.

◀ King Ashoka had edicts carved on tall pillars to promote peace.

Mauryan Empire an empire lasting from about 322 to 187 B.C.E., during which the Mauryan family unified India for the first time

Ashoka ruler of the Mauryan Empire from about 269 to 232 B.C.E., whose edicts reflected Buddhist values

The Mauryan Empire reached its peak under King Ashoka, grandson of Chandragupta Maurya.

17.2 The Mauryas Unify India

The Mauryas were the first leaders to unify India. The Indian subcontinent, once divided into many small kingdoms, covered more than one million square miles. Because India was huge and diverse, the unification of this **vast** land by the Mauryas was a major accomplishment.

Chandragupta (chun-druh-GOOP-tuh) Maurya began to build the **Mauryan Empire** in the 320s B.C.E. He saw that the kingdoms of northern India were weak. Fighting among themselves, they had wasted too much money and lost too many soldiers. Chandragupta used his great army of 700,000 soldiers, with 9,000 elephants, to overthrow the rulers of these kingdoms. He conquered and united all of northern India.

Chandragupta Maurya kept his empire strong by using force whenever necessary. He was deeply afraid of enemies. He used his powerful army, a network of spies, and torture to keep his subjects in line.

Chandragupta's rule was harsh, but it was successful in some ways. He created a strong central government. He wrote laws. He made sure farmers had water for their crops. To help connect the parts of his empire, he built a royal road more than one thousand miles long.

Toward the end of his life, Chandragupta gave up his power. Tradition says that he became an ascetic, or a person who has given up worldly pleasures. He lived in poverty and traveled with monks (simple holy men). Meanwhile, the empire grew even larger. Under the rule of Chandragupta's grandson, King **Ashoka**, it included nearly all of the Indian subcontinent.

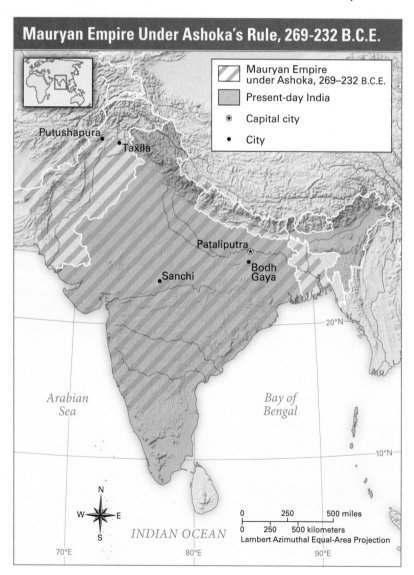

Mauryan Empire Under Ashoka's Rule, 269-232 B.C.E.

Legend:
- Mauryan Empire under Ashoka, 269–232 B.C.E.
- Present-day India
- ⊛ Capital city
- • City

Putushapura
Taxila
Pataliputra
Bodh Gaya
Sanchi
Arabian Sea
Bay of Bengal
20°N
10°N
INDIAN OCEAN

0   250   500 miles
0 250   500 kilometers
Lambert Azimuthal Equal-Area Projection

70°E   80°E   90°E

17.3 Ashoka's Rule

The Mauryan Empire reached its height during the reign of King Ashoka. He ruled the empire from about 269 to 232 B.C.E.

During the early part of his reign, Ashoka expanded the empire to the south and east through a series of wars. Then, after one very brutal battle, he made his decision to **reject** violence and find a more peaceful way to rule.

Ashoka decided to embrace Buddhism. He supported the Buddhist values of love, peace, and nonviolence. As a Buddhist, he respected all living things. He gave up hunting and became a strict vegetarian. (A vegetarian is someone who does not eat meat.) He visited holy Buddhist sites. Perhaps most surprisingly, Ashoka gave up wars of conquest. Never again would he fight another kingdom for its land.

Ashoka wanted his people to follow the Buddhist path. He urged them to be respectful, kind, and moral, which means to know right from wrong ways of behavior. He told the people to treat their servants well, to respect their elders, and to tolerate those who practiced different religions. Ashoka saw himself as a wise and loving father figure. He often referred to the people he ruled as his children.

King Ashoka originally built this dome-shaped structure, called a *stupa*, to hold sacred objects associated with Buddhism.

Ashoka spread Buddhism beyond India. According to tradition, he sent Mahinda, his son, to Ceylon, a large island south of India. (Today, it is called Sri Lanka.) Mahinda converted Ceylon's king to Buddhism, which became the official faith of the kingdom.

Not all of Ashoka's actions reflected Buddhist values. For example, under his rule, the practice of slavery was allowed, and people could be **executed** for serious crimes. Ashoka also continued to maintain a strong army. Although he gave up battles of conquest, he did not return any of the lands the Mauryas had already conquered.

edict a command that is obeyed like a law

17.4 Ashoka's Edicts

Ashoka wanted a strong, united empire guided by Buddhist values. To spread those values to his people, he had **edicts** carved into walls, rocks, and tall pillars throughout the empire, in places where the greatest number of people could see them.

Ashoka's edicts were designed to **promote** four main goals:

- **Buddhist Values** These edicts encouraged the Buddha's teachings. They asked people to be loving and respectful, and to practice nonviolence. They said people should not get attached to worldly things, such as money. They also told people to act morally (do right rather than wrong).

- **General Welfare** These edicts promoted people's well-being. They were intended to make sure people had good health, shelter, clean water, and enough food.

- **Justice** These edicts were in regard to fair-laws. They also described the way people were to be treated in the empire's courts and jails.

- **Security** These edicts were concerned with enemies of the Mauryan Empire and people who were not citizens. They often dealt with issues of peace and conquest.

Ashoka's four goals were intended to give his empire a strong foundation. His reign is still remembered in India as a time of great achievements and progress. But his dream of a united empire did not last. About 45 years after his death, the empire broke apart into separate kingdoms.

A more lasting legacy was Ashoka's support of Buddhism. As you have read, Ashoka sent his son to introduce Buddhism

to Ceylon. Later, around the start of the Common Era, Buddhism spread from northwestern India to Central Asia. From there, it traveled to China, Korea, and Japan.

The symbol seen here on one of Ashoka's pillars and on the flag of India is called the Ashoka Chakra or the Wheel of the Law. It stands for the perpetual movement and change that is part of all life.

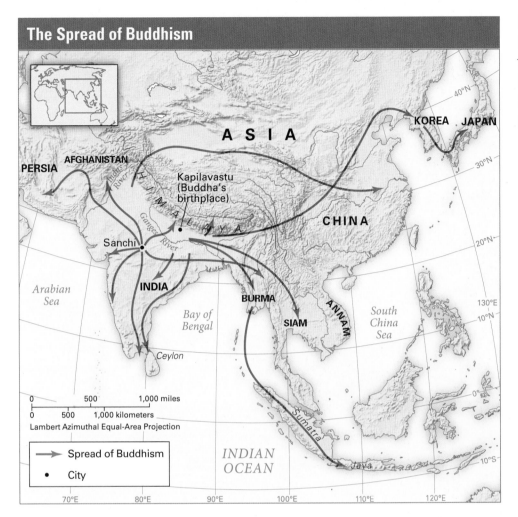

The Spread of Buddhism

During his reign, King Ashoka worked to spread Buddhist beliefs across the Mauryan Empire and beyond its borders.

Chapter Summary

In this chapter, you learned how the Maurya family unified and ruled India, first through the use of force, and later by spreading the ideas of Buddhism.

The Mauryas Unify India The Mauryas were a family of powerful rulers who created an empire through a series of wars and conquests. They reigned over a unified India for several generations, from about 322 to 187 B.C.E.

Ashoka's Rule King Ashoka first expanded his empire through war. Then he embraced Buddhist values of love and nonviolence and spread these ideas. However, he allowed slavery and executions for serious crimes. He also maintained a strong army.

Ashoka's Edicts Ashoka carved edicts into walls and pillars throughout the empire. These edicts promoted Buddhist values, general welfare, justice, and security. The spread of Buddhism in Asia was Ashoka's most lasting legacy.

Chapter 18

The Achievements of the Gupta Empire

Why is the period during the Gupta Empire known as a "golden age"?

18.1 Introduction

Under the Mauryan Empire, India was unified for the first time and Buddhist beliefs became widespread. In this chapter, you will explore the next great empire to unite India. It was called the Gupta (GOOP-tuh) Empire.

The Guptas were a line of rulers who controlled much of India from 320 to 550 C.E. Many historians have called this period a golden age, which is a time of great **prosperity** and **achievement**. In unstable times, people are likely to be busy meeting their immediate needs for food, shelter, and safety. But in times of peace and prosperity, people can turn their attention to more creative activities. For this reason, a number of advances in the arts and sciences occurred during the peaceful golden age of the Gupta Empire. Many of these achievements have left a lasting mark on the world.

Archaeologists have made some notable discoveries that have helped us learn about the accomplishments of the Gupta Empire. For example, they have unearthed palm-leaf books that were created about 550 C.E. Sacred texts often appeared in palm-leaf books. These sacred texts are just one of many kinds of literature that Indians created during the Guptas' reign.

Literature was one of several areas of major accomplishment during India's golden age. In this chapter, you will learn more about the rise of the Gupta Empire. Then you will take a close look at seven achievements that came out of this rich period in India's history.

In this Ajanta cave, richly colored paintings decorate the walls around a statue of Buddha.

◀ An artist of the Gupta Empire painted this delicate image of Buddha.

Gupta Empire the empire covering much of northern India that was ruled by the Guptas from about 320 C.E. to about 550 C.E.

alliance a bond between families, states, or other groups to further their common interests

province a territory that is part of a country or an empire

golden age a period of great happiness, prosperity, and achievement

18.2 The Rise of the Gupta Empire

After the Mauryan Empire fell in about 187 B.C.E., India broke apart into separate kingdoms. For about 500 years, these smaller kingdoms fought each other for land and power. Beginning around 320 C.E., a second great empire arose in India: the **Gupta Empire**.

The empire began under a ruler named Chandragupta I. He and his family, the Guptas, united the northern kingdoms by conquering them through war. The Guptas also formed some **alliances** by arranging marriages between members of their family and the sons and daughters of other rulers.

The Gupta line of kings lasted until about 550 C.E. At the height of their power, the Guptas ruled most of northern India. Their empire was the largest that India had known since the days of the Mauryas.

In some ways, the Gupta Empire was similar to the Mauryan Empire. The Guptas set up a central government to oversee the empire. A council, made up of advisers and members of the royal family, helped the king make decisions.

Unlike the Mauryas, the Guptas gave local areas a great deal of independence. They divided the empire into large sections called **provinces**. Each of these provinces was ruled by a royal governor. Within the provinces, town leaders could make many of their own decisions.

The Guptas' ruling strategy helped them stay in power for nearly 230 years. The relatively peaceful times, as well as the empire's stability, encouraged growth in both the arts and the sciences. The result was a **golden age** that produced some of the greatest advances in Indian history. Let's look at seven areas of achievement for the Gupta Empire.

During their reigns, Gupta kings were often shown on coins.

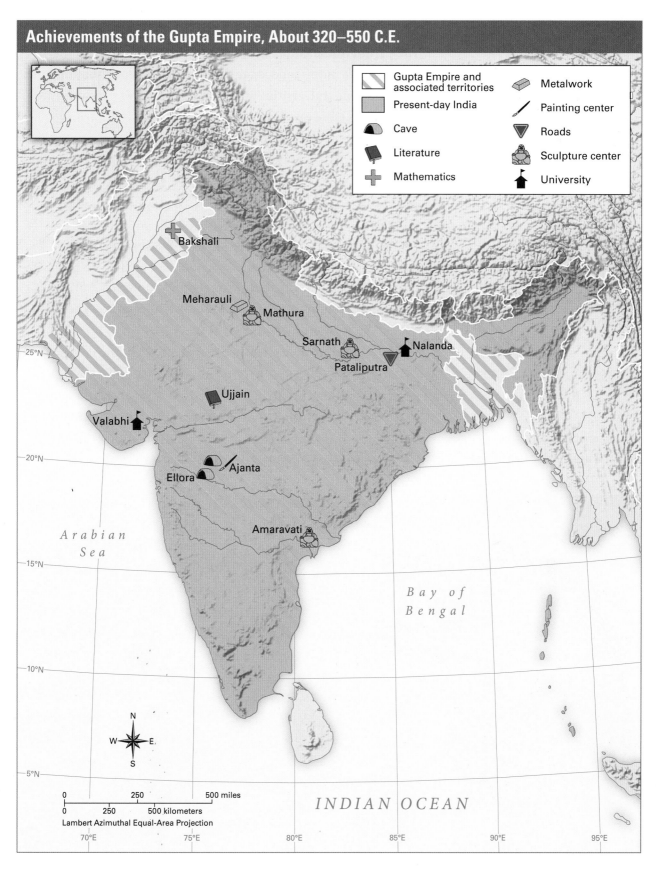

Achievements of the Gupta Empire, About 320–550 C.E.

Legend:
- Gupta Empire and associated territories
- Present-day India
- Cave
- Literature
- Mathematics
- Metalwork
- Painting center
- Roads
- Sculpture center
- University

Bakshali

Meharauli

Mathura

Sarnath

Nalanda

Pataliputra

Ujjain

Valabhi

Ellora

Ajanta

Amaravati

Arabian Sea

Bay of Bengal

INDIAN OCEAN

0   250   500 miles
0   250   500 kilometers
Lambert Azimuthal Equal-Area Projection

Under the rule of the Guptas, India made great advances in many areas, including the arts, education, and the building of roads.

18.3 Universities

The period of the Gupta Empire was a time of learning. The Guptas built many colleges and universities throughout the empire. Some universities were Hindu; others were Buddhist. The schools were open primarily to males. However, teachers' daughters were allowed to attend.

Hindu universities provided the upper classes with religious training. Students attended classes in religion, **mathematics, astronomy,** chemistry, and Sanskrit. They could also study sculpture, painting, music, and dancing.

The most famous university was the Buddhist school at Nalanda, in northern India. The school had eight colleges and three libraries. It also had a hospital and a monastery. Students were instructed in Buddhist and Hindu **philosophy**. They also studied logic, grammar, and medicine.

Students of medicine learned the practices of the day. They were trained in how to question patients about their physical problems. Students were taught how to make cures from bark, roots, leaves, and minerals. They also learned how to use the front claws of giant ants to stitch up wounds. Hindu doctors were especially skilled at performing surgery.

philosophy a theory or set of values by which one lives; the search for wisdom and knowledge

The ruins of the university at Nalanda are impressive in size.

18.4 Literature

Gupta writers created many kinds of literary works. They wrote poetry, fables, and folktales. They also created plays, including both comedies and dramas. Some of the plays were about historical and political subjects. Large audiences gathered to watch the performances.

There were other forms of writing as well. Scholars and lawyers wrote about Hindu law and religion. Some of the great Sanskrit literature took shape during this time. The *Puranas* ("Ancient Lore") was a collection of Hindu legends that taught the lessons of the Vedas, or sacred Hindu texts, through tales of sages and kings. These stories had been passed down orally for generations. The Guptas were the first to gather these stories together and record them. The *Mahabharata* ("Great Work"), a poem composed over hundreds of years, reached its final form during the Gupta era. Its themes relate to Hindu values and the battle between good and evil.

The *Bhagavad Gita* (BAH-guh-vahd GHEE-tuh) is part of the *Mahabharata*. Its name means "Song of the Lord." The *Bhagavad Gita* is one of the most beloved works of Hinduism. In this poem, Prince Arjuna is taught basic truths of Hinduism by Krishna, an earthly form of the deity Vishnu.

Some Gupta literature spread beyond India. Gupta sacred texts influenced cultures of countries as far away as Greece and Persia (present-day Iran). The famous Arabian tale about Aladdin and his magic lamp was inspired by a Gupta folktale.

Manuscripts were written in Sanskrit and often illustrated. This page is from the *Bhagavata Purana*, a sacred Hindu literary text. This work's 18,000 verses about the Hindu god Vishnu have greatly influenced Indian culture.

This detail of an Ajanta cave mural shows a procession of elephants.

18.5 Painting

The Gupta Empire is known for its paintings. This art form was an important part of life for noble families. These families were wealthy people of high birth. No home was complete without a painting board or an easel. Popular subjects included deities and other religious topics. Nobles and members of the royalty also hired artists to create works of art. Some paintings highlighted the luxury of noble life. They were often done on long scrolls.

Perhaps the greatest ancient Indian paintings are those known as the Ajanta (uh-JUHN-tuh) cave murals. The murals cover the walls of the 30 caves that make up an ancient Buddhist monastery in central India. The paintings are done in rich, bright colors including red, purple, and green. Artists made the paints from minerals and clay.

Some of the Ajanta murals show scenes from the Buddha's life. Some murals portray stories that reflect Buddhist values, such as love and understanding. Many of the scenes include graceful images of kings, queens, musicians, and dancers. Other scenes show animals and hunters in the forest. These woodland scenes are decorated with flowers, trees, and complex patterns. Gupta artists were skilled painters.

18.6 Sculpture

Another art form in the Gupta Empire was sculpture. Sculptors created statues out of stone, wood, bronze, and terra-cotta clay. Many of these statues portrayed the Buddha or Hindu deities. Some sculptures showed scenes from important people's lives. Many sculptures were created to stand on their own foundations. Others were carved into the walls of temples and caves.

Gupta sculptures portrayed the human form simply and gracefully. One example is the sculpture of the river deity, Ganga, shown on this page. She is riding on the back of a sea monster. The statue's lines are curved and elegant. Her dress and hair are carved in much detail.

The temple statue of the Buddha shown below reflects the same attention to clean lines and detail. The Buddha sits on a highly decorated seat. His hands and legs are smoothly crossed. His expression is calm and peaceful. The sculptor used lowered eyes and a calm face to portray the Buddha's wisdom.

These sculptures of the river deity, Ganga (right), and the Buddha (left), are typical of Gupta sculptures.

Gupta metalworkers made gold coins to honor the kings who owned the mines.

18.7 Metalwork

One remarkable accomplishment of the Gupta Empire was its metalwork. Gupta kings controlled huge mines of gold, copper, and iron. Metalworkers made gold and copper coins. They engraved the coins with pictures honoring Gupta rulers. The coins often highlighted the rulers' wealth and their achievements in art, politics, and war.

Gupta metalworkers were also famous for their ironwork. An iron pillar at a place called Meharauli is one example of these artisans' unusual skill. The pillar is made of solid iron. It stands 25 feet tall and weighs about 13,000 pounds. The sides are engraved with a story that describes the achievements of a Gupta emperor. The iron is nearly rust free after 1,600 years in the rain and sun. No one knows how Gupta ironworkers acquired such advanced metalworking skills.

18.8 Mathematics

Earlier Hindu mathematicians had created a way of writing whole numbers using the numerals 1 through 9. Some Gupta mathematicians made further advances, one of which was developing the decimal system. The decimal system uses ten basic numerals that have different values depending on their "place." In the number 105, for instance, 1 is in the "hundreds place" and means 100. The system also works for fractions. In the decimal 0.10, 1 means one-tenth. Note the zeros in these examples. Hindu mathematicians were the first to treat zero as a number. Many calculations are impossible without the zero.

In later centuries, Arab peoples learned the Indian system of numbers and spread it to Europe. As a result, Europeans called this way of writing numbers "Arabic numerals." A more accurate name would be "Hindu-Arabic numerals," because the system actually originated with the ancient Indians. We still use this system today.

The use of mathematics allowed ancient Indians to build complex structures such as this temple.

One of the most famous Gupta mathematicians was a man named Aryabhata. He combined mathematics and astronomy to make important discoveries. He figured out that a year was exactly 365.258 days long. He calculated the approximate size of Earth. He proposed that planets were spheres. He was one of the earliest scientists to suggest that Earth spins on its **axis,** an imaginary line through Earth's center.

Mathematics had immediate practical uses as well. For example, Gupta builders applied their knowledge of mathematics to design complex structures like the one shown above.

18.9 Roads

Gupta rulers encouraged trade by creating a system of well-built roads. Care and precision were used to build these roads. First engineers cleared the roadway of plants, trees, and rocks. Then, holes were filled in. Finally, workers smoothed the ground until it was level. The finished roads were made of hard-packed dirt.

The roadways were designed for safety and comfort. They were built a few feet off the ground. Ditches, or canals, ran along either side. These features helped prevent flooding during the rainy monsoon season. Water would run off the road and into the ditches.

Signs along the roadway told travelers where they were. Signs also marked off the distances so people could calculate how far they had traveled. Rest houses gave travelers a place to relax or spend the night. Wells provided water for drinking and cooking.

The empire's roads greatly benefited trade. They enabled busy traders to move easily from city to city within the large empire. Traders could also move goods from the middle of the country to important waterways. From there, traders could ship their goods and sell them in other countries. The roads also connected India to China and the lands east of the Mediterranean Sea.

The network of roads created by Gupta rulers encouraged trade throughout the empire and beyond it. This trade contributed to the empire's prosperity.

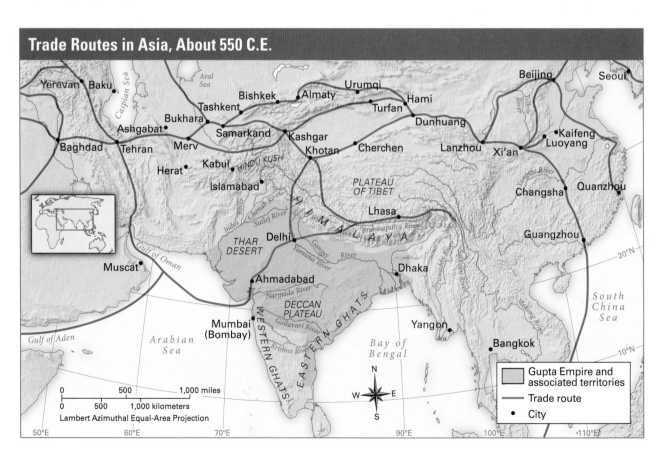

Trade Routes in Asia, About 550 C.E.

Gupta Empire and associated territories

Trade route

City

Lambert Azimuthal Equal-Area Projection

In this chapter, you learned about the many advances made in ancient India during a golden age under the rule of the Gupta Empire.

The Rise of the Gupta Empire The Gupta Empire arose around 320 C.E. under Chandragupta I. Like the Mauryas, the Guptas created a strong central government, while also giving significant independence to local leaders. This strategy helped create an era of stability and prosperity. India experienced a surge of learning and artistic growth in many areas.

Universities The Guptas built many Hindu and Buddhist universities attended by students from the upper classes. Nalanda was the most famous school.

Literature Writers created poetry, fables, folktales, and plays. Scholars wrote about law and religion. Great works of Sanskrit literature, including the *Puranas* and the *Mahabharata,* were recorded. Some of this work spread beyond India and continues to be influential today.

Painting and Sculpture Artists and members of noble families created paintings depicting religious values and noble life. The Ajanta cave murals are among the greatest ancient Indian paintings. Sculptors worked in stone, wood, bronze, and terra-cotta clay. Their work showed Hindu deities, the Buddha, and scenes from important people's lives.

Metalwork Skilled metalworkers engraved gold and copper coins. Artisans were famous for their ironwork, including engravings on iron pillars.

Mathematics Gupta mathematicians developed a decimal system and were the first to treat zero as a number. One astronomer, named Aryabhata, calculated the length of a year and estimated the size of Earth. We still use their advances today.

Roads Engineers designed and built a system of roads that helped improve trade and prosperity.

Each person in this detail of an Ajanta cave mural displays a different mudra, which is a hand position. These Buddhist gestures symbolize beliefs about the gods and communicate such qualities as compassion and fearlessness.

Ancient India

About 1500–1200 B.C.E.
Vedas
The Vedas are the earliest Indian texts, from which Hinduism traces its roots.

About 6500–5000 B.C.E.
Settlement in India
Indian farmers establish early settlements along the Indus and the Ganges rivers.

About 2700–1900 B.C.E.
Harappan Civilization
Harappan civilization flourishes in walled cities with advanced sewer systems.

7000 B.C.E.	6000 B.C.E.	5000 B.C.E.	4000 B.C.E.	3000 B.C.E.

About 563 B.C.E.
Prince Siddhartha Gautama Born
Queen Maya gives birth to Siddhartha, who, tradition says, can already walk and talk.

About 322 B.C.E.
First Unification of India
Chandragupta Maurya, shown here, unites India. His grandson, Ashoka, expands the Mauryan Empire to include nearly all of the Indian subcontinent.

About 528 B.C.E.
Buddhism Founded
According to tradition, Siddhartha Gautama reaches enlightenment, establishing the Buddhist religion.

About 187 B.C.E.
Fall of the Mauryan Empire
The Mauryan Empire falls, and India breaks apart into separate kingdoms.

About 300 B.C.E.
Ramayana **Composed**
The Ramayana and other epic texts are famous stories that become part of Hindu tradition.

About 320–550 C.E.
India's Golden Age
A golden age of peace and prosperity advances the arts and sciences in ancient India.

| 3000 B.C.E. | 2000 B.C.E. | 1000 B.C.E. | 1 C.E. | 1000 C.E. |

269–232 B.C.E.
Reign of Ashoka
King Ashoka posts edicts in public places to unify his empire and spread Buddhist values.

About 320 C.E.
Rise of Gupta Empire
The Gupta family unites northern India and organizes the empire into provinces.

About 499 C.E.
Aryabhatiya Published
Aryabhata publishes his mathematic and scientific discoveries in the *Aryabhatiya*.

Ancient India **195**

Unit 4

Ancient China

The Great Wall of China dates back to ancient times. Extending across northern China, it was built as protection against invasion.

Ancient China

ALTAY MTS.

TAKLIMAKAN DESERT

GOBI DESERT

Huang He (Yellow River)

MANCHURIAN PLAIN

Sea of Japan (East Sea)

K U N L U N   M T S.

PLATEAU OF TIBET

LOESS PLATEAU

NORTH CHINA PLAIN

Yellow Sea

H I M A L A Y A

Mt. Everest (8,850 m, 29,035 ft.)

Chang Jiang (Yangtze River)

East China Sea

30°N

20°N

Pearl River

N
W   E
S

Hainan

0   250   500 miles
0   250   500 kilometers
Albers Conic Equal-Area Projection

90°E

South China Sea

10°N

100°E

110°E

120°E

Elevation

Feet	Meters
Over 10,000	Over 3,050
5,001–10,000	1,526–3,050
2,001–5,000	611–1,525
1,001–2,000	306–610
501–1,000	153–305
0– 500	0–152

▲ Mountain peak

— Silk Road

— Present-day China

Present-day boundary

Ancient China

The land of ancient China is part of a vast region that today is called mainland East Asia. Mainland East Asia includes the present-day countries of China, Mongolia, North Korea, and South Korea. In ancient China, a series of empires controlled territory in mainland East Asia that, at times, included parts of present-day Mongolia and the Korean Peninsula.

The physical geography of mainland East Asia had a dramatic effect on the settlement of ancient China. In the southwestern part of the region, the Himalaya Mountains prevented settlement. A high plateau lies north of these mountains. Because of its awe-inspiring elevation, this region has been called the "roof of the world." The weather is extremely cold here all year round. To the north of this plateau lies desert land, where temperatures are too hot in summer and too cold in winter to make it a good place for people to live. Some groups did roam the area, raising livestock and moving from place to place, but life was hard for them.

To the east of this hostile land, the land is much more moderate. Hills, valleys, and plains are easy to navigate. Rivers provide fertile land for farming. Even the weather is milder, without the extremes of the western part of the country. For these reasons, most ancient Chinese chose to make their homes in this area. Over time, villages developed. Because of China's physical boundaries, including mountains and deserts, the Chinese civilization developed in isolation for thousands of years.

The stability of early villages allowed empires to arise. Powerful leaders unified the country. Advances in civilization allowed empires to conquer more and more territory. The most advanced of these empires, the Han, opened ancient China to trade relations with other cultures to the west. Camel caravans traveled a 4,000-mile-long route known as the Silk Road. From the Huang He (Yellow River) in China, the route extended all the way to the Mediterranean Sea. As people, goods, and ideas traveled back and forth along the Silk Road, the rest of the world soon learned of the achievements of the ancient Chinese.

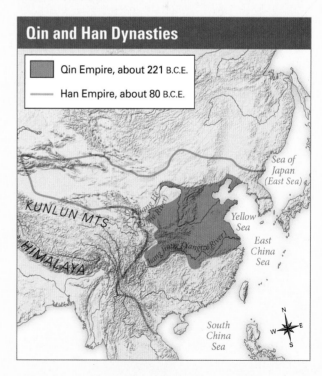

Chapter 19

Geography and the Early Settlement of China

How did geography affect life in ancient China?

19.1 Introduction

In this chapter, you will explore the geography of the vast land of China. You will read about the physical features, climate, and vegetation that greatly influenced the way of life of the early people of China.

China is a large country in eastern Asia. Words like *highest, largest,* and *longest* come to mind when talking about China's geography. The world's highest mountains, the Himalayas, are in China. So is one of the world's largest deserts, the Taklimakan (tah-kluh-muh-KAHN) Desert. China also has some of the longest rivers in the world.

China's climate is just as extreme as its physical features. The weather can vary from ice storms in the high mountains to the dreaded sandstorms of the Taklimakan Desert. The sandstorms darken the skies as if it were nighttime. Hot, howling winds fill the air with sand and gravel. For people caught in a sandstorm, survival may mean wrapping themselves in clothing or blankets and lying down until the storm passes. That could be hours, perhaps even days.

As you can see, China is a land of **contrasts**. In this chapter, you will compare five geographic regions in China. You will learn about the climate, physical features, and vegetation of each region. You will also discover how geography affected the history of the early Chinese people: where they settled, the way they lived, and how they **communicated** with other civilizations.

Extreme climate conditions, like this sandstorm, made travel and trade difficult and helped isolate China from the rest of the world.

◄ The Huang He (Yellow River) flows from west to east across China.

Inner and Outer China, About 1700 B.C.E.–220 C.E.

N
W E
S

0   500   1,000 miles
0   500   1,000 kilometers
Lambert Azimuthal Equal-Area Projection

TURFAN
DEPRESSION

TAKLIMAKAN
DESERT

TIBET-QINGHAI
PLATEAU

HIMALAYA

Mt. Everest

GOBI
DESERT

Huang He (Yellow River)

NORTHEASTERN
PLAIN

40°N

NORTH
CHINA
PLAIN

Chang Jiang (Yangtze River)

CHANG JIANG
BASINS

Yellow
Sea

East
China
Sea

30°N

120°E   20°N

South
China
Sea

110°E

Inner China

Outer China

Most of ancient Chinese history involved Inner China, but the geography of both Inner and Outer China affected early settlement.

19.2 An Overview of China's Geography

Present-day China is the third largest country in the world, after Russia and Canada. China includes about 3.7 million square miles (9.6 million square kilometers). With a population of about 1.2 billion, more people live in China than in any other country.

China's land area was much smaller in ancient times. To understand Chinese history, it's helpful to divide China into two main areas: Outer China and Inner China. Most of ancient Chinese history involves only Inner China. The two areas did not become one country until the 1600s C.E. But the geography of both areas affected the early settlement and history of China.

The Geography of Outer China   Outer China includes the western and northern parts of present-day China. This is an area of great extremes in climate and physical features.

In the southwest, China is bounded by the Himalayas. The key geographical **region** in this area is the Tibet-Qinghai (tih-BET ching-HIE) Plateau. It is the world's largest plateau. This region is a bitterly cold place to live. There are only about fifty days a year without frost. Snowstorms are common, even in July.

In ancient times, the only livable places in China's Northwestern Deserts were areas near water.

In the northwest, the major region is the Northwestern Deserts. This area includes the Turfan Depression, the second-lowest place in China. It is 505 feet below sea level. It can grow so hot here that raindrops **evaporate** before reaching the ground.

In the northeast, the key region is the Northeastern Plain, a land of low hills and plains. It has short, hot summers. Winters are long and dry, with five months of freezing temperatures.

The Geography of Inner China   Inner China includes the southeastern part of present-day China. This part of China is closer to sea level than the western areas. It is a land of rolling hills, river valleys, and plains. Rivers flow through this area from the west. They provide water for irrigation. Floods from these rivers also **enrich** the soil. To early settlers, these physical features made Inner China more attractive than Outer China.

Inner China has two main regions. The northern region is the North China Plain. To the south are the low river plains of the middle and lower Chang Jiang (chahng jyahng) Basins. These regions have very different **climates**. The Chang Jiang Basins are warm and wet. The North China Plain is drier and often cooler.

Each of China's five major regions has its own climate, physical features, and vegetation. Let's take a closer look at each area, starting with the three major regions in Outer China.

The wet, warm Chang Jiang Basins are excellent for growing rice.

region a part or section of a country

climate the average weather conditions at a particular place

The Tibet-Qinghai Plateau is quite cold and dry. In summer, the temperatures often average only 45 degrees Fahrenheit. Winters average 18 degrees. The annual precipitation is only 10 inches.

19.3 The Tibet-Qinghai Plateau

The southwestern part of Outer China is dominated by the high Tibet-Qinghai Plateau. Also known as the Tibetan Plateau, this area is often called the "Roof of the World." Its average elevation of 13,500 feet is more than two miles above sea level. It is a very large area, covering almost a quarter of the land in China.

The Tibet-Qinghai Plateau is a rocky land surrounded by towering mountains. The Himalayas lie on the southern edge of the plateau. The tallest mountain in the world, Mount Everest, is part of this mountain range. Its peak is 29,000 feet in altitude, or more than five miles high.

Because the Tibet-Qinghai Plateau is so high, its climate is very cold. The air is thin and dry. Snow falls even in the summer.

Two of China's major rivers begin in this area: the Huang He (HWAHNG heh), also known as the Yellow River, and the Chang Jiang, also called the Yangtze River. Despite these rivers, the plateau is rather dry. The natural vegetation consists of sparse scrubs and grasses. Antelopes and yaks, a type of ox, roam the area. Sometimes they are prey for wolves and wildcats.

For the people of ancient times, the Tibet-Qinghai Plateau was a challenging place to live. It was too cold and dry to grow crops. But the grasses did provide food for yaks and other livestock. The cold, rocky plateau and the high mountains made travel to Inner China very difficult through this area.

19.4 The Northwestern Deserts

The northwestern part of Outer China is known for its vast deserts, including the Taklimakan and the Gobi (GOH-bee). These deserts are harsh places to live and difficult to cross. The climate varies from sizzling hot in the summer to below freezing in the winter. The **oases** are the only places to grow crops or raise animals such as sheep. Evidence shows that in ancient times, shelters made of mud were sometimes built near oases.

The Taklimakan Desert   The Taklimakan Desert covers an area of about 105,000 square miles. It is considered one of the most dangerous deserts in the world. In fact, its name means "once you go in, you will not come out." Desert winds cause huge sand dunes to shift and change. Sandstorms arise with stunning speed. Legend says that two armies and 300 cities are buried 600 feet beneath the sand dunes.

As you might expect, the desert is too dry to have much vegetation. Bushes, weeds, and trees grow only near oases and along rivers.

The Gobi Desert   Stretching over 500,000 square miles, the Gobi Desert is one of the world's largest deserts. It covers part of China and present-day Mongolia. Unlike the Taklimakan Desert, the Gobi has very few sand dunes. Most of the desert is stony. Its surface is made up of small pebbles and tiny bits of sand. Vegetation is sparse. Plants tend to be small and widely spaced apart.

Temperatures vary greatly here in the Taklimakan Desert, and in other Northwestern Deserts. Summer temperatures can reach 100 degrees Fahrenheit. In winter, the temperatures can be a chilly 15 degrees. The annual precipitation is about 5 inches.

> **oasis** a place, usually in a desert, where water can be found

19.5 The Northeastern Plain

The Northeastern Plain is located east of present-day Mongolia. Today, this area is sometimes called either Inner Mongolia or the Manchurian Plain. It is a land of low hills and plains. The natural vegetation is mostly prairie grass. In ancient times, the grass provided food for horses, sheep, and other animals raised by herders.

The major rivers running through the Northeastern Plain are the Liao (lyow) and the Sungari (SOONG-guh-ree). The Liao is a shallow river, only navigable by small boats. The Sungari is deeper. It can carry larger boats. In the winter, when the waters freeze, people use these rivers as roads.

The Northeastern Plain is an area of great contrasts in its climate. It has short, warm summers. In winter, the northern and eastern parts of the plain are dry and cold. But the southern half, especially the valley of the Liao, has milder weather and more water because of the river. In general, though, the plain is too cold and dry to be suitable for growing crops. In the south, a narrow coastal plain links this area to the rest of China. This plain was used in ancient times by several groups of invaders as a route to Inner China.

The Northeastern Plain generally has a cold, dry climate. In the short summer, temperatures climb to 75 degrees Fahrenheit. In winter, they fall to 10 degrees. The annual precipitation is about 20 inches.

The North China Plain, near the Huang He, is grassy, fertile land. In the summer, the temperature averages 82 degrees Fahrenheit. In the winter, the temperature averages 28 degrees. The annual precipitation is about 23 inches.

19.6 The North China Plain

One of the two major regions in Inner China is the **North China Plain,** a flat region of grassland. Temperatures range from very warm in the summer to quite cold in the winter.

This region is sometimes called the "Land of the Yellow Earth" because the ground is covered by yellow limestone silt. The silt comes from the Gobi Desert. It is carried by the wind to the North China Plain. The river that runs through the plain is also full of yellow silt. The silt gives the river its name, Huang He (Yellow River).

The Huang He is one of the longest rivers in the world. It may also be the world's muddiest. The mud makes the river water look like soup. The river begins in the high western mountains and winds its way down to the eastern plains. The silt it carries helps fertilize the surrounding lands, making the North China Plain a good place in which to settle and grow crops.

While the Huang He does help farmers, it has also been the source of many disasters for the Chinese people. In the past 3,000 years, the river is said to have flooded more than 1,500 times, causing much damage and loss of life.

North China Plain a region in the Huang He River valley, where Chinese civilization began

19.7 The Chang Jiang Basins

The Chang Jiang Basins are areas of low, wet coastal plains. The basins are located along the river called the Chang Jiang.

This river is even longer than the Huang He. In fact, *Chang Jiang* means "Long River." It has hundreds of **tributaries**. People use the river to move goods between eastern and western areas of the region.

Like the Huang He, the Chang Jiang begins in the high western mountains. It flows through three plains and then to a rich delta. Its deposits help make the surrounding lands very fertile. The river floods less often than the Huang He, making the Chang Jiang less dangerous.

The climate in the Chang Jiang Basins is warm and wet. In ancient times, the vegetation may have been thick rainforest. There was little space for farming, and the area was not suitable for grazing animals. But the basins were very good for growing rice, which needs abundant warmth and moisture.

The Chang Jiang Basins have a mild, wet climate. Temperatures range from about 68 degrees Fahrenheit in summer to about 39 degrees in winter. The annual precipitation is about 41 inches.

19.8 Early Settlement in Ancient China

Archaeologists believe that the first inhabitants of China lived in caves more than 500,000 years ago. Remains of these people were found in the 1920s in the northeastern part of China. These cave dwellers are known today as either Peking (pay-king) man or Beijing (bay-jing) man. It is likely that they were nomads who lived by hunting, gathering, and fishing. They made tools and may have used fire.

As people in China turned to farming, they began to settle mostly on the North China Plain in Inner China. They grew crops and lived in villages near the Huang He. This marked the start of settled Chinese society.

It's not surprising that early farmers chose this area to live in. The North China Plain had plenty of water, fertile soil, and a moderate climate. In contrast, both the Tibetan Plateau and the Northeastern Plain in Outer China were too cold and dry to grow crops. The Northwestern Deserts were also too dry. The Chang Jiang Basins were wet and fertile, but heavy rains may have made farming difficult.

19.9 Ancient China's Isolation

China's geography kept the early settlements in Inner China **isolated**. Only a narrow coastal plain linked the Northeastern Plain to Inner China. In the southwest, the towering mountains, rocky plateau, and cold climate formed a natural barrier. In the northwest, the large deserts created another barrier.

Later in Chinese history, the same geographic features that kept ancient China isolated also made it difficult to govern a developing China as a unified state. The harsh geography and huge distances made communication and transportation difficult, and interfered with the movement of military forces.

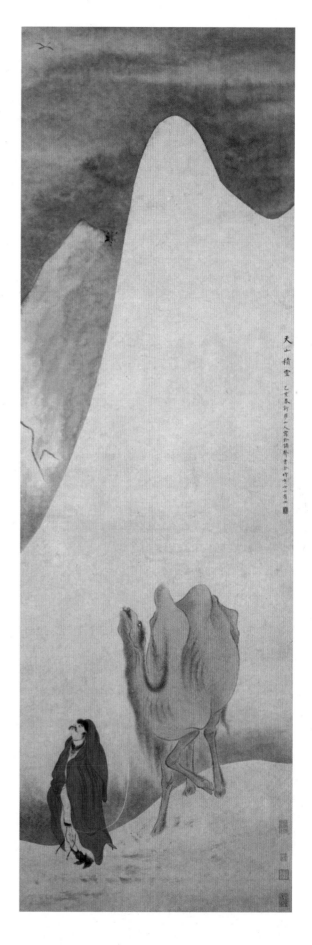

Traveling was difficult and dangerous during China's early history. This 18th-century painting shows a traveler and his camel making their way through towering sand dunes in a desert.

In many parts of Outer China, people lived as nomads. They had to move often to find new grazing land for the animals they raised.

19.10 Different Regions, Different Ways of Life

Although most early inhabitants settled on the North China Plain, some people did live in the other geographic regions. Ways of life for settlers in these regions developed quite differently.

Life in Outer China   Mainly because Outer China did not have good farmland, fewer people settled there than in Inner China. The Tibetan Plateau was not suitable for growing crops, but herders could raise livestock, especially yaks.

The people who lived on the plateau were nomads who had to move frequently to find new grazing land. The animals they herded supplied many of the nomads' needs. They ate meat from the yak, and made butter and yogurt from yak milk. People used yak wool to make the heavy clothing that they needed to survive the cold climate. They also wove yak hair into material for tents.

In the Northwestern Deserts, the only permanent communities were on the oases. There, residents built homes out of mud. People grew cotton and wheat. Their main foods were wheat noodles, bread, and mutton.

The Northeastern Plain was too cold and dry for much farming, but its prairie grass supported livestock. Early inhabitants of this region were also nomads. They raised sheep, goats, cattle, and horses. Because they were constantly moving to find grass for their animals, they lived mostly in tents. Their main food was meat. They often invaded the North China Plain to get needed supplies. Eventually, the people of Inner China built the Great Wall to keep these invaders out.

Life in Inner China   The fertile land of Inner China supported larger, more settled populations on the North China Plain. Farmers grew mainly wheat and millet. They raised cattle, sheep, oxen, pigs, and chickens. They herded cattle, water buffalo, and horses. Settlers built permanent homes out of rammed earth (soil tightly packed to make solid walls).

The Chang Jiang Basins had limited farmland and lacked grazing land for animals such as cattle. But rice thrived in this warm, wet area. As early as 10,000 B.C.E., settlers were able to grow rice in the river valley. They also raised pigs and poultry. Nearby seas provided plentiful seafood. People built permanent houses so they could stay in one place and tend their animals and crops.

In Inner China, most people lived in one place and raised crops such as millet and rice.

Chapter Summary

In this chapter, you explored the climate, physical features, and vegetation in five geographic regions in China. You learned how geography affected settlement, ways of life, and communication in ancient China.

Outer China   This area includes three regions in the western and northern parts of modern China: the Tibet-Qinghai, or Tibetan, Plateau; the Northwestern Deserts (the Taklimakan and the Gobi); and the Northeastern Plain. This area's features— high mountains, a cold and rocky plateau, and large deserts—isolated Inner China.

Inner China   This area includes two regions in the southeastern part of modern China: the North China Plain and the Chang Jiang Basins. The plain has the best conditions for farming.

Early Settlement and Isolation   Archaeologists have found remains of what may be the first inhabitants of China. These hunter-gatherers lived in caves more than 500,000 years ago. Later, farmers established the first permanent settlements on the North China Plain, near the Huang He, or Yellow River. Harsh geography and vast distances isolated these early inhabitants.

Different Regions and Ways of Life   Because of a lack of farmland, most settlers in Outer China were nomads and herders. In Inner China, people farmed and raised animals in permanent settlements. Farmers in the Chang Jiang Basins grew rice.

Chapter 20

The Shang Dynasty

What do Shang artifacts reveal about this civilization?

20.1 Introduction

In ancient times, most of China's early farmers settled on the North China Plain, near the Huang He (Yellow River). In this chapter, you will explore one of China's earliest dynasties, the Shang (shung) dynasty. This dynasty ruled the area centered in the Huang He valley, from 1700 to 1122 B.C.E.

Parts of ancient China were controlled by different clans, or extended families. Rival clans frequently fought each other. Sometimes, one clan became powerful enough to rule all of ancient China and begin a dynasty. The Shang was one example of such clans.

For hundreds of years, the Shang dynasty was considered a legend by Western scholars. Stories about some mysterious markings on animal bones hinted that the Shang might have been the first Chinese to use a system of writing. But still archaeologists had no solid evidence that the ancient culture had ever existed.

Then, in 1899, a Chinese scholar found some bones that had writing on them. He thought that they might be Shang oracle bones. Oracle bones are animal bones and turtle shells with inscriptions carved by engravers. In ancient times, many people believed that these objects could tell the future.

Later, in the 1920s, the ruins of a Shang city were found at Anyang (ahn-yahng). Archaeologists unearthed many artifacts from these ruins. You will learn what these artifacts reveal about Shang civilization.

This oracle bone from the time of the Shang Dynasty is engraved with an inscription.

◀ This beautiful bronze vessel was made by Shang artisans.

Near the king's palace, the nobles in Shang society lived in homes made of wood and earth. Farther away from the palace were the smaller earthen houses of people in the lower classes.

Anyang location where ruins were found from the Shang dynasty, China's first civilization

Shang dynasty one of the first Chinese dynasties, ruled from 1700 to 1122 B.C.E.

clan a large group of family members and friends

bronze a strong metal alloy made from copper

20.2 A Shang Capital City

When archaeologists began excavating the ruins at **Anyang** in 1928, a great deal was learned about the Shang culture. These ruins were the remains of one of the royal cities of the **Shang dynasty**. The city included a palace, a temple, and houses. There were also workshops for artisans who created objects made of metals, pottery, stone, and jade.

The king's palace sat on a platform. The palace was built of mud-plastered walls held up by wooden posts. Beneath its foundations, archaeologists found human bones. The bones suggest that the Shang performed human sacrifices when they constructed a new royal house.

Human sacrifices were also part of Shang burials. While excavating at Anyang, archaeologists found at least nine royal tombs. Each tomb had a large pit with ramps leading down to it from the north and south. When a king was buried, slaves, servants, and animals were led down the ramps into the pit. There, they were sacrificed as part of the Shang belief that the king must continue to be served in the afterlife.

This belief in life after death is likely the reason that metal vessels and containers of food were also buried with or near Shang kings. The treasures found in royal tombs include many weapons, carved jade ornaments, bone carvings, pieces of pottery, stone sculptures, and even chariots.

The artifacts unearthed at Anyang reveal some interesting facts about Shang beliefs and ways of life. Let's find out what conclusions scholars have drawn about this ancient civilization, beginning with the Shang government.

20.3 Shang Government

The Shang government was led by a powerful king. To extend his power, a king set up smaller kingdoms led by his younger brothers and nephews. When a king died, his power was often preserved by passing it to a younger brother or to a son.

Shang kings depended on strong armies to maintain their rule and to defend and **expand** their kingdoms. The kings took part in almost constant warfare with their enemies and fought to keep other **clans** under control. Prisoners of war were used as laborers and in human sacrifices.

The king's armies were especially powerful because Shang nobles had weapons made of **bronze**. The Shang were among the first civilizations in the world to discover how to make bronze from a mixture of copper and tin.

Shang armies were made up of large numbers of foot soldiers, archers, men mounted on horses and elephants, and fighters in chariots. The chariots were two-wheeled carts drawn by horses. Three soldiers rode in each chariot. The driver stood in the middle, with a spear carrier to his left and an archer to his right. Shang armies must have been a terrifying sight to their enemies.

Chinese archaeologists in Anyang examine new excavations of chariots and horses from the Shang Dynasty. The Shang buried nobles with objects they believed would be needed in the afterlife. Find Anyang on the map below.

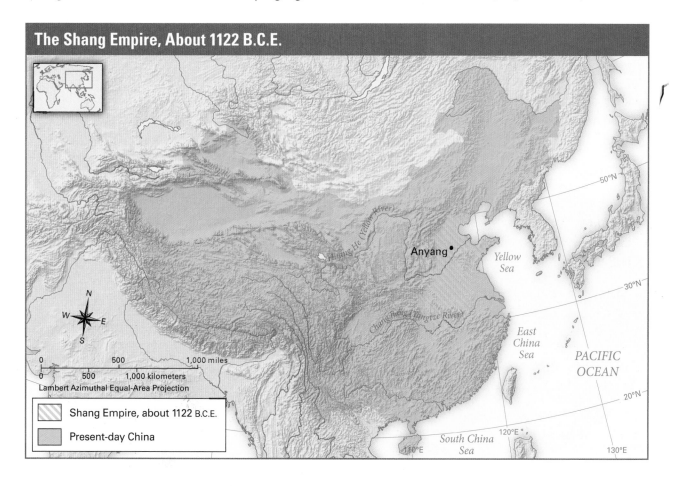

The Shang Empire, About 1122 B.C.E.

Anyang

Huang He (Yellow River)

Chang Jiang (Yangtze River)

Yellow Sea

East China Sea

PACIFIC OCEAN

South China Sea

0   500   1,000 miles
0   500   1,000 kilometers
Lambert Azimuthal Equal-Area Projection

Shang Empire, about 1122 B.C.E.

Present-day China

50°N
30°N
20°N
110°E   120°E   130°E

20.4 Shang Social Classes

Shang society can be divided into six social classes. The king and his relatives were in the highest class. Below them were the nobles, artisans, traders, farmers, and slaves.

Nobles   After the ruling family, the nobles made up the highest-ranking social class. Nobles fought in the king's armies. They also supplied the armies with weapons, foot soldiers, and chariots. In exchange for their **military** help, the king was unlikely to interfere with the nobles' control over the land.

Shang nobles enjoyed a life of luxury. They lived in great palaces and spent time hunting. We know that the Shang were great hunters, because large numbers of wild animal bones have been found at excavation sites. In addition, writings on oracle bones show that the king invited nobles to join him in hunting foxes, badgers, and other wild animals.

The king often gave nobles symbols of power, such as jade discs. The discs might be decorated with a "lucky" creature such as a dragon or tiger. Nobles often mounted the discs on posts in their homes.

Artisans   This talented group formed a small social class that included potters, stonemasons, and workers crafting items of bronze and jade. These skilled workers had lower status than nobles but higher status than farmers. Artisans skilled in bronze were especially valued. They made the weapons used by Shang warriors. They also made and decorated containers for the king and his nobles to use in religious ceremonies, or simply as symbols of their wealth.

This jade disc from the Shang dynasty is inscribed with a poem praising the shape and quality of the jade.

Traders   Like artisans, those who were traders ranked below nobles but above farmers in Shang society. Scholars believe that the Shang traded extensively. One clue comes from the modern Chinese word for "merchant," *shang ren*, which could also mean "Shang man." During the Shang dynasty, people mostly exchanged goods.

The Shang also used cowrie shells, a type of seashell, as money. The shells were valuable because they came from far away. The Shang people had to trade with neighboring regions to get them.

Stone sculptures like this ox have shown archaeologists what kinds of animals Shang farmers raised.

Farmers   Farmers made up the largest social class in Shang society. They worked small plots of land, growing millet, wheat, barley, rice, fruit, vegetables, and nuts. They did not own the land they farmed. The land was under the control of either the king or the nobles. Farmers gave most of their harvest to the nobles, who sent a portion to the king. Farmers could keep only enough food to feed themselves and their families.

Even after the Chinese became highly skilled at making bronze and iron weapons, many farmers continued to use simple tools made of wood and stone. They dug with wooden sticks, weeded with stone-tipped hoes, and harvested grain with stone knives and scythes.

Besides growing crops, farmers learned to raise cattle. They may also have raised pigs and chickens.

Slaves   At the very bottom of Shang society were slaves. Many of these slaves were prisoners of war. They spent their lives building tombs and palaces. When their masters died, the slaves were sometimes sacrificed, in keeping with the Shang belief that slaves should continue to serve their masters in the afterlife.

Along with artifacts, the remains of animals, soldiers, and servants have been found buried in Shang tombs, as this picture illustrates.

20.5 Shang Religion

Shang religion centered on **ancestor worship**. The treasures buried in kings' tombs show that the Shang believed in a life after death. They also believed that dead ancestors had the power to help or harm the living. For this reason, the Shang honored their ancestors. As signs of respect, worshippers gave offerings of food, and sometimes made human sacrifices.

The Shang believed that their king's relationship to ancestral spirits had special significance. The king inherited the right to rule from his ancestors. And among the king's responsibilities was a duty to follow the wishes of his ancestors.

Kings used **oracle bones** to seek their ancestors' advice on important matters such as when to hunt, where to build cities, and whether to go to war. The oracle bones were made from turtle shells or the shoulder blade of a cow. To ask a question, a holy man would make a statement such as this: "Tomorrow is a good day for the hunt." Then he would press a hot needle against the back of the bone. The heat would make the bone crack. The pattern of the crack was believed to be a message, which the holy man or king would translate. The holy man might then carve the message on the oracle bone. Today, these inscriptions reveal valuable information about life during the Shang dynasty.

ancestor worship honoring of ancestors through rituals, such as offering food to the spirits of the dead

oracle bone a piece of bone or shell heated and cracked by holy men to seek advice from a king's ancestors

20.6 Shang Writing

The inscriptions on oracle bones are among the earliest known examples of Chinese writing. In Shang writing, as in modern Chinese, characters stand for words rather than sounds. Early Chinese writing contained only pictographs, images that stand for objects. By the Shang dynasty period, people were also using logographs, characters that stand for words. For example, the character for "good" is a combination of the characters for "woman" and "child."

Having a written language helped unify the Chinese people. Although spoken language varied from place to place, people of the upper classes used the same written language.

20.7 Shang Art

Shang artists showed great skill in working with bronze. Shang artisans made beautiful vessels and other objects. Some bronze vessels had geometric **designs** and pictures of mythical creatures. The most common picture was an animal mask, later known as a taotie. It might have the horns of an ox, the ears of an elephant, the talons of a bird, the eye of a man, and the crest of a dragon. Some scholars say that these masks were symbols of all the beings in the world.

The Shang also produced remarkable jade pieces. Jade is a very hard stone. Workers made jade objects by sawing, filing, and sanding the stone.

The Chinese may have believed that the qualities of jade represented the qualities of a superior person. The hardness of jade stood for wisdom. Jade was also smooth and shiny. These qualities stood for kindness.

Skilled Shang artists worked with bronze and jade. The bronze vessel at left has long masks on its legs. At right is a small jade statue of a person kneeling.

The Shang made a variety of weapons out of bronze. They created these two dagger-axes between the 13th century and the 11th century B.C.E.

20.8 Shang Technology

Working with bronze was an important technology for the Shang. Artisans used bronze to make many tools of war. These included arrowheads, spearheads, ax heads, and helmets. The bronze-making skill of the Shang is one of the reasons they were able to remain in power for more than five hundred years.

20.9 The End of the Shang Dynasty

The Shang excelled in war, enabling the ruling classes to build up great wealth. But, in time, these very strengths helped to bring about the end of the dynasty. Constant warfare eventually weakened the military power of the Shang.

The Shang had a system of money, using valuable cowrie shells that they received as part of their extensive trade with neighbors. The Shang king and his nobles spent extravagant amounts of money on their palaces, furnishings, clothing, and even their tombs. Over time, this lavish spending may have weakened the economy. A later king would say that the final blow was the corruption of the last Shang king. Rather than look after his people, he spent all his time on recreational activities like hunting. But no one knows whether this report was true.

Around 1045 B.C.E., a frontier state called Zhou (joh) rose up against the dynasty. Zhou armies under King Wu caught the Shang unaware, defeating and overthrowing them. One story says that, as Zhou rebels stormed his capital city, the last Shang king ran from the battlefield, put on all his jewelry, and threw himself into the flames of a fire.

In this chapter, you learned about one of China's earliest dynasties, the Shang dynasty, by examining artifacts from that time.

A Shang Capital City The ruins and artifacts found at Anyang show that the Shang believed in an afterlife. Kings were buried with goods, people, and animals that would be useful to them in their life after death.

Shang Government Shang kings were powerful rulers who inherited their power and kept it through family ties and military might.

Shang Social Classes Shang society can be divided into six social classes: the king's clan, nobles, artisans, traders, farmers, and slaves.

Shang Religion, Writing, Arts, and Technology The Shang practiced ancestor worship and, sometimes, human sacrifice. Their writing used logographs as well as pictographs. Shang artisans excelled in working with bronze and jade. The bronze weapons they created enabled the Shang to stay in power.

The End of the Shang Dynasty The Shang ruled in the valley of the Huang He for some five hundred years. They traded widely and grew wealthy. But constant warfare, lavish spending, and corruption in the ruling class may have led to the dynasty's downfall. Around 1045 B.C.E., the Shang were defeated by the Zhou.

Archaeologists unearthed this Shang tomb, which is more than three hundred feet long and sixty feet deep.

Chapter 21

Three Chinese Philosophies

How did Confucianism, Daoism, and Legalism influence political rule in ancient China?

21.1 Introduction

One of China's earliest dynasties was the Shang dynasty. China's next line of rulers belonged to the Zhou (joh) dynasty. In this chapter, you will learn about the Zhou and explore three Chinese philosophies that arose during this dynasty.

The Zhou dynasty lasted from about 1045 to 256 B.C.E. During its later years, different leaders fought for control in China. The country was thrown into disorder. These troubles led Chinese thinkers to ask serious questions about the best way to have peace and order in society. Three very different answers emerged and became the philosophies of Confucianism (kuhn-FYOO-shuh-niz-uhm), Daoism (DOW-iz-um), and Legalism.

The following scene illustrates the differences between these schools of thought. Imagine that it is 250 B.C.E. The ruler of a small kingdom has sent three advisers to learn about the three philosophies. Upon their return, he asks them, "What should I do to rule well?"

The first adviser has learned about Confucianism. He tells the king, "Lead by example." The second adviser has studied Daoism. He says, "If you must rule, rule as little as possible." The third adviser has learned about Legalism. He says, "Set clear laws and harshly punish those who disobey them."

In this chapter, you will learn why the three advisers gave such different answers. You will explore Confucianism, Daoism, and Legalism and learn how each philosophy influenced political rule in ancient China.

Confucianism

Daoism

Legalism

These three philosophies arose during the disorder in the later years of the Zhou empire.

◄ Scholars study the Daoist symbol for yin and yang in this painting.

Zhou dynasty a line of rulers in China, from about 1045 to 256 B.C.E.

Mandate of Heaven a power or law believed to be granted by a god

This diagram shows the cycle of events by which the Mandate of Heaven gave a king the divine right to rule.

21.2 The Zhou Dynasty

Around 1045 B.C.E., the Zhou, a group of people in northwestern China, moved into the central plains. They overthrew the Shang dynasty and established a new dynasty. For several centuries, the **Zhou dynasty** ruled over a group of states in China. But in the later years of the dynasty, wars between these states plunged China into disorder.

The Early Years: Stability and Feudalism After overthrowing the Shang dynasty, the Zhou established their own dynasty to rule over China. To justify their conquest, they claimed that they had been given the **Mandate of Heaven,** a divine right to rule China.

According to this belief, Heaven was a power that controlled human destiny. The king was the son of Heaven. As long as the king governed his people well, Heaven gave him the right to rule. If the king did not govern well, Heaven would send signs of its displeasure, such as earthquakes and floods. When the king lost the support of Heaven, others had the right to overthrow him. The Zhou and later groups believed in the Mandate of Heaven.

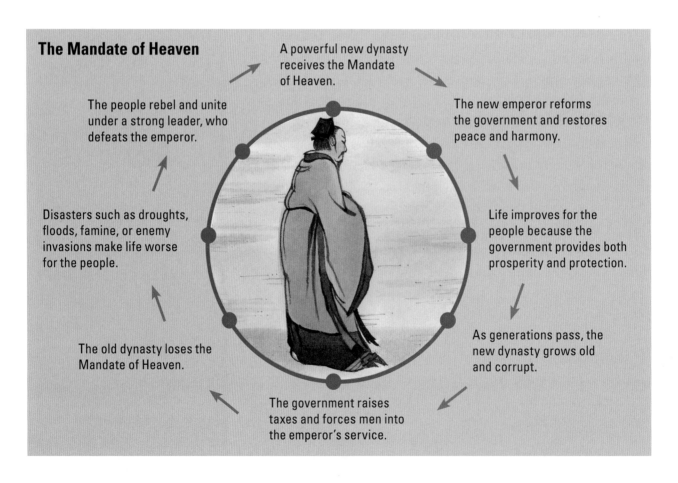

The Mandate of Heaven

A powerful new dynasty receives the Mandate of Heaven.

The new emperor reforms the government and restores peace and harmony.

Life improves for the people because the government provides both prosperity and protection.

As generations pass, the new dynasty grows old and corrupt.

The government raises taxes and forces men into the emperor's service.

The old dynasty loses the Mandate of Heaven.

Disasters such as droughts, floods, famine, or enemy invasions make life worse for the people.

The people rebel and unite under a strong leader, who defeats the emperor.

Using a system of relationships called **feudalism,** the Zhou increased the stability the government. Under feudalism, the king owned all the land. He gave large pieces of the land to loyal supporters, called lords. In exchange, these lords sent soldiers to fight against enemies who threatened their king. The lords were rulers of their own lands, or states. They had absolute power over the peasant farmers who worked those lands. Peasants had their lord's protection. In return, they gave a **portion** of their crops to the lord.

feudalism a system of government based on land-owners and tenants

The Later Years: Conflict and Creative Thought For a time, feudalism maintained political stability in China. But by the 700s B.C.E., the system was starting to break down. The lords of individual states became more ambitious and more powerful. Eventually, the power of some lords rivaled that of the king.

Between about 770 and 453 B.C.E., a number of small states often quarreled with one another. They eventually grouped into six or seven larger states that fought for power. These wars brought some 250 years of disorder to China. This historical time is often called the Warring States period.

The Zhou empire ruled the central plains of China for hundreds of years. The capital, Haojing (Hao), was later called Chang-an and then Xi'an.

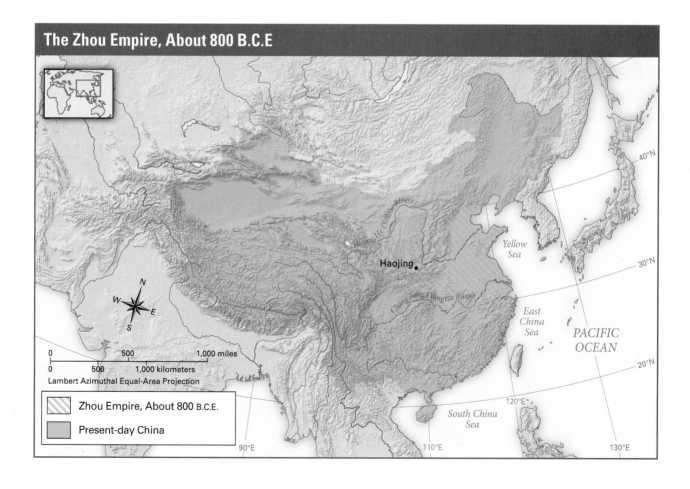

The Zhou Empire, About 800 B.C.E

- Haojing
- Huang He (Yellow River)
- Yellow Sea
- Chang Jiang (Yangtze River)
- East China Sea
- PACIFIC OCEAN
- South China Sea

0   500   1,000 miles
0   500   1,000 kilometers
Lambert Azimuthal Equal-Area Projection

Zhou Empire, About 800 B.C.E.

Present-day China

Confucianism a Chinese philosophy that emphasizes proper behavior

Such unrest led Chinese thinkers to ask important questions about human nature and about how best to govern. Some rulers hired scholars to advise them on how to create order and increase their royal power.

So many ideas were offered that the Chinese later called them the "Hundred Schools of Thought." The three major schools of thought that **emerged** were Confucianism, Daoism, and Legalism. Each of these philosophies had a major influence on Chinese culture. Let's take a closer look at their origins, teachings, and influence, beginning with Confucianism.

21.3 Confucianism

Confucianism is based on the teachings of Kongfuzi, who is called Confucius (kuhn-FYOO-shuhs) by Western society. This philosophy deeply influenced Chinese government and culture.

Confucius is the most famous philosopher in Chinese history.

The Founder of Confucianism   Confucius lived from about 551 to 479 B.C.E. He was born in the small state of Lu, in eastern China. He experienced firsthand the disorder that erupted when lords fought for power. Between 722 and 481 B.C.E., his own state was invaded many times.

Confucius deeply respected Chinese traditions such as reverence for ancestors and learning. But he also saw that society and government had to change, if peace and order were to exist. In particular, rulers needed to govern wisely. Confucius wanted to teach men of good character to serve society as honest and fair government officials.

The Teachings of Confucianism   The goal of Confucianism was to achieve a just and peaceful society. Confucius taught that society worked well when all people used standards of good behavior in their roles and in their relationships with others.

According to Confucianism, there are five basic relationships between people: ruler and subject, husband and wife, father and son, older **sibling** and younger sibling, and friend and friend. All people must respect and obey those who are above them in status. In particular, they must respect their elders. In return, those with authority, such as rulers, fathers, husbands, and older siblings, must set a good example. They should be kind, honest, wise, and faithful. Confucius taught, "Do not do to others what you would not want done to you."

The Influence of Confucianism The philosophy of Confucius attracted a number of students who spread his ideas and teachings. After his death, some of these students collected his sayings in a book called *The Analects*. Later scholars further developed Confucianism.

Confucianism had a very practical effect on the government of a later dynasty, the Han dynasty. In China, **civil servants** were traditionally the sons of nobles. However, that did not ensure that they had the ability and wisdom to do their jobs well. The influence of Confucianism led Han leaders to hire civil servants on the basis of their ability. To be qualified, government workers were expected to know the Chinese classics in detail. For example, they had to know the proper behavior required of people in the various roles in society, from **laborers** to government officials. To prove that candidates had this knowledge, they had to take exams that the emperor himself might grade.

The teachings of Confucius had a major influence on Chinese culture. Values such as respect for elders, proper behavior, and love of scholarship became deeply woven into Chinese society. Even today, the sayings of Confucius are wise and practical. Here are two examples from *The Analects*:

> *Confucius said to his follower:*
> *The gentleman first practices what he preaches*
> *and then preaches what he practices.*

> *Confucius said to his student:*
> *Shall I teach you what knowledge is?*
> *When you know a thing, say that you know it;*
> *when you do not know a thing,*
> *admit that you do not know it.*
> *That is knowledge.*

civil servant a person who works for a government

During the Han dynasty, every candidate for a government position had to pass a hard exam. Here, candidates wait to find out their exam results.

According to Chinese tradition, Laozi was leaving China on a water buffalo when he met a border guard who asked him to write down his thoughts.

21.4 Daoism

The second great philosophy to come out of China's time of trouble was **Daoism** (also spelled Taoism). Like Confucianism, it tried to provide answers to the problems that prevented right living and good government.

The Founder of Daoism

According to tradition, the great sage, or wise man, of Daoism was Laozi (low-dzuh). His name is sometimes spelled "Lao-tzu." Laozi was said to be the author of a work called the *Dao De Jing* (dow duh jing). The English version of the title is *The Classic of the Way and Its Power*.

Some modern scholars think that Laozi was a real man who lived in the late 500s B.C.E. Other historians believe that he was merely a legend. Scholars do agree that the *Dao De Jing* was actually written over time by many writers.

Old stories of Laozi's life tell how he came to write the *Dao De Jing*. These stories say that Laozi worked as an adviser to the Zhou court for many years. When he was 90 years old, he tired of government work and decided to leave China. When he came to the Chinese border, a guard recognized him. The guard was upset that the great teacher's wisdom would be lost to China. He asked Laozi to record his thoughts before leaving. So Laozi sat down and wrote a small manuscript of only 5,000 characters, the *Dao De Jing*.

The *Dao De Jing* preached a return to a simple and natural way of living. Here is an example of one passage:

If you do not want your house to be molested by robbers,
Do not fill it with gold and jade.
Wealth, rank, and arrogance add up to ruin,
As surely as two and two are four.

Daoism a Chinese philosophy that emphasizes living in harmony with nature

The Teachings of Daoism

Daoism was based on the ancient Chinese idea of the Dao (dow), or "the Way." Dao was the force that gave order to the natural universe. Daoism taught that people gained happiness and peace by living in harmony, or agreement, with the way of nature.

To Daoists, nature is full of opposites, like life and death, or light and darkness. True harmony comes from balancing the opposite forces of nature, called **yin and yang**. *Yin* means "shaded," and *yang* means "sunlit." In the same way, human life is a whole made up of opposites. It is impossible to have good without bad, beauty without ugliness, or pleasure without pain.

The Daoists taught that people followed the way of nature by living simple lives of quiet meditation. Notice, the Daoists said, how nothing in nature strives for fame, power, or knowledge. Similarly, people should neither feel self-important nor work to gain possessions or honors. Instead, they should accept whatever comes, like a blade of grass that bends when the breeze blows.

The Daoists believed that everyone must discover the Dao for themselves. Too many laws and social rules conflict with the way of living naturally and following the Dao. According to these teachings, the best rulers were those who ruled the least. The *Dao De Jing* says, "Governing a large country is like frying a small fish. You spoil it with too much poking." It also tells rulers to be weak and let things alone.

The Influence of Daoism

Daoism encouraged rulers to govern less harshly. But Daoism's more important influence was on Chinese thought, writing, and art. In time, Daoism developed into a popular religion.

This painted scroll shows a Daoist scholar asleep in his cottage. He is dreaming that he has gained immortality, or eternal life. In the center of the image, the scholar floats away over a mountain.

yin and yang the Daoist concept of opposing forces of nature

Legalism a Chinese philosophy that emphasizes strict obedience to laws

21.5 Legalism

The third major philosophy that came out of China's time of trouble was **Legalism**. It was very different from Confucianism or Daoism. It offered new answers about how to solve problems that interfere with order and good government.

The Founder of Legalism   Legalism was based on the teachings of Hanfeizi (hahn-fay-dzoo). Hanfeizi (also spelled Han-fei-tzu) lived from 280 to 233 B.C.E. He was a prince of the royal family of the state of Han. Hanfeizi lived to see the end of the Warring States period and of the Zhou dynasty.

Like Confucius, Hanfeizi was very concerned with creating peace and order in society. But he did not think that the Confucian teachings about proper behavior were the answer. Many of his ideas survive today in a book named after him, *Hanfeizi*.

Hanfeizi was a leader of the important Chinese philosophy called Legalism.

The Teachings of Legalism   Those who followed Legalism believed that most people are naturally selfish. Left to themselves, Legalists said, people will always **pursue** their own self-interest. They cannot be counted upon to have a good influence on one another. Therefore, it was not enough for rulers to set a good example. Instead, they should establish strict laws and enforce them, either with rewards for good behavior or with harsh punishments for bad behavior. Civil servants should be watched carefully and punished for doing a poor job. People who were caught criticizing the government should be banished to China's far northern frontier.

In Hanfeizi's time, rulers were frequently overthrown. To solve this problem, Hanfeizi taught that rulers must have absolute power backed by military might. Rulers should trust no one, not even their own families. Hanfeizi wrote, "He who trusts others will be controlled by others."

The Influence of Legalism

Legalist philosophy had an almost immediate influence on government in China. At the end of the Warring States period, the Qin (chin) dynasty seized control of China. Qin rulers read and admired the writings of Hanfeizi. These rulers wanted to build a strong central government and a well-organized society. To achieve these goals, they adopted strict Legalist ideas. People were forbidden to criticize the government. Anyone caught doing so was severely punished. Many people were put to death for disloyalty and other crimes during the rule of the Qin dynasty.

This illustration of the afterlife shows the type of punishment Legalists recommended for those who disobeyed the laws.

Chapter Summary

In this chapter, you read about three major Chinese philosophies—Confucianism, Daoism, and Legalism—and their influence on political rule in ancient China.

The Zhou Dynasty All three schools of thought developed in the later years of the Zhou dynasty. Zhou rulers believed they had the Mandate of Heaven, a divine right to rule China. For a time, the Zhou's practice of feudalism helped stabilize China. But during the dynasty's later years, China collapsed into disorder. Political unrest led many scholars to debate the proper way to rule.

Confucianism Confucius taught his followers that peace and order depended upon proper behavior. Those in authority must lead by example. Those lower in status must obey. Confucianism led Han leaders to hire civil servants based on ability and tested knowledge rather than on family relationships.

Daoism Daoists believed that people should live simply and in harmony with the ways of nature. Harmony could be reached by balancing yin and yang, the opposite forces of nature. Daoists said that the best rulers were those who ruled the least.

Legalism Legalists believed that people were driven by their own self-interest. Legalism taught that rulers could create order in society only through strict laws and harsh punishments.

Chapter 22

The First Emperor of China

Was the Emperor of Qin an effective leader?

22.1 Introduction

In the later years of the Zhou dynasty, China entered a time of unrest that lasted until the Qin dynasty seized power. In this chapter, you will learn how Qin Shihuangdi (chin SHEE-hwahng-dee) unified China.

The Emperor of Qin (chin) ruled over a united China from 221 to 210 B.C.E. His reign was one of great contrasts. He executed hundreds of enemies, and his building projects killed thousands of his own people. But he also unified Chinese government and culture. His construction **projects** were among the most spectacular in the world.

The emperor's biggest project was the Great Wall along China's northern border. The wall was intended to protect China from invasion from the north. Much like a general would prepare for a war, the Emperor of Qin made plans to build his wall. Supply camps were set up to bring food and materials to the workers in the mountains and deserts of the northern **frontier**. Soldiers were posted to fight off bandits and to stop workers from running away. Thousands of Chinese were marched from their homes and forced to work on the wall. It is said that many of them never returned.

Clearly, the Emperor of Qin was both a strong leader and a cruel one. It is little wonder that later Chinese historians would have very differing opinions of this ruler. In this chapter, you will read about the Emperor of Qin and form your own opinion.

The Great Wall, shown here, was rebuilt by Chinese leaders after the rule of Emperor Qin. From its watchtowers, soldiers guarded the frontier. They lit fires to warn of approaching invaders.

◀ China's first emperor, Qin Shihuangdi, was a strong and a cruel ruler.

The Emperor of Qin's wars of conquest cost many millions of lives.

Qin Shihuangdi the first emperor to rule a united China, from 221 to 210 B.C.E.

22.2 Creating an Empire

China's first emperor began life as Prince Zheng (jung) of the royal family of the state of Qin. He was born in 259 B.C.E., near the end of the Warring States period. In 256 B.C.E., Qin rulers took over the state of Zhou, ending the Zhou dynasty. Ten years later, 13-year-old Prince Zheng became king.

Sometimes called the Tiger of Qin, Zheng was quite an ambitious man. He used military might, spies, bribery, and alliances to conquer the remaining rival states. His empire became far larger than the kingdoms of earlier dynasties. In 221 B.C.E., he gained control of all of China. He decided then to take a new title, **Qin Shihuangdi,** or First Emperor of Qin.

As a ruler, the Emperor of Qin was greatly influenced by Legalism. Legalists believed in strict laws, harsh punishments, and a strong central authority. The emperor adopted these ideas. To avoid threats from powerful lords, he replaced the old system of feudalism with a government he controlled personally. He divided his vast territory into 36 districts. Three officials were appointed to govern each district. One official was responsible for the army. Another took care of the laws and agriculture. The duty of the third official was to keep the emperor informed of district activities.

The Emperor of Qin used harsh measures to maintain his power. When he discovered plots against his life, he had the traitors and their families killed. He even exiled his own mother from court, fearful that she was plotting against him.

22.3 Standardizing the Culture

The Emperor of Qin wanted to unify China. He began to **standardize** cultural practices that differed from place to place.

One key step was to create a uniform system of laws. A number of the emperor's new laws were aimed at government officials. Officials were punished if the grain in storehouses spoiled, or if a wall built under their supervision collapsed. Other laws governed everyday life. For example, widows were not allowed to remarry.

The emperor's laws were based on Legalist beliefs. The laws were detailed, and they spelled out exact punishments for people who broke them. Rich and poor were punished in the same way. Typical punishments included fines that were paid in shields, gold, or suits of armor. But there were also physical punishments that included forced labor, whippings, and beheadings.

To make trading easier, the emperor standardized money, weights, and measures. Throughout China, people had used various types of items as money, such as shells, pearls, silver, tin objects, and coins. The Emperor of Qin commanded that metal coins of gold or bronze would be the only acceptable form of money. A hole in the center of each coin enabled people to carry several coins together on a cord. The emperor also ordered that measuring cups be made to hold consistent amounts. To regulate weights, he had metalworkers create bell-shaped bronze or iron weights in a variety of standard sizes.

Shihuangdi also simplified the writing system. He removed many of the written characters that were in use across China. A later dictionary listed 9,000 approved characters.

standardize to make the same

These artifacts show ways in which the Emperor of Qin standardized Chinese coins, weights, measurements, and written language.

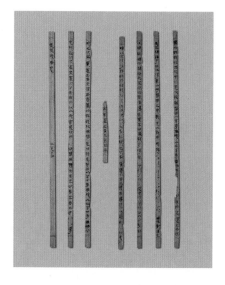

The Great Wall was the Emperor of Qin's most impressive project. Do you think the benefit of the Great Wall was worth the cost in lives?

22.4 Protecting the Northern Border

To protect his empire from invaders, the Emperor of Qin forced workers to build a long wall along China's northern border. Earlier kingdoms had already built smaller walls of their own. The emperor ordered long sections built to connect these walls. He also extended the wall to the west. The structure was called the "10,000 Li Long Wall." (One *li* is about three-tenths of a mile.) It later became known as the **Great Wall**.

Few traces of the original Great Wall survive. The Great Wall as we know it today was built by later rulers. Most likely, the original wall was made of layers of earth pounded into wooden frames that held everything together.

The Emperor of Qin's wall took ten years to build. A workforce of 300,000 men was assembled to **construct** it. Some were soldiers. Many were peasants who were forced to give up farming to work on the project. Still others were musicians, teachers, writers, and artists that the emperor sent into exile in the north.

The men who built the wall worked under difficult conditions. The wall crossed high mountains, deserts, swampland, and quicksand. The weather was bitterly cold in the winter, and blazingly hot in the summer. According to later accounts, tens of thousands of men died while working on the project. Their bodies were buried in the wall.

Combined with strong Chinese armies, the Great Wall proved extremely effective at stopping invasions. Nomads living to the north of the wall were unable to move sheep or cattle over it. Horses could not jump it. Therefore, any invaders who managed to scale the wall would be left without supplies or horses.

22.5 Ending Opposition

The changes that the Emperor of Qin introduced to unify and protect China drew a great deal of opposition. They were especially unpopular with Confucian scholars. The Confucians believed in behaving properly and setting a good example. They did not believe in enforcing harsh laws.

The emperor was determined to end any opposition to his rule. It is said that he executed 460 Confucian scholars for plotting against him.

The **conflict** between the emperor and the scholars grew worse during a royal banquet in 213 B.C.E. During the meal, one Confucian scholar criticized the emperor. The scholar warned that the Qin dynasty would not endure unless the emperor followed the ways of the past.

The scholar's comments angered the emperor's trusted adviser, Li Siu (lee sway). Li told the emperor that scholars' criticisms were causing trouble, and the government should **censor** the scholars. No one, he said, should be allowed to learn about Con-

fucianism. All Confucian books must be brought to the capital city and burned. Only books dealing with medicine, farming, and the history of the Qin kingdom should escape censorship.

The Emperor of Qin agreed to order the book burning. He said that scholars who disobeyed the order would be marked with a tattoo on their faces and sent to do forced labor. Anyone who discussed ancient teachings would be guilty of criticizing the government and would be executed.

The emperor's brutal action shocked the people of China. Some scholars chose to die rather than give up their books. Even the emperor's son became a victim of his father's campaign to end opposition. When the son objected to the killing of scholars, he was sent to oversee work on the Great Wall.

Later emperors said that the Emperor of Qin crushed opposition by executing Confucian scholars. According to legend, he ordered that some scholars be buried alive.

censor to remove or suppress ideas considered harmful or dangerous

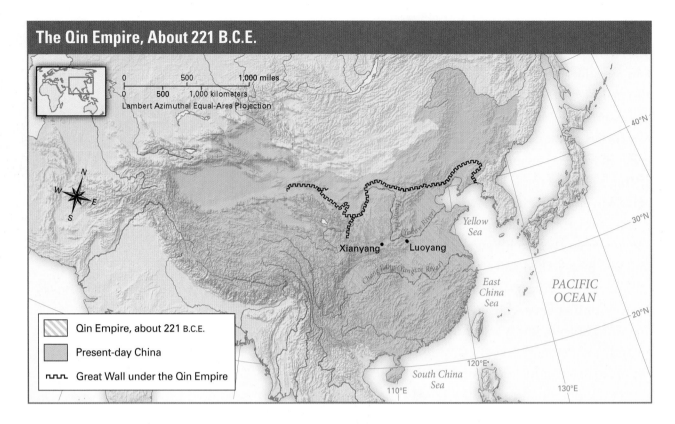

The Qin Empire, About 221 B.C.E.

0 — 500 — 1,000 miles
0 — 500 — 1,000 kilometers
Lambert Azimuthal Equal-Area Projection

40°N
30°N
20°N

Yellow Sea
Xianyang   Luoyang
East China Sea
PACIFIC OCEAN
South China Sea

120°E
110°E
130°E

Qin Empire, about 221 B.C.E.

Present-day China

Great Wall under the Qin Empire

The Great Wall protected the long northern border of the Qin Empire.

immortal able to live forever

22.6 The Emperor's Death and the End of the Qin Dynasty

Despite the Emperor of Qin's many achievements, some ancient Chinese writings say that he could not find happiness. Above all, the emperor was afraid to die. He summoned magicians to his court, asking them how he could become **immortal,** or live forever. Some magicians told him that he should seek a magic potion. The emperor searched far and wide for such a potion. He once sent an expedition all the way to islands in the sea that is east of China.

The Death and Burial of the Emperor of Qin   In 210 B.C.E., the Emperor of Qin died after ruling for just over ten years. He had been off searching for the magic potion, 600 miles from the capital city. No one knows the cause of his death. He may have been poisoned.

The Emperor of Qin's body was taken back to the capital and buried in a huge tomb in a human-made mound. The tomb complex, or group of structures, covered many square miles. Ancient Chinese writings say that more than 700,000 workers helped build it. Some of them were buried with the emperor to prevent grave robbers from learning about the tomb's fabulous treasures.

The treasures in the Emperor of Qin's tomb were not uncovered until 1974 C.E. Among them were tools, precious jewels, and rare objects. The most amazing discovery of all was an entire army made of a kind of clay called terra-cotta. The army included more than six thousand life-size figures such as archers, foot soldiers, chariot drivers, and horses. So far, archaeologists have yet to find any two figures that are exactly alike.

The End of the Qin Dynasty Shihuangdi died in 210 B.C.E. The harshness of the emperor's rule had caused much unhappiness across China. After his death, rebellions broke out in the countryside. Members of royal families from conquered states joined in the **revolt**. As various leaders fought each other for power, civil war raged. Finally, in 206 B.C.E., Liu Bang (LEE-oo bahng), a peasant leader, gained power and established the Han dynasty.

The terra-cotta army in the tomb of the Emperor of Qin leads the emperor east into the next world. Many of the unique soldiers were dressed in terra-cotta armor.

Chapter Summary

In this chapter, you learned about Qin Shihuangdi, China's first emperor.

Creating an Empire Qin Shihuangdi was influenced by Legalism. He replaced feudalism with a strong central government under his control. He divided his territory into 36 districts, each governed by three officials. He used harsh measures to enforce his power.

Standardizing the Culture The Emperor of Qin unified China and also greatly expanded its borders. He standardized Chinese laws, money, weights, measures, and writing.

Protecting the Northern Border Among the emperor's many construction projects was the Great Wall, which he built to protect China's northern border from invaders.

Ending Opposition Many of Emperor Qin's actions aroused opposition. He brutally censored and executed his critics, including Confucian scholars.

The Emperor's Death and the End of the Qin Dynasty Although the emperor searched for a way to become immortal, he died in 210 B.C.E. He was buried in a huge tomb, along with many treasures and an army of 6,000 life-size terra-cotta figures. His amazing tomb was discovered in 1974. Revolt broke out after his death and civil war raged until the Han dynasty was established.

China's Great Walls

Is the Great Wall of China 1,500 miles or 4,000 miles long? It was built by the emperor Qin Shihuangdi more than 2,200 years ago. It was also built by the Ming emperors about 500 years ago. Some people claim you can see it with the human eye from space. "No, you can't," say astronauts who have viewed Earth from space. With so many conflicting claims, you might think that the Great Wall is a legend. It is—but it's also solidly there! What *are* the facts about China's amazing structure? How can we separate the facts from the legend?

Very little of the wall made of pounded earth by the Qin dynasty survives today. Much of the Great Wall seen above was rebuilt by the Ming dynasty in the 16th century.

There is a lot of contradictory information about China's Great Wall. That's because it is not *one* wall but many. The wall once ran the length of all of northern China, from the Pacific Ocean to the western desert. But there were also a lot of branches and extensions. In some places, there were as many as three parallel walls.

The Chinese themselves did not call the structure the "Great Wall of China" until about one hundred years ago. It is likely that awed European travelers in the 17th century first used the name. The Chinese called it the "10,000 Li Long Wall" A *li* was a unit of length equal to about one-third of a mile. But this name did not represent an actual measurement. It was a poetic way of expressing the wall's vast length.

To Keep Out the Barbarians

By the 8th century B.C.E., the Chinese were already experts at wall building. Their sturdy walls were constructed by pounding layers of earth and stones inside wooden frames. These walls marked the boundaries of homes, villages, and independent Chinese kingdoms. Some of the walls were hundreds of miles long. When the Qin emperor Shihuangdi conquered and unified these kingdoms in 221 B.C.E., he ordered most of the walls torn down. But he left standing the sections of wall along China's long northern border.

North of the border were nomadic herding tribes. Now and then, they would raid China's territory. The Chinese considered them "barbarians," or savages. Qin Shihuangdi ordered that a new wall be built to connect the remaining wall sections and keep the raiders out. This was the first "Great Wall of China."

Chinese records mention this wall. Legends tell of the hundreds of thousands of workers who were forced to leave their homes to build it. But there are no documented details about how long the wall was or what route it followed. Very few parts of this wall remain. It is likely that the sections were made of local materials to lower the cost of transporting building supplies. Stone was used where it was available. When stone was not available, pounded earth was used as the building material.

The wall was only as strong as China's ability to defend it. Invading "barbarians" could not drive their herds through it or jump their horses over it. But sometimes, enemies broke through the wall to launch raids. Later dynasties repaired and rebuilt parts of the wall. They added new sections. In the 13th century, the Mongols conquered China by going *around* the wall and attacking from the south and east.

The Ming dynasty regained control of China in 1368. But wars with the Mongols continued. Finally, the Ming emperors decided to build new walls along the northern border. At first, the walls were built in the traditional style—pounded earth. But by the 16th century, the Ming were building in brick and stone. They took particular care to fortify the wall north of their capital, Beijing. Here, the wall averaged 26 feet (8 m) in height and up to 30 feet (9 m) in width. Soldiers could march along the top. There were guard towers at every peak, dip, and turn. The guards could send signals from tower to tower. Messages sent this way could travel 26 miles per hour, faster than a galloping horse.

But even this wall could not stop a determined enemy. In 1644, the "barbarian" Manchus broke through and conquered China. Their land in the north was merged with that of the Chinese empire. No longer was there a need for a defensive wall. Neglected, the Great Wall of China began to fall into ruin.

The Ming emperors had new walls of brick and stone built in the 16th century. Since then, parts of the wall have fallen into ruin. A partly ruined section is shown here.

Graffiti left by tourists (left) and large numbers of visitors (right) are two modern threats to the Great Wall.

Crumbling Walls

In 1912, when the last Manchu emperor was overthrown and China became a republic, the Chinese began to take pride in their walls. But by then, many sections of the wall built by the Ming were gone. In fact, actions taken by the Ming had hastened damage to their huge construction project.

As the new walls were being built, Ming emperors were clearing the forest and the grasslands for 60 miles on either side of the wall. On the north side, this was done so that enemies could not launch a surprise attack. On the south side, the area was planted with crops to feed the soldiers. The cleared land gradually became desert. Long stretches of wall were buried by drifting sand. Harsh winds tore stones from the wall's top and sides. In mountainous areas, the cleared land was eroded by floods. This undermined the base of the wall, causing sections to collapse.

Human activity has also damaged the wall. Farmers dug out stones to use as building material. They hauled away packed earth to build up their fields. Modern industry has taken its toll, too. Pollution from factories has further eroded the wall. One section of the wall was blasted away so that a highway could pass through. Another gap was made for trucks to carry gravel from a nearby quarry.

In other places, the wall hasn't been destroyed as much as treated with disrespect. Tourists scribble graffiti on it. Picnickers litter it with trash. In 2006, golfers shot balls from the wall to advertise a golf tournament. All-night dance parties have taken place on it. Government officials have argued over who had the right to collect tourist fees.

Preserving the Walls

Some people in China have taken it upon themselves to save certain sections of the wall. The Chinese government has begun to pay more attention to this national treasure, too.

The movement to preserve the wall began with the people who live nearby. Some are descended from the families once forced by Ming emperors to move to different locations to help build the wall. Today, these people patrol sections of the wall to protect it from further damage. The Chinese government pays them a small amount of money for this work.

In 2006, the government passed laws to protect the wall. Anyone caught bulldozing away sections of it or damaging it in other ways may have to pay a fine. But China is a big country, and the wall is long. Officials are poorly paid, and there are not enough of them to enforce the laws. Even though companies are fined for blasting holes in the wall, much damage has already been done.

Can You See the Great Wall from Space?

Now, what about those stories about the Great Wall being visible from space? Such claims have often been repeated. However, people were making that statement as early as 1754—more than 200 years before humans first went into space. No astronaut ever confirmed that the Great Wall could be seen by the human eye from space. However, it can easily be seen in radar images taken from space. The Great Wall's steep, smooth sides provide a good surface for reflecting radar beams.

The best way to get a good view of the Great Wall would be to go to China and visit it. Then you would be able to appreciate why Chinese people want to preserve the Great Wall—and what an extraordinary monument it is to human achievement.

This radar image was taken from space. It shows a part of the Great Wall. The wall appears as a thin orange band running across the middle of the picture.

Chapter 23

The Han Dynasty

In what ways did the Han dynasty improve government and daily life in China?

23.1 Introduction

Qin Shihuangdi, a Qin dynasty ruler, was China's first emperor. The Qin dynasty lasted only about fourteen years. In this chapter, you will learn about China's next dynasty, the Han (hahn) dynasty. It lasted over four hundred years, from about 206 B.C.E. to 220 C.E.

The Han dynasty arose during a period of unrest. The Chinese people were unhappy with the harsh, Legalist rule of the Qin. After the first emperor's death, they rebelled against the Qin. Liu Bang (LEE-oo bahng), a rebel who had gained control of the Han kingdom, conquered the Qin army and established the Han dynasty.

Over time, Han emperors began to change the way China was ruled. Gradually, they incorporated Confucian ideals of moral behavior into Chinese government.

Under Han rule, China had a golden age, a long period of stability and wealth. Education, literature, and art flourished. New practices, inventions, and discoveries improved people's lives.

The Han dynasty was also known for its military achievements. Han emperors expanded the empire to include parts of present-day Korea and Vietnam. Once Central Asia was under its control, the Han established trade relationships with the West.

In this chapter, you will explore warfare, government, agriculture, industry, art, medicine, and science under the Han dynasty. You will see how the Han dynasty improved daily life in China.

Han dynasty artists engraved scenes such as this one on bricks used to construct tombs.

◄ The first Han emperor marches his army toward his capital.

Han dynasty the dynasty that ruled China from about 206 B.C.E. to 220 C.E., the period following the Qin dynasty

23.2 Warfare

The Han excelled in warfare. Their military methods and new weapons helped them expand their dynasty. At its height, the **Han dynasty** reached west into Central Asia, east to present-day Korea, and south to present-day Vietnam.

The Han dynasty had a large and well-organized army. All men from about the ages of twenty-five to sixty had to serve two years in the army. Historians **estimate** that Han armies had 130,000 to 300,000 men.

The army was helped by new technologies. Advances in iron making improved the strength and quality of armor. Han iron-workers produced a kind of fish-scale armor that flexed and moved with the body. The Han were among the first people to make iron swords. The strength of iron allowed skilled workers to fashion longer swords. With a long sword, a soldier could swing at an enemy from a safer distance.

Another favorite weapon of the Han was the crossbow. A crossbow is made of two pieces of wood in the shape of a cross. A string is attached to each end of the horizontal piece of wood. When that string is pulled back and **released**, an arrow is shot from the crossbow.

The Han invented the kite and used it in clever ways for military purposes. According to one legend, a Han general once used a kite to measure the width of a heavily guarded wall. Kites were used to send messages from one part of an army to another. They were also used to frighten the enemy. Kites with bamboo pipes were flown over enemy camps at night. Enemy soldiers would hear a ghostly noise coming from the darkness above them. It sounded like "*fu, fu*" ("beware, beware"). The alarmed soldiers often ran away.

The Han Empire, About 80 B.C.E.

0   500   1,000 miles
0   500   1,000 kilometers
Lambert Azimuthal Equal-Area Projection

Chang'an • Luoyang
Yellow Sea
East China Sea
PACIFIC OCEAN
South China Sea

40°N
30°N
20°N
120°E
110°E

Han Empire, about 80 B.C.E.

Present-day China

Great Wall under the Han Empire

Han military skill enabled the dynasty to extend its power over Central Asia, and parts of present-day Korea and Vietnam.

23.3 Government

The Han emperors made significant improvements in Chinese government. They adopted the centralized government established by Emperor Qin Shihuangdi. But they softened the harsh ruling style of the Qin emperor and brought Confucian ideas back into government.

Han emperors needed many government officials to help run the vast empire. The government of China during this time functioned as a **bureaucracy**. A bureaucracy is a large organization that operates using a fixed set of rules and conditions. At each level of the bureaucracy, people direct those who are at the level below them.

The highest-level Han officials lived in the capital and gave advice to the emperor. Lower-level officials lived throughout the empire. They had many responsibilities, including overseeing the maintenance of roads and canals. They also had to make sure that, in case of famine, enough grain was produced and stored.

One key improvement made by the Han concerned the way civil servants, or government workers, were hired. Before the Han dynasty, social status determined which government officials got jobs. The Han, however, based their choices on ability and knowledge. To become officials, young men had to pass a long, difficult civil service exam. It was based on the principles of classic Chinese writings. The candidates had to learn five books by heart. Legend says that the men then had to spend several days taking the exam in tiny rooms. All the while, they were watched by guards to prevent cheating.

Once hired, civil servants were not allowed to serve in their home districts. This rule was intended to prevent officials from giving special favors to friends and relatives. Every three years, civil servants could be promoted or demoted depending upon an evaluation of their work.

> **bureaucracy** a large, complex organization that functions under a given set of rules and conditions

This bronze statue shows an escort walking behind a Han official riding in a chariot.

決水復流和
農候生用莊
桔槹取諸井
翻車而諸塘
吾嘗參分曝
那乘涼糧
在如毛郭字解
嗟何郎
沂陽耿寒柳笑歌間户飲

In this painting, a thatched roof provides shade as men work the pedals of a chain pump, bringing water to their fields.

23.4 Agriculture

Farmers in ancient China faced a number of difficulties. Several important advances made in agriculture during the Han dynasty improved their lives.

Han farmers were expected to grow enough food to feed their families and to help stock the shared granaries, or grain storehouses. In addition to growing crops, farmers had to make their own clothing, build their own homes, and give one month of unpaid labor to the government for building projects such as canals and roads. Hard as this life already was, floods and drought often destroyed crops, presenting farmers with yet another challenge.

One invention that helped farmers was the chain pump. The chain pump made it easier to move water from low irrigation ditches and canals up to the fields. Workers used pedals to turn a wheel, which pulled a **series** of wooden planks that moved water uphill to the fields.

The Han skill in ironwork also came to the farmers' aid. The Chinese were the first to learn how to pour melted iron into molds. This process enabled them to make strong iron plows. Han plows were designed to push the dirt away from the row being plowed so that the soil would not pile up in front of the plow.

The Han also invented the wheelbarrow. The Chinese wheelbarrow had one large wheel in the center. Goods were carried on either side of the wheel. It was much easier for farmers to push a heavy load in a wheelbarrow than to carry it on their backs or in buckets **suspended** from a pole across their shoulders.

23.5 Industry

Like agriculture, Chinese **industry benefited** from advances made during the Han dynasty. The Han government controlled the two most important industries in China, silk and salt. New inventions helped both industries.

Silk is a material produced from the fibers of a silkworm cocoon. For the ancient Chinese, making silk was difficult and time-consuming labor. During the Han dynasty, the Chinese developed a foot-powered machine that could wind the silk fibers onto a large reel, ready for use. Making silk production more efficient was important because there was a high demand for silk outside of China. The valuable silk trade began during the Han dynasty.

Salt was an equally important trade item. Salt was valued in ancient times because people used it to help preserve meat and vegetables. At first, people only knew how to get salt from the sea. During the Han dynasty, the Chinese learned how to mine salt from under the ground.

Salt water, or brine, exists deep beneath Earth's surface. The Chinese used iron-tipped bamboo drills to dig deep wells. When the drills reached salt water (sometimes 1,000 feet below the surface), a hollow bamboo pole was dropped into the well. The pole had a valve that allowed the salt water to enter the pole. The valve was then closed, and the pole filled with the salt water was brought back to the surface. Workers placed the water in large iron pots. The pots were heated until the water evaporated and only the salt remained. In this way, the Chinese people could find salt, even in regions far from the sea.

industry a business that manufactures a particular product, such as silk

Silk production was a key industry during the Han dynasty. This foot-powered reeling machine threaded silk fibers through a series of guides and onto a large reel.

23.6 Art

During the Han dynasty, a key advance was made in art—the invention of paper. Paper was the ideal material for calligraphy, which is the art of fine handwriting. Calligraphy was important in Chinese culture. It was a style of writing especially valued for its natural flow, as if inspired by nature.

Chinese scribes used some of the same tools and techniques as painters did. They wrote their characters by painting them with a brush and ink. Characters were created by one or more strokes, drawn quickly in a particular order. The ideal stroke created both delicate and bold lines. Paper was perfect for this art because of the way it absorbed the ink.

Before the invention of paper, the Chinese wrote on silk. Silk could easily be rolled into scrolls, but it was very costly. People also wrote symbols vertically on bamboo strips. To make books, they tied a series of strips together in a bundle. Bamboo was less expensive than silk, but it was bulky and awkward to use.

The invention of paper, in about the first century C.E., not only benefited calligraphers but also changed the way people communicated. It was cheaper to produce paper than bamboo or silk, so more people could now afford writing materials. Paper was also easier to bind together into books.

A variety of materials were used to make paper. They included silk fibers, hemp, bamboo, straw, and seaweed. These were boiled into a soupy pulp. A screen was dipped into the pulp and then pulled out. When the pulp dried on the screen, the result was paper.

This 19th-century woodblock print shows how Chinese papermakers hang sheets of paper on a wall.

These doctors are performing the healing technique of moxibustion. This method is still used today, often along with acupuncture.

23.7 Medicine

The practice of medicine during the Han dynasty involved some ideas and treatments that are still used in traditional Chinese healing today. The ancient Chinese believed that illnesses occurred when the forces of yin and yang in the body were out of balance. Healers tried to restore the natural balance of these opposite forces.

One technique developed by Chinese healers for this purpose was acupuncture. In acupuncture, thin needles are inserted into specific parts of the body. This procedure is thought to rebalance the forces of yin and yang. Acupuncture is believed to be useful for curing illnesses that strike quickly, like headaches.

A second healing technique was moxibustion. In this method, a moxa—a small cone of powdered leaves or sticks—is placed on or near the skin and burned. The heat is believed to reduce pain and promote healing. This technique is used to treat long-term diseases, such as arthritis.

Chinese doctors also made several discoveries about how the human body works. For example, they learned to judge health by listening to a person's heartbeat or by feeling his or her pulse. The pulse is the little throb in your blood vessels, caused by the contraction of your heart as it pumps blood through the body. The Chinese also discovered that blood circulates from the heart, through the body, and back to the heart. Western science did not make this discovery until the 1600s C.E.

The image on this Chinese postage stamp shows a Chinese "south-pointing spoon," the oldest known compass.

23.8 Science

The Chinese achieved a number of scientific advances during the Han dynasty. Chinese astronomers closely observed the heavens. They recorded the appearance of comets, which they called "broom stars." They discovered that the moon shines because it reflects the light of the sun. They also learned that solar eclipses occur when the moon blocks our view of the sun.

The Chinese of this period also invented two very useful instruments, the seismograph and the magnetic compass. A seismograph is an instrument for detecting earthquakes. The first Chinese seismograph was a circular machine made of bronze. The machine had a pendulum in the center, surrounded by eight sculpted animal heads. During an earthquake, the pendulum vibrated. The vibration triggered the release of one of eight balls. The ball would then fall in the direction of the earthquake. Using this ingenious machine, the Han were able to detect earthquakes up to several hundred miles away.

The magnetic compass is an instrument for determining direction, such as north or south. The Chinese believed that using direction to correctly position their temples, graves, and homes would bring good fortune. By the 200s C.E., Chinese scientists understood that a lodestone, a type of iron ore, tends to align itself in a north-south direction because of Earth's magnetism. With this knowledge, they used lodestones to make compasses. The lodestone was carved into the shape of a spoon with a handle that would always point south.

In this chapter, you read about the golden age in China during the Han dynasty. In this period, the Chinese made many advances that improved their government and daily life. The Chinese word *Han* is still used to describe China's culture.

Warfare and Government New weapons helped Han emperors succeed in war and expand their empire. They organized the government into a bureaucracy. Civil servants who were chosen for their ability worked in the bureacracy.

Agriculture and Industry Several inventions improved production in agriculture and in the silk and salt industries. Farmers used the chain pump for irrigation and iron plows. Workers used foot-powered reeling machines to make silk thread, and iron tipped drills to mine salt.

Art, Medicine, and Science The invention of paper advanced the art of calligraphy and changed the way people communicated. Healers learned about the human body and developed techniques that are still used today. Chinese scientists made careful observations of the heavens, and invented the seismograph and the compass.

Emperor Wudi, at left, was the fifth ruler of the Han dynasty. He set up a university to prepare students for the civil service exam.

Chapter 24

The Silk Road

How did the Silk Road promote an exchange of goods and ideas?

24.1 Introduction

Under Han rule, new trade routes allowed the Chinese to trade with other ancient cultures. In this chapter, you will explore the great trade route known as the Silk Road.

The Silk Road was actually a network of smaller trade routes. It stretched for more than four thousand miles across Asia— from Luoyang (lwaw-yahng) and the Han capital of Chang'an (chahn-ahn) in China to Mediterranean ports such as Antioch (AN-tee-ahk) in Syria. By the first century C.E., the Roman Empire, and its capital, Rome, **dominated** the Mediterranean region. The Silk Road connected the Han and Roman empires.

Both goods and ideas traveled along the Silk Road. The Chinese traded silk and jade for spices from India and glassware from Rome. Ideas, like Buddhism, entered China with this trade.

The Silk Road **linked** the peoples of the East and the West for more than a thousand years. In this chapter, you will learn more about the exchanges between Asian and western cultures.

The Chinese wove delicate fibers from silkworm cocoons into silk. Traders moved such goods across Asia on the Silk Road (below).

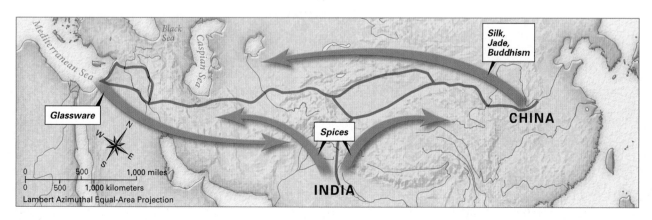

◀ These modern travelers follow an ancient route of the Silk Road.

Silk Road a network of trade routes that stretched for more than four thousand miles across Asia

trade route a network of roads along which traders traveled

24.2 The Opening of the Silk Road

The expansion of the Han empire made the **Silk Road** possible. The military campaigns of the Han drove back nomadic peoples in northwestern China, opening up **trade routes** to the west.

The Father of the Silk Road   A Chinese explorer named Zhang Qian (jahng chee-ehn) is often called the Father of the Silk Road. His travels opened the way for trade between China and its western neighbors.

In 138 B.C.E., a Han emperor sent Zhang Qian west with 100 men. His mission was to persuade western peoples to form an alliance against China's northern enemy, the Huns. Zhang Qian traveled across Central Asia to what is now the country of Iran. Twice, he was taken prisoner by the Huns. Both times, he was able to escape.

Zhang Qian never achieved an alliance. But his trip was a success in other ways, as it helped the Chinese learn about a number of cultures to the west. Zhang Qian brought back word of such places as Persia, Syria, India, and Rome.

Some years later, Zhang Qian went on a second journey to the west. This time, he learned about a type of horse that was more powerful than the smaller Chinese horse and better suited for war. He also discovered grapes, which were unknown in China. Most important, he was able to establish trade relationships with some of the Central Asian peoples he met along the way.

Over time, Chinese traders traveled farther west. Smaller trade routes connected to form larger networks. The most famous of these routes became known as the Silk Road, named after the product that traders valued most of all: Chinese silk.

The carving on this cup shows Zhang Qian floating in a hollow log down the Huang He.

These women are making silk. The Chinese closely guarded the secret of how to produce silk.

Silk as a Trade Good   Silk is a fiber used to make cloth. Silk cloth is strong, but also warm, light, and soft.

Silk was a valuable good for trade because, at first, only the Chinese people knew how to make it. During the Han dynasty, the Chinese had discovered how to make silk out of the fibers taken from the cocoon of the silkworm. To protect the trade value of silk, the Chinese tried to keep their production process a secret. Under Han rule, revealing the silk-making process was a crime punishable by death.

Rome Trades Glassware for Silk   When people of other cultures learned about silk, it became a highly prized material. The Romans, in particular, eagerly traded valuable goods for silk.

The first time the Romans saw silk may have been during a battle near the Euphrates River in Mesopotamia. At a key point in the fighting, the enemy unfurled many colorful silk banners. The Romans lost the battle, but this experience led them to want to **acquire** this remarkable new material.

Chinese silk was a luxury item. It was rare and expensive. Even the richest Romans could afford to wear only a strip or a patch of silk stitched to their white togas, or robes. Silk was so highly valued that traders willingly made the dangerous journey eastward to obtain it.

Besides having gold to trade, the Romans had something else the Chinese prized: glassware. The Romans knew how to blow glass into wonderful, delicate shapes. Just as the Romans had never seen silk, the Chinese did not know the method for glass production. The Romans were happy to trade glassware for silk.

Traders often joined in long caravans to cross the Taklimakan Desert. Some caravans had as many as 1,000 camels.

24.3 The Eastern Silk Road

The Silk Road was not one continuous route. It was a network of shorter trade routes between various stops. Most traders moved between these stops, rather than journeying thousands of miles along the entire length of the route. Goods changed hands many times before reaching their final destination.

The two major parts of the route were the Eastern Silk Road and the Western Silk Road. The Eastern Silk Road connected Luoyang to Kashgar (KASH-gahr), in the western part of the Taklimakan Desert. The Western Silk Road ran from Kashgar to Antioch and other Mediterranean ports.

Traveling the Eastern Silk Road   From Luoyang, the Silk Road led west along the Gobi Desert to Dunhuang (dun-hwang), in northwestern China. This part of the route was protected by the Great Wall to the north.

From Dunhuang, travelers could choose either a northern or a southern route across the Taklimakan Desert to Kashgar. Many chose the northern route, where the distances between oases like Loulan and Kucha were shorter.

Several dangers faced traders crossing the Taklimakan Desert. Bandits often attacked travelers on the northern route between Dunhuang and Kucha. Throughout the desert, sudden sandstorms sometimes buried travelers in sand. Mirages may have lured travelers off the main path to their deaths.

To protect themselves before entering the desert, travelers often formed long **caravans** of camels. One type of camel was especially suited for desert travel. Bactrian camels have double eyelids and nostrils that can close to keep out blowing sand. These camels could also carry enough food and water to ensure a traveler's survival from one oasis to the next.

caravan a group of people traveling together

Goods Exchanged Along the Eastern Silk Road

It was costly to carry goods over the Silk Road. For traders to make a profit, goods had to be valuable. They also had to be easy to carry so that merchants could transport more goods on fewer animals.

Silk was the perfect trading good because it was both light and valuable. Huge quantities of silk traveled along the Eastern Silk Road from China. Traded for other goods, the silk eventually reached the shores of the Mediterranean Sea. Then it was taken by boat to Rome and other Mediterranean cities.

Besides silk, the Chinese also traded fine dishware (which became known as china), ornaments, jewelry, cast-iron products, and decorative boxes. In return, the Chinese received a variety of goods from other traders. The Chinese particularly valued horses from Central Asia. Other items from Central Asia included jade, furs, and gold. Traders from India brought various goods north to Kashgar. These included cotton, spices, pearls (from oysters), and ivory (from elephant tusks). From Kashgar, the goods made their way east to China.

Along the Silk Road (see map below), the Chinese traded their goods for horses, jade, furs, and gold from Central Asia. The bronze Han statue (above) depicts one of the spirited horses the Chinese valued.

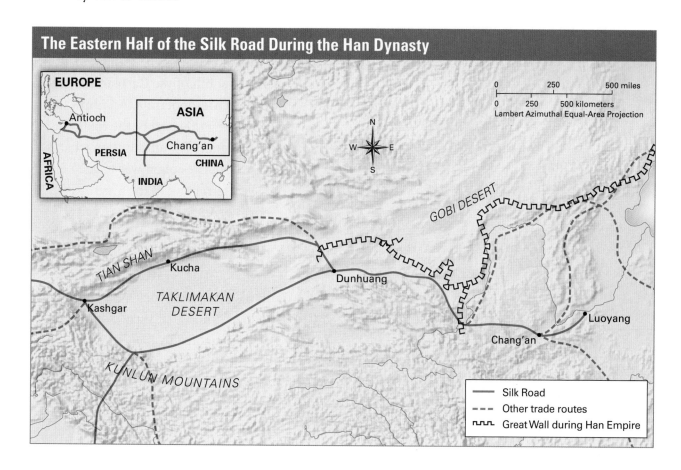

The Eastern Half of the Silk Road During the Han Dynasty

EUROPE
Antioch
AFRICA
PERSIA
ASIA
Chang'an
CHINA
INDIA

0   250   500 miles
0   250   500 kilometers
Lambert Azimuthal Equal-Area Projection

GOBI DESERT

TIAN SHAN
Kucha
Dunhuang
TAKLIMAKAN DESERT
Kashgar
Luoyang
Chang'an
KUNLUN MOUNTAINS

—— Silk Road
----- Other trade routes
ᴧᴧᴧ Great Wall during Han Empire

24.4 The Western Silk Road

Kashgar was the central trading point at which the Eastern Silk Road and the Western Silk Road met. Goods from various areas were exchanged there and sent in both directions along the trade route. Traders traveling westward carried goods by yak rather than camel. The Western Silk Road ended in Mediterranean ports like Antioch.

Traveling the Western Silk Road The journey west from Kashgar began with a difficult trek across the Pamir (pah-meer) Mountains. Some of these mountain peaks rose over twenty thousand feet. Travelers often experienced headaches, dizziness, and ringing in the ears caused by a lack of **oxygen** in the thin air of the high mountains.

Many of the mountain passes were narrow and dangerous. Along this part of the route, sometimes called the "trail of bones," animals and people often died. Pack animals such as donkeys slipped off the narrow trails and tumbled over cliffs. Sometimes, traders unloaded their animals and hand-carried the goods through the passes.

After the Pamir Mountains, the route took travelers through a fertile valley in what is now the country of Afghanistan. Then the route went across the Iranian Plateau, passed south of the Caspian Sea, and crossed Mesopotamia. An important stop along this part of the route was Ctesiphon (TES-uh-fahn), in what is now Iraq. Ctesiphon was located on the eastern bank of the Tigris River, north of ancient Babylon.

From Ctesiphon, the Silk Road turned north and passed through the Syrian Desert. Travelers faced many hardships there. They were threatened by tigers, lions, and scorpions, and also tormented by flies.

The varied goods finally reached Antioch and other Mediterranean ports. From there, ships carried them throughout the Mediterranean world.

Crossing the Pamir Mountains presented many challenges. In winter, travelers caught in snowstorms could freeze to death.

Goods Exchanged Along the Western Silk Road

Many goods traveled along the Western Silk Road and eventually ended up in China. Traders from Egypt, Arabia, and Persia brought perfumes, cosmetics, and carpets. Central Asian traders brought metal items and dyes, and sometimes traded slaves.

Rome sent a number of products to be exchanged for Chinese silk. The Chinese highly valued Roman glass products. These included trays, vases, necklaces, and small bottles. They also prized asbestos, which the Chinese used for making fireproof cloth as well as coral. Chinese doctors used coral to help them treat illness. It was said that coral lost its color when placed on the skin of someone who was sick.

The Romans also sent massive amounts of gold to trade for silk. In fact, so much gold was shipped out of Rome that, in the first century C.E., the Roman emperor Tiberius passed a law forbidding men to wear silk. Legend says that the emperor was afraid that wearing so much finery would make the Romans appear soft and weak. It is more likely that he wanted to reduce the amount of gold that was flowing out of his empire.

Persian carpets, like the one above, were traded along the Silk Road. Traders brought them east to China and west to Europe.

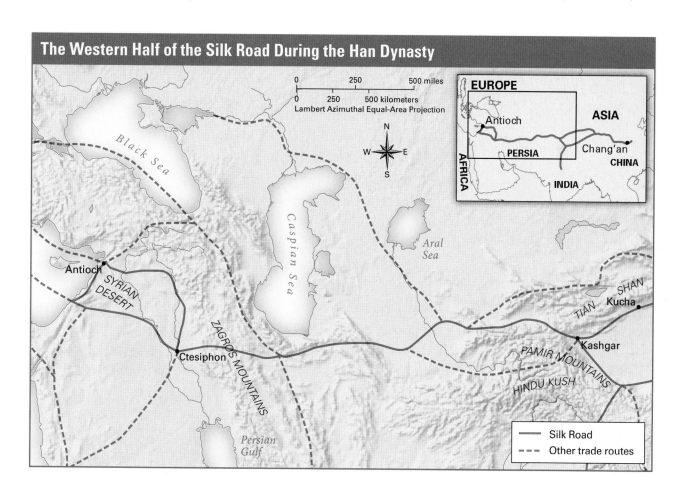

The Western Half of the Silk Road During the Han Dynasty

0   250   500 miles
0   250   500 kilometers
Lambert Azimuthal Equal-Area Projection

N
W   E
S

EUROPE

ASIA

Antioch

PERSIA

Chang'an

AFRICA

CHINA

INDIA

Black Sea

Caspian Sea

Aral Sea

Antioch

SYRIAN DESERT

ZAGROS MOUNTAINS

Ctesiphon

TIAN SHAN

Kucha

Kashgar

PAMIR MOUNTAINS

HINDU KUSH

Persian Gulf

— Silk Road
--- Other trade routes

The spread of Buddhism from India to China is an example of cultural diffusion. These two Buddha statues from China (left) and India (right) reflect the spread of ideas.

cultural diffusion the spreading of cultural traits, such as goods and ideas, from one culture to another, or within one culture

24.5 Cultural Exchanges and the Silk Road

The trade between East and West along the Silk Road created **cultural diffusion,** in which ideas and knowledge—as well as goods—spread from one culture to another. For example, China and Rome did not merely trade new products with each other. In time, they learned how to make these products for themselves. By 500 C.E., the Chinese had learned how to make glass. About the same time, the West had learned how to produce silk. Such cultural diffusion **occurs** in many cultures, past and present, and in many different ways.

Diets, gardening, and agriculture also changed as trade introduced new plants into different areas. For example, China imported many new foods and spices. Among them were grapes, cucumbers, figs, pomegranates, walnuts, chives, sesame, and coriander. The West imported oranges, peaches, pears, and different kinds of flowers, including roses, chrysanthemums, azaleas, peonies, and camellias.

The Silk Road also helped spread Buddhist beliefs. Buddhism had its origins in India. Because the Silk Road passed through many different nations, religious travelers using the route shared their teachings.

The spread of Buddhism is a good example of how cultural diffusion takes place. Buddhism was introduced to China around the middle of the first century C.E. Some Chinese Buddhists journeyed on foot across Central Asia to India to learn more about their new religion. They returned to China with copies of sacred Buddhist texts. Buddhism would eventually become a major religion in China.

In this chapter, you learned how the Silk Road, an ancient network of trade routes, promoted an exchange of goods and ideas between China and the West.

The Opening of the Silk Road The Silk Road was opened during the Han dynasty and remained a major route of trade for more than one thousand years. The eastern and western parts of the Silk Road presented many dangers and hardships for those who traveled along it. To make a profit from trade, goods had to be valuable and easy to carry. Silk and ornaments traveled from China to Rome, India, and central Asia. Gold, horses, cotton, and spices traveled back to China.

The Eastern Silk Road The Eastern Silk Road connected the capital of China to Kashgar. Travelers formed camel caravans for protection from bandits and the harsh conditions of desert travel.

The Western Silk Road From Kashgar, the Western Silk Road crossed mountains and a desert on its way to Mediterranean ports like Antioch. Travelers faced high, slippery mountain trails and dangerous desert wildlife, such as tigers and lions.

Cultural Exchanges Along the Silk Road Many goods were exchanged along the Silk Road, including both silk from China and glassware from Rome. In addition to new products, ideas and knowledge were exchanged. In this way, trade brought cultural changes to both East and West. One of the most important examples of cultural diffusion was the introduction of Buddhism to China.

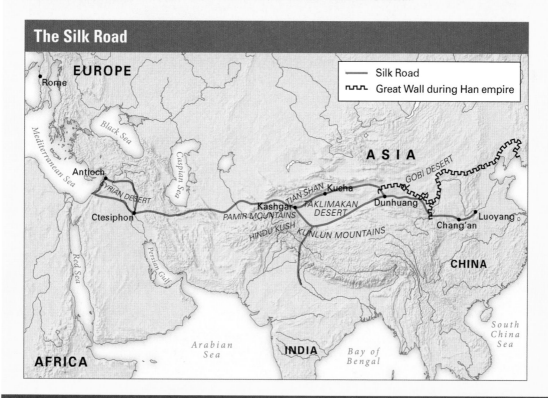

The Silk Road

Unit 4 Timeline Challenge

Ancient China

About 1700–1122 B.C.E.
Shang Dynasty
The Shang, one of China's earliest civilizations, rule the Huang He Valley.

About 1400 B.C.E.
Early Chinese Writing
Early Chinese writing includes about 3,000 characters. Oracle bones have writing in the form of logographs.

About 1045–256 B.C.E.
Zhou Dynasty
The Zhou claim the Mandate of Heaven and rule China under a system of feudalism.

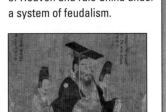

| 1800 B.C.E. | 1600 B.C.E. | 1400 B.C.E. | 1200 B.C.E. | 1000 B.C.E. | 800 B.C.E. | 600 B.C.E. |

551–479 B.C.E.
Life of Confucius
Confucius teaches that people should act properly and respect relationships.

280–233 B.C.E.
Life of Hanfeizi
Hanfeizi proposes Legalism, a philosophy emphasizing a system of strong central government.

About 6th century B.C.E.
Life of Laozi
According to Chinese legend, Laozi teaches about the Dao and yin and yang.

About 206 B.C.E.–220 C.E.
Han Dynasty
The Han develop a bureaucratic system of government and improve life in China.

About 80 B.C.E.
Expansion of Han Empire
Military technology and strategy allow the Han empire to expand into Central Asia and parts of Korea and Vietnam.

65 C.E.
Spread of Buddhism into China
Cultural diffusion occurs as Buddhism spreads from India to China.

600 B.C.E.   **400 B.C.E.**   **200 B.C.E.**   **1 C.E.**   **200 C.E.**   **250 C.E.**

221–210 B.C.E.
First Unification of China
Emperor Qin Shihuangdi unites northern China, standardizes the culture, and builds the Great Wall.

138 B.C.E.
First Trade Along Silk Road
Chinese explorer Zhang Qian establishes trade relationships with Central Asian peoples, using a network of routes that become known as the Silk Road.

About 105 C.E.
Chinese Invent Paper
The Chinese invent paper during the Han dynasty, making it easier for people to communicate and create documents and records.

Unit 5

Ancient Greece

The Parthenon is the most famous building in Greece. The ancient Greeks built the Parthenon as a temple to the goddess Athena. Its ruins stand in Athens, the present-day capital of Greece. People come from all over the world to see it.

Ancient Greece

As sunlight falls on the mountains, hills, and coasts of Greece, reflecting off the surfaces of the glittering sea, white-washed buildings, and ancient ruins, it is dazzling, brilliant, and vibrant. In ancient times, the light of Greece was unaffected by the haze of modern pollution, and was surely even more magical than it is today.

Greece has three main parts: the mainland, which is part of southern Europe; the peninsula, which nearly touches the mainland and is connected to it by just a thin strip of land; and the islands, which number more than 2,000. The peninsula is called the Peloponnesus. The largest island, Crete, lies in the Mediterranean Sea, south of the mainland. Most of the islands of ancient Greece, however, were not suitable places for people to make their homes.

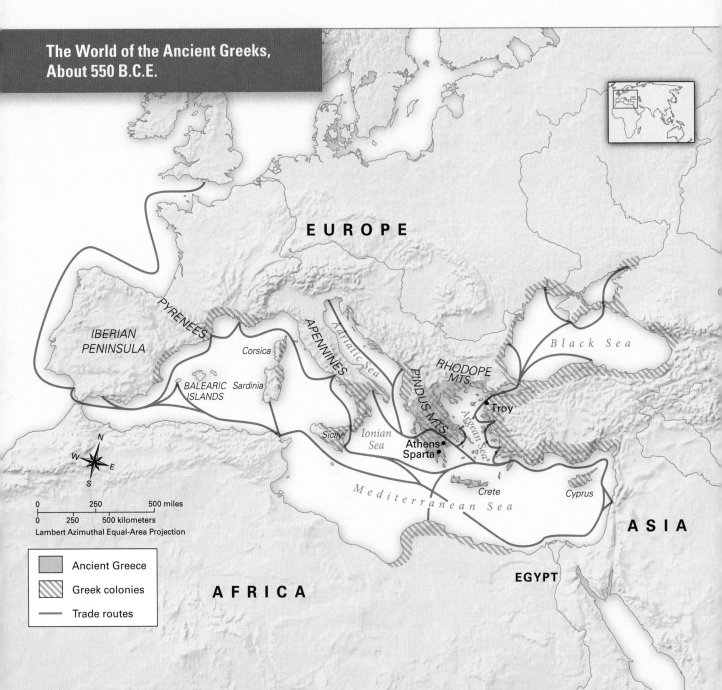

The World of the Ancient Greeks, About 550 B.C.E.

Legend:
- Ancient Greece
- Greek colonies
- Trade routes

0   250   500 miles
0   250   500 kilometers
Lambert Azimuthal Equal-Area Projection

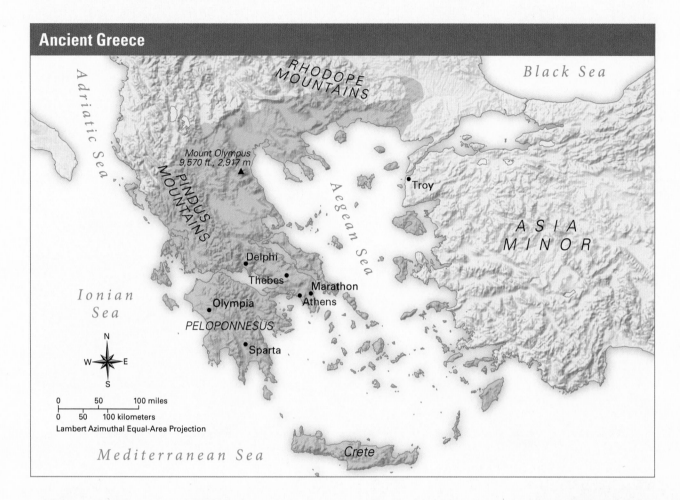

Ancient Greece

Mount Olympus
9,570 ft., 2,917 m

Adriatic Sea

RHODOPE MOUNTAINS

Black Sea

PINDUS MOUNTAINS

• Troy

Aegean Sea

ASIA MINOR

• Delphi

Thebes •

• Marathon
• Athens

Ionian Sea

• Olympia

PELOPONNESUS

• Sparta

N
W E
S

0   50   100 miles
0   50   100 kilometers
Lambert Azimuthal Equal-Area Projection

Mediterranean Sea

Crete

Settlement in ancient Greece was influenced by geography, just as it was for people of other ancient cultures. High mountains separated Greek communities from one another, making it easier for the Greek people to interact with outsiders than with each other.

Most of Greece is covered with steep mountains. Mount Olympus is the highest, rising about 9,500 feet above sea level. The rest of Greece is made up of lowlands along its many miles of coastline. Greece is surrounded by seas on three sides: the Aegean to the east, the Mediterranean to the south, and the Ionian to the west. Carved out of the land where it meets the sea are many deep inlets and protected bays. It is understandable why shipbuilding, fishing, and seafaring were important in ancient Greece.

In early times, coastal villages were separated by the high mountains. The soil was poor, and level land was scarce, but farmers grew olives, grapes, and fruit and nut trees along the coast. Cattle could not graze on the steep hillsides of Greece, so the Greeks raised sheep and goats.

Over time, as the population of ancient Greece increased, it became harder to produce enough food for everyone. So the Greeks took to the seas, traveling to Asia Minor (present-day Turkey), France, Italy, Spain, and Africa to set up trading colonies. The map opposite shows Greek colonies and trading routes about 550 B.C.E.

In this unit, you will learn more about the "land of light" and the ways in which the mountains and the sea shaped the history of ancient Greece.

Chapter 25

Geography and the Settlement of Greece

How did geography influence settlement and way of life in ancient Greece?

25.1 Introduction

In this chapter, you will learn about how geography affected the early settlement of ancient Greece. This remarkable culture flourished between 750 and 338 B.C.E. Ancient Greek art, ideas, and writings continue to influence many aspects of the modern world today.

Greece is a small country in southern Europe. It is shaped somewhat like an outstretched hand, with fingers of land that reach into the Mediterranean Sea. The mainland of Greece is a peninsula. A peninsula is land that is surrounded on three sides by water. Greece also includes many islands throughout the Mediterranean and the Aegean (ih-JEE-uhn) seas.

Mainland Greece is a land of steep, rugged mountains, almost entirely surrounded by turquoise blue seas. The ancient Greeks lived on farms or in small villages scattered throughout the country. These farms and villages were isolated, or separated, from each other by the mountains and seas.

In this chapter, you will explore how Greece's geography influenced settlement and way of life in ancient Greece. You will learn why people lived and farmed in isolated communities. You will also discover how the Greeks used the sea to establish colonies and trade relations with people from other lands.

The ancient Greeks learned to use the sea as a major route for travel and trade.

◀ Farmers in ancient Greece grew olives and grapes on rocky hillsides.

peninsula a body of land that is surrounded on three sides by water

Aegean Sea an arm of the Mediterranean Sea, east of Greece

Most ancient Greeks traveled by and lived near the water. What three seas surround Greece?

25.2 Isolated Communities and the Difficulties of Travel

The mountains and the seas of Greece contributed greatly to the isolation of ancient Greek communities. Because travel over the mountains and across the water was so difficult, the people in different settlements had little communication with each other.

Travel by land was especially hard. People mostly walked, or rode in carts pulled by oxen or mules. Roads were unpaved. Sharp rocks frequently shattered wooden wheels, and thick mud could stop a wagon in its tracks. Only wealthy people could afford to ride horses.

Travelers could stop at inns on the main roads, but many inns provided only shelter. People had to bring their own food and other supplies with them. Slaves or pack animals carried bedding, food, and other necessities. With all these goods to take with them, the Greeks often traveled in groups, moving at a slower pace than someone traveling alone.

Traveling by water was easier than traveling by land. You can see on the map on this page that mainland Greece is a **peninsula,** made up of smaller peninsulas. Ancient Greeks were never far from the water. To the south of Greece is the Mediterranean Sea; to the east, the **Aegean Sea;** and to the west, the Ionian (ahy-OH-nee-uhn) Sea. The ancient Greeks soon learned to travel by ship.

The Greeks understood the dangers of the sea and treated it with great respect. Sudden storms could drive ships off course or send them smashing into the rocky shoreline. Even in open waters, ships could sink. These hazards encouraged Greek sailors to navigate close to shore, sail only during daylight, and stop at night to anchor.

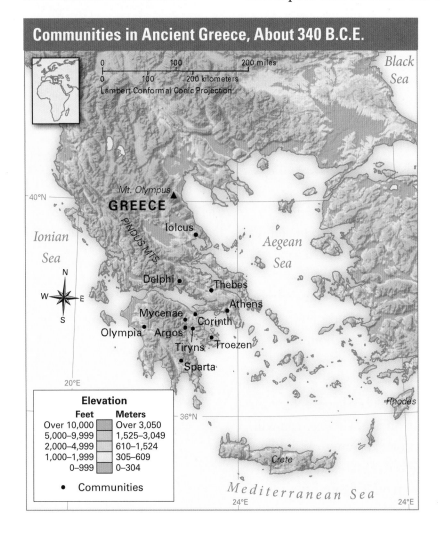

Communities in Ancient Greece, About 340 B.C.E.

Black Sea

Ionian Sea

GREECE
Mt. Olympus
PINDUS MTS.
Iolcus
Aegean Sea
Delphi
Thebes
Athens
Mycenae
Corinth
Olympia Argos
Tiryns Troezen
Sparta

Rhodes

Crete

Mediterranean Sea

0   100   200 miles
0   100   200 kilometers
Lambert Conformal Conic Projection

40°N
20°E
36°N
24°E
24°E

Elevation

Feet	Meters
Over 10,000	Over 3,050
5,000–9,999	1,525–3,049
2,000–4,999	610–1,524
1,000–1,999	305–609
0–999	0–304

• Communities

The images on this ancient Greek vase show women gathering fruit.

25.3 Farming in Ancient Greece

Most people in ancient Greece made their living by farming. But farming wasn't easy in that mountainous land. Even in the plains and valleys, the land was rocky, and water was scarce. There were no major rivers flowing through Greece, and the rains fell mostly during the winter months.

With limited flat land available, Greek farmers had to find the best ways to use what little land they had. Some farmers built wide earth steps into the hills to create more flat land for planting. A few farmers were able to grow wheat and barley, but most grew crops that needed less land, particularly grapes and olives. Greek farmers produced a lot of olive oil, which was used for cooking, to make soap, and as fuel for lamps.

Ancient Greek farmers grew food for their own families. In addition to small vegetable gardens, many farmers planted hillside orchards of fruit and nut trees. Some Greek families kept bees to make honey. Honey was the best-known sweetener in the ancient world.

Greek farmers also raised animals. But because cattle need wide flat lands for grazing, the ancient Greeks had to raise sheep and goats, which can graze on the sides of mountains. Sheep supplied wool for clothing, while goats provided milk and cheese. Greek farmers kept some oxen, mules, and donkeys for plowing and transportation. Many Greek families also kept pigs and chickens.

The shortage of good farmland sometimes led to wars between Greek settlements, with each one claiming land for itself. As you will see, some settlements also had to look beyond the mainland for new sources of food and other goods.

colony a settlement under the control of a usually distant country

25.4 Starting Colonies

As the populations of Greek communities increased, the existing farmland no longer produced enough food to feed all of the people. One solution was to start colonies, or settlements in distant places. Many Greek communities sent people across the sea, in search of new places to farm so that they could ship food back home. People who set up colonies are called colonists.

The ancient Greeks made many preparations before starting a journey to a new land. Often, they began by **consulting** an oracle to ask the Greek gods whether their efforts would be successful. An oracle was a holy person who the Greeks believed could communicate with the gods.

Next, the colonists gathered food and supplies. They took a flame from their town's sacred fire so they could start a sacred fire in their new home.

Greek colonists faced many hardships. They had to take a long sea voyage and then find a good location for their colony. They looked for areas with natural harbors and good farmland. They tried to avoid places where the local people might oppose the new colonies. Finally, they had to build their new community and make it successful.

Many ancient Greeks started colonies across nearby seas in order to farm and trade.

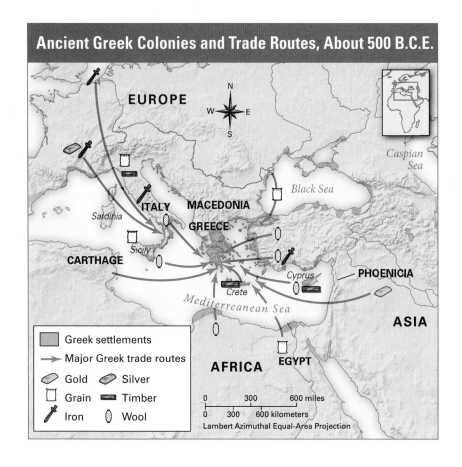

Ancient Greek Colonies and Trade Routes, About 500 B.C.E.

Greek settlements
→ Major Greek trade routes
Gold   Silver
Grain   Timber
Iron   Wool

0   300   600 miles
0 300 600 kilometers
Lambert Azimuthal Equal-Area Projection

The Greeks established colonies over a period of more than 300 years, from 1000 to 650 B.C.E. The first group of settlers started a colony called Ionia, in Asia Minor, in what is present-day Turkey. Later groups started colonies in Spain, France, Italy, and Africa, and along the coast of the Black Sea.

These colonies helped spread Greek culture. Some flourished through farming and trade. Colonists continued to enjoy whatever rights they once held in their home country of Greece, including the right to **participate** in Greek athletic games.

25.5 Trading for Needed Goods

Many Greek settlements on the mainland **relied** on trade with each other to get needed goods. Some had enough farmland to meet their own needs, so they were less dependent on trade.

The Greeks traded among the city-states, with Greek colonies, and in the wider Mediterranean region. Olive oil and pottery from the mainland were exchanged for such goods as grain, timber, and metal.

Most goods were carried on ships owned by merchants. These ships were built of wood, with large rectangular cloth sails. Merchants had ships built, not for speed, but for space to hold goods. Because these ships traveled only about three to five miles per hour, journeys were long. A one-way trip from the mainland could take two months.

Merchant ships, like the one shown here, sailed on the Mediterranean Sea around 500 B.C.E.

Navigating these ships was difficult. The Greeks had no compasses or charts. They had only the stars to guide them. The stars could tell sailors a ship's location, but not what hazards lay nearby. No lighthouses warned sailors of dangerous coastlines. Despite these dangers, adventurous sailors carried more and more goods, and trade flourished along the Mediterranean coast.

Chapter Summary

In this chapter, you learned about the ways in which geography influenced settlement and way of life in ancient Greece.

Isolated Communities and the Difficulties of Travel Greece's steep mountains and surrounding seas forced Greeks to settle in isolated communities. Travel by land was hard, and sea voyages were hazardous.

Farming in Ancient Greece Most ancient Greeks farmed, but good land and water were scarce. They grew grapes and olives, and raised sheep, goats, pigs, and chickens.

Starting Colonies Many ancient Greeks sailed across the sea to found colonies that helped spread Greek culture. Colonists settled in lands that include parts of present-day Turkey, Spain, France, Italy, and northern Africa.

Trading for Needed Goods To meet their needs, the ancient Greeks traded with other city-states, their colonies, and with other peoples in the Mediterranean region. They exchanged olive oil and pottery for such goods as grain, timber, and metal.

Chapter 26

The Rise of Democracy

How did democracy develop in ancient Greece?

26.1 Introduction

Geography affected how settlements developed in ancient Greece. Isolated communities, separated from each other by steep mountains, grew in diverse ways. For example, differences arose in how people governed themselves. In this chapter, you will learn about the various forms of government in these ancient Greek communities.

The ancient Greeks had many things in common. For example, they spoke the same language. But the Greek people did not view Greece as one country. Rather, they identified with a hometown that they called their "city." Each of these cities included both a settlement and its surrounding farmland.

Most Greeks were fiercely proud of their cities. Each city had its own laws, its own army, and its own form of money. For these reasons, ancient Greek cities are called city-states. The ancient Sumerians in Mesopotamia were the first people to form city-states. Like the Sumerian city-states, individual Greek city-states had their own form of government.

In this chapter, you will explore the four forms of government that developed in the Greek city-states: monarchy, oligarchy, tyranny, and democracy. You will also trace how one form of rule led to another, until the Greeks eventually developed democracy.

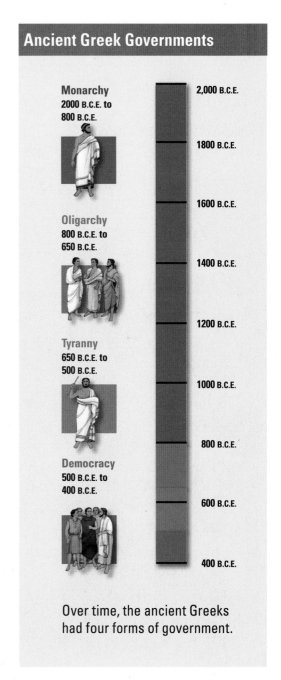

Ancient Greek Governments

Monarchy
2000 B.C.E. to
800 B.C.E.

Oligarchy
800 B.C.E. to
650 B.C.E.

Tyranny
650 B.C.E. to
500 B.C.E.

Democracy
500 B.C.E. to
400 B.C.E.

2,000 B.C.E.
1800 B.C.E.
1600 B.C.E.
1400 B.C.E.
1200 B.C.E.
1000 B.C.E.
800 B.C.E.
600 B.C.E.
400 B.C.E.

Over time, the ancient Greeks had four forms of government.

◀ Olympia, at left, was an ancient Greek city-state.

monarchy a government in which the ruling power is in the hands of one person

aristocrat a member of the most powerful class in ancient Greek society

26.2 Monarchy: One Person Inherits Power

From about 2000 to 800 B.C.E., most Greek city-states were ruled by a monarch, or king. In a **monarchy,** the governing power is in the hands of one person, usually a king. Greek settlements did not allow queens to govern.

At first, Greek kings were chosen by the people of a city-state. When a king died, another leader was selected to take his place. In time, however, kings demanded that, after their death, their power be passed to their children, usually to the oldest son. Consequently, Greek monarchs rose to power through inheritance.

The kings of ancient Greece had many powers. They had the authority to make laws and act as judges. They also conducted religious ceremonies. They led their armies during wars. They could use force to punish people who disobeyed the laws or didn't pay their taxes.

Kings had councils of **aristocrats** to advise them. The word *aristocrat* is formed from a Greek word that means "best." The aristocrats were wealthy men who had inherited large pieces of land.

At first, councils of aristocrats had little actual power. But during wartime, kings depended on their support, as only the rich aristocrats could afford to supply soldiers with horses and armor. The aristocrats soon realized that, as a group, they were stronger than their king. They wanted a share of the king's power.

In some city-states, aristocrats **insisted** that their king obtain the crown through an election rather than an inheritance. Then they limited a king's rule to a certain number of years. Eventually, aristocrats in many city-states overthrew the monarchy and took the power for themselves. By 800 B.C.E., most of the Greek city-states were no longer ruled by kings.

Agesilaus II was king of the city-state of Sparta.

26.3 Oligarchy: A Few People Share Power

Between about 800 and 650 B.C.E., most Greek city-states were ruled by a small group of wealthy men. These men were called oligarchs, from a Greek word that means "few." In an **oligarchy,** the ruling power is in the hands of a few people.

Most Greek oligarchs were aristocrats, rich men who had inherited land from their families. A few oligarchs were wealthy merchants.

Compared with the poor, oligarchs had very comfortable lives. They often spent their days either hunting or taking part in chariot races. In the evenings, they might host or attend parties, during which slaves and hired performers entertained guests with music, dance, and acrobatics.

Unlike the aristocrats, the poor had to work long hours in the fields. They saw the unfair differences between their difficult lives and the easy lives of the wealthy aristocrats.

To make matters worse, the oligarchs **ignored** the needs of the majority of the people. By passing laws that favored the rich, the oligarchs protected and increased their own wealth. They used the army to force others to obey these unjust laws. In some city-states, such laws forced farmers who were unable to pay their debts to sell themselves into slavery.

Under the rule of the oligarchs, the rich became richer and the poor became poorer. Hate for the oligarchs grew. Eventually, the poor turned to other leaders who promised to improve their lives. Typically, these leaders were in the army. Backed by the people, they used their soldiers to throw the oligarchs out of power.

26.4 Tyranny: One Person Takes Power by Force

During the mid-600s B.C.E., people in many Greek city-states turned to the men who had promised to change the government. These men who forced the oligarchs from power were called tyrants. In a **tyranny,** the ruling power is in the hands of one person who is not a lawful king. A tyranny is sometimes called a dictatorship. A tyrant is another name for a dictator. This form of government in ancient Greece lasted until about 500 B.C.E.

oligarchy a government in which the ruling power is in the hands of a few people

tyranny a government in which absolute ruling power is held by a person who is not a lawful king

The Granger Collection, New York

This ancient Greek bowl shows a woman playing a flute. Oligarchs in ancient Greece enjoyed musical performances at parties.

Most tyrants were forced out of power by the people. The artwork on this vase shows the killing of the Greek tyrant Hipparchus.

A tyranny is different from a monarchy in several ways. A tyrant cannot claim that the laws of the land give him the right to rule. There are no legal limits on his powers. Also, a tyrant's son does not usually inherit his father's power.

Although tyrants in ancient Greece were likely to take and keep control by force, they were often popular. Most Greek tyrants were military leaders who gained the support of the people by promising them more rights. Once they were in power, many Greek tyrants were good rulers. They made changes that improved the lives of the poor. Some canceled the debts of struggling farmers. Others were **hostile** to aristocrats and took away their land.

Some tyrants, though, did not use their power to help the people. Hippias (HIP-ee-uhs), the last tyrant to rule the city-state of Athens, is one example. Along with his brother, Hipparchus (hih-PAHR-kuhs), Hippias ruled well, at first. But then, two enemies of the brothers murdered Hipparchus. After that, Hippias ruled more harshly. He paid spies to report anyone who criticized him. His rule became more and more cruel. The people finally drove him from power. Soon after, Athens would try another form of government, one that shared power among all the people.

26.5 Democracy: All Citizens Share Power

Around 500 B.C.E., the people of Athens were the first in Greece to try governing themselves. They developed a form of government called **democracy,** or "rule by the people." In a democracy, all **citizens** share in the ruling power.

Ancient Greek democracy was different from democracies today. The government of Athens was a direct democracy. In that type of government, every citizen is allowed to vote on every issue. Unlike Athens, the United States is a representative democracy. In this type of government, people may vote for representatives who then decide issues on behalf of the people.

democracy a government in which power is held by the people, who exercise power directly or through elected representatives

citizen a person who has certain rights and duties in a city-state or nation

assembly a group of citizens, in an ancient Greek democracy, with the power to pass laws

How did direct democracy work in Athens? The city had an **assembly,** or lawmaking group. Any free man could speak in this assembly and vote on a possible new law or a proposal to go to war. Free men also ran the city's day-to-day business.

Not all Greeks believed that democracy was a good type of government. Powerful speakers sometimes persuaded ordinary citizens to vote unwisely. Often, an assembly **reversed** important decisions after just a few weeks. Problems like these led most city-states to return to earlier forms of government, such as dictatorships and oligarchies.

But the idea that people can and should rule themselves would survive. In time, the ideal of democracy would become one of the great gifts from ancient Greece to the modern world.

The painting on this piece of pottery shows Greek citizens casting votes in an election.

Chapter Summary

In this chapter, you read about four forms of government used by ancient Greek city-states.

Monarchy: One Person Inherits Power Most Greek city-states were monarchies until about 800 B.C.E. In a monarchy, one person, usually a king, holds the power. Ancient Greek kings had councils of aristocrats to help them rule.

Oligarchy: A Few People Share Power Between about 800 and 650 B.C.E., most Greek city-states were ruled by oligarchies, in which power is held by a few people. Most oligarchs were wealthy aristocrats who ignored the needs of poor people. The poor eventually turned to leaders who promised to improve their lives.

Tyranny: One Person Takes Power by Force From the mid-600s to about 500 B.C.E., many Greek city-states were ruled by tyrants. Tyranny is a form of government in which a person who is not a lawful king holds the power.

Democracy: All Citizens Share Power The people of Athens were the first Greeks to develop a form of democracy, known as a direct democracy, in which every citizen was allowed to vote on every issue.

Chapter 27

Life in Two City-States: Athens and Sparta

What were the major differences between Athens and Sparta?

27.1 Introduction

In this chapter, you will learn about two of the most important Greek city-states, Athens and Sparta. They had different forms of government. Their citizens also had very different ways of life.

Athens was a walled city near the sea. Close by, ships came and went from a busy port supporting trade. Inside the city walls of Athens, talented master potters and sculptors labored in workshops. Wealthy Athenians and their slaves strolled through the marketplace. Citizenship was enjoyed by free men. Often, the city's citizens gathered to loudly debate the issues of the day.

Sparta was located in a fertile farming area on an inland plain. No walls surrounded the city. Its buildings were simple compared with those of Athens. The same was true about the clothes worn by the people. Spartan soldiers wore stern expressions behind their bronze helmets as they marched in columns through the streets.

Even a casual visitor would have noticed that Athens and Sparta were very different. Let's take a closer look at the way people lived in these two city-states. We will examine each city's government, economy, education, and treatment of women and slaves to discover how they differed.

The art on this graceful Athenian jar shows the harvesting of olives.

◀ Fierce Spartan terra-cotta masks were used in worship.

Athens a city-state of ancient Greece that was first to have a democracy; also known as the birthplace of Western civilization; the capital of present-day Greece

Sparta a city-state of ancient Greece, known for its military oligarchy

Peloponnesus a peninsula forming the southern part of the mainland of Greece

27.2 Comparing Two City-States

Both Athens and Sparta were Greek cities, only about 150 miles apart. Yet they were as different as they could be. Why?

Part of the answer is geography. **Athens** is in central Greece, only four miles from the Aegean Sea. Its location encouraged Athenians to look outward toward the world beyond the city. Athenians liked to travel. They were eager to spread their own ideas and to learn from others. They encouraged artists from other parts of Greece to come and share their knowledge of art and architecture. Athens developed strong relationships with other city-states, and it grew large and powerful through trade. A great fleet made it the leading naval power in Greece.

In contrast, **Sparta** was more isolated. It was located on a narrow plain on a peninsula in southern Greece known as the **Peloponnesus** (pel-uh-puh-NEE-suhs). Sparta was surrounded on three sides by mountains, and its harbor was about 25 miles away. Spartans were suspicious of outsiders and their ideas. They could already grow much of what they needed in the fertile soil around Sparta. What they could not grow, Sparta's powerful armies would often take by force from their neighbors. While Athenians boasted of their art and culture, Spartans valued simplicity and strength. They taught their sons and daughters to fight, and they were proud to produce soldiers rather than artists and thinkers.

For most of their histories, these two city-states were bitter rivals. As you will see, the major differences between Athens and Sparta were reflected in almost every part of life.

The locations of the ancient city-states of Athens and Sparta help to explain their many differences.

Athens and Sparta, About 500 B.C.E.

27.3 Athenian Government

Athens became a democracy around 500 B.C.E. But unlike modern democracies, Athens allowed only free men to be citizens. All Athenian-born men over the age of 18 were considered Athenian citizens. Women and slaves were not permitted citizenship.

Every citizen could take part in the city's government. A group called the **Council of 500** met every day. Each year, the names of all citizens 30 years of age or older were collected. Then, 500 citizens were **selected** to be on the council. The council ran the daily business of government and suggested new laws.

Proposed laws had to be approved by a much larger group, the Assembly of Athens. The Assembly met on a hill every ten days. According to law, at least 6,000 citizens had to be present for a meeting to take place. If fewer people attended a meeting, slaves armed with ropes dipped in red paint would be sent out to round up more citizens. Athenian men were said to be embarrassed to appear in red-stained clothes at these meetings.

The Assembly debated issues and voted on laws proposed by the council. Every citizen had the right to speak at Assembly meetings. Some speakers were more skilled than others. Some spoke longer than others. A water clock was sometimes used to time a speaker. It worked by placing a cup filled with water above another cup. The top cup had a small hole drilled into the bottom. A speaker was permitted to talk only during the time it took for all the water in the top cup to drain into the bottom cup.

Most Athenian men enjoyed taking part in the city's democratic government. They liked to gather and debate the issues. They were proud of their freedom as Athenian citizens.

The Granger Collection, New York

Desmosthenes, an Athenian leader, speaks to the Assembly.

Council of 500 in Athens, a group of 500 citizens chosen to form a council responsible for running the day-to-day business of government

27.4 Athenian Economy

An important part of life in any community is its economy. An economy is the way in which a community or region organizes the manufacture and exchange of money, food, products, and services to meet people's needs.

Because the land around Athens did not provide enough food for all of the city's people, Athens's economy was based on trade. Athens was near the sea, and it had a good harbor. This enabled Athenians to trade with other city-states and with several foreign lands to **obtain** the goods and natural resources they needed. Athenians acquired wood from Italy and grain from Egypt. In exchange, Athenians traded honey, olive oil, silver, and beautifully painted pottery.

Athenians bought and sold goods at a huge marketplace called the **agora** (A-guh-ruh). There, merchants sold their goods from small stands. Athenians bought lettuce, onions, olive oil, and other foods. Shoppers could also buy household items such as pottery, furniture, and clay oil lamps. Most people in Athens made their clothes at home, but leather sandals and jewelry were popular items at the market. The agora was also the place where the Athenians bought and sold slaves.

Like most other city-states, Athens developed its own coins to make trade easier. Gold, silver, and bronze were some of the metals used to make coins. Athenians decorated the flat sides of their coins. One such coin had an image of the goddess Athena. The other side of the coin pictured Athena's favorite bird, the owl.

agora a marketplace in ancient Greece

Athenians shopped for food and household goods in the agora. The shopper at right on this vase is inspecting a piece of pottery.

27.5 Education in Athens

Athenian democracy depended on having well-prepared citizens. People in Athens believed that producing good citizens was the main purpose of education. Since only boys could grow up to be citizens, boys and girls were educated quite differently.

Athenians believed that a good citizen should have both an intelligent mind and a healthy body. Therefore, book learning and physical training were important. Boys were taught at home by their mothers or male slaves until the age of 6 or 7. Then, boys went to school until about the age of 14. Teachers taught reading, writing, arithmetic, and literature. Because books were rare and very expensive, students had to read subjects out loud and memorize everything. Writing tablets helped boys learn. To build boys' strength, coaches taught sports such as wrestling and gymnastics. Boys also studied music. They learned to sing and to play the lyre, a stringed instrument like a harp.

At 18, Athenian men began their military training. After their army service, wealthy young men might study with private teachers. These teachers charged high fees for lessons in debating and public speaking that would help young men become future political leaders.

Unlike boys, most girls did not learn to read or write. Instead, girls grew up helping their mothers with household tasks. They were taught to cook, clean, spin thread, and weave cloth. Some also learned ancient secret songs and dances performed for religious festivals. Girls usually married around the age of 15. Those from wealthy families married men chosen by their fathers. Girls from poor families often had more choice.

In addition to reading and writing, Athenian boys studied poetry and music. The stringed instrument near the top of this ancient Greek painting is a lyre.

27.6 Women and Slaves in Athens

Only men were considered citizens in Athens. Citizenship was not possible for women and slaves, so they had far fewer rights than free men did.

Women   Athenian women could not inherit or own much property. They could not vote or attend the Assembly. Most could not even choose their own husbands.

A few women had jobs. Some women sold goods in the market. A few very important women were priestesses. But most Athenian women had their greatest influence in the home. They spent their days managing the household and raising their children. An Athenian wife had separate rooms at home. Her responsibilities included spinning, weaving, and supervising the slaves. She never went out alone. She taught her sons until they were about 6 or 7 and ready for school. She educated her daughters until they were 15 and ready to be married.

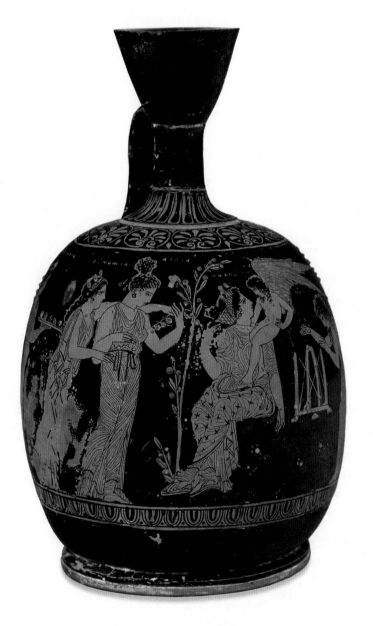

The women of Athens had their greatest influence in the home.

Slaves   There were many slaves in ancient Athens. Most Athenians who weren't poor owned at least one slave. Some people were born into slavery. Others were forced into slavery as captives of war.

Slaves performed a wide variety of jobs in Athens, including tasks that required a great deal of skill. Some ran households and taught Athenian children. A number of slaves were trained as artisans. Others worked on farms or in factories. Some slaves worked for the city as clerks.

Some slaves worked in the silver mines. They might work ten hours a day, in cramped tunnels 300 feet below the surface. They had little air to breathe and were often harshly punished if they stopped to rest.

27.7 Spartan Government

Sparta was different from Athens in almost every way, beginning with its government. While Athens was a democracy, Sparta was an oligarchy. In an oligarchy, the ruling power is in the hands of a few people.

Sparta's government—as well as Spartan society—was dedicated to military strength. Founded in the 800s B.C.E., Sparta was the leading military power in the Mediterranean area until about 370 B.C.E.

Like Athens, Sparta had an Assembly. But the important decisions were actually made by a much smaller group called the **Council of Elders**.

The Council of Elders consisted of two kings and 28 other men. The two kings inherited their position and shared equal powers. The other 28 members of the council were elected by members of the Assembly.

To be elected to the Council of Elders, men had to be at least 60 years old and from a noble family. Some scholars believe that members of the Assembly voted for candidates by shouting. Those men who received the loudest support were elected. Once elected, they served for life.

The Council of Elders held the real power in Sparta. It prepared laws for the Assembly to vote on, and it had the power to stop any laws passed by the Assembly that council members didn't like.

The Assembly in Sparta was made up of male citizens. Because the Assembly was large, it met in a spacious outdoor area away from the center of the city. The Assembly had little power. Unlike the Assembly in Athens, it did not debate issues. Members of the Assembly could only vote yes or no on laws suggested by the Council of Elders.

Council of Elders a small group of Spartans who made all the important governing decisions

The agora in Sparta was a place where people could gather. The men of Sparta men often debated government issues there.

27.8 Spartan Economy

While Athens's economy depended on trade, Sparta's economy relied on farming and on conquests of other people. Although Sparta had fertile soil, there was not enough land to provide food for everyone. When necessary, Spartans took the lands they needed from their neighbors, who were then forced to work for Sparta. Because Spartan men were expected to serve in the army until the age of 60, Sparta had to rely on slaves and noncitizens to produce the goods it lacked.

Conquered villagers became slaves, called helots. The helots were allowed to live in their own villages, but they had to give much of the food they grew to Sparta.

The Spartans also made use of a second group of people—noncitizens who were free. Noncitizens might serve in the army when needed, but they could not take part in Sparta's government. They were responsible for making such necessary items as shoes, red cloaks for the soldiers, iron tools like knives and spears, and pottery. They also conducted some trade with other city-states for goods that Sparta could not provide for itself.

In general, though, Sparta discouraged trade. The Spartans feared that contact with other city-states would lead to new ideas that might weaken the government. Trading with Sparta was already difficult because of its system of money. Rather than use coins, Spartans used heavy iron bars as money. According to legend, an ancient Spartan leader decided to use this form of money to discourage stealing. An iron bar had little value. A thief would have needed to steal a wagonload of bars to make the theft worthwhile. As you might guess, other city-states were not anxious to receive iron as payment for goods.

Spartans used iron rods like those above as money. This discouraged trade. Instead, Sparta's economy depended on farming, as shown by the figures on the cup from ancient Greece, at right.

27.9 Education in Sparta

In Sparta, the purpose of education was to produce **capable** men and women who could fight to protect the city-state. Spartans were likely to **abandon** sickly infants who might not grow up to be strong soldiers.

Spartans highly valued discipline and strength. From the age of 7, all Spartan children trained for battle. Even girls were given some military training. They learned wrestling, boxing, footracing, and gymnastics. Spartan boys lived and trained in buildings called barracks. Boys learned to read and write, but those skills were not considered as essential as military skills.

The most important Spartan goal was to be a brave soldier. Spartan boys were taught to suffer any amount of physical pain without complaining. They marched without shoes. They were not well fed; in fact, they were encouraged to steal food, as long as they did not get caught. One Spartan legend tells of a boy who was so hungry, he stole a fox to eat. But seeing his teacher coming, the boy quickly hid the fox under his cloak. The boy chose to let the fox bite him in the stomach rather than be caught stealing by his teacher.

At about the age of 20, Spartan men were given a difficult test of fitness, military ability, and leadership skills. If they passed, they became Spartan soldiers and full citizens. Even then, they continued to live in soldiers' barracks, where they ate, slept, and trained with their classmates. A man could not live at home with his wife and family until he was 30 years old. At the age of 60, Spartan men could retire from the army.

Boys in Sparta often exercised in outdoor areas.

27.10 Women and Slaves in Sparta

Spartan women lived the same simple life as Spartan men. They wore plain clothing with little decoration. They did not wear jewelry or use cosmetics or perfume. Like Spartan men, women were expected to be strong and healthy—and ready to fight when needed. A wife was expected to look after her husband's property in times of war. She also had to guard it against invaders and revolts by slaves.

Spartan women had many rights that other Greek women did not have. They were free to speak with their husbands' friends. Women could own and control their own property. They could even marry again, should their first husband be away at war for too long a time.

Spartan slaves, the helots, were people the Spartans had conquered. There were many more helots than citizens in Sparta. The Spartans treated the helots harshly, fearful that the helots would revolt.

Sometimes, the Spartan government declared war on the helots so that any slaves it thought might rebel could be legally killed. In fact, the Spartan government once asked the helots to choose their best fighters. The Spartans said that these slaves would be set free as thanks for fighting for Sparta. The helots chose two thousand men. Immediately, the Spartans killed every one of them to **eliminate** the possibility of any future helot leaders.

Despite this harsh treatment, helots did have some rights. They could marry whomever and whenever they wanted. They could pass their names on to their children. They could sell any leftover crops after giving their owner his share. Helots who saved enough money could even buy their freedom.

Like Spartan men, Spartan women were expected to be strong, healthy, and ready to fight. At left is a statue of a Spartan woman athlete.

In this chapter, you learned about Athens and Sparta, two very different city-states in ancient Greece.

Comparing Two City-States Its location near the sea made it easier for Athens to develop relationships with other city-states. Sparta's inland location and its culture made it more isolated than Athens. The people of Athens valued art, culture, and education. The people of Sparta valued strength, simplicity, and military skills.

Government Athens was a democracy, though only free men could take part in government. Sparta was primarily a military state. Its government was an oligarchy in which a few men held most of the power.

Economy The economy of Athens relied on trade with other city-states and several foreign lands. The Spartan economy relied on farming and conquest. Sparta depended on slaves and other noncitizens to provide for many of its needs.

Education In Athens, boys were educated to be good citizens. Education balanced book learning and physical training. Girls learned skills for managing the household. In Sparta, boys and girls alike were educated to protect the city-state. Spartan boys began their military training at age 7, and men served in the army until age 60.

Women and Slaves In Athens, women and slaves had far fewer rights than men had. Spartan women had more rights than other Greek women, such as owning property.

This bronze statue is of a Spartan soldier.

Chapter 28

Fighting the Persian Wars

What factors influenced the outcome of the Persian wars?

28.1 Introduction

Athens and Sparta were two very different city-states in ancient Greece. Their differences sometimes led to a distrust of each other. But between 499 and 479 B.C.E., these city-states had a common enemy—the Persian Empire.

At that time, Persia was the largest empire the world had ever seen. Its powerful kings ruled over lands in Africa, the Middle East, and Asia. During the 400s B.C.E., the Persians invaded Greece, and the Persian wars began.

To fight the Persians, the Greek city-states eventually joined together as allies. Allies are states that agree to help each other against a common enemy.

Compared with Persia, these tiny Greek city-states had much less land and far fewer people. How could they possibly turn back such a powerful invader? In this chapter, you will learn about important battles during the Persian wars and discover who won them. You will also learn about the factors that influenced the outcome of the Persian wars.

In the 400s B.C.E., the vast Persian Empire extended from the Middle East and northeastern Africa to modern-day Pakistan. The Persians wanted to claim Greece as well.

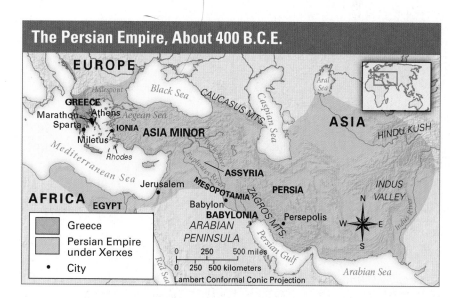

The Persian Empire, About 400 B.C.E.

Greece

Persian Empire under Xerxes

• City

On this pottery, a Greek soldier defeats a Persian soldier.

28.2 The Persian Empire and the Ionian Revolt

The Persians started out as a small group of nomads, in what is now Iran. They built a large empire by conquering neighbors. By unleashing a storm of arrows that surprised their enemies, Persian archers won many battles, often before their opponents could get close enough to use their lances, or spears.

At its height, the **Persian Empire** extended from Egypt, in North Africa, east to the Indus River in present-day Pakistan. The empire was ruled by powerful kings who conquered Mesopotamia, Asia Minor, Egypt, and parts of India and Europe.

To rule such a large area, King **Darius** (duh-RAHY-uhs), one of the greatest of all the Persian kings, divided the empire into 20 provinces. He established a system of tax collection and appointed officials to rule local areas. He allowed conquered peoples to keep their own customs and religions. King Darius ruled Persia from 522 to 486 B.C.E.

The Ionian Revolt, which began in 499 B.C.E., led to the start of the **Persian wars**. Earlier, in 546 B.C.E., the Persians had conquered the wealthy Greek settlements in Ionia, a small coastal region bordering the Aegean Sea, in Asia Minor. The Persians took the Ionians' farmland and harbors. They forced the Ionians to pay tributes, or the regular payments of goods. The Ionians also had to serve in the Persian army.

The Ionians knew that they could not defeat the Persians by themselves, so they asked mainland Greece for help. Athens sent soldiers and a small fleet of ships. Unfortunately for the Ionians, the Athenians went home after an **initial** success, leaving the small Ionian army to continue fighting alone.

In 493 B.C.E., the Persian army defeated the Ionians. To punish the Ionians for rebelling, the Persians destroyed the city of Miletus (my-LEE-tuhs).

This detail from a piece of painted pottery shows King Darius of Persia conducting a council of war.

28.3 The Battle of Marathon

After the Ionian Revolt, King Darius of Persia was determined to conquer the city-states of mainland Greece. He sent messengers to Greece to ask for presents of Greek earth and water. These gifts would be a sign that the Greeks had agreed to accept Persian rule. But the Greeks refused to hand over the tribute. Instead, they threw the Persian messengers into pits and wells. According to legend, the Greeks then shouted, "If you want Greek earth and water, help yourselves!"

Darius was furious. In 490 B.C.E., he sent about 15,000 foot soldiers and **cavalry** across the Aegean Sea by boat to Greece. The Persian army assembled on the plain of Marathon, near the city-state of Athens. (See the map at the end of this chapter.)

A brilliant Athenian general named Miltiades (mil-TAHY-uh-deez) **convinced** the Athenians that it was vital to fight the Persians at Marathon. The Athenians quickly gathered an army of about 11,000 soldiers. Although the Athenians were outnumbered, two factors helped them defeat the Persians. The first was better weapons. The Greeks' swords, spears, and armor were superior to the Persians' weapons.

The second factor that helped the Athenians defeat the Persians was military strategy. Miltiades assembled his army across a narrow valley. For several days, both sides hesitated to attack.

Finally, Miltiades decided to attack. He commanded the center portion of his army to advance. As the Persians came forward to meet them, Miltiades ordered soldiers from the left and from the right portions of his army to sweep down as well, attacking the Persians on three sides.

The Battle of Marathon, between the Greeks and the Persians, was the first battle in the Persian wars. In this painting, the Greeks are in red and the Persians are in blue. To the left is a Persian ship; to the right, the battlefield.

cavalry soldiers who ride on horses

Xerxes son of Darius, and ruler of Persia from 486 to 465 B.C.E.; eventually defeated by the Greeks at the end of the Persian wars

Hellespont a long, narrow body of water between Europe and the present-day country of Turkey

In this painting of the Battle of Thermopylae, a smaller force of Spartans (in the background) fights to hold off the huge invading Persian army (in the foreground).

It was not long before the Persian soldiers began running for their ships. Then the Greeks marched back to Athens, in time to defend the city against the Persian cavalry. The Persians lost about 6,400 soldiers. The Greeks lost 192.

A clever military strategy and better weapons helped the Athenians win a stunning victory. But this battle with the Persians marked only the beginning of the Persian wars.

28.4 The Battle of Thermopylae

After King Darius died, his son, **Xerxes** (zurk-seez), organized another attack on Greece. King Xerxes gathered a huge army of more than 180,000 soldiers. To get this army from Persia to Greece, Xerxes chose to cross the **Hellespont** (HEL-uh-spont), a narrow sea channel between Europe and Asia. (See the map at the end of this chapter.) There, he created two bridges by roping hundreds of boats together and laying wooden boards across their bows. In this way, his army was able to "walk" across the channel into Europe.

In 480 B.C.E., Xerxes marched west from the Hellespont and then turned south. His forces overwhelmed several Greek city-states. Hearing the news, Athens and Sparta decided to work together to fight the enemy. Their strategy had two parts. The Athenian **navy** would try to stop the Persian navy. In the meantime, the Spartan king, Leonidas (lee-ON-ih-duhs), would try to stop the Persian army.

The Spartans made their stand at Thermopylae (ther-MOP-uh-lee). At this site, the Persian army would have to go through a narrow pass between the mountains and the sea. Leonidas had only about 6,000 to 7,000 soldiers to stop nearly 180,000 Persians. Even so, when the Persians got to the pass, the Greeks drove them back. Then a Greek traitor showed the Persians a secret path in the mountains. The path allowed the Persians to surround the Greeks, attacking them from the front and the rear.

Leonidas knew he could only delay the attackers now. To save his army, he ordered most of his troops to escape. He prepared to fight with his remaining soldiers, including about 300 Spartans.

Legend says that the Spartans fought until every weapon was broken. Then they fought with their hands. In the end, all the Spartan soldiers were killed. The Persians' strategy had worked. By having the advantage of the path through the mountains, the Persians won the battle and could now advance to Athens.

28.5 The Battle of Salamis

In 480 B.C.E., as news of the Greek defeat at Thermopylae reached Athens, its citizens panicked. They boarded ships and sailed for nearby islands. Only a small army of Athenians was left to defend the city. Within two weeks, the Persians had burned Athens to the ground.

An Athenian navy leader, Themistocles (thuh-MIS-tuh-kleez), thought that he knew a way to defeat the Persians. He wanted to fight their navy in the narrow channels between the Greek islands and the Greek mainland. The Persians would find it hard to move their ships around to attack the Greek navy.

For his plan to work, Themistocles had to get the Persian ships into a channel near a place called Salamis (SAL-uh-mis). So he set a trap. He sent a loyal servant to Xerxes' camp, with a message saying that Themistocles wanted to change sides and join the Persians. If Xerxes attacked now, the message said, half the Greek sailors would surrender.

Believing the message, Xerxes ordered his ships to attack. They quickly sailed into the narrow waterway between Salamis and the mainland.

At the Battle of Salamis, the Greeks lured the Persians into a narrow channel, where the Greek ships rammed the Persian ships. Here, a Greek ship is about to destroy a Persian ship.

As the Persians **approached,** the Greek ships appeared to retreat. But this was another trick to draw the Persians farther into the channel. Soon, the Greeks had them surrounded. The Greeks had attached wooden rams to the front of their ships. They rammed into the Persian boats, crushing their hulls and sinking 300 ships. The Greeks lost only 40 ships.

Once again, the Greeks had defeated the mighty Persian Empire. At Salamis, the Greeks combined military strategy with their knowledge of coastal geography to influence the outcome of the battle.

28.6 The Battle of Plataea

In 480 B.C.E, after the defeat of the Persians at Salamis, Xerxes fled with some of his soldiers. He was afraid that the Greeks would reach the Hellespont first and destroy the bridges he had built. As it turned out, the bridges had already been wrecked by a bad storm. Xerxes had to ferry his men across the water by boat.

Xerxes left the rest of the Persian army in Greece, with orders to attack again in the spring. When spring arrived, the Persians approached Athens once more. The Spartans feared that the Athenians, with their city already in ruins, would surrender to Persia. But the Athenians proudly declared their "common brotherhood with the Greeks." They joined with the Spartans to fight the Persians once again.

The decisive battle took place outside the town of Plataea (pluh-TEE-uh), in 479 B.C.E. Led by the Spartans, a force of 80,000 Greek troops destroyed the Persian army. The alliance between the Athenians and Spartans was a key factor in winning the Battle of Plataea. Most importantly, the Greek victory ended the Persian wars and any future threat from the Persian Empire.

The Greeks paid a high price for their defeat of the Persians. Thousands of Greeks were dead, and the city of Athens had been destroyed. But the Athenians would soon rebuild their city and raise it to an even greater glory.

The Spartans led the fight against the Persians, in a fierce battle outside the city of Plataea. In this image, the well-armed Greek forces are to the left, and the Persian army is to the right.

Chapter Summary

In this chapter, you learned about the factors that helped the smaller Greek forces defeat the powerful Persian Empire during the Persian wars.

The Persian Empire and the Ionian Revolt The vast Persian Empire extended from Egypt east to the Indus River. In 546 B.C.E., the Persians conquered the Greek settlements of Ionia. The Ionians revolted, and in 493 B.C.E., the Persians defeated them. This triggered the first of the Persian wars in 490 B.C.E.

The Battle of Marathon In 490 B.C.E., the Persian king Darius invaded Greece. At the Battle of Marathon, better Greek weapons and strategy defeated the Persians.

The Battle of Thermopylae In 480 B.C.E., the Persian army used a secret mountain path to surround a small Spartan force and win the Battle of Thermopylae. Then the Persians advanced to Athens.

The Battle of Salamis In the same year, 480 B.C.E., the Persian king Xerxes burned down Athens. The Persian navy was later defeated at the Battle of Salamis, when Greek ships rammed and sank the Persian vessels.

The Battle of Plataea In 479 B.C.E., an army of 80,000 allied Athenian and Spartan troops destroyed the Persian army in this decisive battle that ended the Persian wars.

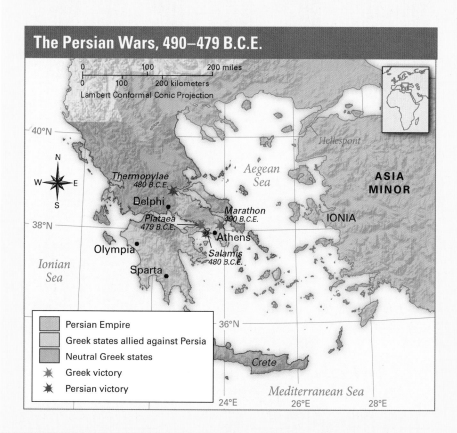

The Greek allies used military strategy, superior weapons, and knowledge of the region's geography to defeat the larger Persian forces.

Chapter 29

The Golden Age of Athens

What were the major cultural achievements of Athens?

29.1 Introduction

At the end of the Persian wars, the city of Athens was in ruins. A great Athenian named Pericles (PER-uh-kleez) inspired the people of Athens to rebuild their city. Under his leadership, Athens entered its Golden Age, a period of peace and wealth. Between 479 and 431 B.C.E., Athens was the artistic and cultural center of Greece.

Suppose that you were able to visit Athens during its Golden Age. Passing through the city's gates, you would wind your way through narrow streets to the agora, the public meeting place in the center of the city. The agora is a large square. On two sides you would see magnificent public buildings. The other two sides have covered walkways where you would meet and talk with friends about current issues. In the center of the square are market stalls with a variety of goods for sale, from all over Greece and beyond. Nearby, you would see the acropolis, a high, craggy hill crowned with great temples, rising above the city.

In this chapter, you will explore several important sites in ancient Athens. At each site, you will learn about major cultural achievements accomplished during Athens's Golden Age. You will learn about Greek religion, architecture, sculpture, drama, philosophy, and sports.

This image shows Pericles, a great leader during the Golden Age of Athens.

◄ Note the Greek columns in the ruins of the Parthenon.

Pericles a great leader who developed Athens's culture, democracy, and power during its Golden Age

Parthenon the temple built on the acropolis above Athens, honoring the goddess Athena

acropolis the hill above a Greek city, on which temples were built

29.2 Athens After the Persian Wars

During the Persian wars, the Persians burned Athens to the ground, in 480 B.C.E, after defeating the Greeks in the Battle of Thermopylae. The Greeks eventually defeated the Persians, but the wars left Athens in ruins.

Pericles, Leader of Athens From about 460 to 429 B.C.E., Pericles was the leader of Athens's government. One of his chief contributions was to direct the rebuilding of the city. Pericles promoted constructing many public and religious buildings, including the Parthenon, the most famous temple in Athens.

Pericles believed that Athens was a model—in culture and in government—for all the Greek city-states. While the leader of Athens, he encouraged creativity in all of the arts, including music and drama. He was a strong supporter of democracy and made **reforms** to encourage its growth. He believed that all citizens had an equal right to participate in government. Under Pericles' leadership, Athens paid the salaries of men who held public office. This enabled poor men, who would otherwise have been unable to afford to leave their jobs and farms, the chance to serve in government positions.

A City of Contrasts Ancient Athens was a city of great contrasts. Many people lived in small, uncomfortable houses that lined narrow streets. Yet the city's public spaces and buildings were large and stately.

Most homes in Athens were one story high and made of mud bricks. The homes of poor families were very simple. The wealthier people had larger houses with rooms built around a central courtyard. Athenian houses had few windows, so homes were usually lit by oil lamps.

The public spaces and buildings were the pride of Athens. The Athenians built large government buildings around the agora. These buildings were made of stone. On the acropolis, the hill above the city, the Athenians built magnificent temples as earthly homes for their gods and goddesses.

In this engraving, Pericles, seated, reviews building plans for the Parthenon, under construction in the background.

Zeus Ruler of the gods

Hera Wife of Zeus; goddess of marriage

Poseidon Brother of Zeus; god of the sea

Hestia Sister of Zeus; goddess of the hearth (the family fire)

Demeter Sister of Zeus; goddess of agriculture

Ares Son of Zeus; god of war

Athena Daughter of Zeus; goddess of wisdom and war

Apollo Son of Zeus; god of the sun, poetry, and music

Artemis Daughter of Zeus; goddess of the moon and the hunt

Hephaestus Son of Zeus; god of fire and metalworkers

Aphrodite Daughter of Zeus; goddess of love and beauty

Hermes Son of Zeus; messenger of the gods and god of travel

This Parthenon frieze shows Poseidon, Apollo, and Artemis.

29.3 Greek Religion

The ancient Greeks thought that the gods and goddesses they worshipped looked and often acted like humans, but did not age and die. Every city-state honored a god or goddess, who was thought to give its people special protection. For example, Athens was named for the goddess Athena.

The Greeks believed that each god or goddess had power over a particular area of life. Athena was the goddess of war and wisdom. The Greeks placed a colossal (huge) statue of her inside the Parthenon, the temple they built in her honor.

Another famous temple was in the city of Delphi. This temple was **dedicated** to the god Apollo. People would visit the temple to ask Apollo for advice. A priestess, called the oracle of Delphi, would answer their questions by going into a trance. The words spoken by the priestess were thought to come from Apollo.

The Greeks told **myths,** or stories, about the gods. According to these stories, the home of the gods was Mount Olympus, a real mountain in Greece. Twelve of the gods and goddesses were particularly important. They are often called the Olympian gods.

The Olympian gods and goddesses were part of everyday life in ancient Greece. For example, before setting out on journeys by land or sea, the Greeks would ask them for help. The Greeks dedicated their festivals and sporting events to their deities. Greek artists decorated the temples with images of them.

myth a traditional story that helps explain a culture's beliefs

29.4 Greek Architecture

Temples are good examples of the Greeks' talent for architecture. The Greeks built their temples, not as places in which to worship, but as beautiful dwelling places for the gods and goddesses. Religious ceremonies were **conducted** outside.

The temples show the importance of balance and order in the Greeks' idea of beauty. Temples were built with rows of tall **columns**. The Greeks used three styles of columns. The Doric column was the simplest. It had no base and got slimmer toward the top. The Ionic column was thinner. It sat on a base and had scrolls carved into the top. The Corinthian column was the most complex, with carvings that looked like leaves at the top.

Athenians built three temples on the acropolis to honor Athena. As you have read, one of these was the Parthenon. One of the most beautiful temples in ancient Greece, the Parthenon was built on a long rectangular platform. There were 8 columns across both the front and the back, and 17 along each side. The roof was slanted, creating triangles, called pediments, at the front and back of the building. Above the columns was a band of sculptures called a frieze (freez). The sculptures themselves are called metopes (MEH-tuh-pees).

Features of Greek architecture seen in the Parthenon above include pediments, friezes, and three kinds of columns. Below, from left to right, are Doric columns, Ionic columns with scrolled tops, and decorative Corinthian columns.

There were many different sizes of Greek temples, but their basic shape was similar. Most had a main room with a statue of the temple's god or goddess. The Parthenon, for example, had a magnificent statue of Athena that stood 30 feet high. Made of wood, the statue was covered with ivory to make it more lifelike. Then it was dressed in clothes and decorated with gold. Like the temple itself, the statue expressed both the Greeks' love of beauty and their awe of the gods.

29.5 Greek Sculpture

The statue of Athena in the Parthenon was a wonderful example of another important Greek art: sculpture. Sculptors in Athens often set up a workshop near the site where the finished statue would be placed. Sculptor apprentices first made a life-size clay model supported by wooden or metal frames. The general outline of the statue was then roughed out in marble. A master sculptor added details and finishing touches.

Greek statues were colorful. Metalworkers attached appropriate bronze pieces to the statue, like spears and shields. Painters applied wax and bright colors to a statue's hair, lips, clothes, and headdress.

Creating lifelike statues was one of the great achievements of Greek sculptors. The earliest Greek statues had been influenced by Egyptian styles. Like the Egyptians, the Greeks created larger-than-life figures that faced front, with their arms held stiffly at their sides. Later Greek sculptors made more realistic statues in natural poses, showing **muscles**, hair, and clothing in much greater detail.

One of the most famous Athenian sculptors was a man named Phidias (FIH-dee-uhs). He designed the figures that line the frieze on the Parthenon. He also sculpted the statue of Athena that stood inside the temple. The statue carried a shield of gold, with carvings of two faces—those of the great Athenian leader Pericles and of Phidias himself.

The sculptor Phidias created the huge statue of Athena that stood inside the Parthenon. Above is a replica completed in 1990 by an American artist.

The ruins of the Theater of Dionysus are still visible in Athens. Built in the mid-300s B.C.E., it could hold as many as 17,000 spectators.

drama the art of writing, acting in, and producing plays

29.6 Greek Drama

In addition to architecture and sculpture, the ancient Greeks excelled in **drama,** the art of the theater. Going to the theater was a regular part of Athenian life. The Theater of Dionysus (dy-uh-NIE-suhs), in Athens, could hold thousands of people.

Dionysus was the god of merriment. Greek plays grew out of the songs and dances that the Greeks performed at harvest time to honor him. As Greek playwrights developed their art, they began to write plays that told stories. The plays included a few main characters and a chorus. The chorus was a group of men who recited lines that commented on the actions of the main characters. The words spoken by the chorus helped explain and expand on the story.

There were no women actors in ancient Greece. Men played all the characters, both male and female. That was one reason actors wore masks. The masks also showed the audience whether a character was happy or sad.

Plays were staged in open-air theaters built into the sides of hills. A Greek theater was shaped like a bowl so that everyone could hear what was said. The seats rose in a semicircle around a stage at the bottom of the bowl. Scenery was painted on canvas and hung behind the actors.

Plays were often a form of competition that could last for days. Judges chose winners in four categories: tragic playwright, comic playwright, leading tragic actor, and leading comic actor. The winning writers and actors were crowned with olive leaves and given prizes such as figs.

29.7 Greek Philosophy

Athenians, like other Greeks, loved to talk and argue. In the sheltered spaces to one side of the agora, men often gathered to discuss the world around them. They talked about nature, often trading ideas about the natural world, such as what it was made of and how it worked. They also talked about things they couldn't see, such as the meaning of life, justice, truth, and beauty. This kind of thinking is called philosophy, which means "the love of wisdom."

One of the greatest philosophers in Athens was a man named **Socrates** (SAH-kruh-teez). Socrates encouraged people to question the very things they thought they knew. He taught others by asking them such questions as, *What makes a good life? What is truth? How do you know?* In this way he led his students to think about their beliefs.

Even in Athens, where people loved new ideas, this constant questioning got Socrates into trouble. His enemies accused him of not honoring the gods and of leading young people into error and disloyalty. In 399 B.C.E., Socrates was brought to trial for these crimes. In defending himself, Socrates said that he was the wisest man in Greece because he recognized how little he knew.

Socrates a great ancient Greek philosopher who taught by asking his students thought-provoking questions

Socrates calmly drank poison after being sentenced to death by an Athenian jury.

The jury found Socrates guilty and sentenced him to death. Friends encouraged him to escape from Athens, but Socrates insisted on honoring the law. He died by drinking hemlock, the juice of a poisonous plant.

The example of Socrates inspired many other important Greek thinkers, especially his student Plato (PLAY-toh). In turn, Plato taught the great philosopher, Aristotle (ar-uh-STOT-uhl).

29.8 Greek Sports

The Greeks' interest in philosophy shows how much they valued the mind. Their love of many kinds of sports shows that they also prized physical fitness.

The Greeks often held athletic events to honor their gods and goddesses. In Athens, games were held as part of a festival called the Panathenaea (pan-ath-uh-NEE-uh), which honored the goddess Athena. The high point of the festival was the procession, or solemn parade. The Athenians attached a new robe, as a gift for the statue of Athena, to the mast of a ship and pulled it through the city to the temple.

The **Panathenaic Games** included many events. There were horse races and chariot races, including one event in which men jumped on and off a moving chariot. Men also competed in footraces. In one race, men ran in their armor.

The games also included combat sports, such as boxing and wrestling. In an event called the *pancratium,* men were allowed to punch, kick, and even choke each other. The event ended when one fighter surrendered, lost consciousness, or died.

Another set of games, to honor the god Zeus, was played every four years at Olympia. Called the Olympics, these games were so important to the Greeks that they would call a truce from all wars so athletes could travel safely to the games.

A piece of pottery like this may have been awarded to the winner of a footrace at the Panathenaic Games.

> **Panathenaic Games** athletic events, including horse races and chariot races, held as part of the festival called Panathenaea, honoring the goddess Athena

In this chapter, you explored major achievements in ancient Greek culture during the Golden Age of Athens.

Athens After the Persian Wars Pericles was a great leader who promoted both the rebuilding of Athens and the growth of Greek culture and democracy.

Greek Religion The Greek worship of gods and goddesses was part of everyday life. Athens was named for the goddess Athena. The Parthenon honored her. The temple at Delphi honored the god Apollo. The Greeks told myths, or stories, about their many gods.

Greek Architecture and Sculpture The temples on the acropolis in Athens were examples of the Greek talent for architecture. The lifelike marble statues made in workshops displayed the art of sculpture.

Greek Drama and Philosophy Athenians enjoyed dramas staged in large open-air theaters. Only male actors performed. The Greeks also enjoyed discussing philosophy. Socrates was one of the greatest philosophers in Athens.

Greek Sports The Greeks competed in athletic events at the Panathenaic Games and the Olympics. Events included races and combat sports.

This present-day photograph shows the ruins of the Parthenon as they stand today, at the top of the acropolis in Athens.

Chapter 30

Alexander the Great and His Empire

How did Alexander build his empire?

30.1 Introduction

As the power of Athens grew, other city-states, especially Sparta, became jealous and fearful. Athens and Sparta had mistrusted each other for a long time. After joining together to defeat the Persians, they soon began to quarrel.

In 431 B.C.E., Sparta declared war on Athens. Many of the smaller city-states were drawn into the fight. This conflict is called the Peloponnesian (pel-uh-puh-NEE-zhuhn) War. The war continued for 27 years.

While the city-states were at war, a new threat was growing to the north, in a kingdom called Macedonia (mas-ih-DOH-nee-uh). A Macedonian king, Philip II, realized that constant wars had left the Greeks divided and weak. He seized the chance and brought Greece under his control.

Philip's son, Alexander, was even more ambitious. Today, he is known as Alexander the Great. Alexander extended Macedonian rule over a vast area. In time, his power reached from Macedonia and Greece, through Central Asia, all the way to parts of India.

In this chapter, you will learn how Alexander built and tried to rule this vast empire. How did he plan to unite so many different peoples under his rule?

This sculpture honors the powerful leader Alexander the Great.

◀ A detail of a Roman mosaic shows Alexander the Great in battle.

Peloponnesian War (431 to 404 B.C.E.) the war fought between Athens and Sparta that involved other city-states

Macedonia an ancient kingdom located north of Greece

Aristotle a great Greek philosopher; a tutor of Alexander the Great; and the author of works on logic, science, and politics

30.2 The Peloponnesian War and the Rise of Macedonia

In 431 B.C.E., the quarrel between Athens and Sparta grew into a conflict called the **Peloponnesian War**. The name comes from the Peloponnesus, the peninsula that extends south from mainland Greece. Sparta was located here. Other city-states were drawn into the war as **allies** of either Athens or Sparta.

The war lasted for 27 years, from 431 to 404 B.C.E. Sparta won. It became the most powerful Greek city-state, until it was defeated by Thebes.

While the Greek city-states fought one another, **Macedonia** grew stronger. For a long while, the Macedonians had lived in scattered tribes. Then King Philip II took the throne. He unified the warlike tribes of the north and created a well-trained army.

Philip then looked south to mainland Greece. Years of war had left the Greeks divided and weak. Philip used this weakness.

By 338 B.C.E., King Philip had conquered most of mainland Greece. He let the Greek city-states keep many freedoms. But Philip now ruled them. Never again would a Greek city-state become a great power.

Philip wanted to attack Persia next, but, in 336 B.C.E., he was murdered. His son, Alexander, was the new Macedonian king.

30.3 Alexander Creates an Empire

Alexander was only 20 years old when he became king. But he was well prepared for his new duties. He had been tutored by **Aristotle** (ar-uh-STOT-uhl), the famous Greek philosopher. Aristotle had taught him public speaking, science, and philosophy. He had also taught Alexander to **appreciate** Greek culture.

As king, Alexander put down a rebellion by some of the Greek city-states. Then he focused on the east. Alexander wanted to carry out his father's plan to invade Persia. Fighting Persia would help to unite the Greeks by giving them a common enemy. And a victory over Persia would add to Alexander's wealth.

In 334 B.C.E., Alexander, with a united Macedonian and Greek army, invaded Asia Minor. His plan was to create an empire by using a strategy of both terror and kindness. The towns and cities that resisted him would be burned to the ground, and their people sold into slavery. The towns and cities that surrendered to him would keep their government officials, and Alexander would help them rebuild damaged property.

Coins in ancient Greece were often decorated with portraits of important leaders. This coin shows King Philip on horseback.

30.4 Alexander's Plan to Unite His Empire

In a short time, Alexander extended his rule over Asia Minor, Egypt, and Central Asia. Still not satisfied, he pushed on. He marched to the farthest limit of the Persian Empire. His armies even reached western India.

Many leaders in history have dreamed of ruling the world. Alexander came as close as anyone to fulfilling that dream. He brought much of the known world at that time under his rule. His achievements gave him the name **Alexander the Great**.

Alexander was a bold and brilliant general, but his many conquests created new challenges. How could he control such a large territory? And how could he unite so many different peoples and cultures?

Alexander wanted all the people he conquered to accept him as their ruler. He also intended to spread Greek culture. But he did not want to destroy the local **customs** and traditions of the various cultures across his empire. His goal was to bring the different peoples of these many cultures together under a single government.

Alexander created a plan to achieve his goals. The plan had three key parts. First, he would spread Greek culture and ideas. Second, he would use religion to inspire loyalty. Third, he would show respect for the cultures he had conquered, and even adopt some of their customs. Let's look at each part of his plan.

Alexander the Great the ruler of a vast empire that extended from Macedonia to India in the 300s B.C.E.

custom a practice that is common to people of a particular group or region

Alexander the Great ruled a vast empire. It extended from his home in Macedonia to western India.

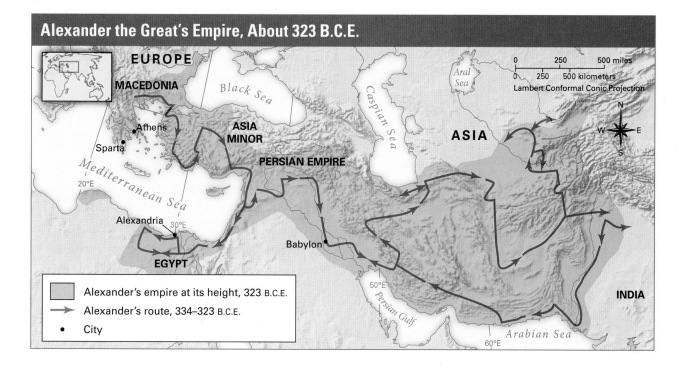

Alexander the Great's Empire, About 323 B.C.E.

EUROPE
MACEDONIA
Black Sea
Athens
Sparta
ASIA MINOR
Mediterranean Sea
20°E
Alexandria
30°E
PERSIAN EMPIRE
Caspian Sea
Babylon
EGYPT
50°E
Persian Gulf
60°E
Aral Sea
ASIA
0   250   500 miles
0   250   500 kilometers
Lambert Conformal Conic Projection
N W E S
INDIA
Arabian Sea

Alexander's empire at its height, 323 B.C.E.
Alexander's route, 334–323 B.C.E.
City

This mosaic, or tile art, from a church floor shows the city of Alexandria in Egypt.

30.5 How Alexander Spread Greek Ideas

Alexander deeply admired Greek culture and wanted to spread Greek ideas throughout his empire. He hoped that Greek ideas, customs, and traditions would blend with the diverse cultures of the people he had conquered.

Alexander thought that the building of Greek-style cities would be one way to accomplish his goal. He established many cities in different parts of the empire. Like the cities in Greece, they had marketplaces, temples, and theaters.

People from Greece flocked to settle in Alexander's cities. They brought with them their Greek laws, art, and literature. Alexander insisted that local soldiers and government officials speak only Greek.

The most famous of the new cities was **Alexandria**. Founded by Alexander in 332 B.C.E., Alexandria was located in Egypt, near the sea. Alexandria was designed in a grid of intersecting wide and narrow streets. It had many Greek features, including a marketplace, a university, a gymnasium, and a theater. The city also boasted law courts and a library. There was even a temple dedicated to Poseidon (puh-SY-din), the Greek god of the sea.

In time, the city of Alexandria became one of the ancient world's most important centers of trade and learning. Its library contained more than half a million books. This was one of the largest libraries in the world at that time.

Alexandria a city in Egypt, founded in 332 B.C.E. by Alexander the Great; also, an ancient center of learning

30.6 How Alexander Used Religion

The second part of Alexander's plan—to inspire loyalty among his followers and the people he had conquered—**involved** religion. Alexander used religion in two ways.

First, he honored Egyptian and Persian gods, with the same respect he paid to Greek gods. To show his respect, he visited oracle sites, made sacrifices, and had temples built to honor these gods. On one occasion, he visited the oracle site of the Egyptian god Ammon. When he arrived, an Egyptian priest welcomed him as "God's son." The priest's words helped Alexander gain the loyalty of the Egyptian people.

Second, Alexander promoted the idea that he himself was a god. After his visit to the Egyptian oracle, he began wearing a crown with two ram's horns. This crown looked much like the sacred headdress of Ammon. Seeing Alexander wearing the crown encouraged the Egyptians to accept him as a god.

Alexander spread the story of the Egyptian priest's greeting throughout the empire. Later on, he also **required** all Greeks to accept him as the son of Zeus.

On the silver coin above is one of the earliest-known images of Alexander the Great. The ram's horn is a sign that he is a god. The engraving below depicts a meeting between Alexander, kneeling in respect, and a Jewish high priest.

His marriage to the daughter of King Darius III of Persia was a symbol of Alexander's efforts to blend cultures in his empire.

30.7 How Alexander Adopted the Ways of Conquered Cultures

The third part of Alexander's plan was to show respect for the cultural practices of the people he had conquered. He did this by adopting some of these practices himself.

For example, in Persia, he adopted the Persian system of government. He allowed Persian governors to run the day-to-day business of their lands. However, he was careful to appoint Macedonians to head the army. He also made sure his own people controlled the taxes that were collected.

Alexander also borrowed Persian customs. He began wearing decorative Persian-style clothing. He received official visitors in a luxurious tent, much as a Persian king would have done. The tent was supported by tall columns. The columns were covered in gold and silver and decorated with precious stones.

Alexander demanded that each of his visitors greet him according to Persian custom. A visitor had to kneel in front of the throne and bend over until his head touched the ground. Alexander would then raise the visitor to his feet, kiss him, and address him as "kinsman."

Finally, Alexander encouraged marriage between the people of Macedonia and Persia. He himself married the eldest daughter of Darius III, a Persian king he had defeated.

Historians are not sure why Alexander behaved in these ways. Some think that by adopting the customs of his former enemies, Alexander was simply trying to be a more acceptable ruler. Other historians think that he truly considered all of the peoples he conquered to be equal to the Greeks and the Macedonians.

30.8 Alexander's Empire Crumbles

By 324 B.C.E., Alexander's armies were in northern India. After ten years of fighting, the exhausted soldiers refused to go on. **Reluctantly,** Alexander returned to Babylon, in Persia. In 323 B.C.E, he died at the age of 33.

After his death, Alexander's empire fell apart. Settlers left the cities he had built, and the cities fell into ruin. His generals fought to control the empire. Eventually, his land was divided into three kingdoms. Egypt became one kingdom. Syria in the Middle East was the second kingdom. Macedonia and Greece made a third kingdom.

Alexander had spread Greek ideas throughout a vast area. In the centuries to come, Greek power would slowly fade away. But Greek culture would continue to influence the lands that Alexander had once ruled.

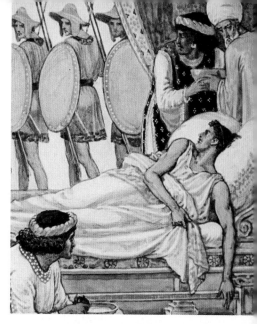

Alexander the Great died at the age of 33, leaving behind an empire that soon crumbled.

Chapter Summary

In this chapter, you learned how Alexander the Great built and ruled his empire.

The Peloponnesian War and the Rise of Macedonia Athens and Sparta and their allies fought one another in the Peloponnesian War, lasting from 431 to 404 B.C.E. Then, King Philip II of Macedonia took advantage of the Greeks' weakness after years of warfare and conquered most of Greece.

Alexander Creates and Unites an Empire Alexander, son of Philip, became king. Educated by the Greek philosopher Aristotle, Alexander enlarged his empire by invading Asia Minor. He conquered Persia, Egypt, Central Asia, and western India. He planned to unite his vast empire by spreading Greek culture, by inspiring loyalty through religion, and by adopting some of the customs of conquered peoples.

Spreading Greek Ideas, Using Religion, and Adopting the Ways of Conquered Cultures Alexander built Greek-style cities, such as Alexandria, in Egypt. Greeks settled in these cities and brought their laws and arts. Alexander made Egyptian and Persian gods equal to Greek gods. He also encouraged the idea that he himself was a god. He adopted customs from the cultures of the people he had conquered, such as the Persian system of government.

Alexander's Empire Crumbles After Alexander's death in 323 B.C.E., his generals fought among themselves for control of the empire. Settlers left the cities Alexander had built. The empire divided into three kingdoms. But the Greek culture that he had spread would continue to influence the lands Alexander had ruled.

Chapter 31

The Legacy of Ancient Greece

How did ancient Greece contribute to the modern world?

31.1 Introduction

In this chapter, you will explore the advances made by the ancient Greeks in many aspects of their civilization. You will also discover how these achievements continue to affect us today.

There is an ancient story, still told today, about a Greek thinker named Archimedes (ar-kuh-MEE-deez), who climbed into a bath filled to the top with water. As the water overflowed onto the floor, he realized something. The **volume** of his body could be measured by the amount of water that left the tub. "Eureka!" Archimedes is said to have shouted. In Greek this means, "I have found it!" By being curious and observing events closely, Archimedes had discovered an interesting fact about the natural world.

Curiosity and careful observation are important in the study of science. This way of thinking is one of the gifts that we have received from the ancient Greeks. The Greeks left us valuable ideas in many other fields as well.

Not only have important ideas come from the Greeks, but so have many of the words we use to describe those ideas. The world of the ancient Greeks may seem far away, but it is as close as the thoughts we think and the words we speak. Let's look at Greek contributions to our lives in the areas of language, government, medicine, mathematics and science, architecture, entertainment, and sports.

Note the Greek architectural features—columns, pediment, and frieze—in the ruins of an ancient Greek temple in Sicily, Italy.

◀ Greek architecture influenced the columns of the U.S. Capitol.

Herodotus is known as the "father of history." He wrote a history of the wars between the Greeks and the Persians.

31.2 Literature and History

Did you know that the word *alphabet* comes from the first two letters of the Greek alphabet, *alpha* and *beta*? Our alphabet grew out of the one that ancient Greeks used. In addition, many English words have Greek roots. For example, the word *telephone* is made up of the Greek words *tel,* meaning "far off," and *phone,* meaning "voice."

Even the way we write sentences comes from the language of ancient Greece. The rules of English grammar, punctuation, and paragraphing are all based on Greek writing. And don't forget literature. The Greeks created drama, including both tragedy and comedy. They also developed historical writing. Modern historians follow in the footsteps of great Greek writers such as Herodotus (huh-ROD-uh-tuhs), known as the "father of history," and Thucydides (thoo-SID-ih-deez).

Thucydides was one of the greatest historians of ancient Greece. He wrote *History of the Peloponnesian War,* an account of the conflict between Athens and Sparta in the 400s B.C.E. Thucydides himself took part in the war, serving in the Athenian army. Although he was an eyewitness to history, he was careful to present facts rather than his own viewpoint or opinion. He is remembered today as one of the founders of historical writing.

31.3 Government

Democratic government was a Greek idea. Democracy, or rule by the people, began in Athens. The practice of having citizens serve on juries also began in Greece.

Democratic government in the United States has roots in ancient Greece. There are a number of important differences, however, between American democracy and ancient Greek democracy. For example, in Athens, all citizens debated and voted on every issue. But in the United States, citizens elect representatives to speak for them and make laws. Another difference is that only native-born men could be citizens in Athens. But in the United States, all men and women born in this country are U.S. citizens, and people from other countries can become citizens, too.

Still, the basic **principles** of democracy were developed by the ancient Greeks. Athenians were proud that their government allowed citizens to control their own destiny. This idea remains the basis of democracy today.

Hippocrates emphasized principles of medicine, including ethical conduct. At left, a vase painting shows a Greek doctor treating a patient.

31.4 Medicine

For centuries, the Greeks believed that gods and goddesses controlled natural events, including health and sickness. In fact, the earliest Greeks thought that illnesses and accidents were punishments sent by the gods. Ancient Greeks didn't know about the natural causes of disease and healing.

A Greek man named Hippocrates (hih-POK-ruh-teez) changed the way people thought about health and medicine. Hippocrates is often called the "father of medicine." He brought a scientific way of thinking to his work as a doctor. Hippocrates believed that diseases had natural causes. He taught his students to carefully observe their patients and write down what they saw.

Even more important, Hippocrates established principles of medicine that are still followed. Today, people who become doctors take the Hippocratic Oath, based on these ideas of ethical behavior. Doctors promise to be honest, to preserve life, and to keep information about their patients private.

The Greeks loved to participate in and watch competitions in sports. Their interest in athletics gave them some knowledge about how the human body moves. But their understanding of the body was limited, partly because it was forbidden to look inside the body to see how it worked. The early Greeks believed that cutting open a human body offended the gods. As these beliefs changed over time, the Greeks made new discoveries.

Several centuries after Hippocrates, Greek **medical** students were able to name and describe organs inside the body. They discovered that the heart was a pump that sent blood flowing throughout the body. They also learned that the brain was the center of the nervous system.

31.5 Mathematics

The Greeks loved reasoning, or looking for logical answers to nature's mysteries. Greek scientists often found those answers in the field of mathematics.

One such scientist, Pythagoras (pih-THAG-er-uhs), believed that numbers were the key to understanding nature. He started a school where students developed mathematical **theories**.

geometry the branch of mathematics involving points, lines, planes, and figures

Like many Greeks, Pythagoras was especially fascinated by **geometry**. *Geometry* comes from a Greek word that means "to measure land." Geometry began as a system for measuring areas of land. The Egyptians could also measure shapes and spaces, but the Greeks created new and improved methods. Using geometry, they could figure out problems such as how much seed to buy for planting a field or how to lay out a city.

Another famous Greek mathematician was Euclid (YOO-klid). His geometry textbook has been used as the basis for the teaching of geometry for more than 2,000 years.

Greek culture produced the first woman to earn fame as a mathematician, Hypatia (hie-PAY-shuh). Born in Egypt in about 370 C.E., she taught Greek philosophy and mathematics in the city of Alexandria.

31.6 Astronomy

Astronomy comes from the Greek word for "star." Astronomy is the scientific study of outer space. Ancient Greeks were pioneers in this field.

People in all civilizations observed the sun, moon, and stars. But a Greek scientist named Aristarchus (ayr-uh-STAHR-kuhs) was the first person to suggest that Earth moves around the sun. This idea upset many Greeks who believed that Earth was the center of the universe.

Another Greek, Hipparchus (hih-PAHR-kuhs), is often called one of the greatest scientists of the ancient world. He studied and named more than 850 stars. He also figured out how to estimate the distances from Earth to both the sun and the moon. His theories allowed later scientists to **accurately** predict eclipses of the moon.

Hypatia was a highly respected philosopher and mathematician in Alexandria, Egypt.

31.7 Geography

The study of geography has roots in ancient Greece. The word *geography* comes from Greek words that mean "writing about the earth." The Greek historian Herodotus created the first map of the known world, in about 450 B.C.E. To gather the information for his map, Herodotus asked geographic questions. He found some answers to his questions by traveling and talking with other travelers. He organized the information by displaying it on a map.

Another great geographer of ancient times was Ptolemy (TAH-luh-mee), a Greek scientist who lived in Alexandria, Egypt. He wrote a book called *Geographia* that listed about 8,000 places around the world. His book contained maps that showed how to represent the curve of Earth on a flat surface.

Ptolemy also designed a system of lines drawn on a map called **latitude** and **longitude**. With this system, he recorded the specific locations for the thousands of places he listed in his book. Centuries later, Arab scholars would further develop the study of geography, especially in the field of mapmaking.

31.8 Biology

Ancient Greeks developed the science of **biology**. About 600 B.C.E., Greek thinkers believed each event has a cause and an effect. They used this idea to study the natural world.

Curiosity led Greeks to study plants and animals. Scientists learned about the anatomy, or body structure, of animals and humans. This knowledge helped doctors in their medical studies.

The Greeks identified plants and also named their parts. The Greeks learned that plants reproduce by spreading seeds. Greek doctors used plants, such as herbs, as medicines and for pain.

A 15th-century mapmaker created this replica of Ptolemy's map of the world. Compare it with a modern world map. Can you find Africa?

latitude a measure of how far north or south a place on Earth is measured from the equator

longitude a measure of how far east or west a place on Earth is from an imaginary line that runs between the North and South Poles

biology the study of living things; their structure, growth, and function

Greek actors wore masks that showed which character they were playing.

The Greek philosopher Aristotle was fascinated by living things. He collected information about many types of animals and plants. Then he organized animals into groups, such as "those with backbones" and "those without backbones." He divided plants into such groups as "herbs," "shrubs," and "trees." The way we classify, or group, animals and plants today reflects the work of Aristotle.

31.9 Architecture

The word *architecture* comes from a Greek word that means "master builder." Greek architecture was one of the achievements of the Golden Age of Athens. One feature was the way that the Greeks used columns to make their temples look balanced and stately. Another feature was the pediments, the triangular shapes where roof lines come together. And a third architectural feature was the decorated bands called friezes.

Today, Greek styles are still used in many buildings. They are common in public structures such as government buildings, schools, churches, libraries, and museums. The U.S. Capitol has elements of Greek architecture, such as columns and pediments. The building that houses the U.S. Supreme Court is another example of a public structure inspired by Greek architecture.

You can also see Greek building styles in homes and stores. For example, many houses have covered porches. The design of these porches reflects a feature of Greek architecture called a stoa. This is a covered line of columns.

31.10 Theater

The word *theater* comes from a Greek word that means "a viewing place." Greek theaters were built as semicircles. The rows of seats rose steeply from the stage so that everyone in the audience could see and hear. These ideas are used in theaters built today.

The Greeks even invented special effects. For example, they used hoists to lift actors off the stage, so that they appeared to be flying. They also created scenery that revolved, or turned. Revolving the scenery let them quickly change where the action in a play was taking place. Perhaps the greatest Greek contributions to the theater are their stories and plays. Writers throughout the ages have been inspired by Greek myths and stories. Greek dramas are still performed all over the world.

31.11 Sports

Many modern sports trace their roots back to ancient Greece. The most famous example is the Olympic Games.

The first Olympics were held in 776 B.C.E. to honor the Greek god Zeus. Today's Olympic Games reflect ancient Greek customs. During the opening ceremony, an athlete lights the Olympic flame. This custom comes from the time in ancient Greece when the first Olympic athletes lit a fire on the altar of Zeus.

Many modern Olympic events grew out of Greek contests. One example is the pentathlon. *Pentathlon* is a Greek word that means "five contests." The Greek pentathlon included the footrace, discus throw, long jump, javelin throw, and wrestling. The Greeks invented this event as a test of all-around athletic skill. Although the five contests are different today, the pentathlon is still an Olympic event.

Two Chinese athletes take part in the torch relay to light the flame for the 2008 Beijing Olympics.

Chapter Summary

In this chapter, you learned how ancient Greek civilization affects today's world.

Literature, History, and Government The modern alphabet, English grammar, drama and historical writing, and democratic government all trace their roots to the ancient Greeks.

Medicine Hippocrates applied scientific thinking to medicine and established a code of ethics used by doctors today. Centuries later, Greek medical students made discoveries about the heart and the brain.

Mathematics Pythagoras and Euclid made important advances in geometry that are still taught today.

Astronomy and Geography Greek scientists suggested that Earth moves around the sun. They named hundreds of stars and estimated the distances from Earth to both the sun and the moon. Greeks created the first maps and the system of latitude and longitude that is still used today to find locations on Earth.

Biology Greeks developed the scientific study of plants, animals, and humans called biology. The way we classify animals and plants is based on the work of Aristotle.

Architecture, Theater, and Sports Greek building styles, including columns and pediments, are seen today in public and private structures. Greek plays, stories, and myths are read today. Even the Olympic Games first began in ancient Greece.

This is the original marble statue Peplos Kore as she looks today in the Acropolis Museum in Athens. The statue was created around 530 B.C.E.

Painting the Gods

Because the ancient Greeks left behind stone images of their deities, we can see how this ancient culture pictured its gods and goddesses. Classical Greek sculpture is so realistic, the figures so distinct, it is easy to assume that we are seeing these sculptures as they appeared in their original form. But now, experts in the fields of art and archaeology are proving us wrong. How is a German archaeologist challenging our ideas about ancient art? What did these statues actually look like when they were created?

The colors are dazzling. The young woman is wearing a long yellow-gold dress with a detailed design of animals in shades of red, green, and blue. Her hair hangs down in auburn braids. Her red lips are curved in an inviting smile.

The woman (or is she a goddess?) is called the Peplos Kore. A *kore* is a type of ancient Greek statue depicting a female figure. This one was carved in marble by an unknown artist, around 530 B.C.E. She once stood on the acropolis, the hill above Athens, among the temples the Athenians built to honor their gods. She is still in Athens today, in the Acropolis Museum. But if you look for her there, you won't see her in her richly colored dress. The original statue is now plain white marble. The painted copy is made of plastic. It is a creation of two German archaeologists, Vinzenz Brinkmann and his wife, Ulrike Koch-Brinkmann.

People have viewed white marble Greek sculpture for 500 years or more. But Vinzenz Brinkmann believes his brightly colored copies are more similar to what the ancient Greeks created. What's more, art historians think he's right!

Why White Marble?

Few Greek sculptures have survived from ancient times. Wind, rain, and the passage of time have worn away the colors that once brightened them. These same factors have also damaged the buildings in which the sculptures stood. For a thousand years after the fall of the Roman Empire, people didn't care much about ancient art. Temples were torn down to recycle the building stone. Marble statues were burned to produce lime, which could then be used to make mortar, glass, and other useful things.

In the 1400s, interest in ancient Greek art revived. People found ancient statues buried under the ground and pulled them from the sea. When artists such as Michaelangelo saw these statues, they assumed that bare white marble had been the style of the ancient artists. So leaving stone in its natural color became the standard practice.

As more ancient art pieces were uncovered, experts sometimes noted traces of color on their surfaces. But this color faded or disappeared when the sculptures were exposed to light and air. Sometimes art restorers scrubbed the color off because people of this time considered bare stone more beautiful.

But there was evidence showing that the Greeks had not agreed. One example of the Greek preference for color is found in a play by the Athenian dramatist Euripides, who lived in the fifth century B.C.E. In the play, the beautiful Helen of Troy wishes that the gods had made her ugly, "as a statue from which the color has been wiped off."

Many art experts understood that ancient Greek sculpture and buildings had been brightly painted. Now and then, scholars tried to picture how these statues must have looked. A few 19th-century artists made copies of Greek statues and colored them in the current style of the artists' time. These efforts were laughed at or ignored. White marble was how people preferred to think of ancient Greek art. Besides, how could anyone know what the original colors had been?

Enter Vinzenz Brinkmann

Vinzenz Brinkmann believed he could figure out what colors had appeared on pieces of Greek art. Beginning in the 1980s, he and his team of archaeologists researched the pigments that Greek artists had used to color ancient statues. He used special lamps, high-tech cameras, and computers to bring out traces of the original colors. In some cases, the color had completely faded. But even then, Brinkmann's cameras often revealed changes in the chemistry on the surface of the stone.

These changes were like clues in a detective story. They showed what minerals artists had worked with in making the original pigments. The ancients used a mineral called malachite to make green. They used cinnabar to make red. Arsenic traces on the stone showed that the color had been gold or yellow.

This re-creation of Peplos Kore shows how Vinzenz Brinkmann believes she looked in ancient Greece. He figured out the missing colors through scientific research.

The Brinkmanns researched both ancient Greek and Roman art. Above is the original Roman statue, Augustus of Prima Porta, as it looks today, side by side with its color replica.

Behold the Gods!

After years of research, Vinzenz Brinkmann was ready to repaint Greek sculptures, to show them in their original colors. Of course, he would not touch the actual ancient statues. He used laser technology to make reproductions of the statues he wanted to study.

First Brinkmann made three-dimensional scans of the statues. Then he used the data from these scans to create full-size copies. They were made from a kind of plastic that looks like marble.

To paint the reproductions, Brinkmann chose an archaeologist-artist he knew well—his wife, Ulrike Koch-Brinkmann. She was assisted by other artists. They used only pigments the ancients would have used. There were some details for which Vinzenz Brinkmann could not confirm the original color. Ulrike left these areas white.

When the Brinkmanns had finished more than 20 reconstructions, they decided to present their work. In 2003, the couple opened an exhibit at a museum in Munich, Germany, that specializes in Greek and Roman sculpture. The museum displayed the colored copies side by side with the original ancient white marble statues. The exhibit traveled to other museums in Europe. By 2007, it had reached the United States. The exhibit was called "Gods in Color."

The colorful sculptures caused a sensation. As one art critic put it, "The exhibition forces you to look at ancient sculpture in a totally new way."

Several of the sculptures were copied from originals in the temple of the goddess Aphaia on the Greek island of Aegina. There is a battle scene featuring warriors in deadly combat. Eyes are drawn to the figure of a kneeling archer. He wears a full-body tunic with a pattern of diamonds in red, green, blue, and yellow. His gold helmet is decorated with a flower. He shoots gold-tipped blue arrows from a red and gold bow.

Another battle scene is carved on the lid of a sarcophagus, or stone coffin. It depicts the famous king Alexander the Great fighting the Persians. In the center, Alexander wears a red and blue tunic, a gold helmet, and red and gold leggings. His white horse rears up above a fallen warrior who holds a gold shield trimmed in red. Alexander raises his sword to strike. To his left and right, Persian and Greek soldiers fight to the death.

The Brinkmanns' work is changing the way people think about ancient Greek art—and about the ancient Greeks. Today, when we look at bare white marble statues of Zeus, Apollo, or Aphrodite, we think of how they might have once been painted. And that leads us to wonder what the Greeks *really* thought about their gods and goddesses.

Even Greece itself has embraced these colorful images of its past. When the Brinkmanns' collection arrived in Athens, many government officials turned out to welcome it. Cameras snapped as Vinzenz Brinkmann posed some of his pieces on the acropolis. It was as if the gods and the heroes of ancient Greece were returning home after a long journey.

Below is the Brinkmanns' painted replica of an archer posed by the Parthenon on the acropolis in Athens. The original statue was in the Temple of Aphaia in Greece.

Unit 5 Timeline Challenge

Ancient Greece

By 800 B.C.E.
Oligarchies Replace Monarchies
Oligarchies replace monarchies as the form of government in most Greek city-states.

By Mid-600s B.C.E.
Tyrannies Replace Oligarchies
Tyranny becomes the form of government in many Greek city-states.

About 500 B.C.E.
Greek City-States Flourish
Greek city-states establish colonies and conduct trade in the wider Mediterranean region.

900 B.C.E.   800 B.C.E.   700 B.C.E.   600 B.C.E.   500 B.C.E.

By 500 B.C.E.
Democracy Develops in Athens
Democracy develops in Athens and gives shared ruling power to all citizens.

499–479 B.C.E.
Persian Wars
The Persian wars end with a Greek victory aided by the alliance of Athens and Sparta.

479–431 B.C.E.
Golden Age of Athens
The Golden Age of Athens makes the city-state the artistic and cultural center of Greece.

431 B.C.E.
Pericles' Funeral Oration
Pericles praises the greatness of Athens in his Funeral Oration honoring Athenian soldiers killed in the Peloponnesian War.

About 400 B.C.E.
Death of Thucydides
The historian Thucydides writes about the history of the Peloponnesian War.

399 B.C.E.
Death of Socrates
A jury finds the philosopher Socrates guilty and sentences him to death.

500 B.C.E.   400 B.C.E.   300 B.C.E.   200 B.C.E.

431–404 B.C.E.
Peloponnesian War
The Peloponnesian War between Athens and Sparta, each with its own allies, weakens the Greek city-states.

334–323 B.C.E.
Empire of Alexander the Great
Alexander the Great builds a vast empire and spreads Greek culture to Asia and Africa.

About 300 B.C.E.
Euclid Writes About Geometry
The mathematician Euclid writes *The Elements*, a collection of 13 books about geometry.

Unit 6

Ancient Rome

The ancient Romans built the Colosseum as an arena for gladiator fights and mock naval battles. The gigantic structure seated about 50,000 people. Today the ruins of the Colosseum are one of the leading sights in Rome.

Unit 6 Setting the Stage

The Italian Peninsula

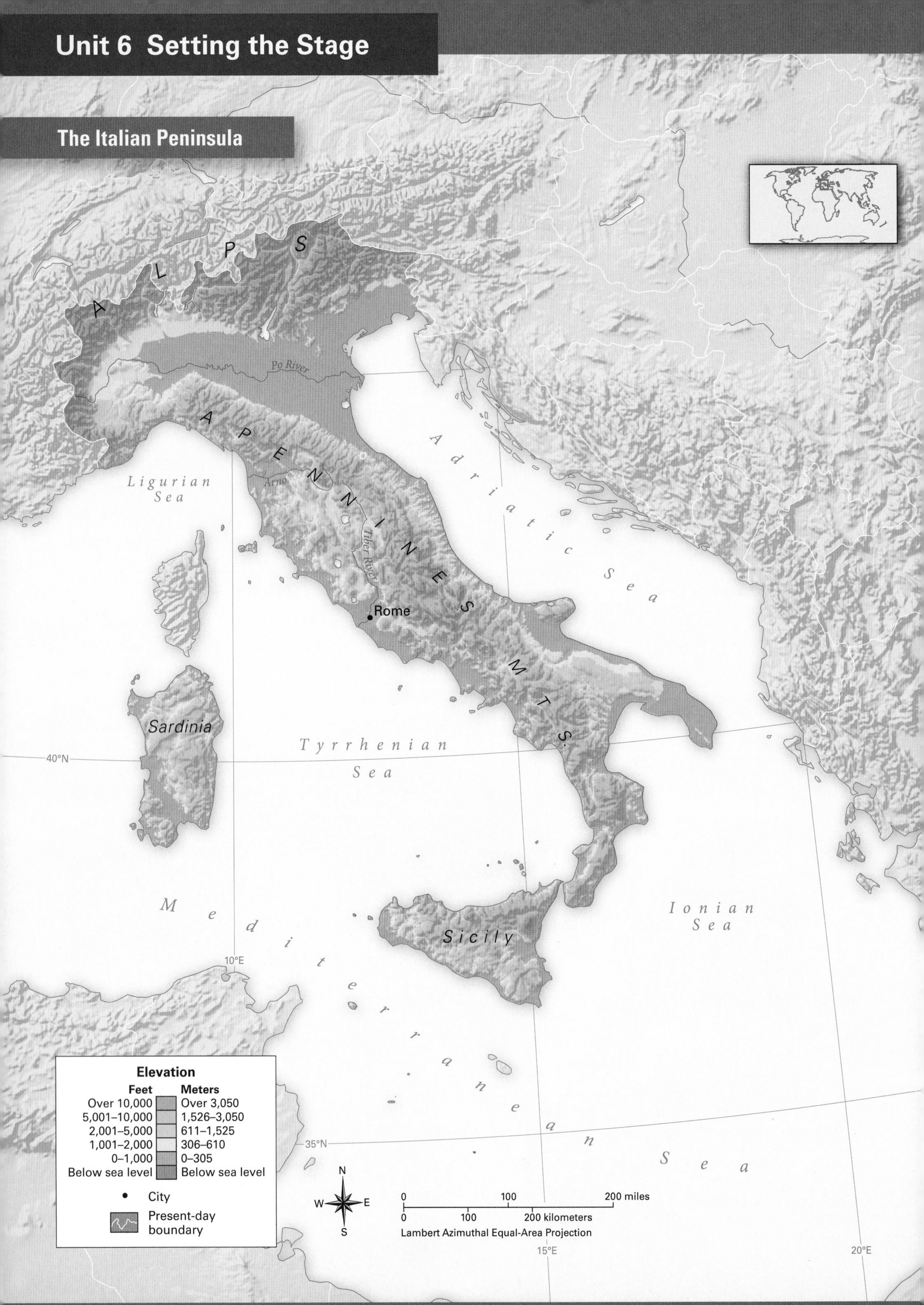

ALPS
APENNINES MTS.
Po River
Arno
Tiber River
Rome
Ligurian Sea
Adriatic Sea
Tyrrhenian Sea
Ionian Sea
Mediterranean Sea
Sardinia
Sicily
40°N
35°N
10°E
15°E
20°E
Elevation
Feet
Meters
Over 10,000
Over 3,050
5,001–10,000
1,526–3,050
2,001–5,000
611–1,525
1,001–2,000
306–610
0–1,000
0–305
Below sea level
Below sea level
City
Present-day boundary
N
S
E
W
0
100
200 miles
0
100
200 kilometers
Lambert Azimuthal Equal-Area Projection

Ancient Rome

The civilization of Rome developed on the Italian peninsula, a long, boot-shaped piece of land in Europe, surrounded on three sides by water. To the north of Italy lies the rest of northern Europe. To the south, east, and west lay the seas.

On this small peninsula are two major mountain ranges: the lofty Alps, which extend from west to east along Italy's northern border; and the Apennines, which stretch like a backbone down the length of Italy. Their peaks and hillsides cover most of the peninsula.

The small amount of Italy that is not mountainous is made up of high, rocky coastland or level plains. Several rivers, including the Po and the Tiber, flow through these areas to the sea.

Find the city of Rome on the map on the opposite page. You can see that it is located about midway down the peninsula, on the Tiber River and close to the sea. This was a good place to found a city. Its hillside location made it easy to defend. It sat at the very point at which crossing the Tiber was easiest. Rome also lay on the route from the Apennine Mountains to the sea.

As you will learn in this unit, several different cultures converged in Rome. The Greeks, for example, settled nearby, on other parts of the peninsula.

As the map below shows, Rome gradually grew from a city into an empire that extended into Europe and parts of Africa and Asia. Today, the legacy of ancient Rome lives on in the contributions it has made to western civilization—for example, in the modern culture of Western Europe and North America. In this unit, you will learn how Rome grew into an empire. You will also learn about Rome's lasting influence on the world today.

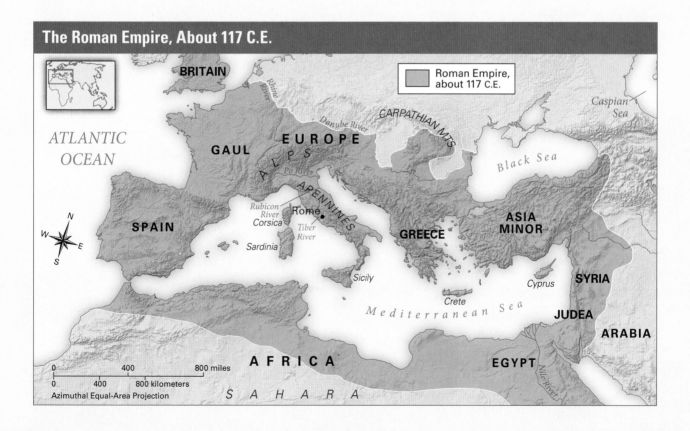

The Roman Empire, About 117 C.E.

Roman Empire, about 117 C.E.

BRITAIN

ATLANTIC OCEAN

GAUL

EUROPE

ALPS

Rhine River

Danube River

CARPATHIAN MTS

Caspian Sea

Black Sea

Po River

APENNINES

Rubicon River

Rome

Corsica

Tiber River

Sardinia

SPAIN

GREECE

ASIA MINOR

Cyprus

SYRIA

Crete

JUDEA

ARABIA

Sicily

Mediterranean Sea

AFRICA

EGYPT

Nile River

SAHARA

0   400   800 miles
0   400   800 kilometers
Azimuthal Equal-Area Projection

Chapter 32

Geography and the Early Development of Rome

How did the Etruscans and Greeks influence the development of Rome?

32.1 Introduction

In this unit, you will explore the Roman civilization, which flourished from about 700 B.C.E. to about 476 C.E. It began in the ancient city of Rome.

Rome is located in Italy, which includes a peninsula and islands in southern Europe. The Italian peninsula is shaped a lot like a boot. It reaches into the Mediterranean Sea—its toe pointed toward the island of Sicily.

The Romans have a myth about the founding of their city. Long ago, the story goes, a princess gave birth to twin sons, Romulus and Remus. The boys' father was Mars, the Roman god of war. The princess's uncle—the king—was afraid the boys would grow up to take his throne, so he ordered his men to drown them in the Tiber (TIE-bur) River. But before the twins drowned, a wolf rescued them.

When Romulus and Remus grew up, they decided to build a town on the banks of the Tiber River where the wolf had found them. But they quarreled over who would rule their settlement. Romulus killed his brother. He became king of the city, which he named Rome.

The tale of Romulus and Remus is a colorful myth. In this chapter, you will learn about the real founding of Rome. You will also learn how two important groups, the Etruscans and the Greeks, influenced the development of Roman culture.

The twins Romulus and Remus, shown on this ancient coin, are the legendary founders of Rome.

◀ The Baths of Carcalla show both Etruscan and Greek influences on Rome.

Rome the capital city of the Roman civilization, founded about 700 B.C.E.

Etruscan an ancient inhabitant of Etruria, a land in north and central Italy

In the 6th century B.C.E., the Etruscans and Greeks controlled much of the Italian peninsula.

32.2 The Early Romans and Their Neighbors

Over the years, historians have tried to discover the truth about the founding of **Rome**. No one really knows who the first king of Rome was. We do know that the first people to live in the area that became Rome were the Latins. The Latins were one of several groups who had invaded Italy sometime before 1000 B.C.E.

Perhaps around 700 B.C.E., a Latin tribe built the village that eventually became Rome. They built their village on the Palatine, a hill in central Italy. The Palatine overlooks the Tiber River, at a location about a dozen miles inland from the sea. In time, the village of thatched huts grew into a mighty city that spread over seven hills.

As Rome grew, Roman culture was greatly influenced by two of Rome's neighbors, the **Etruscans** (eh-TRUH-skans) and the Greeks. The Romans borrowed many ideas and skills from these two groups, beginning with the Etruscans.

The Etruscans had come to control Etruria, a land just north of the Palatine, by about 800 B.C.E. No one knows exactly where they came from. They built some city-states and conquered others. By 600 B.C.E., they ruled much of northern and central Italy, including the town of Rome.

The Greeks also were a major influence on Roman culture. The Romans learned about Greek culture when Greek colonists established towns in southern Italy and on the island of Sicily. Romans also learned about Greek ways from traders and the many Greeks who came to Rome. Let's look at some of the ideas and customs the Romans learned from these two groups.

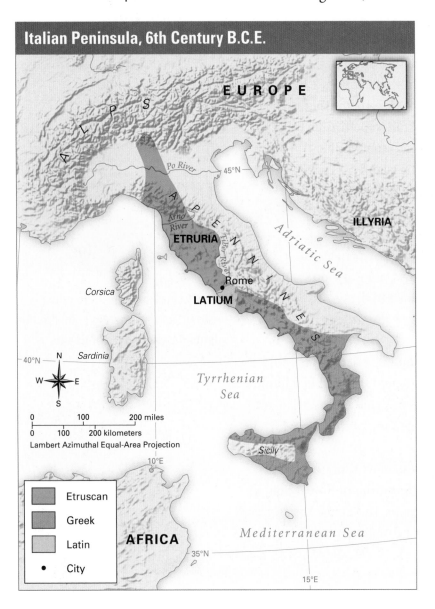

Italian Peninsula, 6th Century B.C.E.

Etruscan
Greek
Latin
• City

32.3 The Influence of Etruscan Engineering

The Romans became great builders. They learned many techniques about engineering, or the science of building, from the Etruscans. Two important Etruscan structures the Romans adapted were the arch and the **cuniculus**.

Etruscan arches rested on two pillars. The pillars supported a half-circle of wedge-shaped stones. A keystone in the center held the other stones of the arch tightly in place.

A cuniculus was a long underground trench. Vertical shafts connected it to the ground above. Etruscans used these trenches to irrigate land. They also used them to drain swamps and to carry water to their cities.

The Romans **adapted** both of these structures. In time, they became even better engineers than the Etruscans. They used arches to build huge public works, including bridges, stadiums, and aqueducts to carry water over long distances.

This arched city gate was built by the Etruscans. The arch is held in place by the pressure of the stones against each other.

32.4 The Influence of Etruscan Sporting Events

Romans also adapted two bloody Etruscan sporting events. The first was slave fighting. The Etruscan custom was to stage slave fights during funerals. Two slaves of the dead master fought to the death with swords and small shields. After being congratulated, the winner was executed.

The Etruscans also enjoyed watching chariot races. The charioteers, or drivers, were strapped to their chariots. If a chariot overturned, a driver could be dragged under the chariot's wheels or trampled by the horses. These fierce competitions often resulted in injury or death.

These Etruscan sports became popular in Rome. In Roman stadiums, thousands of slaves died fighting as **gladiators**. These professionally trained fighters battled either each other or wild animals. Romans also flocked to see charioteers risk their lives racing four-horse teams.

cuniculus an underground irrigation system invented by the Etruscans

gladiator a person trained to fight for public entertainment

Etruscan charioteers like this one risked their lives racing around the track during a chariot race.

32.5 The Influence of Greek Architecture

The Romans borrowed and adapted ideas from the Greeks, as well as the Etruscans. Greek architecture was one important influence on the Romans. The Greeks built marble temples as homes for their gods. Temples like the Parthenon had stately columns that added to their beauty.

The Romans used Greek designs in their own public buildings. In time, they learned to use concrete to make even larger structures, such as the Pantheon in Rome.

The Romans also used concrete to build huge stadiums like the Colosseum, where gladiators fought. The Circus Maximus, where people watched chariot races, could seat more than two hundred thousand spectators.

32.6 The Influence of Greek Writing

Sometimes, the Greek influence on Roman culture was indirect. For example, the Greek alphabet was adopted and then changed by the Etruscans. The Romans then borrowed and altered the Etruscan alphabet.

The Greek alphabet had a more direct influence on Roman culture. Like the Greeks, the Romans wrote in all capital letters. The Greeks carved important **documents,** such as laws and treaties, into bronze or stone plaques. The plaques were **displayed** in the public squares. The Romans also carved inscriptions in walls and columns for all to see.

Many Roman writers were inspired by Greek poetry and myths. The Roman poet Virgil built on Greek tales of a long-ago conflict, the Trojan War. Virgil's poem, the *Aeneid*, told how Aeneas (ay-NEE-ahs), a Trojan prince, fled to Italy after the war. According to Virgil, Aeneas was the ancestor of the first Romans.

In the ruins of the Parthenon from ancient Greece, we can see the architectural details that influenced building designs in Rome and, later, around the world.

Greeks and Romans wrote in all capital letters. This example of Greek writing is inscribed on a voting token called an *ostrakon.*

32.7 The Influence of Greek Art

Both the Etruscans and the Romans admired Greek pottery, painting, and sculpture. The Romans got some Greek ideas from Etruscan art. They borrowed others directly from the Greeks.

Greek pottery was valued throughout the Mediterranean world for its usefulness and beauty. Greek potters created large clay vessels for storing food, water, and wine. They often painted black figures on the red clay. Some of their designs showed pictures of gods and heroes. Others showed people in their daily lives. The Romans eagerly took the work of Greek potters into their homes. Roman artists imitated the technique, but had their own style.

The Greek influence on Roman painting and sculpture was so great that historians speak of "**Greco-Roman** art." Wealthy Romans often collected Greek art. They built monuments in a Greek style. Roman sculptors and painters used Greek art as models for their own work.

Roman artists also created a lively and realistic style of their own. Greek artists often tried to show an ideal, or perfect, human being or god. As Rome's power grew, much of Roman art celebrated great leaders and events. Roman sculptors became especially skilled in creating lifelike portraits. They made realistic busts, or statues showing the subject's head and shoulders. They also carved life-sized statues of famous military leaders. The statues often seemed just as powerful as the leaders themselves.

The vase and cup show the two most common styles that Greeks and Romans used on their pottery. On the left, the figures are painted black on red clay. On the right, the cup is painted black, leaving the red clay showing through.

Greco-Roman having the characteristics of Roman culture with a strong Greek influence

The Greek gods and goddesses of Mount Olympus, shown in this painting, were adapted into Roman religion.

32.8 The Influence of Greek Religion

The religion of the Romans was a blend of many influences. For example, they followed Etruscan religious rituals in founding their cities. But it was Greek religion that especially influenced Roman ideas about the gods.

The Greeks worshipped a number of gods and goddesses. The gods governed every part of Greek life. The Greeks performed rituals and sacrifices to gain the gods' favor for everything from a good harvest to curing the sick.

The early Romans had their own gods and rituals. But their ideas about the gods changed as they came in contact with other cultures. When the Romans encountered a similar god from another culture, they blended that god's characteristics with those of their own.

The Romans adapted many of the Greek gods as their own, but they gave them Roman names. The greatest Greek god, Zeus, became Jupiter. Aphrodite, the goddess of love, became Venus. Aries, the god of war, became Mars.

The Romans were much less interested in telling stories about the gods than were the Greeks. Romans were more concerned with performing exactly the right ritual for a particular occasion.

In this chapter, you learned about the beginnings of ancient Rome and the Roman civilization. Rome was founded by people called the Latins who settled near the Tiber River on the Italian peninsula.

The Early Romans and Their Neighbors Over time, the Romans borrowed many ideas and skills from their neighbors. Two groups who greatly influenced Roman culture were the Etruscans and the Greeks.

The Influence of Etruscan Engineering Romans learned a great deal about engineering from the Etruscans. Etruscan ideas included the arch and the cuniculus.

The Influence of Etruscan Sporting Events The Romans also adapted some Etruscan sporting events. Most popular were chariot racing and slave fighting, which later became gladiator contests in Rome.

The Influence of Greek Architecture and Writing Greek civilization had a huge influence on Roman culture. The Romans used Greek temple designs in their own buildings. They used Greek-style capital letters in their writing, and many Roman poets were inspired by Greek poetry and stories.

The Influence of Greek Art and Religion The Romans greatly admired Greek art. The blend of Greek and Roman styles became known as "Greco-Roman" art. The Romans also made many Greek gods and goddesses their own, although they were more interested in rituals than in stories.

The Etruscans developed the sport of chariot racing, which the Romans later adapted.

Chapter 33

The Rise of the Roman Republic

What were the characteristics of the Roman Republic and how did they change over time?

33.1 Introduction

Early Rome was ruled by Etruscan kings from northern Italy. In this chapter, you will learn how the Romans overthrew the Etruscans and created a republic around 509 B.C.E. A *republic* is a form of government in which leaders are elected to represent the people.

Ancient Romans told an interesting story about the overthrow of their Etruscan rulers. One day, two Etruscan princes went to see the famous oracle at Delphi (DEL-fie), in Greece. A Roman named Lucius Junius Brutus traveled with them.

At Delphi, the princes asked the oracle which one of them would be the next king of Rome. The oracle answered, "The next man to have authority in Rome will be the man who first kisses his mother." Hearing this prediction, Brutus pretended to trip. He fell on his face, and his lips touched Earth, "the mother of all living things."

Back in Rome, Brutus led the revolt that drove out the Etruscan kings. He became one of the first leaders of the new republic. In this way, the oracle's mysterious words came true. The Roman people were now free to govern themselves. But not all Romans were equal. Power in the early republic belonged to rich men called patricians (pah-TRIH-shens). The majority of Romans, the plebeians (pleh-BEE-anz), had no voice in the government. In this chapter, you will see how a long struggle between patricians and plebeians shaped the government of Rome.

Lucius Junius Brutus led the overthrow of the Etruscan kings and the establishment of the new republic of Rome.

◀ In the Roman Republic, senators debated and interpreted the laws.

patrician in the Roman Republic, a member of the upper, ruling class

plebeian in the Roman Republic, one of the common people

republic a form of government in which leaders are elected to represent the people

Senate a group of 300 men elected to govern Rome

consul one of two chief leaders in Rome

Brutus denounced the Etruscan kings and was elected one of the first consuls in the new republic.

33.2 Patricians and Plebeians Under Etruscan Rule

Between 616 and 509 B.C.E., the Etruscans ruled Rome. During this time, Roman society was divided into two classes, patricians and plebeians.

Upper-class citizens, called **patricians,** came from a small group of wealthy landowners. *Patrician* comes from the Latin word *pater,* which means "father." The patricians chose from among themselves the "fathers of the state," the men who advised the Etruscan king. Patricians controlled the most valuable land. They also held the important military and religious offices.

Free non-patricians called **plebeians** were mostly peasants, laborers, craftspeople, and shopkeepers. The word *plebeian* comes from *plebs,* which means "the common people." Plebeians made up about 95 percent of Rome's population. They could not be priests or government officials. They had little voice in the government. Yet they still were forced to serve in the army.

33.3 The Patricians Create a Republic

Over time, the patricians came to resent Etruscan rule. In 509 B.C.E., a group of patricians, led by Lucius Junius Brutus, rebelled. They drove out the last Etruscan king. In place of a monarchy, they created a republic. In a **republic,** elected officials govern for the people.

To the patricians, "the people" meant themselves, not the plebeians. The patricians put most of the power in the hands of the Senate. The **Senate** was a group of 300 patricians elected by patricians. The senators served for life. They also appointed other government officials and served as judges.

Two elected leaders, called **consuls,** shared command of the army. The Senate was supposed to advise the consuls. In fact, the Senate's decisions were treated as law.

The creation of the republic gave Rome a more democratic form of government. But only the patricians could participate in that government.

33.4 The Plebeians Rebel

Rome was now a republic, but the patricians held all the power. They made sure that only they could be part of the government. Only they could become senators or consuls. Plebeians had to obey their decisions. Because laws were not written down, patricians often changed or interpreted the laws to benefit themselves. As a result, a small group of families held all the power in Rome.

The plebeians had to fight for what they wanted. They began to demand more political rights. The struggle between plebeians and patricians is known as the Conflict of the Orders, a conflict between the two social classes.

The conflict grew especially heated during times of war. The new republic frequently fought wars against neighboring tribes. Plebeians had to fight in the army even though the patricians decided whether to go to war. Plebeians resented this.

The struggle took a **dramatic** turn in the year 494 B.C.E. By then, Rome was a city of twenty to forty thousand people. Most of the population was plebeian. Angry over their lack of power, the plebeians marched out of the city and camped on a nearby hill. They refused to come back until the patricians met their demands.

Rome was in **crisis**. Work in the city and on the farms came to a halt. Without the plebeians, patricians feared that the army would be helpless if an enemy struck at Rome. "A great panic seized the city," wrote Livy, a noted Roman historian. The patricians had little choice but to compromise.

For years, plebeians struggled to gain a share of the political power enjoyed by patricians.

33.5 The Plebeians Gain Political Equality

The plebeians' revolt led to a major change in Roman government. The patricians agreed to let the plebeians elect officials called Tribunes of the Plebs. The **tribunes** spoke for the plebeians in the Senate and with the consuls. Later, tribunes gained the power to **veto,** or overrule, actions by the Senate and other government officials. Over time, the number of tribunes grew from two to ten.

Plebeians could also elect a lawmaking body, the Council of Plebs. However, the council made laws only for plebeians, not for patricians.

The plebeians had gained some important rights. However, they still had less power than the patricians. Over the next 200 years, the plebeians staged a series of protests to gradually win political equality.

First, they demanded that the laws be written down. In that way, the patricians couldn't change them at will. Around the year 451 B.C.E., the patricians agreed. The laws were **published** on tablets called the Twelve Tables.

Plebeians won a major victory when patricians agreed to post Rome's laws on the Twelve Tables.

Next, in 367 B.C.E., a new law said that one of the two consuls had to be a plebeian. Former consuls held seats in the Senate, so this change also allowed plebeians to become senators.

Finally, in 287 B.C.E., the plebeians gained the right to pass laws for all Roman citizens. Now, assemblies of all Roman citizens, such as the Citizens' Association, could approve or reject laws. These plebeian assemblies also nominated the consuls, the tribunes, and the members of the Senate. More and more plebeians served alongside patricians in the Senate. After 200 years of struggle, the plebeians had won their fight for equality.

Rome's republican form of government inspired future leaders in Europe and America. Rome became an example of a type of government ruled by a set of basic laws, or a **constitution**. Future political thinkers also pointed to Roman ideals of elected assemblies, citizenship, and **civic** duty. They adopted the model of governmental bodies that could check each other's power. Above all, they were inspired by the spirit of republicanism. This means that government should rule for the good of the people. Cicero (SIS-eh-roh), a famous Roman statesman, captured this spirit when he wrote, "The people's good is the highest law."

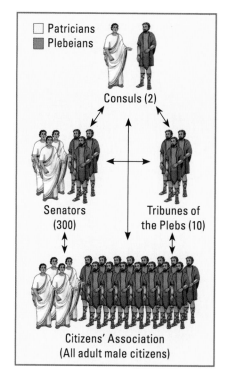

In the Roman Republic, eventually patricians were forced to share power with the plebeians.

Chapter Summary

In this chapter, you learned how the Romans overthrew the Etruscans and created a republic. Romans were proud of their republic, which lasted for about 500 years.

Patricians and Plebeians Under Etruscan Rule Under the Etruscans, Roman society was divided into two classes, patricians and plebeians. Plebeians made up about 95 percent of Rome's population, but had little voice in the government.

The Patricians Create a Republic In 509 B.C.E., patricians drove out the last of the Etruscan kings and created a republic. Most of the power was held by the patrician Senate and the consuls. Only patricians could participate in the new government.

The Plebeians Rebel The plebeians began to demand more political rights in a struggle with the patricians known as the Conflict of the Orders. In 494 B.C.E., angry over their lack of power, the plebeians rebelled.

The Plebeians Gain Political Equality The patricians agreed to let the plebeians elect Tribunes of the Plebs and the Council of Plebs. Around 451 B.C.E., the Twelve Tables were published. By 287 B.C.E., assemblies of all citizens could pass laws. Plebeians governed with patricians. The plebeians had won their fight for equality.

Chapter 34

From Republic to Empire

Did the benefits of Roman expansion outweigh the costs?

34.1 Introduction

In this chapter, you will discover how the ancient republic of Rome expanded its power. By the early 1st century C.E., it had become a mighty empire that ruled the entire Mediterranean world.

The expansion of Roman power took place over **approximately** five hundred years, from 509 B.C.E. to 14 C.E. At the start of this period, Rome was a tiny republic in central Italy. Five hundred years later, it was the thriving center of a vast empire. At its height, the Roman Empire included most of Europe, together with North Africa, Egypt, much of the present-day Middle East, and Asia Minor.

The growth of Rome's power happened gradually, and it came at a price. Romans had to fight countless wars to defend their growing territory and to conquer new lands. Along the way, Rome itself changed. The Romans had once been proud to be governed under a republic of elected leaders. Their heroes were men who had helped to preserve the republic. By 14 C.E., the republic was just a memory. Power was in the hands of a single supreme ruler, the emperor. Romans even worshiped the emperor as a god.

In this chapter, you'll see how this dramatic change occurred. You'll trace the gradual expansion of Roman power. You will also explore the costs of this expansion, both for Romans and for the people they conquered.

The Romans celebrated their military victories by building structures such as Trajan's Column (center). It was erected in Rome in 113 C.E.

◄ As Rome grew, power flowed into the hands of one supreme ruler.

34.2 From Republic to Empire: An Overview

The growth of Rome from a republic to an empire took place over 500 years. The story has four major periods.

The First Period of Expansion   The first period of expansion, or becoming larger, began in 509 B.C.E. At this time, the Romans drove the last Etruscan king out of power, and Rome became a republic.

The Romans wanted to protect their borders and to gain more land. This led to a series of wars. During the next 245 years, the Romans fought one enemy after another. They conquered their Latin neighbors in central Italy. They also defeated their old rulers, the Etruscans.

Wisely, the Romans eventually made allies, or friends, of their former enemies. By 264 B.C.E., Rome and its allies controlled all of the Italian peninsula.

Rome gained power over new lands through three savage wars with Carthage, across the Mediterranean Sea.

The Second Period of Expansion   Rome's growth threatened another great power, the city of Carthage (KAR-thidge), in North Africa. During the second period of expansion, from 264 to 146 B.C.E., Rome and Carthage fought three major wars. Through these wars, Rome gained control of North Africa, much of Spain, and the island of Sicily. Roman armies also conquered Macedonia and Greece.

Roman general Julius Caesar helped expand Roman power by conquering Gaul and by invading Britain.

The Third Period of Expansion During the third period of expansion, from 145 to 44 B.C.E., Rome came to rule the entire Mediterranean world. In the east, Rome took control of Asia Minor, Syria, and Egypt. In the west, the Roman general Julius Caesar conquered much of Gaul (modern-day France).

Proud Romans now called the Mediterranean "our sea." But the republic was in trouble. **Civil wars** divided the city. Roman generals were becoming **dictators**. They set their armies against the power of the Senate. Caesar himself ruled as a dictator for life until he was assassinated in 44 B.C.E.

The men who murdered Caesar thought they were saving the power of the Senate. However, several more years of civil war followed. Then Caesar's grandnephew, Octavian, seized total power. The Senate named him Augustus, or "honored one." Rome was now an empire governed by one supreme ruler.

The Fourth Period of Expansion The fourth period of expansion began with the start of the empire. It lasted until 14 C.E. The first emperor, Augustus, added a great deal of new territory by pushing the borders of the empire all the way to natural boundaries, like rivers, to make it easier to defend. Later emperors added more territory. At its height, the Roman Empire stretched from the island of Britain in the northwest to the Black Sea in the east.

Each period of expansion involved cost and sacrifice. The next four sections give more details about each expansion. As you read, ask yourself what Romans of the time might have thought about these events.

> **civil war** a war between groups in the same country
>
> **dictator** a ruler with absolute power

Julius Caesar's grandnephew, Octavian, became Caesar Augustus, the supreme ruler of the Roman Empire.

34.3 Rome's Conquest of the Italian Peninsula, 509 B.C.E. to 264 B.C.E.

Rome's first period of expansion included more than two hundred years of almost constant warfare. During this time, Rome gradually took control of the entire Italian peninsula.

After the last Etruscan king was overthrown in 509 B.C.E., the Romans began to expand their territory and influence. In 493 B.C.E., Roman leaders signed a treaty, or agreement, with their Latin neighbors to the south. The treaty said, "There shall be peace between the Romans and all the communities of Latins as long as heaven and earth endure." These new allies agreed to band together against their common enemies. During the next 100 years, the Romans fought a number of wars against the Etruscans, as well as against tribes living in hills around Rome.

Then, in 390 B.C.E., Rome nearly came to an end. A band of Gauls (gawlz), a warlike people from the north, crushed a Roman army and surged into the city. Most of Rome's people fled into the countryside. The Gauls looted the city and burned most of it down.

In 458 B.C.E., the Roman Senate made Lucius Quintius Cincinnatus dictator, or supreme ruler, to lead the defense of the city during an attack. After defeating the enemy, Cincinnatus willingly gave up power and returned to his farm. His sense of duty and respect for the republic made Cincinnatus one of Rome's great heroes.

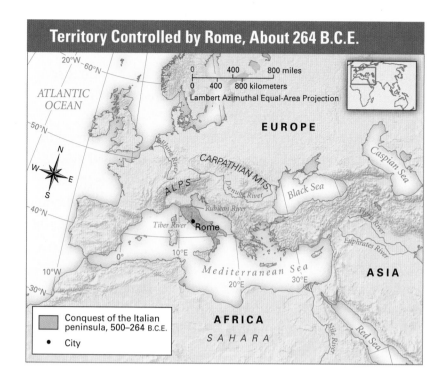

Territory Controlled by Rome, About 264 B.C.E.

0   400   800 miles
0   400   800 kilometers
Lambert Azimuthal Equal-Area Projection

EUROPE

ATLANTIC OCEAN

CARPATHIAN MTS.

ALPS

Rhine River
Danube River
Rubicon River
Tiber River
Rome

Black Sea

Caspian Sea

Tigris River
Euphrates River

Mediterranean Sea

ASIA

AFRICA

SAHARA

Nile River

Red Sea

Conquest of the Italian peninsula, 500–264 B.C.E.
• City

By 264 B.C.E., the Romans had taken over the entire Italian peninsula.

With the city in ruins, the Romans considered fleeing. Instead, they bravely decided to start over. They rebuilt their city and surrounded it with walls. They also built up their army. Before long, Roman soldiers were on the march again.

During the 300s B.C.E., Rome conquered the Etruscans and many neighboring tribes. To the south, they battled a people called the Samnites and several Greek city-states. By 275 B.C.E., Rome's conquest of the Italian peninsula was complete. But expansion came at great cost. Romans had been fighting for two centuries. And the Gauls had once destroyed their capital city.

As Rome's territory expanded, the city had to keep a large, permanent army to defend it and the conquered lands. As a result, more and more Romans were forced to serve in the army. Most of the soldiers were plebeians. Many plebeians resented this fact, leading to civil unrest.

Roman citizens were not the only ones who paid a cost for Rome's expansion. Rome allowed the people of some defeated cities to become Roman citizens. But other cities were not treated so well. Many received more limited privileges, such as the ability to trade with Rome. And Roman allies had to pay Roman taxes and supply soldiers for Roman armies.

By 264 B.C.E., Rome had more citizens and well-trained soldiers than any other power in the Mediterranean world. But very soon, the Romans would face their greatest challenge yet.

Punic Wars a series of wars fought between Rome and Carthage for control of the Mediterranean

In 218 B.C.E., the Carthaginian general Hannibal led his troops across the Alps to attack Rome.

34.4 Expansion During the Punic Wars, 264 B.C.E. to 146 B.C.E.

During Rome's second period of expansion, it fought three savage wars with Carthage, a powerful city-state in North Africa, for control of the Mediterranean region.

When the wars began, Carthage held North Africa, most of Spain, and part of the island of Sicily. It also controlled most of the trade in the western Mediterranean. The Greek cities in southern Italy had frequently clashed with Carthage over trading rights. When Rome conquered these cities, it was drawn into the fight with Carthage.

Rome's wars with Carthage are called the **Punic Wars,** after the Greek name for the people of Carthage. The First Punic War began in 264 B.C.E. It was fought mostly at sea. Carthage had a very powerful navy. But the Romans built up their own navy by copying and improving on the Carthaginians' ship designs. A decisive victory at sea in 241 B.C.E. won the war for the Romans. The triumphant Romans took over Sicily, as well as other islands in the area.

The Second Punic War started 23 years later. This time, the Carthaginians decided to attack Italy itself. In 218 B.C.E., Hannibal, a brilliant Carthaginian general, surprised the Romans by marching his army from Spain across the Alps (a high mountain range) and into Italy. His troops rode elephants and braved snowstorms, landslides, and attacks by local tribes. For 15 years, Hannibal's men fought the Romans in Italy.

In 202 B.C.E., Hannibal had to return home to defend Carthage against an attack by a Roman army. There he was defeated in the battle that ended the Second Punic War. Carthage was forced to give up Spain to Rome, along with huge sums of money.

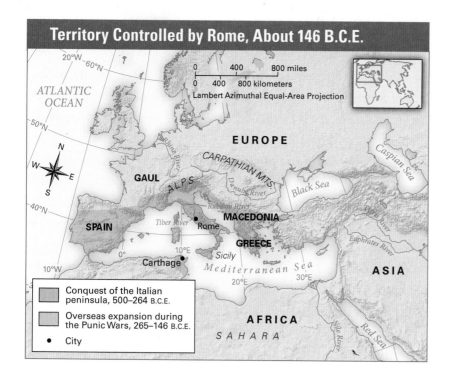

Territory Controlled by Rome, About 146 B.C.E.

0   400   800 miles
0   400   800 kilometers
Lambert Azimuthal Equal-Area Projection

ATLANTIC OCEAN

EUROPE

CARPATHIAN MTS.

GAUL

ALPS

Rhine River

Danube River

Rubicon River

Tiber River

Rome

SPAIN

MACEDONIA

GREECE

Sicily

Carthage

Mediterranean Sea

Black Sea

Caspian Sea

ASIA

Euphrates River

Tigris River

AFRICA

SAHARA

Nile River

Red Sea

Legend:
- Conquest of the Italian peninsula, 500–264 B.C.E.
- Overseas expansion during the Punic Wars, 265–146 B.C.E.
- City

By 146 B.C.E., Roman power had spread across much of the northern Mediterranean.

For about fifty years, there was peace between Rome and Carthage. Then, spurred on by Cato (KAY-toh), a senator who demanded the complete destruction of Carthage, the Romans attacked once more.

The Third Punic War lasted three years. In 146 B.C.E., the Romans burned Carthage to the ground. They killed many people and sold others into slavery. Rome was now the greatest power in the Mediterranean region. It controlled North Africa, much of Spain, Macedonia, and Greece.

The Punic Wars expanded Roman power and territory, but Rome's victories came at a price. Countless young men had died in the long wars. In addition, people living outside Rome suffered huge losses in population and property. Hannibal's army had destroyed thousands of farms. Other farms had been neglected while farmers went off to fight in Rome's armies. By the time the soldiers returned home, Rome had been forced to import grain from Sicily and other places. Small farms were being replaced by large estates, where the wealthy planted vineyards and raised livestock. Unable to compete with the wealthy landowners, many poor farmers had to sell their land.

While riches and slaves flowed into Rome from the conquered lands, so did new customs. Many of the new ideas came from Greece. Wealthy Romans competed with one another to build Greek-style homes and beautiful temples.

Julius Caesar a Roman general who ended the Roman Republic when he seized power and became dictator for life

34.5 Expansion During the Final Years of the Republic, 145 B.C.E. to 44 B.C.E.

By 145 B.C.E., Roman conquests had brought great wealth to the city of Rome. But they had also put the ideals of the republic under great strain. By the end of Rome's third period of expansion, the republic **collapsed**.

The final years of the republic were marked by still more wars. Many of Rome's allies resented having to pay Roman taxes and fight in Roman armies without enjoying the rights of citizenship. In 91 B.C.E., some rebelled. To end the revolt, Rome agreed to let all free Italians become Roman citizens.

Rome also had to fight to put down slave revolts. As Romans conquered new territory, they brought hundreds of thousands of prisoners to Roman lands. They turned them into slaves who labored on farms and in the city. Although some slaves were respected, Romans often treated their slaves very harshly. A slave named Spartacus led a famous revolt in 73 B.C.E. After crushing his army and killing Spartacus in battle, the Romans put thousands of the surviving rebels to death on crosses.

Julius Caesar was stabbed 23 times and bled to death at the door of the Senate.

There was trouble in the city, too. With so many slaves to do the work, thousands of farmers and laborers had no jobs. They crowded into Rome, becoming a mob that an ambitious leader could turn into an army.

Rome's army was producing many such leaders. Generals used their armies to gain fame and power in far-off lands and then to fight for influence in Rome. In one such civil war in the 80s B.C.E., 200,000 Romans were killed.

Forty years later, another civil war broke out between two ambitious generals, Pompey (POM-pee) and **Julius Caesar** (SEE-zer). Pompey had expanded Roman rule in such eastern lands as Syria and the island of Cyprus. Caesar had conquered much of Gaul.

Territory Controlled by Rome, About 44 B.C.E.

Conquest of the Italian peninsula, 500–264 B.C.E.

Overseas expansion during the Punic Wars, 265–146 B.C.E.

Expansion during the final years of the Republic, 145–44 B.C.E.

• City

By the time Julius Caesar seized power in the 40s B.C.E., Rome ruled most of the Mediterranean world and much of Europe.

By 49 B.C.E., Pompey was back in Rome, while Caesar commanded an army to the north of Italy, across the Rubicon River. Both men wanted to control Rome, but Pompey had the support of the Roman Senate.

Urged on by Pompey, the Senate forbade Caesar to enter Italy with his army. Caesar disobeyed. On January 11, 49 B.C.E., he crossed the Rubicon with his army. After three years of fighting, he defeated Pompey. The frightened Senate named Caesar dictator for life. With Caesar in control, and after nearly five hundred years, the republic was at an end.

As dictator, Julius Caesar introduced many reforms. He gave work to thousands of Romans by starting projects to make new roads and public buildings. To keep the poor happy, he staged gladiator contests they could watch for free. He also adopted a new calendar that is still used today.

Caesar had a **vision** of Rome as a great empire. He started new colonies and granted citizenship to the people of cities in Gaul and Spain. But he did not live to see his vision come true. On March 15, 44 B.C.E., a group of enemies stabbed Caesar to death as he was entering the Senate.

The men who killed Caesar thought they were saving the republic. But they were wrong. Instead, real power would never return to the Senate, as an emperor eventually emerged to take Caesar's place.

As emperor, Augustus encouraged education and literature. Here, he reads to a group of citizens. Augustus ruled for 41 years, until his death in 14 C.E.

34.6 Rome Becomes an Empire, 44 B.C.E. to 14 C.E.

Caesar's murder plunged Rome into civil wars that lasted over ten years. When the fighting ended, Caesar's grandnephew and adopted son Octavian was the sole ruler of Rome. So began the Roman Empire, and Rome's fourth period of expansion.

To gain power, Octavian had to defeat jealous rivals. One of them was Marc Antony, a popular general. Antony had married Queen Cleopatra of Egypt. In 31 B.C.E., Octavian defeated Antony and Cleopatra in a sea battle near Actium, Greece. His army chased the couple to Egypt, where they killed themselves. Octavian was now the supreme ruler of the Mediterranean region.

Octavian knew that the Romans prized their republic. He told them he was restoring the authority of the Senate. But in fact, he was in complete control. The Senate gave him the title *Augustus*, which means "revered" or "honored." He ruled for life as **Caesar Augustus**, and historians call him Rome's first emperor.

Augustus encouraged education, art, and literature. He completed grand construction projects, repairing more than eighty temples. "I found Rome brick and left it marble," he boasted. He also gave Rome its first police force, firefighters, and library.

Augustus ruled over more than fifty million people. He turned eastern kingdoms, such as Judea and Armenia, into Roman provinces. To better defend the empire, he pushed its borders to natural boundaries: the Rhine and Danube rivers in the north, the Sahara in the south, and the Atlantic in the west.

The empire needed a strong economy. The Romans improved trade by building harbors, canals, and roads. Goods flowed across the empire and from as far away as China. Romans made trade easier by establishing a single system of currency.

But Rome's final expansion brought new problems. To reform Roman morals, Augustus harshly punished people for being unfaithful to their husbands or wives. To protect himself and his family, he established a private army, the Praetorian (pray-TOR-ee-uhn) Guard. Later, this same Guard sometimes took part in murder **plots** against the emperors it was supposed to protect.

Under Rome, the Mediterranean world was mostly at peace for 200 years. This period is called the *Pax Romana*, or Roman Peace. But keeping the peace cost the Romans a great deal. During Augustus's reign, one rebellion in the east took three years and 100,000 soldiers to put down.

Caesar Augustus Julius Caesar's grandnephew and adopted son, Octavian; Rome's first emperor

Pax Romana a 200-year period of peace and stability established and maintained by the Roman Empire

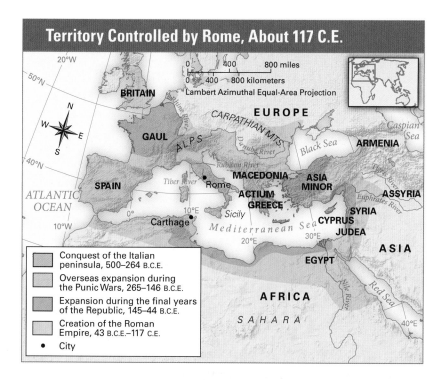

Territory Controlled by Rome, About 117 C.E.

20°W
50°N
BRITAIN

0   400   800 miles
0   400   800 kilometers
Lambert Azimuthal Equal-Area Projection

EUROPE

CARPATHIAN MTS.

GAUL
ALPS

Danube River

Black Sea

Caspian Sea

ARMENIA

40°N

Rubicon River

MACEDONIA
Tiber River • Rome

ASIA MINOR

ASSYRIA

Euphrates River

ATLANTIC OCEAN

SPAIN

0°

10°E

ACTIUM
GREECE

Tigris River

SYRIA

10°W

Sicily

Carthage

Mediterranean Sea

30°E

CYPRUS

JUDEA

20°E

ASIA

EGYPT

AFRICA

Nile River

Red Sea

SAHARA

40°E

Conquest of the Italian
peninsula, 500–264 B.C.E.

Overseas expansion during
the Punic Wars, 265–146 B.C.E.

Expansion during the final years
of the Republic, 145–44 B.C.E.

Creation of the Roman
Empire, 43 B.C.E.–117 C.E.

• City

At its largest, Rome was a mighty empire that ruled over the entire Mediterranean, large parts of the Middle East, and most of Europe.

Later emperors added to the territory controlled by Rome. From Britain to the Red Sea, a single power ruled over the greatest empire the world had ever known.

Chapter Summary

In this chapter, you read about four main periods of Roman expansion. In each period, the costs of expansion were great. Yet, the Roman Empire lasted 500 years.

Conquest of the Italian Peninsula The first period of expansion began in 509 B.C.E. The Romans rebelled against the Etruscans, and Rome became a republic. The Romans then conquered central Italy. By 264 B.C.E., Rome controlled all of Italy.

The Punic Wars During the second period of expansion, from 264 to 146 B.C.E., Rome fought Carthage in the three Punic Wars. As a result, Rome gained North Africa, much of Spain, and Sicily. Rome also conquered Macedonia and Greece.

The Final Years of the Republic During the third period of expansion, from 145 to 44 B.C.E., Rome took control of Asia Minor, Syria, Egypt, and Gaul. But civil wars divided the republic. Julius Caesar made himself dictator for life. Then Octavian seized power, becoming the first emperor, Caesar Augustus.

Rome Becomes an Empire The fourth period of expansion began with the start of the empire and lasted until 14 C.E. The emperors continued to add a great deal of new territory. At its height, around 117 C.E., the Roman Empire stretched from Britain to the present-day Middle East.

Chapter 35

Daily Life
in the Roman Empire

How did wealth affect daily life in the Roman Empire?

35.1 Introduction

In this chapter, you'll explore the daily life of people living in the Roman Empire at the height of its power—around 100 C.E. "All roads lead to Rome," boasted the Romans. For thousands of miles, road markers showed the distance to Rome. But more than roads connected the empire's 50 million people. They were also connected by Roman law, Roman customs, and Roman military might.

If Rome was the center of the empire, the Forum was the center of Rome. The word *forum* means "gathering place." The original Forum was an open area used for merchants' stalls, and for viewing races, games, and plays. In time, the Forum became a sprawling complex of government buildings, meeting halls, temples, theaters, and monuments. This was the heart of life in Rome.

In this chapter, you will visit this bustling center of Rome's vast empire. You'll learn about eight areas of daily life in ancient Rome and discover how life differed for the rich and the poor.

A vast network of roads helped to unite the Roman Empire.

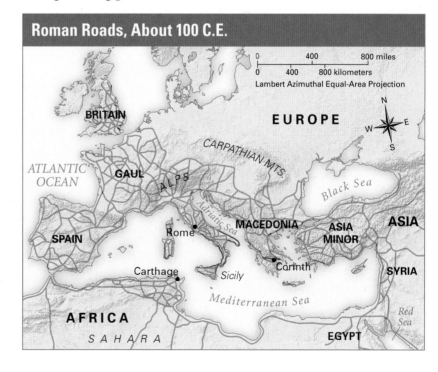

Roman Roads, About 100 C.E.

◄ The Forum was the center of the city and the empire of Rome.

35.2 Daily Life in Ancient Rome

If you had visited Rome in the 1st century C.E., you would have seen a city of great contrasts. Nearly one million people lived in the empire's capital city. Rome was full of beautiful temples, stately palaces, and flowering gardens. Yet most of its people lived in tiny apartments crammed into narrow, dirty streets.

In the city's **Forum,** or public gathering place, wealthy Roman women shopped for goods, **accompanied** by their slaves. Proud senators strolled about, protected by their bodyguards, while soldiers marched through the streets. Merchants and craftspeople labored at their trades. Foreigners roamed the streets from such faraway places as Britain, Spain, and Egypt. And in the midst of it all were Rome's slaves—hundreds of thousands of them, many of them captured in war.

People and goods flowed into Rome from the four corners of the empire. Wealthy Romans spent great sums of money on silks, perfumes, jeweled weapons, and musical instruments. They decorated their homes with statues, fountains, and fine pottery.

But the rich were only a small part of Rome's population. Most of the city's people lived in filthy neighborhoods filled with crime and disease. Their children were lucky to live past age ten. To keep the poor from turning into an angry, dangerous mob, Roman emperors gave away food and provided entertainment, such as gladiator contests and chariot races.

The empire had many large cities, but most people lived in the countryside. There, too, most of the people were poor. Some worked their own small farms. Others labored on huge estates owned by the rich.

Forum the center of most of the important public activities of the city Rome and its empire

The area known as the Forum was the heart of Rome's business, government, and religious life.

35.3 Law and Order

The Romans always believed in the **rule of law**. In the days of the republic, the Senate and the assemblies were important sources of law. But in the empire, the **ultimate** source of law was the emperor. As one Roman judge said, "Whatever pleases the emperor is the law."

Even in the empire, however, Romans honored some of their old traditions. The Senate continued to meet, and senators had high status in society. They had their own styles of clothing. They might wear special rings, pins, or togas (robes) trimmed with a wide purple stripe. Important senators had their own body-guards. These guards carried *fasces,* bundles of sticks with an ax in the center. The fasces were symbols of the government's right to punish lawbreakers. When carried inside the city, the ax was removed, to symbolize the right of Roman citizens to appeal a ruling against them.

Roman laws were strict, but crime was common in Rome. The most frequent crimes were stealing, assault, and murder. Roman police kept an eye on wealthy neighborhoods, but rarely patrolled the poor sections of the city. Some streets were so dangerous that they were closed at night.

Romans tried to protect themselves against crime. Rich men tried to hide their wealth by wearing old, dirty togas when they traveled at night. Women and children in rich families were told never to go outdoors alone, even during the day.

Any Roman, including the poor, could accuse someone else of a crime. A jury of citizens decided the case. Accused persons sometimes tried to win the jury's sympathy. They might wear rags or dirty clothes to court or have their wives and children sob in front of the jury.

Romans believed that one law should apply to all citizens. Still, under the empire, Roman law was not applied equally. The poor, who were often not citizens, faced harsher punishments than the rich; sometimes even torture.

> **rule of law** the idea that people should live according to a set of agreed-upon laws

In Rome's law courts, lawyers represented both accused persons and their accusers.

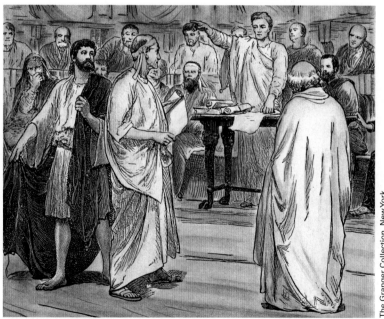

The Granger Collection, New York

35.4 Religion

Religion was important to the Romans. As you may know, the Romans adopted many Greek gods. They also adopted gods from other cultures to create their own group of gods.

Romans wanted to please their gods because they believed that the gods controlled their daily lives. At Rome's many temples and shrines, people made offerings and promises to the gods. They often left gifts of food, such as honey cakes and fruit. They also sacrificed animals, including bulls, sheep, and oxen.

When someone was sick or injured, Romans would leave a small offering at a temple in the shape of the hurt part of the body. For instance, they might leave a clay foot to remind the god which part of the body to cure.

Festivals and holidays, or "holy days," were held throughout the year to honor the gods. But religion was also a part of daily life. Each home had an altar where the family worshipped its own household gods and spirits. The family hearth, or fireplace, was sacred to the goddess Vesta. During the main meal, the family threw a small cake into the fire as an offering to Vesta.

In time, the Romans came to honor their emperors as gods. One emperor, Caligula (kah-LIG-yoo-lah), had a temple built to house a statue of himself made of gold. Every day the statue was dressed in the type of clothes that Caligula was wearing that day.

As the empire grew, foreigners brought new forms of worship to Rome. The Romans welcomed most of these new religions, as long as they didn't encourage disloyalty to the emperor.

Bulls were often sacrificed to Mars, the Roman god of war.

35.5 Family Life

Family life in Rome was ruled by the **paterfamilias** (pah-ter-fah-MEE-lee-us), or "father of the family." A Roman father's word was law in his own home. Even his grown sons and daughters had to obey him.

Roman men were expected to provide for the family. In richer families, husbands often held well-paid political positions. In poor families, both husbands and wives had to work in order to feed and care for themselves and their children.

Wealthy Roman women ran their households. They bought and trained the family's slaves. Many had money of their own and were active in business. They bought and sold property.

Roman babies were usually born at home. The Romans kept only strong, healthy babies. If the father didn't approve of a newborn, it was left outside to die or to be claimed as a slave. Romans found it strange that other people, such as the Egyptians, raised all their children.

Babies were named in a special ceremony when they were nine days old. A good-luck charm called a *bulla* (BOO-lah) was placed around the baby's neck. Children wore their bullas throughout childhood.

Between the ages of 14 and 18, a Roman boy celebrated becoming a man. In a special ceremony, he offered his bulla, along with his childhood toys and clothes, to the gods.

Roman girls did not have a ceremony to mark the end of childhood. They became adults when they were married, usually between the ages of 12 and 18.

Weddings were held at a temple. The bride wore a white toga with a long veil. The groom also wore a white toga, along with leather shoes that he had shined with animal fat. But the new husband did not become a paterfamilias until his own father died.

paterfamilias the oldest male of a Roman household; his word was law for the family

For young men and women in Rome, getting married was a step into adulthood.

35.6 Food and Drink

What Romans cooked and ate depended on whether they were rich or poor. Only the rich had kitchens in their homes. The poor cooked on small grills and depended on "fast-food" places called *thermopolia* (therm-op-oh-LEE-ah), where people could buy hot and cold foods that were ready to eat. Even the rich often bought their daytime meals at thermopolia because the service was fast and convenient.

The main foods in ancient Rome were bread, beans, spices, a few vegetables, cheeses, and meats. Favorite drinks included plain water and hot water with herbs and honey.

For breakfast, Romans usually ate a piece of bread and a bowl of beans or porridge. Porridge was an oatmeal-like cereal made from grains like barley or wheat. Lunch might include a small bit of cheese and bread, and perhaps some olives or celery.

For dinner, poor Romans might have chunks of fish along with some asparagus and a fig for dessert. Wealthy Romans ate more elaborate dinners. Besides the main part of the meal, they had special appetizers. Some favorites were mice cooked in honey, roasted parrots stuffed with dates, salted jellyfish, and snails dipped in milk.

Roman markets offered many choices to those who could afford them. Wealthy Roman women or their slaves shopped for the perfect foods for fancy dinner parties. Merchants often kept playful monkeys or colorful birds on display to attract customers. Shelves were packed with fruits, live rabbits, chickens, geese, baskets of snails, and cuts of meat. Large clay jars were filled with a salty fish sauce, called *garum,* that the Romans liked to pour over the main dish at dinner.

In Rome's bustling marketplace, merchants sold many kinds of food and other goods.

35.7 Housing

Like food, housing was very different in Rome for the rich and for the poor. The spacious, airy homes of the rich stood side by side with the small, dark apartments that housed the poor.

Wealthy Romans lived in grand houses, built of stone and marble. Thick walls shut out the noise and dirt of the city.

Inside the front door was a hall called an *atrium* where the family received guests. An indoor pool helped to keep the atrium cool. An opening in the roof let in plenty of light.

Beyond the atrium, there were many rooms for the family and guests. The fanciest room was the dining room. Its walls were covered in pictures, both painted murals and mosaics made of tiles. Mosaics also decorated the floors. Graceful statues stood in the corners. Some dining rooms had beautiful fountains in the center to provide guests with cool water.

During dinner parties, guests lay on couches and ate delicious meals prepared by slaves. While they ate, they listened to music played by slaves on flutes and stringed instruments, such as the lyre and the lute.

Nearby, many of the poor crowded into tall apartment buildings. Others lived in small apartments above the shops where they worked. Without proper kitchens, the poor cooked their meals on small portable grills, which filled the rooms with smoke.

The apartments were cramped, noisy, and dirty. Filth and disease-carrying rats caused sickness to spread rapidly. Fire was another danger. Many of the buildings were made of wood, and the cooking grills caught fire easily. In 64 C.E., a disastrous fire broke out that burned down much of the city.

In this atrium of a wealthy Roman's home, you can see the roof opening that let in light and the indoor pool that helped to cool the house.

Unlike the rich, the empire's poor lived in crowded, dirty apartment buildings.

35.8 Education

If you had grown up in ancient Rome, your education would have depended on the type of family you were born into. Many poor children in Rome were sent to work instead of to school. They learned trades, such as leatherworking and metalworking, to help earn money for their families.

In wealthier families, boys and girls were tutored by their fathers, or often by slaves, until they were about six years old. Then boys went off to school. Classes were held in public buildings and private homes. Many of the tutors were educated Greek slaves.

A typical school day in Rome began very early in the morning. Students walked through crowded streets, carrying their supplies in a leather shoulder bag. On the way, they stopped at local breakfast bars. There they bought beans, nuts, and freshly baked bread to munch on while they walked to class.

Once at school, students sat on small stools around the tutor. They used a pointed pen, called a stylus, to copy down lessons on small, wax-covered wooden boards. When the lesson was over, they rubbed out the writing with the flat end of the stylus so they could use the board again. The school day lasted until two or three o'clock in the afternoon.

Roman boys learned Latin, Greek, math, science, literature, music, and public speaking. They typically became soldiers, doctors, politicians, or lawyers. Girls might become dentists, real estate agents, or tutors. Some female slaves or freedwomen could become midwives (nurses who helped with childbirth).

Upper-class boys stayed in school until age 12 or 13. Boys from very wealthy families often continued their studies until they were 16, when they began to manage their own properties.

Wealthier Roman families hired tutors to teach their children.

35.9 Recreation

There were many forms of recreation in Rome. Wealthy Romans had a lot of **leisure**, because slaves did the work. The rich enjoyed plays in theaters and musical performances in one another's homes.

Both rich and poor often relaxed at Rome's public baths. There they could bathe, swim, exercise, and enjoy a steam bath or a massage. The baths also had gardens, libraries, shops, and art galleries.

Roman emperors made sure to give the poor "bread and circuses"—food and entertainment—to keep them busy and happy. Besides the many festivals throughout the year, rich and poor alike flocked to two spectacles: gladiator contests and chariot races.

Romans watched gladiators fight in large public arenas, like the **Colosseum**. Both men and women were gladiators. Usually, they were slaves or prisoners of war, although some won or bought their freedom in time. The crowd shouted as the gladiators fought each other and wild animals to the death. Many thousands of gladiators died bloody and painful deaths for the entertainment of the spectators.

A favorite gathering place was the **Circus Maximus,** a huge racetrack with room for 200,000 spectators. There, Romans watched thrilling chariot races. Wealthy citizens sat on plush cushions close to the track, with shades protecting them from the sun. The poor sat on wooden benches high above the track.

Men and women sat in separate sections at the Colosseum, but could sit together at the Circus Maximus. A Roman poet said the Circus Maximus was the best place to meet a new boyfriend or girlfriend because you never knew who would sit next to you.

At the Circus Maximus, chariot races (top) thrilled thousands of spectators. Rome's gladiator contests (bottom) were bloody— and deadly.

Colosseum a large arena in Rome where gladiator contests and other games and sporting events were held

Circus Maximus a large Roman stadium primarily used for chariot races

Daily Life in the Roman Empire **373**

35.10 Country Life

Rome was one of many cities scattered throughout the Roman Empire. But 90 percent of the empire's people lived in the country. There, too, rich and poor had very different lives.

Wealthy Romans often owned country **estates** with large homes, called villas. A villa was a place for Romans to invest their money in raising crops and livestock. And it was a pleasant place to relax in the summer's heat.

When they went to the country, wealthy estate owners checked up on how their farms were being managed. But they had plenty of time left over for reading and writing, as well as for hunting, picnicking, and taking long walks in the fresh air.

The empire's farms provided much of the food for Rome and other cities. They produced grain for bread, grapes for wine, and olives for oil. Goats and sheep provided cheese, and their skins and wool were made into clothing. Cattle and pigs were raised for their meat. Farmers also kept bees for making honey, the sweetener used by the Romans.

Slaves did much of the actual work of farming. Overseers, or supervisors, kept a close eye on the slaves and often treated them cruelly.

Many people in the countryside were not slaves, but their lives were hard. They lived in huts and worked their own small farms, trying to earn enough to survive. Or, they labored on the estates, tending the animals, helping with the crops, or working as servants. In the 1st century C.E., Paul of Tarsus, a Christian writer, summed up the lives of the empire's poor. He wrote, "He who does not work shall not eat."

At a Roman villa, lush landscaping surrounds the large house.

In this chapter, you learned about daily life for the rich and the poor in the Roman Empire. Rome was a large, thriving capital city.

Many wealthy Romans, such as this woman, were attended by personal servants and slaves.

Daily Life in Ancient Rome Nearly one million people lived in the city of Rome. The Forum was its center. The empire had many large cities, but most people lived in the country.

Law and Order Romans believed in the rule of law. Laws were strict, but crime was common. Any Roman could accuse someone else of a crime. A jury decided the case.

Religion Religion was part of daily life. Romans made offerings to the gods. Festivals and holy days were held throughout the year. Each home had an altar for household gods and spirits. The Romans also honored their emperors as gods.

Family Life Each family was ruled by the paterfamilias. At nine days old, a baby was given a bulla, which he or she wore throughout childhood. Between 14 and 18, a boy became a man. Girls became adults when they were married, between 12 and 18.

Food, Drink, and Housing Only the rich had kitchens. The poor cooked on small grills or bought "fast food." The main foods were bread, beans, spices, vegetables, cheeses, meats, and garum. Drinks included water and hot water with herbs and honey. The rich lived in large houses, built around a central atrium. The poor crowded into apartment buildings.

Education and Recreation Many poor children in Rome learned trades, instead of going to school. Wealthier boys and girls were tutored by their fathers or by slaves until they were about 6. Then boys went to school. Roman boys learned Latin, Greek, math, science, literature, music, and public speaking. Upper-class boys stayed in school until age 12 or 13. The rich enjoyed plays and musical performances. Both rich and poor often relaxed at Rome's public baths. Besides celebrating many festivals, rich and poor alike enjoyed viewing gladiator contests and chariot races.

Country Life Ninety percent of the empire's people lived in the country. The wealthy often owned villas. Farms provided much of the food for the cities. Slaves did much of the farm work. Many country people were not slaves, but their lives were hard. They lived in huts and worked their own small farms or on the great estates.

Chapter 36

The Origins and Spread of Christianity

How did Christianity originate and spread?

36.1 Introduction

In this chapter, you will discover how a new religion, Christianity, spread throughout the Roman Empire. Christianity was founded by Jesus, a man who lived from about 6 B.C.E to about 30 C.E. The New Testament of the Christian Bible tells that Jesus was put to death by crucifixion, a form of execution in which a person is tied or nailed to a cross. Christians believe that Jesus was the Son of God and call him Jesus Christ.

As time went on and Christianity gained followers, many Romans saw the faith as a threat to Roman order and tradition. Several emperors tried to stop the spread of the new religion through violent persecutions. Then, in 312 C.E., the day before going into battle against a rival, the emperor Constantine had a vision of a cross hanging in the sky. Around the cross were the words "In this sign, you will conquer." That night he had a dream about Jesus. The emperor saw the vision and dream as a sign that he would win the battle if he accepted Christian beliefs.

Constantine's soldiers went into battle with the first two letters of the word *Christ* on their shields. At the Battle of Milvian Bridge, near Rome, they won a great victory. From that time on, Constantine favored the Christian God over all others. His mother became a leader in the faith. By 380 C.E., Christianity was the official religion of the Roman Empire.

How did this happen? Where did Christianity begin? How did it gradually spread throughout the Roman Empire? In this chapter, you will find answers to these questions.

The emperor Constantine was the first Roman ruler to follow the new religion of Christianity.

◀ The Church of the Holy Sepulchre in Jerusalem is sacred to Christians.

36.2 Judea: The Birthplace of Christianity

The birthplace of **Christianity** was a remote territory at the eastern end of the Mediterranean Sea. According to the New Testament, **Jesus,** the founder of Christianity, was born in this region. The Romans called it Judea. It had once been part of the ancient kingdom of Israel ruled by kings David and Solomon.

The Jews of the region were devoted to their homeland and to their belief in a single God. This belief, together with their religious customs, set them apart from their neighbors in the ancient world.

Once an independent kingdom, Judea came under Roman rule in 63 B.C.E. The Romans tried to govern the country by putting in charge Jewish rulers who agreed with Roman rule. But several times, groups of Jews rebelled against Roman control.

In 37 B.C.E., Rome appointed a man named Herod to be the king of Judea. Although Herod was not Jewish by birth, he practiced the Jewish religion and rebuilt the Temple of Jerusalem. However, many Jews distrusted him. They saw him as a puppet of the Romans.

When Herod died in 4 B.C.E., his kingdom was divided among his three sons. Once again, unrest broke out. Finally, Rome sent soldiers to Judea to take control. They replaced Herod's sons with a military governor.

The military governor kept order and made sure Judeans paid taxes to Rome. But he usually left local affairs to the Jews themselves. For example, a council of Jewish leaders ruled the holy city of Jerusalem. The council was headed by a high, or chief, priest.

Judea was outwardly peaceful. But many Jews hated the Romans. In their sacred writings, they saw prophecies that one day God would send a savior to restore the glorious kingdom of David. This savior was called the **Messiah,** or "anointed one." *Anointed* means "blessed with oil." More generally, it means specially chosen by God.

Judea, where the New Testament says Jesus was born, was located in the present-day Middle East.

Judea, About 1 C.E.

0   400   800 miles
0   400   800 kilometers
Lambert Azimuthal Equal-Area Projection

BRITAIN

GAUL

ALPS

Rhine River

Danube River

Black Sea

Caspian Sea

SPAIN

Tiber River   Rome   MACEDONIA   ASIA MINOR   ASSYRIA

Rubicon River

Euphrates River

Tigris River

Sicily

Nazareth   GALILEE

Mediterranean Sea   Jerusalem

Bethlehem

EGYPT

Red Sea

Nile River

S A H A R A

- Roman Empire, 1 C.E.
- Judea (ruled by Rome)
- • City

According to the Gospel of Luke, Jesus was born in a stable, where his parents had taken shelter because there was no room inside the inn. There, humble shepherds and three kings came to see him.

36.3 The Birth of Jesus

No one knows exactly when Jesus was born. Our modern calendar dates the start of the Common Era from the supposed year of Jesus's birth. But after careful study, historians now believe that Jesus was probably born in about 6 B.C.E., during the reign of King Herod.

Historical records tell us a great deal about the days of the Roman Empire. The lives of the emperors, for example, were recorded in detail. But there were few historians to write about Jesus. Instead, most of the information about him comes from the writings of his followers.

These writings make up the New Testament of the Christian Bible. Among them are four **Gospels**. The Gospels are accounts of Jesus's life that were written in Greek by four of his followers, some years after Jesus's death. The followers' names have come down to us as Matthew, Mark, Luke, and John.

Gospel an account of the life and teachings of Jesus; four of them are included in the New Testament of the Christian Bible

The Gospel of Luke tells the story of Jesus's birth. According to Luke, Jesus's mother, Mary, lived in a town called Nazareth in the Roman territory of Galilee. There, the Gospels claim, an angel appeared to her. The angel told Mary she would have a child and that she should name him Jesus.

Luke's gospel says that around this time the Roman emperor Augustus ordered a census, or head count, of all the people in the Empire. Each man was supposed to go to the town of his birth to be counted. Mary's husband, a carpenter named Joseph, set out from Nazareth to his hometown of Bethlehem (BETH-lih-hem), in the territory of Judea. Mary went with him. In Bethlehem, she gave birth to Jesus.

According to the Gospel of Luke, Jesus's family returned to Nazareth after his birth. The New Testament gospels say little about Jesus's childhood. It is likely that he grew up in Nazareth and learned carpentry. According to Luke, at age 12, Jesus astonished the rabbis, or teachers, in the great Temple of Jerusalem with his wisdom and his knowledge of Jewish law.

When Jesus was about 30, a preacher known as John the Baptist identified Jesus as the Messiah—the savior the Jews had been waiting for. After 40 days of praying in the wilderness, Jesus began to preach in Galilee.

36.4 The Life and Death of Jesus

According to the Gospels, Jesus began preaching in Galilee, an area in present-day Israel. At first, he preached in synagogues, or Jewish places of worship. Larger and larger crowds gathered to hear him. So Jesus began teaching in open areas—in the street, on hillsides, and by the Sea of Galilee.

disciple a person who helps spread the religious teachings of another

Jesus called a small number to be his followers, or **disciples**. The disciples were mostly simple people, such as laborers and fishermen. Throughout his life, Jesus spent time with ordinary people, the poor, and the sick, rather than those who were wealthy and important.

The Teachings of Jesus Jesus based his teachings on traditional Jewish beliefs. But the Gospels say he put special **emphasis** on love and mercy. Of all the Jewish laws, he said, two were the most important. The first was, "You shall love your God with all your heart and all your soul." The second was, "You shall love your neighbor as yourself."

According to the Gospels, Jesus told his followers that the kingdom of God was coming soon. But to Jesus, God's kingdom was not an earthly kingdom of power and riches. Instead, the kingdom of God meant a time when people would live according to God's will. Then, Jesus said, everyone would know God's love for all people, even those who suffer or who are looked down upon by others.

One of Jesus's favorite ways of teaching was through **parables,** simple stories with moral or religious messages. Jewish law says that you should love your neighbor as yourself. When asked, "Who is my neighbor?" Jesus told the Parable of the Good Samaritan. Once a traveler was beaten and robbed on the road. Two people passed by and ignored him. Then a Samaritan stopped and helped the injured traveler. In Jesus's time, the Judeans and Samaritans did not get along. Because of the Samaritan's good deed, however, Jesus considered him a neighbor, worthy of love.

Teachings like this shocked and angered some of Jesus's listeners. To some Jews, this way of thinking was wrong and dangerous. Others worried that Jesus's growing following would cause trouble with the Romans. Jesus did not preach revolt against the Romans. Still, it was easy for some people to see him as a troublemaker.

The Crucifixion and Resurrection   According to the Gospels, after a year or two of traveling and preaching, Jesus went to Jerusalem for the Jewish festival of Passover. The festival celebrated God's rescue of the Jews from Egypt more than a thousand years before Jesus's time. Every year, thousands of Jews came to Jerusalem to celebrate Passover. Roman soldiers kept a sharp eye out for anyone who might start a demonstration against Rome.

The Granger Collection, New York

The Gospels tell about crowds that gathered to hear Jesus preach and to ask him to cure the sick.

parable a simple story that explains a moral or religious lesson

This 15th-century painting by Piero della Francesca is called *The Resurrection of Christ*. It is his interpretation of the Christian belief that Jesus rose from the dead and appeared to his disciples.

Resurrection in Christian belief, Jesus's rise from the dead

According to the Gospels, Jesus said that his enemies would come together to destroy him and that he would be killed. The Gospels then tell that one of Jesus's disciples, Judas, had decided to betray him. After a final meal with his disciples, Jesus went to pray in a garden. Judas then reported where Jesus could be found. As Jesus was led away under guard, the other disciples ran away. Christians call Jesus's final meal with his disciples "the Last Supper."

Jesus had gained a large following in Jerusalem. The city's Roman rulers feared that his supporters might stir up trouble. They worried that Jesus might lead a revolt. To end this threat, they decided that he must die. According to the Christian Bible, Pontius Pilate, the Roman governor of Judea, ordered that Jesus be executed. In Roman times, a common form of execution was to be crucified, or tied or nailed to a cross until dead.

According to the New Testament, the Romans took Jesus to a hill outside the city walls. There, they nailed him to a cross and left him to die between two other condemned men who were also crucified. A few faithful followers took his body and buried it in a tomb carved out of rock.

The Gospels say that three days later Jesus rose from the dead and then appeared to his disciples. Christians call this event the **Resurrection**. Belief in the Resurrection convinced Jesus's disciples that he was the Son of God. According to the Gospels, Jesus left them again some time later to join his Father, God, in heaven. His disciples then began spreading the news of his life and teachings.

36.5 The Missionary Work of Paul

The early converts to Christianity were Jews, just as Jesus and his disciples had been. One such **convert** was Paul. He is one of the most important people in Christianity. He devoted his life to spreading the teachings of Jesus. After his death, the Roman Catholic Church named him a saint.

Paul came from Tarsus, a town in present-day Turkey. At first, he opposed Christianity and helped to persecute Christians. According to the New Testament, one day Paul was traveling to Damascus in present-day Syria. He saw a blinding light and heard the voice of Jesus. The vision changed Paul's life. He adopted the Christian faith and became a **missionary**.

As an educated man with Roman citizenship who spoke Greek, Paul made it his special mission to convert non-Jews, called Gentiles, to the new religion. He spent 17 years visiting cities throughout the Greek-speaking world. Wherever he went, he made new converts and started new churches.

In his preaching and letters, Paul **stressed** the need to believe in Jesus as the Son of God. He taught that all people, Jews and Gentiles alike, were God's children. Jesus, he said, was the Christ, God's chosen one. He was a Messiah for everyone, not just his fellow Jews.

Paul's journeys took him through much of the empire. He preached throughout Asia Minor, in Greece, and in Rome. Sometimes his visits caused riots when angry Jews protested what they considered blasphemous, or unholy, teaching.

For a time Paul was jailed in Rome, where he continued to write letters to other Christians. Tradition says that he was beheaded by the Romans in about 65 C.E. By that time, the Romans were beginning to persecute Christian believers.

missionary someone who tries to convert others to believe in a particular religion or set of beliefs

In this enamel plaque from the 12th century, Paul speaks with Jews and Gentiles. Paul also wrote letters to Christian communities in which he taught about the life, death, and Resurrection of Jesus. These letters became part of the Christian Bible.

Emperor Constantine supported Christianity and was baptized before he died.

36.6 Christianity Spreads

By the 60s C.E., Christians were beginning to attract the notice of the Romans. Christian preachers traveled along the roads of the empire, winning converts to their new religion. Both Paul and Peter, a close friend of Jesus, preached in Rome. At first, Rome was not unfriendly to Christians. What was another god, among so many?

But Christians refused to worship the other Roman gods. Worse, they would not accept that the emperor was a god. Their way of life seemed to be an insult to Roman customs. Instead of wealth and luxury, they preferred simplicity. Recalling Jesus's message of peace and love, many refused to serve in the army.

As the number of Christians grew, many Romans saw them as a threat to Roman order and patriotism. Eventually, the Christian religion was declared illegal.

Some emperors were determined to make an example of these disloyal citizens. For refusing to honor the Roman gods, Christians were sentenced to die in cruel and painful ways. Some were crucified. Some were burned to death. Others were brought into arenas, where they were devoured by wild animals in front of cheering crowds.

But the persecutions failed to destroy the new religion. Instead, Christians won new admirers by facing death bravely. Christianity offered many people in the empire a sense of purpose and hope. It taught that even the poor and slaves could look forward to a better life after death if they followed the teachings of Jesus.

Gradually, people of all classes began to adopt the new faith. By 300 C.E., possibly as many as 30 million Christians lived in the Roman lands of Europe, North Africa, and western Asia.

At the beginning of the chapter, you read about the emperor **Constantine** and how a victory in battle made him favor the Christian religion. In 313 C.E., Constantine announced the Edict of Milan. An *edict* is an order. In this edict, Constantine gave Christians the freedom to practice their religion openly. Future emperors also accepted the new faith. Emperor Theodosius I banned all pagan sacrifices. By 380, Christianity was the official religion of the Roman Empire.

Constantine Roman emperor from about 280 to 337 C.E.; the first Roman emperor to become a Christian

Chapter Summary

In this chapter, you learned how Christianity began and how it spread across the Roman Empire.

Judea: The Birthplace of Christianity Christianity began in Judea in the present-day Middle East. Jews there told prophecies about a Messiah who would remove the Romans and restore the kingdom of David.

The Birth of Jesus What we know about Jesus's life and his birth around 6 B.C.E., comes from the four Gospels. Not much is known about his childhood, but when Jesus was about 30, John the Baptist identified him as the Messiah.

The Life and Death of Jesus Jesus preached with his disciples in present-day Israel. He emphasized love and mercy, and often taught in parables. His teachings angered some. In his early 30s, the Romans executed Jesus by crucifixion. According to the Christian Bible, three days later, he arose from the dead and appeared to his disciples. His disciples began to spread his teachings.

The Missionary Work of Paul Paul of Tarsus was a Jew. He persecuted Christians. But after a vision, he became an important Christian missionary, spreading the religion around the empire. His letters to early churches are part of the Christian Bible.

Christianity Spreads The new religion survived harsh persecution and spread across the Roman Empire. In 313 C.E., the emperor Constantine gave Christians freedom of religion in the Edict of Milan. It was the official Roman religion by 380.

Chapter 37

Learning About World Religions: Christianity

How are Christians' lives shaped by the beliefs and practices of Christianity?

37.1 Introduction

In this chapter, you will learn how Christianity shapes the lives of Christians around the world today. Christianity is the most **widespread** of the world's major faiths. Christian churches are found in most parts of the globe. With two billion followers, Christianity is the largest religion, as well. About a third of the world's people call themselves Christians.

Christianity is a diverse religion. One scholar has counted over thirty thousand separate Christian denominations, or religious groups, worldwide. Each group has its own views on how the faith should be practiced. Some denominations are quite small. Others have many millions of members.

All Christians are bound by their belief in the teachings of Jesus. These are found in the New Testament of the Christian Bible. This Bible tells how, through his life and words, Jesus brought a message of love. He told followers of God's love for all people. He urged them to let that love flow through themselves to others, even enemies. In his most famous sermon Jesus said:

> Love your enemies, do good to those who hate you, bless those who curse you, pray for those who mistreat you.
> —*The Gospel of Luke, Chapter 6, Verse 27*

In this chapter, you will learn more about Christian beliefs. You will see how the early Christian community became a religion with many branches. You will also examine the beliefs and practices that have given meaning to the lives of Christians for nearly two thousand years.

Christianity has spread around the globe. About one of every four people in Asia is a Christian. Shown here is a priest in China.

◄ St. Peter's Basilica in Rome is the "mother church" of Catholicism.

37.2 The Central Beliefs of Christianity

Although there are differences of **interpretation,** most Christians today accept a set of central beliefs about God and his relationship with humankind. Let's examine some of these basic Christian beliefs, including the Holy Trinity, the Resurrection, and Salvation.

Trinity in Christianity, the unity of the Father, Son, and Holy Spirit as three beings in one God

salvation being saved from sin; in Christianity, to be specifically saved by Jesus, the source of salvation

The Holy Trinity   Christians believe in one God. They see God as three beings in one—Father, Son, and Holy Spirit. This union of three beings in one God is known as the **Trinity**.

Christians believe that God the father is the creator of the universe. They believe that world and everything in it reveal his power and love. Christians believe that God the son is Jesus, known to his followers as Jesus Christ.

Most Christians believe that Jesus was both divine and human. He lived and died like a human being. Christians also believe that he is the son of God, who took a human form.

Christians believe that the Holy Spirit is God's power at work in the world today. They believe that when they feel God present in their lives, the Holy Spirit has touched them.

The Resurrection and Salvation   Christians believe that, after his execution and burial, Jesus rose from the dead and appeared to his disciples before joining his father in heaven. To Christians, this is a miracle known as the Resurrection.

Christians believe that they, too, can look forward to life after death. After the end of this life, each person faces God's judgment. God decides who should be saved from sin and evil to enjoy eternal life in heaven, according to their beliefs.

The belief that God can save people from sin and grant them everlasting life is known as **salvation**. Christians believe that salvation is a gift from God. This gift is open to all who have faith in Jesus and repent, or ask God to forgive their sins.

This image of the Trinity shows symbols for God the Father (top), Jesus the Son (left), and the Holy Spirit (right).

37.3 From One Church to Many

Christianity became the official religion of the Roman Empire in 380 C.E. As the religion spread across Europe, however, conflicts arose over differences of opinion about Christian beliefs.

German priest Martin Luther began the separation from the Roman Catholic Church that developed into the Protestant Reformation.

The Great Schism of 1054   One such conflict occurred between church leaders in eastern and western Europe. Church leaders in western Europe insisted that the Christian church had one leader—the pope. The pope lived in Rome. But he claimed authority over Christians everywhere.

Church leaders in eastern Europe rejected this claim by the pope. Their leaders were called the patriarchs. The patriarch of Constantinople claimed authority over all Christians in eastern Europe.

In 1054, a quarrel between these leaders split the church into two separate branches. The western branch became the **Roman Catholic Church**. The eastern branch became the **Eastern Orthodox Church**. This division of the Christian church is remembered as the Great Schism of 1054.

The Reformation   Another conflict began in 1517. In that year, a German priest named Martin Luther called for reforms in the Roman Catholic Church. The pope demanded that Luther give up his reform efforts. Luther refused. Instead, he rejected the pope's authority over him. He and his followers formed their own church. They were called **Protestants** because their church began as a protest against the Roman Catholic Church.

Other religious reformers followed Luther's example. Today, the Protestant branch of Christianity includes thousands of denominations. Protestant churches differ from one another in their beliefs and practices. But they share a belief in the Trinity, the Resurrection of Jesus, and salvation as a gift from God.

37.4 Christian Sacraments

By Luther's time, Christianity had spread across Europe. From there, Christian missionaries carried their faith around the world. Today, most people in North and South America are Christians. There are many Christians in Africa and Asia, as well. Wherever Christians live, sacred rituals called **sacraments** shape their lives. Let's learn about two of the most widely practiced sacraments.

Roman Catholic Church a Christian church headed by the pope in Rome

Eastern Orthodox Church a Christian church that grew out of Christianity in eastern Europe and present-day Turkey

Protestant any member of a Christian church founded on the principles of the Reformation

sacrament a sacred rite, or ritual, of Christian churches

Baptism by full immersion is practiced in many Christian denominations. These people are being baptized as Christians in Africa.

baptism the Christian sacrament that makes a person a member of the Christian Church

Holy Communion a Christian sacrament in which bread and wine are consumed as memorials of Jesus's Last Supper with his disciples

Baptism **Baptism** involves the use of water to **symbolize** a new phase in a person's life. The New Testament tells how Jesus himself was baptized in the Jordan River by John the Baptist before he began his preaching. The sacrament of baptism marks a person's entry into the Christian Church. Churches differ on when they baptize their members. Some baptize children while they are still infants. Others wait until a person is old enough to choose to be baptized.

Churches also differ on how they carry out this sacrament. Some churches sprinkle water on the person's head. Others immerse the person completely underwater. Either way, Christians see baptism as central to their identity as members of the Christian community.

Holy Communion The sacrament of **Holy Communion,** known as the Eucharist, is central to Christian worship. The New Testament tells us that Jesus began this sacrament at the Last Supper. He gave bread to his disciples, saying, "This is my body." He poured them wine, saying, "This is my blood." He told them to practice this sacrament in remembrance of him.

Almost all Christian churches celebrate Holy Communion in some way. Generally, this involves sharing bread and wine or grape juice that has been specially blessed. Christians differ in their vision of Holy Communion and its meaning. They perform the sacrament differently and at different **intervals** during the year. Some see the bread and wine as the body and blood of Christ. Others see both as symbolic. But all Christians believe that the presence and power of Christ is conveyed through the sacrament of Holy Communion.

37.5 Christian Worship

For most Christians, going to church and worshipping with others is an important part of Christian life. Some Christians attend church regularly, while others do not. When Christians refer to "the church," they sometimes have in mind the world community of Christians. At other times, they have in mind a specific group of Christian believers. Such a group can gather anywhere—outdoors, at home, or in a building.

Places of Worship Most Christians gather in churches built as places of worship. Churches around the world range in size from simple huts to vast cathedrals. But almost all display a cross, the universal symbol of Christianity.

Some churches are richly decorated with paintings and stained glass windows to celebrate the glory of God. Others are kept very plain so that nothing will distract worshippers from focusing on the word of God in the Bible.

Sunday Services Most churches hold their worship services on Sunday. That is the day Christians believe Jesus rose from the dead. Christians worship in many different ways. But most Sunday services combine hymns and readings from the Bible. Hymns are songs of praise to God. Some churches celebrate Holy Communion every Sunday. Others do so only once or twice a year. Many services also include a sermon given by the church leader, such as a priest or a minister. A *sermon* is a speech intended for religious instruction.

Prayer is a part of every worship service. Prayers may be read or spoken aloud. Or worshippers may pray in silence. However Christians pray, they believe that God hears their prayers.

Churches vary in size, shape, and decoration. But all are places where Christians can gather to worship. This shared sense of community is an important part of Christianity.

The Christmas pageant is a holiday tradition for students at this Christian school in Honolulu, Hawaii.

37.6 The Christian Year

The Christian year is marked by events in the life of Jesus and his followers. Christmas and Easter are by far the most widely celebrated holidays. But over the centuries, Christians have found other people and events to celebrate, as well.

Christmas Christmas is the holiday that celebrates the birth of Jesus. The story of Jesus's birth is told in the Gospels of both Matthew and Luke.

The story of the first Christmas is told in the Gospel of Luke. It begins with Mary and Joseph traveling to the town of Bethlehem for a Roman census. There, Mary gave birth to Jesus in a humble stable. That same night, angels appeared in the sky saying, "Glory to God in the highest, and on Earth peace, goodwill toward men."

Today, Christians gather with family and in churches to retell this story in songs and plays. They rejoice in the birth of Jesus and in his later message of God's love. And they strive to let peace and goodwill shine through their hearts to all people.

Easter Easter is the most important holiday in Christianity. It celebrates the Resurrection of Jesus. In the United States and Europe, Christians celebrate Easter in the spring. Prior to Easter, many Christians observe a season known as Lent.

Lent marks the 40 days that Jesus spent in the wilderness before he began to preach. During that time, Jesus fasted, or went without food. In the past, Christians observed Lent by giving up favorite foods, such as sugar or meat. Today, during Lent, many Christians choose to give up other things they enjoy.

The last week of Lent is known as Holy Week. It begins with Palm Sunday. This holiday recalls Jesus's arrival in Jerusalem to celebrate the Jewish holiday of Passover. According to the Gospels, cheering crowds welcomed him by lining his path with palm branches. On Palm Sunday, some Christians wear crosses made from palm leaves.

At the end of Holy Week, Good Friday marks the day Jesus was crucified. Many churches hold services on that day to remember and mourn Jesus's suffering and death.

In contrast, Easter Sunday is a day of rejoicing. On that day, Christians celebrate the Resurrection of Jesus. Some Christians stay awake through the night to greet Easter morning at dawn with song and celebration. Others attend special Easter morning church services. However they celebrate, Easter is a time for Christians to renew their belief that, through his death and Resurrection, Jesus brings the promise of everlasting life.

The Eastern Orthodox Church often celebrates Easter a week later than other Christian churches.

Chapter Summary

In this chapter, you learned that Christianity has grown into the world's largest religion. It has also become a diverse faith with many denominations.

Christian Central Beliefs Christians believe in one God with three parts—Father, Son, and Holy Spirit—known as the Trinity. Christians believe in the Resurrection of Jesus. They also believe in salvation from sin and in eternal life.

From One Church to Many In 1054, Eastern Orthodox Christianity split from Roman Catholic Christianity in the Great Schism. Beginning in the 1500s, Martin Luther and others began the Reformation that separated Protestants from the Roman Catholic Church and led to the creation of thousands of Protestant denominations.

Christian Sacraments Most Christians practice the sacraments of baptism and Holy Communion. Baptism brings a person into the Christian Church. In Holy Communion, Christians share bread and wine or grape juice as Jesus did in his Last Supper.

Christian Worship and the Christian Year Many Christians make group worship at church services part of their lives. The most important Christian holidays of the Christian year are Christmas and Easter.

Chapter 38

The Legacy of Rome in the Modern World

To what extent does ancient Rome influence us today?

38.1 Introduction

In this chapter, you will learn about contributions the Romans made to the modern world. These were in the areas of art, architecture, engineering, language, government, and the law.

In the year 1764, long after the Roman Empire had fallen, a young Englishman named Edward Gibbon visited the city of Rome. Gibbon saw the ruins of ancient buildings, such as the Roman Colosseum. He marveled at Roman statues and the remains of aqueducts and bridges. He wondered, "How did such a great empire come to an end?"

Gibbon decided to write a book about the Roman Empire. More than twenty years later, Gibbon finally laid down his pen. His work filled six books. He called it *The History of the Decline and Fall of the Roman Empire*. It became a very important work of history.

Why did Gibbon spend so many years learning and writing about ancient Rome? One reason is that Rome has had an **enormous** influence on western civilization. As one historian said, "Rome perished, yet it lived on."

In this chapter, you will discover how and why the Roman Empire came apart. Then you will learn how Rome's influence lives on in modern architecture, art, engineering, language, philosophy, and law.

The ancient Roman Pantheon is one example of Roman architecture and engineering that has influenced modern buildings.

◀ The U.S. Capitol dome shows the influence of Roman architecture.

38.2 The End of the Empire in the West

At the height of Rome's power in the 100s C.E., Romans believed that the empire would last forever. Yet by the year 500, the western half had collapsed. What happened to cause the fall of one of the mightiest empires the world has ever known?

Problems in the Late Empire   Most modern historians believe that a number of problems combined to bring about Rome's fall. Here are three of the main reasons.

Political Instability Rome never solved the problem of how to peacefully **transfer** political power to a new leader. When the emperor died, rivals might fight each other to replace him. Real power fell into the hands of the armies, who could help leaders seize power—or destroy them. Sometimes, rivals did not wait for an emperor to die. Emperors were regularly murdered.

Economic and Social Issues Political instability led to other problems. To finance Rome's huge armies, citizens had to pay heavy taxes. These taxes hurt the economy and drove many people into poverty. Trade also suffered.

Weakening Frontiers The huge size of the empire made it hard to defend. By the 300s, Germanic tribes were pressing hard on the western borders. Many of these people settled inside the empire and were recruited into the army. But these soldiers often had little loyalty to Rome.

As shown in the painting below, the city of Rome was attacked and looted in 410 C.E. by a Germanic tribe. In 476 C.E., the last emperor in Rome lost his throne. This is the event that Gibbon marked as the official fall of the western Roman Empire.

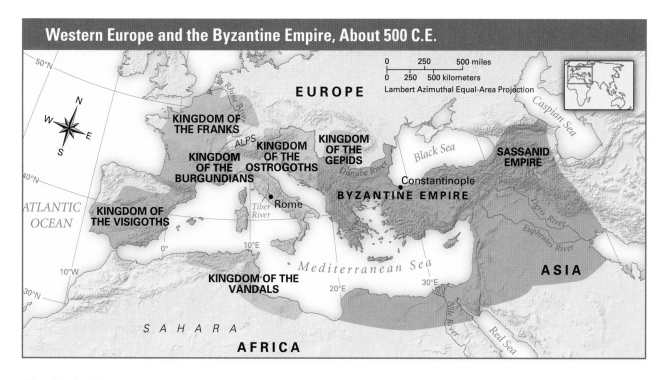

Western Europe and the Byzantine Empire, About 500 C.E.

The Fall of Rome In 330 C.E., the emperor Constantine took a step that changed the future of Rome. He moved his capital 850 miles to the east, to the ancient city of Byzantium (bih-ZAN-tee-uhm), in what is now Turkey. He renamed the city New Rome. Later it was called Constantinople. Today, it is known as Istanbul.

Before Constantine, emperors had tried sharing power over the vast empire between co-rulers. After Constantine's reign, power was usually divided between two emperors, one based in Rome and one in Constantinople. Rome became the capital of just the western part of the empire.

Soon, Rome itself was threatened by Germanic tribes. In 410 C.E., the Visigoths attacked and looted the city. Finally, in 476, the last emperor in the west, Romulus Augustus, lost his throne to a Germanic leader, Odoacer (OH-duh-way-sir). Then, the western half of the empire began to **dissolve** into separate kingdoms ruled by different tribes.

In the east, the empire continued for another 1,000 years. Today, we call this eastern empire the **Byzantine Empire,** after Byzantium, the original name of its capital city. The Byzantines wove the Roman heritage into their own rich civilization. But they were never able to put the old empire back together. For historians, the fall of Rome marks the end of the ancient world.

Yet the influence of Rome lived on. Let's look now at how Rome's legacy continues to affect our lives today.

By the year 500, the Roman Empire had split in two, and the western half was collapsing into separate kingdoms.

Byzantine Empire the name for the eastern Roman Empire, located at the crossroads of Europe and Asia; it lasted from about 500 to 1453 C.E.

patron a person who promotes artistic activities by paying for new works and supporting artists

38.3 Art

The Romans adopted aspects of other cultures. They modified and blended them into their own culture. This was true of Roman art. The Romans were especially influenced by the art of the Greeks. In fact, historians often speak of "Greco-Roman" art.

The Romans were skilled in creating realistic statues. They imitated Greek sculpture, but they were particularly good at making their sculptures true to life.

The homes of wealthy Romans were decorated with colorful murals and mosaics. Again, the Romans took existing artforms and made them their own. They painted beautiful frescoes, a type of mural. Frescoes are painted on moist plaster with water-based paints.

Roman frescoes often showed three-dimensional landscapes and other scenes. Looking at one of these frescoes was almost like looking through the wall at a scene outside. You have probably seen similar murals in modern restaurants, banks, on the sides of buildings, and in other public places.

Romans were also great **patrons,** or sponsors, of art. They paid thousands of painters, sculptors, and craftspeople to create their works. As a result, the Romans left behind many examples to inspire future **generations**.

American artists have often used a Roman style in sculptures and paintings of heroes. Here you see a Roman statue of the emperor Caesar Augustus (left) and an American statue of George Washington (right). In what ways are they alike?

A thousand years after the fall of the empire, Roman art was rediscovered during the period called the **Renaissance**. Great artists, such as Michelangelo, revived the Greco-Roman style in their paintings and sculptures.

A famous example is the ceiling of the Sistine Chapel in Rome. The ceiling shows scenes from the Bible painted by Michelangelo in the 1500s. A Roman would feel right at home looking up at this amazing creation.

Roman art has continued to influence painters and sculptors. Roman styles were especially popular during the early days of the United States. Americans imitated these styles to give their art dignity and nobility. For example, many statues in the capital, Washington, D.C., reflect a strong Roman influence.

The Romans also brought a sense of style and luxury to everyday objects. They made highly decorative bottles of blown glass. For example, a bottle might be shaped like of a cluster of grapes. Romans also developed the arts of gem cutting and metalworking. One popular art form was the cameo. A cameo is a raised, carved portrait of a person's head or a carved scene. The Romans wore cameos as jewelry and used them to decorate vases and other objects. You can find examples of all these art forms today.

With their frescoes and mosaics, wealthy Roman homes were like art galleries.

Renaissance a great flowering of culture based on classical Greek and Roman ideas that began in Italy around 1300 and spread throughout Europe

The Roman Colosseum has inspired stadium builders throughout history.

38.4 Architecture and Engineering

The Romans' greatest contributions to science and technology came in the fields of architecture and engineering. Roman builders learned from the Greeks, Etruscans, and others. Then they added their own genius to take construction in new directions.

Architecture The Romans learned how to use the arch, the vault, and the dome. A vault is an arch used to support a roof. A dome is a series of vaults that form a high, rounded roof.

The Romans were the first to make widespread use of concrete. They made it by mixing broken stone with sand, cement, and water and then allowing the mixture to harden. With the use of concrete, they were able to build much bigger arches than anyone had attempted before. Roman baths and other public buildings often had great arched vaults. The Pantheon, a magnificent temple, now a church that still stands in Rome, is famous for its huge dome.

The Romans also invented a new kind of building, a stadium. This was a large, open-air structure. The Romans used concrete to build tunnels into the famous Colosseum in Rome. The tunnels made it easy for spectators to reach their seats. Modern football stadiums still use this feature.

Roman arches (left) have been copied and adapted around the world. The Arc de Triomphe in France (right) is one famous modern example.

The grand style of Roman buildings has inspired many architects throughout the centuries. One Roman innovation that was widely copied is the **triumphal arch**. This is a huge monument built to celebrate great victories or achievements. One modern example is the Arc de Triomphe (Arch of Triumph) in Paris, France. This monument celebrates the victories of the French emperor Napoleon in the early 1800s. Today, it is the national war memorial of France.

You can see a Roman influence in the design of many modern churches, banks, and government buildings. A fine example is the Capitol building, the home of the U.S. Congress in Washington, D.C. It includes arches, columns, and a dome.

Engineering   The Romans changed engineering as well as architecture. They were the greatest builders of roads, bridges, and **aqueducts** in the ancient world.

About fifty thousand miles of road connected Rome with the frontiers of the empire. The Romans built their roads with layers of stone, sand, and gravel. Their techniques set the standard of road building for 2,000 years. In some parts of Europe, vehicles still drive on freeways built over old Roman roads.

The Romans also set a new standard for building aqueducts. They did not invent the aqueduct, but once again, the Romans learned the technique and improved it. They created a system of aqueducts for Rome. The aqueducts brought water from about sixty miles away to the homes of the wealthiest citizens, as well as to the city's public baths and fountains. The Romans built aqueducts in other parts of the empire, as well. The water system in Segovia, Spain, still uses part of an ancient Roman aqueduct. Remains of Roman aqueducts can also be seen in Europe, North Africa, and Asia Minor.

> **triumphal arch** a large monument in the shape of an arch that celebrates a leader or a military victory
>
> **aqueduct** a pipe or channel built to carry water over a long distance

Ancient Roman aqueducts were so well built that some still stand in Europe today.

Latin the language originally spoken in ancient Rome, on which many words in modern languages are based

38.5 Language

One legacy of Rome that affects us every day is the Roman language, **Latin**. We use the Latin alphabet, although Roman Latin used 23 letters, and English uses 26. Many of our words come from Latin. Latin proverbs are still in use. For example, look at the reverse side of a U.S. dime. You will see the words *E pluribus unum*. It is Latin for "out of many, one." This is the official motto of the United States. The motto reminds Americans of how the colonies joined together to form the United States.

Several modern European languages developed from Latin, including Italian, Spanish, and French. English is a Germanic language, but it was strongly influenced by the French-speaking Normans, who conquered England in 1066 C.E. English has borrowed heavily from Latin, both directly and by way of French.

You can see the influence of Latin in many words we use today. For example, our calendar comes from the one adopted by Julius Caesar. The names of several months come from Latin. *August* honors Caesar Augustus. *September* comes from Latin words meaning "the seventh month." (The Roman year started in March.) *October* means "the eighth month" in Latin.

Many English words start with Latin prefixes. A *prefix* is a set of letters at the beginning of a word that carries its own meaning. Attaching a prefix to a root word creates a new word with a new meaning. In fact, the word *prefix* is formed this way. It comes from *pre-* ("in front of") and *-fix* ("to fasten" or "to attach"). The table on the opposite page shows other examples.

As you can see from the table, other English words come from Latin root words. For instance, *manual* developed from *manus,* the Latin word for "hand."

Finally, we still often use Roman numerals. The Romans used a system of letters to write numbers. Look at the bottom section of the table. You may see Roman numerals, such as these, on clocks, sundials, and the first pages of books, like this one. You might also find Roman numerals on buildings and in some movie credits to show the year in which they were made.

The Romans combined the seven letters shown in the table to express larger numbers. Putting letters *after* another adds the value of the additional letters. For example, VIII means 5 + 3 = 8 and XX means 10 + 10 = 20. Putting a letter *before* a letter with a greater value subtracts its value. For example, IV means 5 – 1 = 4 and IX means 10 – 1 = 9.

Romans wrote in all capital letters. This Latin inscription on the Arch of Constantine dedicates the arch to the emperor in the name of the Senate and the people of Rome.

Latin Prefixes

Latin	Meaning	English Words
in, im, il	not	inactive, impossible, illogical
inter	among, between	international, Internet
com, co	together, with	communicate, cooperate
pre	before	precede, prepare
post	after, behind	postpone, post-graduate
re	back, again	remember, retreat
semi	half	semicircle
sub	under, less than	submarine
trans	across, through	transportation, transnational

Latin Roots

Latin	Meaning	English Words
anima	life, breath, soul	animal, animated
civis	citizen, community	civic
lex, legalis	law, legal	legislature
manus	hand	manual
militare	to serve as a soldier	military
portare	to carry	portable
unus	one	united
urbs	city	urban
verbum	word	verb, verbal

Roman Numerals

Basic Numerals	Meaning	Other Numerals	Meaning
I	1	II	2
V	5	III	3
X	10	IV	4
L	50	VI	6
C	100	VII	7
D	500	VIII	8
M	1,000	IX	9

Stoicism a philosophy that flourished in ancient Greece and Rome and that focused on developing virtue, self-control, and courage as a way to achieve happiness

38.6 Philosophy and Law

Like art and architecture, Roman philosophy and law were greatly influenced by the Greeks. But the Romans made contributions of their own that they passed on to future generations.

Philosophy   Many Romans followed a philosophy known as **Stoicism** (STOH-ih-sism). First developed by the ancient Greeks, this system of thinking was adopted by the ancient Romans and followed until about 200 C.E.

Stoics believed that a divine intelligence ruled all of nature. A person's soul was a spark of that divine intelligence. Stoics believed that the right way to live was in a way that agrees with nature and its laws.

To the Stoics, the key to life was to have a good character. This meant having virtues such as self-control and courage. Stoics disagreed with those who said that happiness meant only avoiding pain and only experiencing pleasure. They highly prized duty and the welfare of the community over their personal comfort. They believed that true happiness was the peace of mind that came from living up to Stoic ideals.

The most famous Roman Stoic was the emperor Marcus Aurelius. Aurelius wrote down his private thoughts in a book he called "To Himself." Later, it was retitled *Meditations*. In his writings, Aurelius constantly reminded himself of Stoic ideals. He said not to worry if you encounter ungratefulness, insults, disloyalty, or selfishness. If you think and act rightly, none of these things can hurt you.

Stoics were famous for bearing pain and suffering bravely and quietly. To this day, we call someone who behaves in this way a "stoic."

The emperor Marcus Aurelius reigned from 161 to 180 C.E. His book on the practice of Stoicism still inspires people today.

Law and Justice   The Stoics' beliefs about justice and nature fit very well with Roman ideas about law. Roman law covered marriages, inheritances, contracts, and countless other aspects of daily life. Modern law codes in European countries, such as France and Italy, are partly based on Roman laws.

Another legacy of the Romans was their concept of justice. The Romans believed that nature provides a universal law of justice. Under this **natural law,** they believed, every person has natural rights. Romans spread this idea by applying it to all citizens of the empire. Judges in Roman courts tried to make just, or fair, decisions that respected individual rights.

Like most people, the Romans did not always live up to their ideals. Their courts did not treat the poor or slaves equally with the rich. Emperors often made bad laws. But the Roman ideals of justice and natural law live on. The U.S. Declaration of Independence and U.S. Constitution were influenced by Roman ideas about law and government. Like judges in Roman courts, modern-day judges make decisions based on these ideals, as well as on written law. Similarly, many people today believe that all humans have basic rights that no written law can take away.

> **natural law** the concept that there is a universal order built into nature that can guide moral thinking

Chapter Summary

In this chapter, you learned about the fall of Rome and explored its legacy.

The End of the Empire in the West By 500, the Roman Empire had split. The eastern empire lasted for over 1,000 years. But the western empire collapsed due to political instability, economic and social issues, and the weakening of the frontiers.

Art Modern artists still follow Roman or Greco-Roman styles in the arts. Murals and mosaics, much like Roman ones, decorate modern buildings and public spaces.

Architecture and Engineering Roman architectural influences are seen in the structures of many modern buildings. The Romans also were talented engineers, whose construction methods and standards lasted thousands of years.

Language Many words and word parts in modern languages, such as English, French, and Spanish, came from Latin. Roman numerals appear today on clocks, in books, and in movie credits.

Philosophy and Law Roman ideals, such as Stoicism, the rule of law, and justice, shaped law and government in many modern nations. Examples include today's law courts and documents, such as the U.S. Declaration of Independence and the U.S. Constitution.

Lessons from Pompeii

About 2,000 years ago in Italy, a volcano named Mount Vesuvius erupted and completely destroyed the city of Pompeii, killing thousands of people. As much as 16 feet of hot ash and rock buried the city, wiping it from the face of the Earth. Pompeii lay forgotten until archaeologists uncovered it in 1748. Excavations have continued since then, revealing a city preserved like a time capsule. What can this long-dead Roman city tell us about life in cities today?

This artwork depicts the eruption of Mount Vesuvius 2,000 years ago that covered Pompeii in 16 feet of rock and ash and killed thousands of people.

Pompeii lies southeast of Rome, near the present-day city of Naples. At the time it was destroyed, about 20,000 people lived in Pompeii. Many Romans also took vacations there. Pompeii was already an old town when the Romans took control of it in 89 B.C.E. But they rebuilt the existing city in a particularly Roman way.

At the center of every Roman city was a gathering space called a *forum*. This was where the most important public buildings were located. Meeting at the forum were two main streets, one going north and south (the *cardo*), and one going east and west (the *decumanus*). The Romans laid out Pompeii's streets in a grid paralleling these two streets. In pre-Roman times, there were shops in and around the forum, but the Romans moved them all to a single large building that faced the forum.

Pompeii's residential neighborhoods had their own smaller public centers. Shops were placed on side streets, or on the ground floors of buildings where people lived. There were bakeries, grocery stores, and taverns. There were gyms, theaters, and a library.

The Romans gave Pompeii a public water system. An *aqueduct* brought water into the city. It branched into three main pipes. These served more than 25 public fountains, from which most citizens got their water for drinking and cooking. The water system also served public baths, a swimming pool, and some private homes and shops.

Urban Planners Study Pompeii

How can an ancient city destroyed 2,000 years ago have anything to teach us today? Think about the town or city where you live. Its street system must be well organized for traffic to flow smoothly.

There is a mix of public and private spaces. There is probably a forum—though you may call it "downtown," "city center," or "Main Street." In the neighborhoods, too, there are local centers of business and public life. And there is *infrastructure,* the term used to describe the physical systems and facilities that make a city livable.

During the 1990s, scholars at the University of Virginia made a detailed study of Pompeii's archaeology. This study was called the Pompeii Forum Project. One of its goals was to find out what Pompeii could teach us about today's problems in urban design.

Urban planners working on the project were guided by two main principles, or ideas. The first principle is that a city is a public place. Many people must live and work there. For that reason, any new building should serve the needs of the people who use it—not the architect who designs it. The second principle is that a city as a whole is more important than its pieces. Therefore, new buildings must not look out of place among the old ones.

Planners on the Pompeii Forum Project learned that the Romans followed both of these principles in Pompeii. For instance, buying and selling is important to the life of any city. But the Romans did not let shops clutter up Pompeii's forum or residential streets. Pompeii's buildings all used similar forms, materials, and parts. The buildings served different functions and were built at different times, but the overall look was coordinated.

Mount Vesuvius rises above the ruins of the forum that was located in the center of Pompeii.

Built in 1901, Savannah's city hall (top) blends with older buildings dating from the 1700s. The city of Santa Barbara was settled by the Spanish. Its county courthouse (bottom) was built in 1929 in a Spanish colonial style.

The Pompeii Forum Project compared two American cities to Pompeii. They were Savannah, Georgia, and Santa Barbara, California. While not nearly as old as Pompeii, both cities date back to the 18th century. By American standards, that makes them old. Did these cities follow the principles of urban planning used in Pompeii?

Savannah was a carefully planned city. Neighborhoods were made up of family homes grouped around central squares. Each had a similar mix of lot sizes, block sizes, and street types. Businesses were along the river, or in buildings that looked more like homes. Some public buildings served one neighborhood. Others served larger areas. But none stood out from the city as a whole.

Modern Savannah has spread far beyond its original core. But the city has adapted well. For example, a pedestrian path runs along the length of its main street. Walkers do not need to step on or off curbs to cross streets. Newer buildings blend in well with the character of the old. One exception is a shopping strip that cuts the old main street in two. Its buildings were designed in what was once considered a modern style, but one that is no longer in fashion. It broke both the rules observed in Pompeii. Today, urban planners call it an embarrassing eyesore.

Santa Barbara was first settled by the Spanish. Its older buildings were designed in a Spanish or Mediterranean style. In 1925, an earthquake damaged the city. Since then, construction of new buildings has largely followed Spanish architecture. A Spanish-style plaza lies at the city's heart. Many public buildings are located on or near the plaza. They include a city hall, a courthouse, a post office, a firehouse, and an art museum. You would have no trouble telling their purposes apart. But they all share some design elements in common. Their similarities help to link the city's blocks together. As in Savannah, buildings whose size or design stands out seem out of place.

Under the Volcano

Any American city can learn from Pompeii. As older areas are torn down and replaced with new buildings and street patterns, urban planners hope that this ancient model can make modern cities better places to live. But some cities have another lesson to learn from Pompeii.

Towering above Tacoma, Washington, is 14,410-foot Mount Rainier. It's one of a line of 27 volcanoes stretching from Canada to California. Mount Rainier last erupted less than 200 years ago. If it were to erupt again, it could let loose a flow of hot mud and rock that would bury Tacoma. Many scientists believe that this next eruption is a question of "when," not "if."

So what has Tacoma learned from Pompeii? Mainly that there isn't anything one can do to stop a volcano. Organizations such as the Red Cross publish information about how to survive a volcanic eruption. The surest way to survive is to evacuate—to get out of the way when the mountain starts rumbling.

Mount Rainier towers over the city of Tacoma, Washington. Scientists believe that one day this volcano will erupt again, as it did almost 200 years ago.

Ancient Rome

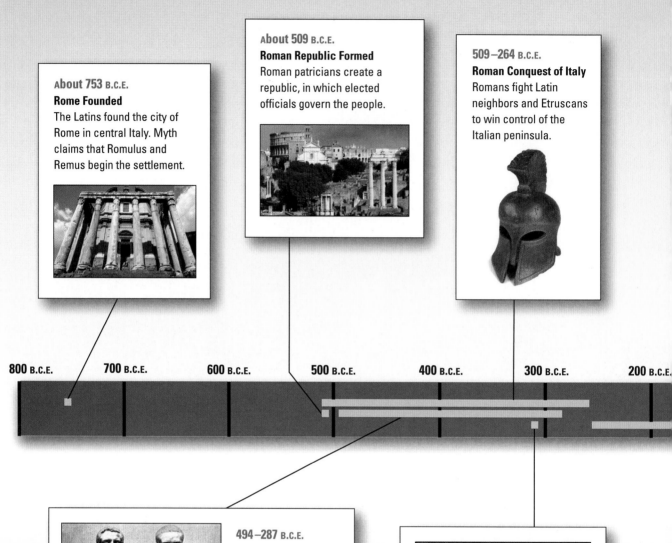

About 753 B.C.E.
Rome Founded
The Latins found the city of Rome in central Italy. Myth claims that Romulus and Remus begin the settlement.

About 509 B.C.E.
Roman Republic Formed
Roman patricians create a republic, in which elected officials govern the people.

509–264 B.C.E.
Roman Conquest of Italy
Romans fight Latin neighbors and Etruscans to win control of the Italian peninsula.

800 B.C.E.   700 B.C.E.   600 B.C.E.   500 B.C.E.   400 B.C.E.   300 B.C.E.   200 B.C.E.

494–287 B.C.E.
Plebeians Rebel
The government of the Roman Republic becomes more democratic as laws are written that protect plebeians' rights.

312 B.C.E.
First Roman Road
The Roman military builds the Appian Way, first of the Roman roads. About 50,000 miles of paved roads are built by the Romans, setting the standard of road building for the next 2,000 years.

49 B.C.E.
Julius Caesar Named Dictator
Julius Caesar becomes dictator of Rome, institutes reforms, and grants citizenship to Gaul and Spain.

About 6 B.C.E.–30 C.E.
Life of Jesus
Jesus and his teachings lay the foundations of Christianity.

About 47 C.E.
Missionary Work of Paul
Paul begins his missionary work, traveling throughout the Greek-speaking world and spreading Christianity.

313 C.E.
Edict of Milan
Emperor Constantine gives Christians the freedom to practice their religion openly. By 395 C.E., Christianity becomes the official religion of the Roman Empire.

100 B.C.E.　1 C.E.　100 C.E.　200 C.E.　300 C.E.　400 C.E.　500 C.E.

264–146 B.C.E.
Punic Wars
In a series of three wars, Rome defeats Carthage to become the greatest power in the Mediterranean region.

31 B.C.E.–14 C.E.
Reign of Emperor Augustus
After Caesar's death in 44 B.C.E., Augustus begins the Roman Empire and expands its boundaries during the Pax Romana.

476 C.E.
Fall of Western Roman Empire
The western part of the Roman Empire falls. The eastern part of the empire continues as the Byzantine Empire.

Ancient Rome **411**

Resources

Boys in ancient Egypt who wished to be scribes, the official writers and record keepers, attended special schools for 12 years to master the Egyptian system of writing that used hieroglyphs.

Physical Features of the World

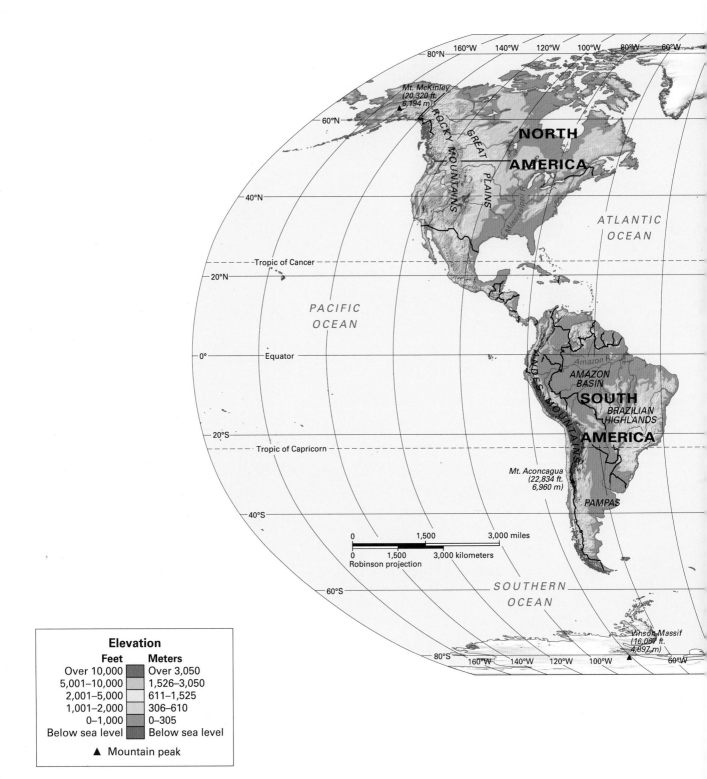

80°N   160°W   140°W   120°W   100°W   80°W   60°W

Mt. McKinley
(20,320 ft.
6,194 m)

60°N

ROCKY MOUNTAINS

GREAT PLAINS

NORTH

AMERICA

ATLANTIC
OCEAN

40°N

Mississippi R.

Tropic of Cancer

20°N

PACIFIC
OCEAN

0°   Equator

Amazon R.

AMAZON
BASIN

SOUTH

ANDES MOUNTAINS

BRAZILIAN
HIGHLANDS

AMERICA

20°S

Tropic of Capricorn

Mt. Aconcagua
(22,834 ft.
6,960 m)

PAMPAS

40°S

0   1,500   3,000 miles

0   1,500   3,000 kilometers
Robinson projection

SOUTHERN
OCEAN

60°S

Vinson Massif
(16,067 ft.
4,897 m)

80°S   160°W   140°W   120°W   100°W   60°W

Elevation

Feet		Meters
Over 10,000		Over 3,050
5,001–10,000		1,526–3,050
2,001–5,000		611–1,525
1,001–2,000		306–610
0–1,000		0–305
Below sea level		Below sea level

▲ Mountain peak

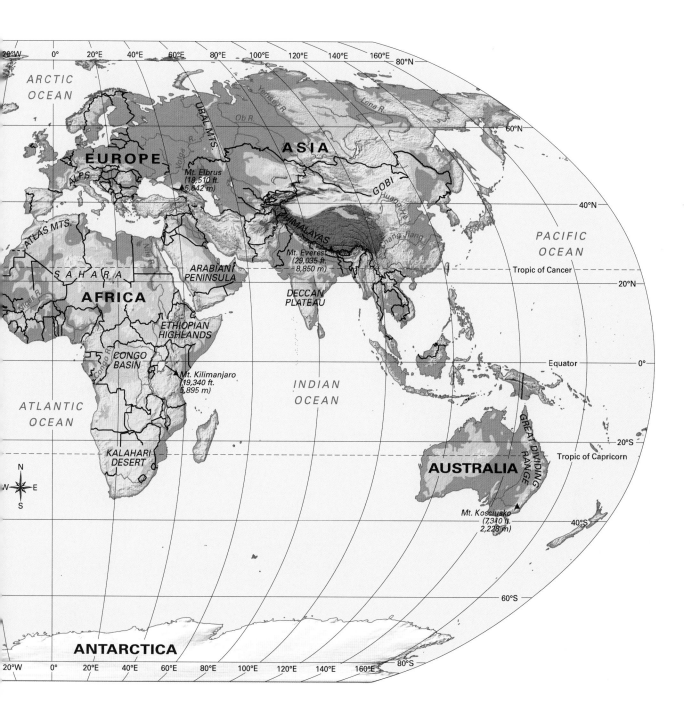

ARCTIC OCEAN

EUROPE

ALPS

Mt. Elbrus
(18,510 ft.
5,642 m)

URAL MTS.

Volga R.

Ob R.

Yenisey R.

Lena R.

ASIA

GOBI

Huang He

80°N

60°N

40°N

ATLAS MTS.

Niger R.

SAHARA

ARABIAN
PENINSULA

HIMALAYAS

Mt. Everest
(29,035 ft.
8,850 m)

Chang Jiang

PACIFIC
OCEAN

Tropic of Cancer

AFRICA

DECCAN
PLATEAU

20°N

ETHIOPIAN
HIGHLANDS

Congo R.

CONGO
BASIN

Mt. Kilimanjaro
19,340 ft.
5,895 m)

INDIAN
OCEAN

Equator

0°

ATLANTIC
OCEAN

20°S

KALAHARI
DESERT

AUSTRALIA

GREAT DIVIDING RANGE

Tropic of Capricorn

N
W   E
S

Mt. Kosciusko
(7,310 ft.
2,228 m)

40°S

60°S

ANTARCTICA

20°W   0°   20°E   40°E   60°E   80°E   100°E   120°E   140°E   160°E   80°S

Political Boundaries of the World

Abbreviations	
ALB.	ALBANIA
AUS.	AUSTRIA
BEL.	BELGIUM
B.H.	BOSNIA and HERZEGOVINA
CR.	CROATIA
CZ. REP.	CZECH REPUBLIC
DEN.	DENMARK
HUNG.	HUNGARY
LUX.	LUXEMBOURG
MAC.	MACEDONIA
MONT.	MONTENEGRO
NETH.	NETHERLANDS
SERB.	SERBIA
SLK.	SLOVAKIA
SLO.	SLOVENIA
SWITZ.	SWITZERLAND

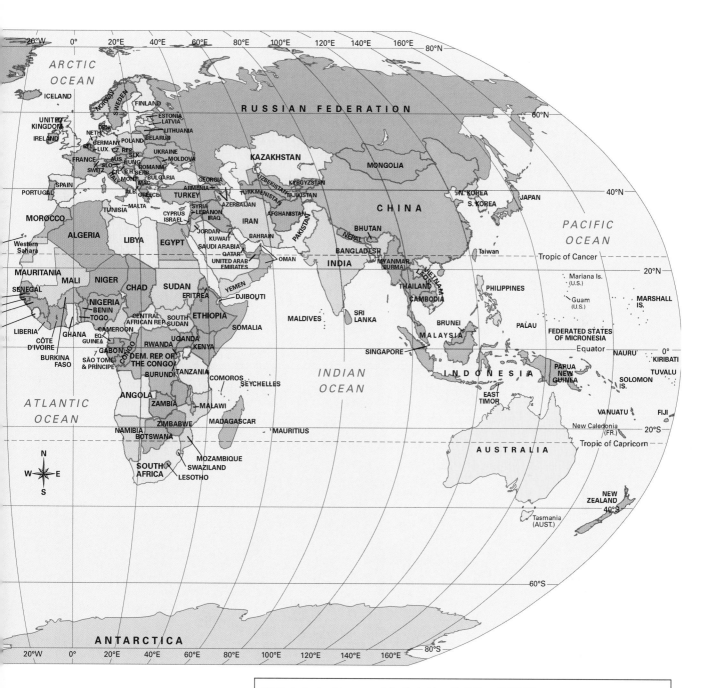

ARCTIC OCEAN

20°W 0° 20°E 40°E 60°E 80°E 100°E 120°E 140°E 160°E 80°N

ICELAND

NORWAY SWEDEN FINLAND

RUSSIAN FEDERATION

60°N

UNITED KINGDOM
IRELAND

DEN.
NETH.
GERMANY POLAND
BEL. LUX. CZ. REP.
FRANCE AUS. SLK.
SWITZ. CR. HUNG.
SLO. ROMANIA
ITALY SERB. BULGARIA

ESTONIA
LATVIA
LITHUANIA
BELARUS

UKRAINE
MOLDOVA

KAZAKHSTAN

MONGOLIA

N. KOREA
S. KOREA

JAPAN

40°N

SPAIN
PORTUGAL

MONT. MAC.
ALB. GREECE
MALTA
TUNISIA

GEORGIA
ARMENIA
TURKEY AZERBAIJAN
CYPRUS SYRIA LEBANON
ISRAEL IRAQ
JORDAN

UZBEKISTAN
TURKMENISTAN
KYRGYZSTAN
TAJIKISTAN
AFGHANISTAN

CHINA

PACIFIC OCEAN

MOROCCO

Western
Sahara

ALGERIA LIBYA EGYPT

IRAN
KUWAIT
SAUDI ARABIA
QATAR
UNITED ARAB
EMIRATES OMAN
BAHRAIN

PAKISTAN
NEPAL

BHUTAN

BANGLADESH

INDIA

MYANMAR
(BURMA)

Taiwan

Tropic of Cancer

20°N

MAURITANIA
MALI NIGER
SENEGAL
NIGERIA
BENIN
TOGO
GHANA
EQ.
GUINEA
LIBERIA
CÔTE
D'IVOIRE
BURKINA
FASO
SÃO TOME
& PRINCIPE
GABON

CHAD SUDAN
ERITREA
YEMEN
DJIBOUTI
CENTRAL
AFRICAN REP.
SOUTH
SUDAN ETHIOPIA
CAMEROON
SOMALIA
UGANDA
RWANDA KENYA
DEM. REP. OF
THE CONGO
BURUNDI TANZANIA
CONGO

THAILAND
LAOS
VIETNAM
CAMBODIA

PHILIPPINES

Mariana Is.
(U.S.)

Guam
(U.S.)

MARSHALL
IS.

MALDIVES

SRI
LANKA

BRUNEI

MALAYSIA

PALAU

FEDERATED STATES
OF MICRONESIA

Equator

NAURU

0°

KIRIBATI

SINGAPORE

INDONESIA

SOLOMON
IS.

TUVALU

COMOROS
SEYCHELLES

INDIAN
OCEAN

PAPUA
NEW
GUINEA

EAST
TIMOR

ATLANTIC
OCEAN

N
W E
S

ANGOLA
ZAMBIA
MALAWI
ZIMBABWE
NAMIBIA MADAGASCAR
BOTSWANA

MAURITIUS

VANUATU

New Caledonia
(FR.)

FIJI

20°S

Tropic of Capricorn

AUSTRALIA

SOUTH
AFRICA
MOZAMBIQUE
SWAZILAND
LESOTHO

NEW
ZEALAND

40°S

Tasmania
(AUST.)

60°S

ANTARCTICA

20°W 0° 20°E 40°E 60°E 80°E 100°E 120°E 140°E 160°E 80°S

• Independent nations are printed in bold capital letters: **FRANCE**.
• Nations whose independence or governing rule is in dispute are printed in bold type: **Taiwan**.
• Territories, provinces, and the like governed by an independent nation are printed in bold type, with an abbreviation for the ruling nation: **French Guiana (FR.)**.
• Areas whose governing rule is in dispute are printed in nonbold type: Falkland Islands.
• Areas that are part of an independent nation but geographically separated from it are printed in nonbold type, with an abbreviation for the ruling nation: Hawaii (U.S.).

Physical Features of North America

Political Boundaries of North America

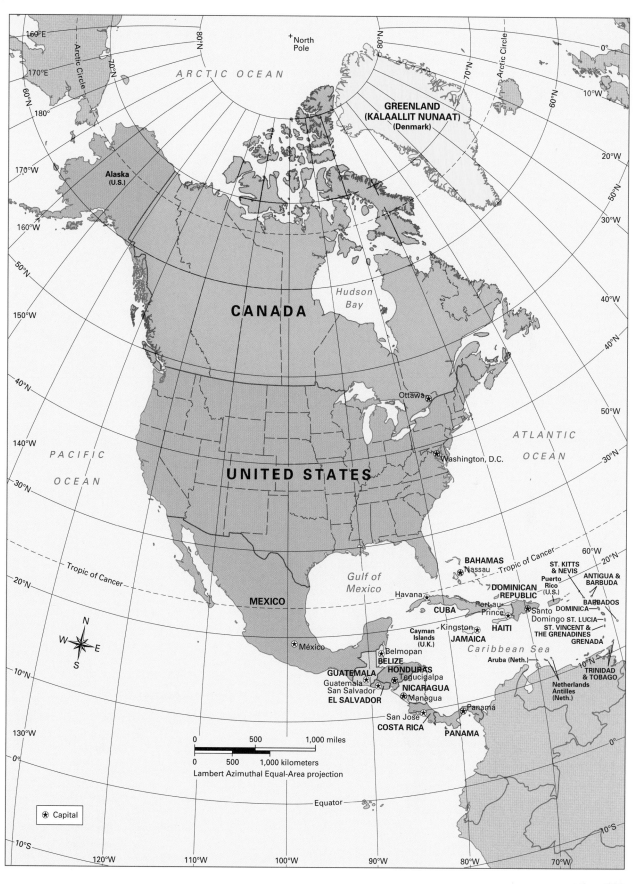

ARCTIC OCEAN

+ North Pole

GREENLAND
(KALAALLIT NUNAAT)
(Denmark)

Alaska
(U.S.)

Hudson
Bay

CANADA

PACIFIC
OCEAN

UNITED STATES

Ottawa ⊛

Washington, D.C. ⊛

ATLANTIC
OCEAN

Tropic of Cancer

MEXICO

Gulf of
Mexico

N
W   E
S

México ⊛

Tropic of Cancer

BAHAMAS
⊛ Nassau

ST. KITTS
& NEVIS
Puerto
Rico
(U.S.)

ANTIGUA &
BARBUDA

Havana

DOMINICAN
REPUBLIC

BARBADOS

CUBA

Port-au-
Prince ⊛

⊛ Santo
Domingo ST. LUCIA

DOMINICA

HAITI

ST. VINCENT &
THE GRENADINES

Cayman
Islands
(U.K.)

Kingston ⊛

GRENADA

JAMAICA

Caribbean Sea

⊛ Belmopan

Aruba (Neth.)

BELIZE

TRINIDAD
& TOBAGO

GUATEMALA ⊛

HONDURAS

Teguçigalpa ⊛

Netherlands
Antilles
(Neth.)

Guatemala
San Salvador
EL SALVADOR

NICARAGUA
⊛ Managua

⊛ Panamá

San José ⊛
COSTA RICA

PANAMA

0   500   1,000 miles

0   500   1,000 kilometers

Lambert Azimuthal Equal-Area projection

Equator

⊛ Capital

Physical Features of South America

Caribbean Sea

90°W 80°W 70°W 60°W 50°W 40°W

10°N

ATLANTIC

OCEAN

LLANOS

Orinoco R.

GUIANA HIGHLANDS

Equator 0°

Galápagos
Islands

AMAZON

BASIN

Amazon R.

Equator 0°

PACIFIC

OCEAN

10°S

ANDES MOUNTAINS

Lake Titicaca

BRAZILIAN

São Francisco R.

HIGHLANDS

10°S

20°S

ATACAMA DESERT

GRAN CHACO

Tropic of Capricorn

Iguazú
Falls

Tropic of Capricorn

30°W

N
W E
S

Mt. Aconcagua
(22,835 ft.
6,960 m)

ANDES MOUNTAINS

Paraná R.

PAMPAS

Uruguay R.

30°S

ATLANTIC

OCEAN

500 1,000 miles

0

0 500 1,000 kilometers
Lambert Azimuthal Equal-Area projection

PATAGONIA

Laguna del Carbón
(-344 ft. -105 m)

50°S

Strait of
Magellan

Tierra del Fuego

Falkland
Islands

50°S

Cape Horn

100°W
60°S

90°W 80°W 70°W 60°W 50°W 40°W

60°S

20°W
40°S

Elevation

Feet	Meters
Over 10,000	Over 3,050
5,001–10,000	1,526–3,050
2,001–5,000	611–1,525
1,001–2,000	306–610
0–1,000	0–305
Below sea level	Below sea level

▲ Mountain peak

Political Boundaries of South America

Physical Features of Europe and Russia

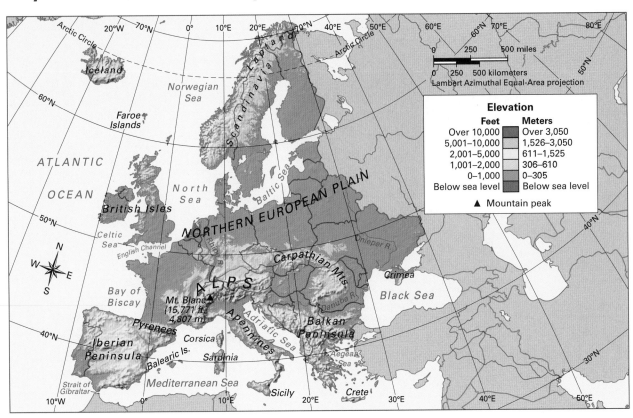

Elevation

Feet	Meters
Over 10,000	Over 3,050
5,001–10,000	1,526–3,050
2,001–5,000	611–1,525
1,001–2,000	306–610
0–1,000	0–305
Below sea level	Below sea level

▲ Mountain peak

Lambert Azimuthal Equal-Area projection

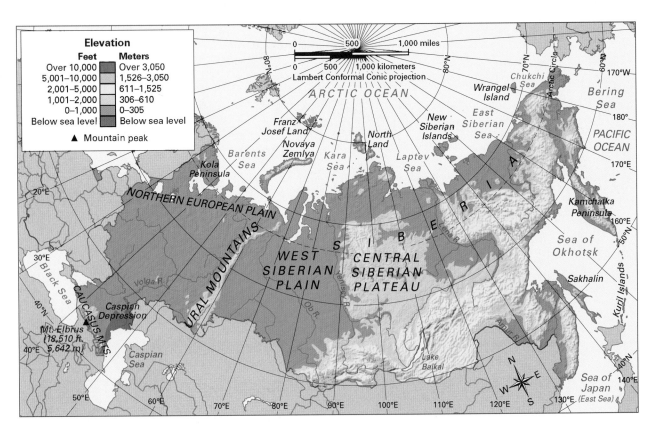

Elevation

Feet	Meters
Over 10,000	Over 3,050
5,001–10,000	1,526–3,050
2,001–5,000	611–1,525
1,001–2,000	306–610
0–1,000	0–305
Below sea level	Below sea level

▲ Mountain peak

Lambert Conformal Conic projection

Political Boundaries of Europe and Russia

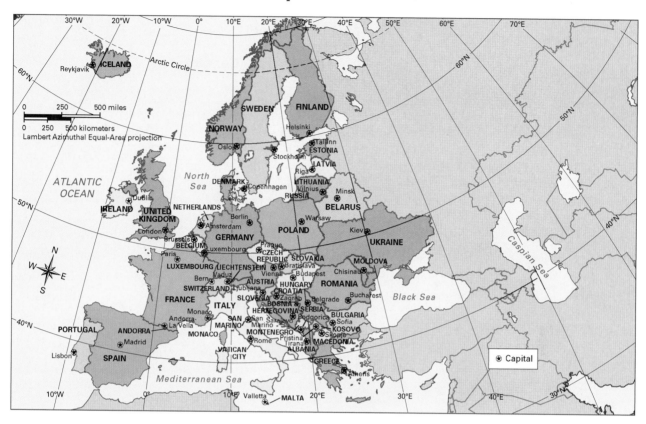

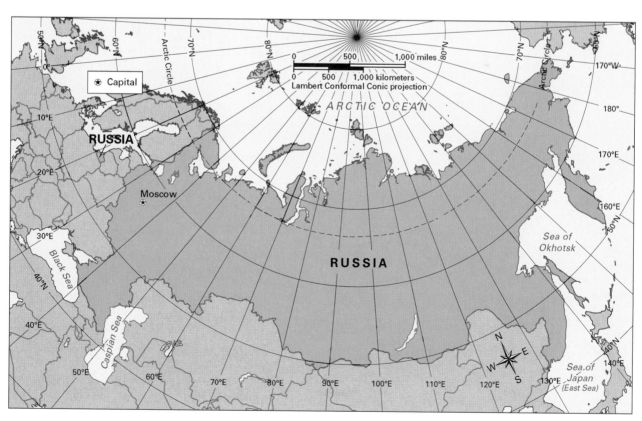

Physical Features of Africa

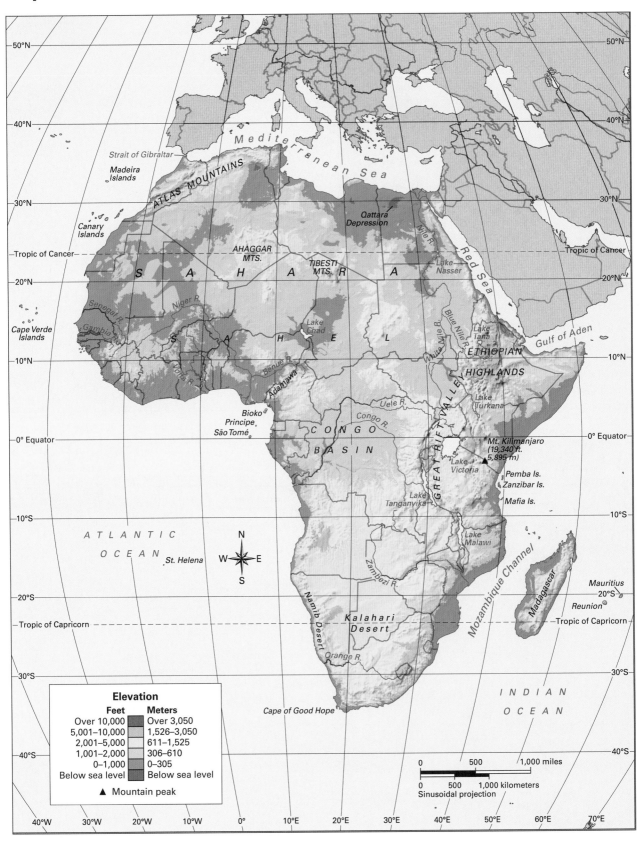

Elevation

Feet	Meters
Over 10,000	Over 3,050
5,001–10,000	1,526–3,050
2,001–5,000	611–1,525
1,001–2,000	306–610
0–1,000	0–305
Below sea level	Below sea level

▲ Mountain peak

0   500   1,000 miles

0   500   1,000 kilometers
Sinusoidal projection

Political Boundaries of Africa

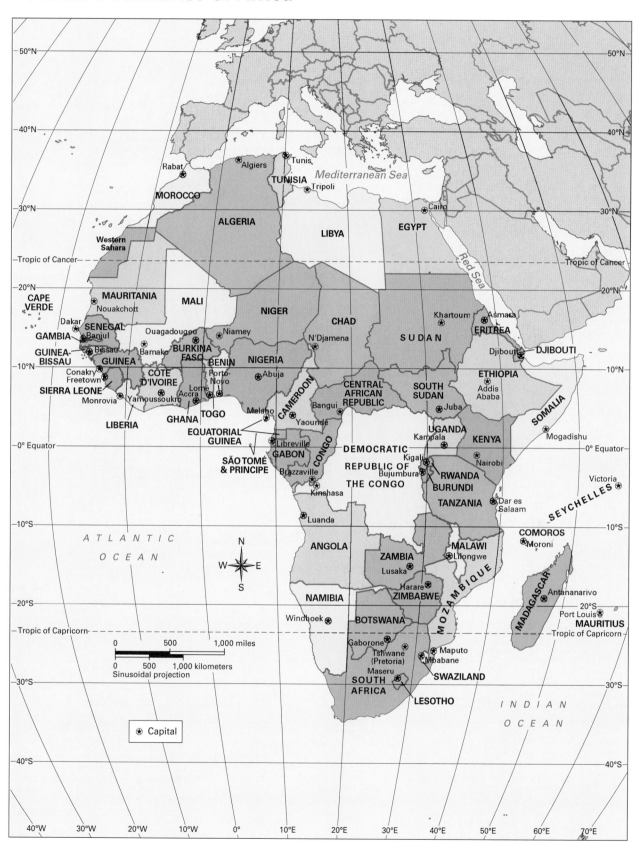

Capital

Physical Features of Southwest and Central Asia

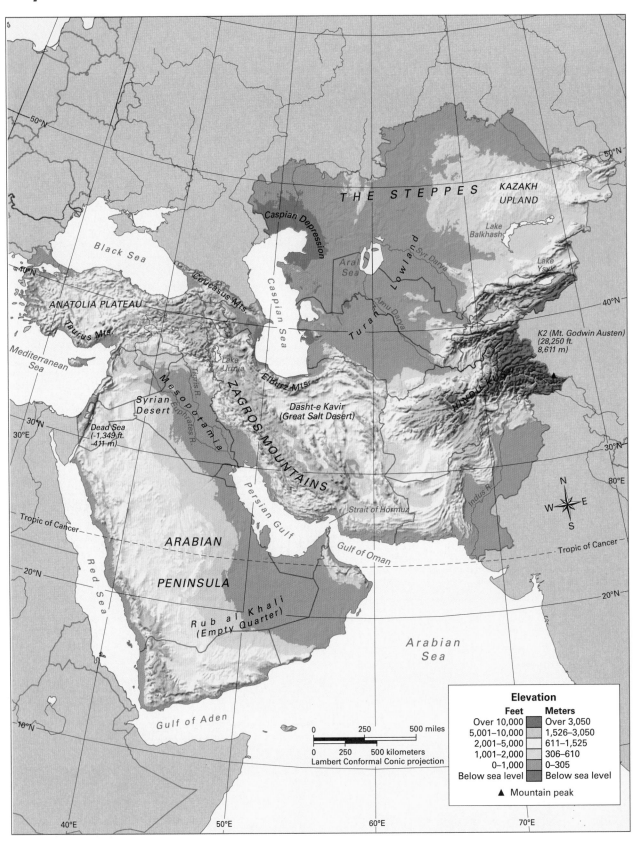

THE STEPPES

KAZAKH UPLAND

Caspian Depression

Lake Balkhash

Aral Sea

Turan Lowland

Syr Darya

Lake Ysyk

Black Sea

Caucasus Mts.

Caspian Sea

Amu Darya

ANATOLIA PLATEAU

K2 (Mt. Godwin Austen)
(28,250 ft.
8,611 m)

Taurus Mts.

Lake Urmia

Elburz Mts.

Mediterranean Sea

HINDU KUSH

Mesopotamia

ZAGROS MOUNTAINS

Dasht-e Kavir
(Great Salt Desert)

Syrian Desert

Tigris R.

Euphrates R.

Dead Sea
(-1,349 ft.
-411 m)

Indus R.

Persian Gulf

Strait of Hormuz

Tropic of Cancer

ARABIAN

Gulf of Oman

Tropic of Cancer

Red Sea

PENINSULA

Rub al Khali
(Empty Quarter)

Arabian Sea

Gulf of Aden

50°N
40°N
30°N
20°N
10°N
30°E
40°E
50°E
60°E
70°E
80°E

N W E S

Elevation

Feet	Meters
Over 10,000	Over 3,050
5,001–10,000	1,526–3,050
2,001–5,000	611–1,525
1,001–2,000	306–610
0–1,000	0–305
Below sea level	Below sea level

▲ Mountain peak

0   250   500 miles
0   250   500 kilometers
Lambert Conformal Conic projection

Political Boundaries of Southwest and Central Asia

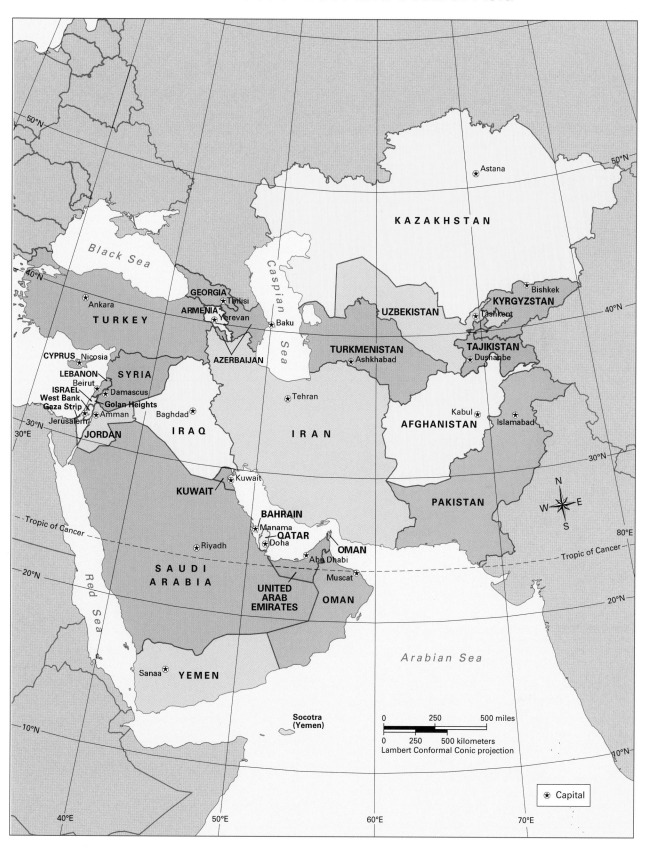

Black Sea

Caspian Sea

KAZAKHSTAN

⊛ Astana

GEORGIA
⊛ Tbilisi
ARMENIA
⊛ Yerevan

TURKEY
⊛ Ankara

⊛ Baku

UZBEKISTAN
⊛ Tashkent

Bishkek ⊛
KYRGYZSTAN

CYPRUS ⊛ Nicosia

TURKMENISTAN
⊛ Ashkhabad

TAJIKISTAN
⊛ Dushanbe

AZERBAIJAN

SYRIA
LEBANON
Beirut ⊛
ISRAEL
⊛ Damascus
West Bank
Golan Heights
Gaza Strip
⊛ Amman
Jerusalem ⊛
JORDAN

⊛ Tehran

⊛ Baghdad

IRAQ

IRAN

Kabul ⊛
AFGHANISTAN
Islamabad ⊛

⊛ Kuwait
KUWAIT

PAKISTAN

N
W   E
S

Tropic of Cancer

BAHRAIN
⊛ Manama
QATAR
⊛ Doha

⊛ Riyadh

SAUDI
ARABIA

Abu Dhabi ⊛
UNITED
ARAB
EMIRATES

OMAN
⊛ Muscat

OMAN

Tropic of Cancer

Red Sea

Arabian Sea

Sanaa ⊛ **YEMEN**

Socotra
(Yemen)

0	250	500 miles

0	250	500 kilometers
Lambert Conformal Conic projection

⊛ Capital

50°N   50°N
40°N   40°N
30°E
30°N   30°N
20°N   20°N
10°N   10°N

80°E

40°E   50°E   60°E   70°E

Physical Features of South Asia, East Asia, and Southeast Asia

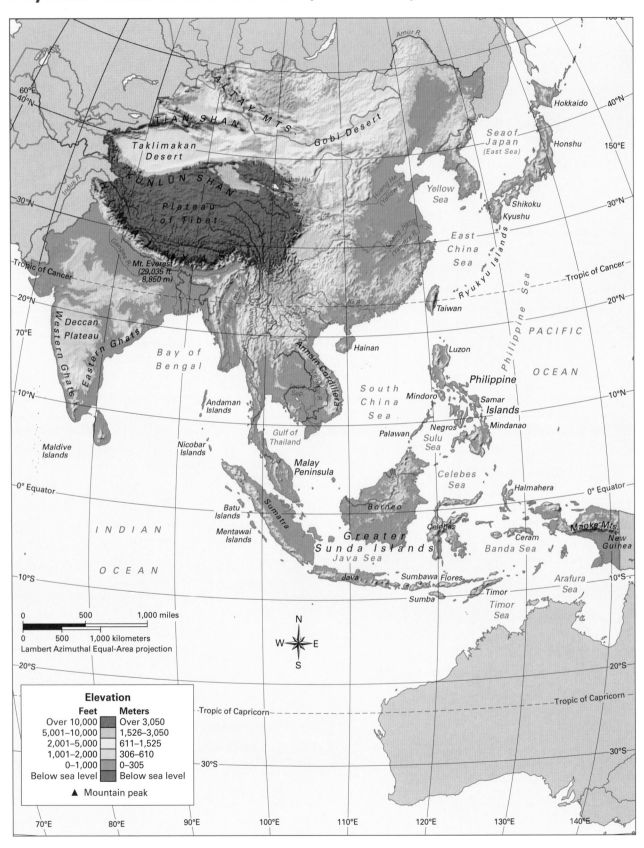

ALTAY MTS.
Amur R.
Gobi Desert
TIAN SHAN
Taklimakan Desert
KUNLUN SHAN
Indus R.
Plateau of Tibet
Qinghai Hu
Huang He (Yellow R.)
Chang Jiang (Yangtze R.)
Hokkaido
Sea of Japan (East Sea)
Honshu
Yellow Sea
Shikoku
Kyushu
East China Sea
Ganges R.
Mt. Everest (29,035 ft. 8,850 m)
HIMALAYAS
Brahmaputra
Ryukyu Islands
Tropic of Cancer
Taiwan
Deccan Plateau
Western Ghats
Eastern Ghats
Bay of Bengal
Godavari R.
Hainan
Philippine Sea
PACIFIC OCEAN
Luzon
South China Sea
Annam Cordillera
Mindoro
Samar
Philippine Islands
Maldive Islands
Andaman Islands
Mekong R.
Tonle Sap
Palawan
Negros
Mindanao
Nicobar Islands
Gulf of Thailand
Malay Peninsula
Sulu Sea
Celebes Sea
Halmahera
INDIAN OCEAN
Batu Islands
Mentawai Islands
Sumatra
Greater Sunda Islands
Borneo
Celebes
Ceram
Banda Sea
Maoke Mts.
New Guinea
Java Sea
Java
Sumbawa
Flores
Timor
Arafura Sea
Sumba
Timor Sea

0   500   1,000 miles
0   500   1,000 kilometers
Lambert Azimuthal Equal-Area projection

N
W   E
S

Elevation

Feet	Meters
Over 10,000	Over 3,050
5,001–10,000	1,526–3,050
2,001–5,000	611–1,525
1,001–2,000	306–610
0–1,000	0–305
Below sea level	Below sea level

▲ Mountain peak

Tropic of Capricorn

Political Boundaries of South Asia, East Asia, and Southeast Asia

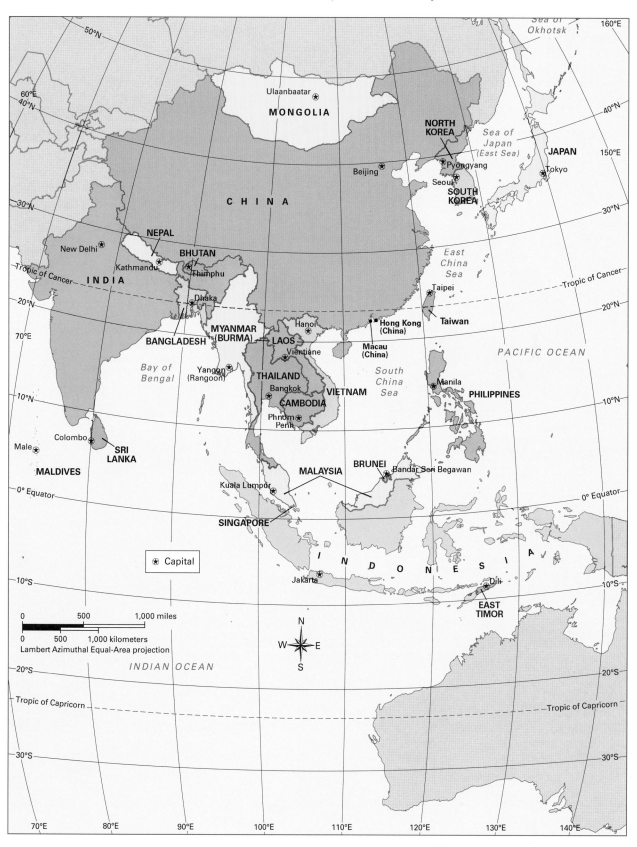

⊛ Capital

0   500   1,000 miles
0   500   1,000 kilometers
Lambert Azimuthal Equal-Area projection

Physical Features of Oceania and Antarctica

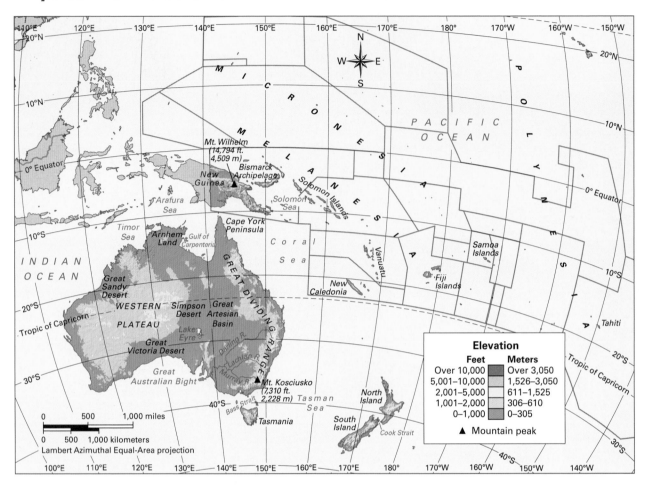

Mt. Wilhelm
(14,794 ft.
4,509 m)

New
Guinea

Bismarck
Archipelago

Solomon Islands

Arafura
Sea

Solomon
Sea

Timor
Sea

Arnhem
Land

Gulf of
Carpenteria

Cape York
Peninsula

Coral

Sea

Vanuatu

Samoa
Islands

INDIAN

OCEAN

Great
Sandy
Desert

WESTERN

PLATEAU

Simpson
Desert

Great
Artesian
Basin

New
Caledonia

Fiji
Islands

Great
Victoria Desert

Lake
Eyre

Darling R.

Lachlan R.

Murray R.

Tahiti

Great
Australian Bight

Mt. Kosciusko
(7,310 ft.
2,228 m)

Bass Strait

North
Island

Tasman
Sea

Tasmania

South
Island

Cook Strait

PACIFIC
OCEAN

MICRONESIA

MELANESIA

POLYNESIA

GREAT DIVIDING RANGE

Tropic of Capricorn

Tropic of Capricorn

0   500   1,000 miles

0   500   1,000 kilometers
Lambert Azimuthal Equal-Area projection

Elevation

Feet		Meters
Over 10,000		Over 3,050
5,001–10,000		1,526–3,050
2,001–5,000		611–1,525
1,001–2,000		306–610
0–1,000		0–305

▲ Mountain peak

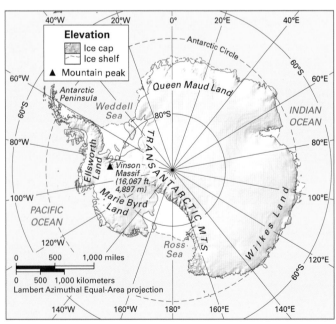

Elevation

Ice cap
Ice shelf
▲ Mountain peak

Antarctic
Peninsula

Weddell
Sea

Queen Maud Land

Antarctic Circle

INDIAN
OCEAN

Ellsworth
Land

Vinson
Massif
(16,067 ft.
4,897 m)

TRANSANTARCTIC MTS

Marie Byrd
Land

Wilkes Land

PACIFIC
OCEAN

Ross
Sea

0   500   1,000 miles

0   500   1,000 kilometers
Lambert Azimuthal Equal-Area projection

Political Boundaries of Oceania and Antarctica

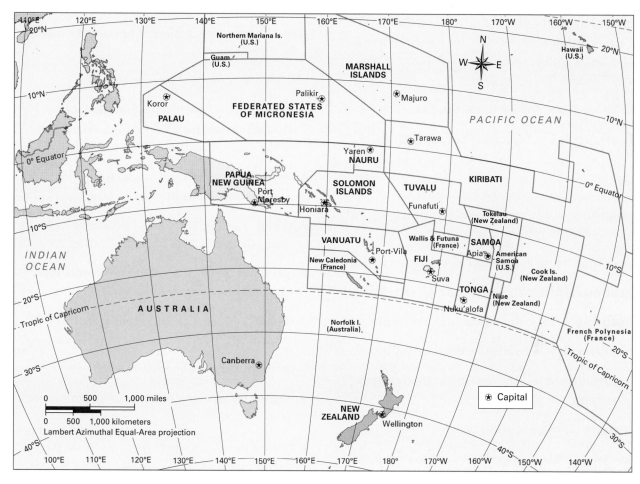

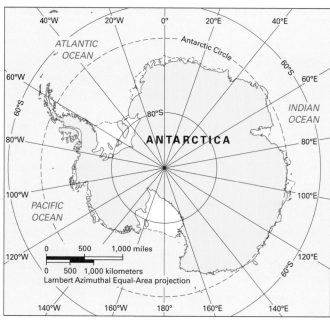

Glossary

Some words in this book have been respelled to help you pronounce them. Respelled words have been adapted from *Merriam-Webster's Collegiate Dictionary, Eleventh Edition; The American Heritage Dictionary of the English Language, Fourth Edition;* and *Random House Dictionary.*

Blue words are defined in the margins.

Black words are Academic Vocabulary terms.

A

abandon to leave someone or something without intending to return

accompany to join someone in going somewhere

accomplish to complete something successfully

accurately correctly, without any mistakes

achievement a positive result gained by hard work

acropolis the hill above a Greek city, on which temples were built

acquire to come into possession of something

adapt to make changes to an existing object or way or doing things

Aegean Sea an arm of the Mediterranean Sea, east of Greece

affect to produce a change in something or someone

afterlife an existence after death

agora a marketplace in ancient Greece

agriculture the business of farming; growing crops and raising animals

Alexander the Great the ruler of a vast empire that extended from Macedonia to India in the 300s B.C.E.

Alexandria a city in Egypt, founded in 332 B.C.E. by Alexander the Great; also, an ancient center of learning

alliance a bond between families, states, or other groups to further their common interests

ally a country that is friendly to another country in times of war

alms goods or money given to the poor

ancestor worship honoring of ancestors through rituals, such as offering food and wine to the spirits of the dead

anthropologist a scientist who studies human development and culture

Anyang location where ruins were found from the Shang dynasty, China's first civilization

appreciate to be aware of the worth and importance of something or someone

approach to move closer to someone or something

approximately a close estimate

aqueduct a pipe or channel built to carry water over a long distance

archaeologist an expert who studies the past by examining objects that people have left behind

aristocrat a member of the most powerful class in ancient Greek society

Aristotle a great Greek philosopher; a tutor of Alexander the Great; and the author of works on logic, science, and politics

artifact an object made or used by people in the past

artisan a craftsperson

ascetic a person who gives up worldly pleasure

Ashoka the ruler of the Mauryan Empire from about 269 to 232 B.C.E., whose edicts reflected Buddhist values

aspect one part of something

assemble to bring together

assembly a group of citizens, in an ancient Greek democracy, with the power to pass laws

astronomy the study of the stars and planets

Athens a city-state of ancient Greece that was first to have a democracy; also known as the birthplace of Western civilization; the capital of present-day Greece

authority the government or controlling power

axis a line on which an object spins

B

baptism the Christian sacrament that makes a person a member of the Christian Church

benefit something that improves someone's life

biology the study of living things; their structure, growth, and function

Brahmanism ancient ritual traditions in which Brahmins played a key role; it grew out of older Vedic religious beliefs and helped lead to Hinduism

brief a short length of time

bronze a strong metal alloy made from copper

Buddha a Sanskrit word meaning "enlightened"; the name given to the man who founded Buddhism

Buddhism the religion founded by Siddhartha, which teaches that life brings suffering that one can escape by seeking nirvana through enlightenment

bureaucracy a large, complex organization that functions under a given set of rules and conditions

Byzantine Empire the name for the eastern Roman Empire, located at the crossroads of Europe and Asia; it lasted from about 500 to 1453 C.E.

C

Caesar Augustus Julius Caesar's grandnephew and adopted son, Octavian; Rome's first emperor

Caesar, Julius a Roman general who ended the Roman Republic when he seized power and became dictator for life

Canaan a land northeast of Egypt, settled by the ancient Israelites, from about 1800 B.C.E. to 70 C.E.

capability ability or skill

capable having the ability or skill necessary to do something well

capital a city that is the center of government

capture to take by force

caravan a group of people traveling together

caste a class, or group, in Hindu society

Catal Hoyuk a Neolithic town discovered in central Turkey

cavalry soldiers who ride on horses

censor to remove or suppress ideas considered harmful or dangerous

challenge a task or problem that tests a person's abilities

channel a passage dug into the earth, through which liquids flow

chapter one section of a book

Christianity the religion based on the life and teachings of Jesus

Circus Maximus a large Roman stadium primarily used for chariot races

citadel a fortress built to protect a city

citizen a person who has certain rights and duties in a city-state or nation

city-state an early city that was like a small, independent country with its own laws and government

civic having to do with the community

civil servant a person who works for a government

civil war a war between groups in the same country

civilization a society marked by developed arts, sciences, government, and social structure

clan a large group of family members and friends

climate the average weather conditions at a particular place

code of laws a collection of written laws and rules

colony a settlement under the control of a usually distant country

collapse a sudden break down or failure

Colosseum a large arena in Rome where gladiator contests and other games and sporting events were held

column a tall, upright structure used to support a building. Some columns have carved decorations on them.

communicate to exchange or share thoughts, feelings, or information with people, using words, writings, or other methods

community a group of people who live in the same area and are united by common interests

complex arranged in a difficult way

complicate to make something more difficult and involved

conduct to carry out an activity in a particular way

conflict a disagreement or fight caused by opposing points of view

Confucianism a Chinese philosophy that emphasizes proper behavior

Constantine Roman emperor from about 280 to 337 C.E.; the first Roman emperor to become a Christian

constitution a set of basic laws

construct to build; usually some kind of structure, such as a house

consul one of two chief leaders in Rome

consult to get an opinion and information from someone

contrast the differences between people or things, when they are compared

contribute to give, along with others, to a common cause

convert someone who has changed their religious beliefs so they accept a different or new religion

convince to persuade someone that something is true

Council of 500 in Athens, a group of 500 citizens chosen to form a council responsible for running the day-to-day business of government

Council of Elders a small group of Spartans who made all the important governing decisions

covenant an agreement or promise

create to bring something new into being

crisis a dangerous moment with a high chance of an unwanted result

cultural diffusion the spreading of cultural traits, such as goods and ideas, from one culture to another, or within one culture

culture a characteristic of civilization that includes the beliefs and behaviors of a society or group of people

cuneiform writing that uses wedge-shaped characters

cuniculus an underground irrigation system invented by the Etruscans

custom a practice that is common to people of a particular group or region

cycle repeating events that occur regularly

D

Daoism a Chinese philosophy that emphasizes living in harmony with nature

Darius a great Persian king who ruled from about 522 to 486 B.C.E.

dedicate to honor someone by recognizing a place in their name

democracy a government in which power is held by the people, who exercise power directly or through elected representatives

deny to hold back and refuse something

design a pattern that is used for an artistic purpose

dharma a belief found in Hinduism and other Indian traditions that a person has a duty or obligation to live an honorable life

dictator a ruler with absolute power

disciple a person who helps spread the religious teachings of another

disperse to spread out

display to show something in a place where people can see it

dispute a strong disagreement

dissolve to separate into smaller pieces

diverse a group of people or elements with obvious differences between one another

divine heavenly or god-like

document a written work that contains important information

domesticate to train a wild animal to be useful to humans

dominate to have control or power over something

drain a pipe that is used to carry away flowing water, often dirty water

drama the art of writing, acting in, and producing plays

dramatic noticeable and remarkable

dynasty a family or group that rules for several generations

E

Eastern Orthodox Church a Christian church that grew out of Christianity in eastern Europe and present-day Turkey

economy the way a region or country uses resources to produce and sell or trade goods and services to meet people's needs and wants

edict a command that is obeyed like a law

efficiently working well; producing very little waste

Egypt a nation in northeast Africa, first settled around 3100 B.C.E.

Eightfold Path a key idea of Buddhism whereby followers should live their lives according to these eight teachings

elevate to raise

eliminate to completely remove or put an end to something

embrace to gladly take in ideas, beliefs, or opinions

emerge to come into existence

emphasis extra attention or importance placed on something

empire a large territory in which several groups of people are ruled by a single leader or government

enable to provide the means or ability to do something

enlightenment the state of gaining spiritual insight and finding universal truth; the goal of Buddhists

enormous great in size or degree

enrich to improve the quality of something

environment all of the physical surroundings in a place, including land, water, animals, plants, and climate

establish to create something secure and long-standing

estate land in the country that usually has a large house on it

estimate a guess as to the value or size of something

ethics a set of moral principles or values

Etruscan an ancient inhabitant of Etruria, a land in north and central Italy

Euphrates River one of the two largest rivers in Southwest Asia that flow from mountains in Turkey to the Persian Gulf

evaporate when a liquid such as water, turns into a vapor, or gas

eventually at a later time

execute put to death, usually as a legal punishment

exile to banish or expel from one's own country or home

expand to grow larger

Exodus the escape of the Israelites from Egyptian slavery to freedom

F

factor something that influences or causes a result

feature an important part or characteristic of something

fertile able to grow crops well

Fertile Crescent an arc-shaped region in Southwest Asia, with rich soil

feudalism a system of government based on landowners and tenants

Forum the center of most of the important public activities of the city Rome and its empire

foundation the solid support on which things are built

Four Noble Truths the four basic doctrines, or principles, of Buddhism

frontier the part of a country that borders another country or territory

function the purpose of an object and how it's used

fundamental at the most basic level

G

generation a group of individuals around the same age, living at the same time

geographer an expert who studies and creates maps of Earth's natural and human-made features

geography the study of the features of Earth's surface

geometric having a form composed of one or a number of simple shapes, such as triangles, squares, or circles

geometry the branch of mathematics involving points, lines, planes, and figures

gladiator a person trained to fight for public entertainment

golden age a period of great happiness, prosperity, and achievement

Gospel an account of the life and teachings of Jesus; four of them are included in the New Testament of the Christian Bible

granary a place to store grain

Great Wall a stone-and-earth wall about 1,500 miles long, first built during the Qin dynasty to defend China's northern boundary

Greco-Roman having the characteristics of Roman culture with a strong Greek influence

Gupta Empire the empire covering much of northern India that was ruled by the Guptas from around 320 C.E. to around 550 C.E.

H

Han dynasty the dynasty that ruled China from about 206 B.C.E. to 220 C.E., the period following the Qin dynasty

Hatshepsut the first woman pharaoh of ancient Egypt

Hellespont a long, narrow body of water between Europe and the present-day country of Turkey

hieroglyph a symbol used in hieroglyphics, a system of writing developed around 3000 B.C.E.

Hinduism a religion that developed in India over many centuries; it traces its roots to older traditions, such as Vedic beliefs and Brahmanism

historian an expert who studies and records the past

Holy Communion a Christian sacrament in which bread and wine are consumed as memorials of Jesus's Last Supper with his disciples

hominid an early ancestor of humans

horror a feeling of great fear and surprise

hostile to act in a way that is unfriendly and angry toward a particular person or object

I

ignore to knowingly not pay attention to something or someone

immortal able to live forever

Indus valley civilization an early civilization, known for its advanced culture, that developed in the Indus River valley in India

industry a business that manufactures a particular product, such as silk

initial occurring first, or at the beginning

insist firmly and repeatedly stating a point of view

instruct to teach

intelligence a strong mental ability to reason and gain knowledge

intense a very strong effect

interpret to judge the meaning of written or spoken words or an event

interpretation the way in which someone understands something

interval a period of time between events

invader someone who forces entry into a place where they are unwanted

involve to be a part of something

irrigation a means of supplying land with water

isolate to set apart from other people or things

Israel the Israelites' kingdom; divided about 930 B.C.E. into two kingdoms called Judah and Israel

Israelite an early name for the Jewish people

J

Jerusalem the holiest city of the Jews; capital of the ancient kingdoms of Israel and then Judah

Jesus the founder of Christianity upon whose life and teachings the religion is based

Jewish Diaspora the scattering of the Jewish people outside their homeland, beginning in 586 B.C.E.

Jordan River a river in southwestern Asia that flows from the Lebanon Mountains, south through the Sea of Galilee, into the Dead Sea

Judaism the first religion to worship one God, developed among the ancient Israelites

K

kandake a powerful female leader who co-ruled Kush with her husband or sons

karma a belief found in Hinduism and other Indian traditions that the good and evil done in a past life determines the nature of that person's next life

Kush a society along the Nile River, south of Egypt, from about 2000 B.C.E. to 350 C.E.

L

laborer someone who does physical work

Latin the language originally spoken in ancient Rome, on which many words in modern languages are based

latitude a measure of how far north or south a place on Earth is measured from the equator

layer a substance that lies between or above other things

Legalism a Chinese philosophy that emphasizes strict obedience to laws

leisure time spent not working

levee a wall of earth built to prevent a river from flooding its banks

link to connect two or more people or things

longitude a measure of how far east or west a place on Earth is from an imaginary line that runs between the North and South Poles

luxury a way of life that offers much more than what is necessary

M

Macedonia an ancient kingdom located north of Greece

maintain to keep something in good condition by making necessary repairs

major very important

Mandate of Heaven a power or law believed to be granted by a god

material a resource that can be used to make something else

mathematics the study of numbers

Mauryan Empire an empire lasting from about 322 to 187 B.C.E., during which the Mauryan family unified India for the first time

medical relating to the practice and treatment of medicine

Mediterranean Sea a body of water north of Africa

merchant a person who makes money by selling goods

Meroë a city on the Nile River that became the center of Kushite culture and industry

Mesopotamia in ancient times, the geographic area located between the Tigris and Euphrates rivers

Messiah a savior who many Jews believe had been promised to them by God

migrate to move from one geographic region to another

military relating to the army

missionary someone who tries to convert others to believe in a particular religion or set of beliefs

Mohenjodaro one of the first major settlements in ancient India that became a center of the Indus valley civilization

monarchy a government in which the ruling power is in the hands of one person

monotheism the belief that there is only one God

monsoon a strong wind that brings heavy rain to southern Asia in the summer

muscle body tissue that connects bones and provides strength

myth a traditional story that helps explain a culture's beliefs

N

natural law the concept that there is a universal order built into nature that can guide moral thinking

navy the part of a nation's military that fights at sea

Neolithic Age the later part of the Stone Age, called the New Stone Age, lasted from around 8000 B.C.E. to 3000 B.C.E.

network an interconnected system of channels or lines

neutral not taking sides or getting involved in disagreements

Nile River the longest river in the world, flowing through eastern Africa to a delta in northeastern Egypt

nirvana an ideal state of happiness and peace

noble of high birth or rank

nomad one who moves from place to place with no permanent home

North China Plain a region in the Huang He River valley, where Chinese civilization began

O

oasis a place, usually in a desert, where water can be found

obtain to get something, usually by making an effort or working for it

occupy to take up or fill

occur to take place

oligarchy a government in which the ruling power is in the hands of a few people

oracle bone a piece of bone or shell heated and cracked by holy men to seek advice from a king's ancestors

oxygen a gas in the air that people and animals need to breathe to live

P

Paleolithic Age the first period of the Stone Age, called the Old Stone Age, from about 2 million years ago to around 8000 B.C.E.

Panathenaic Games athletic events, including horse races and chariot races, held as part of the festival called Panathenaea, honoring the goddess Athena

parable a simple story that explains a moral or religious lesson

Parthenon the temple built on the acropolis above Athens, honoring the goddess Athena

participate to take part in something, such as a game or activity

paterfamilias the oldest male of a Roman household; his word was law for the family

patrician in the Roman Republic, a member of the upper, ruling class

patron a person who promotes artistic activities by paying for new works and supporting artists

Pax Romana a 200-year period of peace and stability established and maintained by the Roman Empire

peasant a person who does farm work for wealthy landowners

Peloponnesus a peninsula forming the southern part of the mainland of Greece

peninsula a body of land that is surrounded on three sides by water

Pericles a great leader who developed Athens's culture, democracy, and power during its Golden Age

period a length of time

Peloponnesian War (431 to 404 B.C.E.) the war fought between Athens and Sparta that involved other city-states

Persian Empire a vast empire in the 400s B.C.E. that ruled over lands in Africa, the Middle East, and Asia

Persian wars (490–479 B.C.E.) the period of fighting waged between the Persian Empire and the allied Greek city-states for control of land in Greece

pharaoh a ruler of ancient Egypt

philosophy a theory or set of values by which one lives; the search for wisdom and knowledge

physical of or related to natural science

plebeian in the Roman Republic, one of the common people

pictograph a symbol that stands for an object

pilgrimage a journey to a holy place

plateau a flat area of land that is elevated, or raised, above the land around it

plot a secret plan made for a specific purpose, to bring about a certain outcome

polytheism the belief that there are many gods

portion a part of a larger whole

prediction a guess as to what will happen in the future

prehistoric before written history

principle a strong belief on the right way to act

professional someone who is trained in a particular career

project a planned undertaking

promote to help something grow or prosper

prosperity a situation of wealth and success

Protestant any member of a Christian church founded on the principles of the Reformation

province a territory that is part of a country or an empire

publish something that is written and distributed

Punic Wars a series of wars fought between Rome and Carthage for control of the Mediterranean

pursue to follow; as in a goal or purpose

Q

Qin Shihuangdi the first emperor to rule a united China, from 221 to 210 B.C.E.

R

Ramses II an ancient Egyptian pharaoh, known as "Ramses the Great"; skilled as a military leader; and responsible for building many monuments, including the temple at Abu Simbel

rectangular having the shape of a rectangle

reform to improve a system or organization

region a part or section of a country

reign the period of time someone rules, usually royalty

reincarnation the belief that a person's soul is reborn into a new body after death

reject to refuse to have or accept

release to let go of something being held

reluctant to have hesitation or an unwillingness to do something

rely to depend on something or someone

Renaissance a great flowering of culture based on classical Greek and Roman ideas that began in Italy around 1300 and spread throughout Europe

republic a form of government in which leaders are elected to represent the people

require to have to do something based on a rule or command

researcher someone who searches for information on a particular subject

resource something that can be used to fulfill a need

Resurrection in Christian belief, Jesus's rise from the dead

reveal to show something that had been hidden

reverse to act or decide in a way that is the opposite of what has been established

revolt a violent action in opposition of a government or law

rigid stiff; unable to bend

ritual relating to a ceremony, such as a religious ceremony

role a position based on socially expected behavior

Roman Catholic Church a Christian church headed by the pope in Rome

Rome the capital city of the Roman civilization, founded about 700 B.C.E.

rule of law the idea that people should live according to a set of agreed-upon laws

S

sacrament a sacred rite, or ritual, of Christian churches

salvation being saved from sin; in Christianity, to be specifically saved by Jesus, the source of salvation

Sanskrit an ancient Indian language

scribe a person who writes

seek to actively search for something or someone

select to choose from a group, based on a liking for one over another

Senate a group of 300 men elected to govern Rome

series a number of like things ordered one after another

Shang dynasty one of the first Chinese dynasties, ruled from 1700 to 1122 B.C.E.

sibling a brother or sister

siege a military blockade and attack on a city to force it to surrender

Silk Road a network of trade routes that stretched for more than four thousand miles across Asia

silt fine particles of rock

skeleton the bones that make up the body of a person or animal

slavery the state of a person who is treated as the property of another

social class a group in a society that is ranked by factors such as wealth, property, and rights

social pyramid a pyramid outline showing the positions of social classes according to their status in a society

social structure the way a civilization is organized

Socrates a great ancient Greek philosopher who taught by asking his students thought-provoking questions

source the place or point where something starts

Sparta a city-state of ancient Greece, known for its military oligarchy

specific exact and detailed

standardize to make the same

status importance

Stoicism a philosophy that flourished in ancient Greece and Rome and that focused on developing virtue, self-control, and courage as a way to achieve happiness

strategy a planned approach

stress to place importance on something

structure something that has been built

subcontinent a large landmass that is smaller than a continent

superior better; in rank or quality

supreme the highest ruling level

survive to live through a difficult experience

suspend to hang something in the air from a single point of support

Sumer an area in southern Mesopotamia, where cities first appeared

symbol a character or picture that is used to represent something else

symbolize to use a character or picture to represent something else

T

Talmud the collection of ancient Jewish writings, or commentaries, that interpret the laws and teachings of the Hebrew Bible, or Tanakh

technique a skilled way of doing something

technology the use of tools and other inventions for practical purposes

temporary for a limited time

Ten Commandments ten laws and teachings said to have been given to Moses by God

texture the characteristics of an object's surface that can be identified by feeling or viewing it

theory a proposed explanation for something

Tigris River one of the two largest rivers in Southwest Asia that flow from mountains in Turkey to the Persian Gulf

topography the shape and elevation of surface features, such as mountains or deserts, of a place or region

Torah Judaism's most sacred text, consisting of the first five books of the Hebrew Bible

trait a special feature or characteristic

trade the business of buying and selling or exchanging items

trade route a network of roads along which traders traveled

tradition an inherited or customary pattern of thought, action, or behavior

transfer to move from one person or place to another

transform to change in appearance or character

transport to move goods or people from one place to another

treaty a written agreement by which two or more states agree to peaceful relations

tribune an official of Rome elected by plebeians to represent them

tributary a stream or river that feeds into a larger stream, river, or lake

tribute wealth sent from one country or ruler to another as a sign that the other is superior

Trinity in Christianity, the unity of the Father, Son, and Holy Spirit as three beings in one God

triumphal arch a large monument in the shape of an arch that celebrates a leader or a military victory

tyranny a government in which absolute ruling power is held by a person who is not a lawful king

U

ultimate something that cannot be outdone

unify to join together

unique one of a kind

V

vast a very large area

Vedas a collection of ancient writings viewed as sacred by many Hindus

vegetation the plants of a place or region

veto to refuse to approve proposals of government

vision the idea someone has for the way something should be

volume the amount of space an object fills

W

widespread spread out over a large area or among many people

X

Xerxes son of Darius, and ruler of Persia from 486 to 465 B.C.E.; eventually defeated by the Greeks at the end of the Persian wars

Y

Yavneh an ancient city in Israel that became a center for Jewish learning

yin and yang the Daoist concept of opposing forces of nature

Z

Zhou dynasty a line of rulers in China, from about 1045 to 256 B.C.E.

ziggurat an ancient Mesopotamian temple tower with outside staircases and a shrine at the top

Index

Standard of Ur, 44–45
Stele of the Vultures, 38
steles, 38, 57–58
Sumerian, 45, 53
of Tutankhaten, 78–79, 86
from Ur, 42
Zhou dynasty, 222–223,
226–231
Artemis, Greek goddess, 305c
artisans, **48**
about, 92, 100–101
ironworkers, 108, 190, 246, 248
metalworkers, 48, 51, 190
sculptors, 307, 343
Shang dynasty, 216
stone carvers, 100
weavers, 59
arts and culture, 51, 82–83
Aryabhata, 191
Aryans, 160
ascetic, **172**–173, 178
Ashoka, King of India, 177–181,
178
Ashoka Chakra (Wheel of Law),
180
Asia Minor, 269, 274, 296, 314–
315, 353, 355
assembly, **280**–281
Assembly of Athens, 285
Assembly of Sparta, 289
Assyrian Empire, 55m, 60–61,
60m, 107, 121
astronomy, 63, 186, 191, 252, 324
Athena, Greek goddess, 266–267,
305c, 307, 310
Athens, **284**
about, 283–284
economy, 286
education, 287
forms of government, 280–281,
285
gods and goddesses, 305c, 323
Golden Age, 302–311
homes and public spaces, 304
maps, 284m

military training, 287
Peloponnesian War, 313–314
Persian wars, 297–300, 304
physical geography, 284
slaves, 288
women, 288
atrium, 371
Augustus, Caesar, Emperor of
Rome, 355, **362,** 380, 398
Australopithecus afarensis, 15
authority, 81
axis, 191

B

Babylonian Empire, 55m, 58–59,
58m, 62, 121, 124
bacteriophages, 144
Bangladesh, 133
baptism, **390**
barbarians, 241
Baths of Carcalla, 338–339
Battle of Mailvian, 377
Battle of Marathon, 297–298
Battle of Plataea, 300
Battle of Salamis, 299–300
Battle of Thermopylae, 298, 304
Bay of Bengal, 133, 144
Beijing, China, 241, 327
Beijing man, 209
ben Zaccai, Yohanan, 126–127
Bethlehem, 380, 392
Bhagavata Gita, 187
Bhagavata Purana, 187
Bhutan, 133
bibles
Christian, 377, 379–383
Hebrew, 111–112, 118–119,
122–123
biology, **325**–326
bipeds, 15
Birla Temple (Laxminarayan
Temple), 162
Black Sea, 274, 355
Bodhi (Enlightenment) tree, 173
Brahma, Hindu god, 163

Brahmanism, **160**–163
Brahmaputra River, 133, 136
Brahmins, 165, 167, 171
Brinkmann, Vinzenz, 328–331
Britain, 355
bronze, **214**–216, 220
Brutus, Lucius Junius, Roman
leader, 347–348
Buckley, Stephen, 86
Buddha, 169–174, **170,** 182–183,
189
Buddhism, **174**
about, 133, 169
in China, 262
Eightfold Path, 174–175
Four Noble Truths, 174–175
in Mauryan Empire, 177,
179–181, 181m
monks, 169
Siddhartha, Prince (Buddha),
169–175
values of, 180
building and construction, 34,
341
bulla, 369
bureaucracy, **247**
burial practices, 96–97, 214,
238–239
bust, 89
Byzantine Empire, **397**
Byzantium, 397

C

Caesar, Julius, 355, **360**–361
calendars, 402
Caligula, Emperor of Rome, 368
camels, 258
Canaan, 62, 69, 71, **76**–77, 76m,
111–113, 117–118. *See also*
Israel and Israelite (Hebrew)
people
capability, **15**
capital, **57**
caravan, **258**
Carter, Howard, 86–89

Correlations

California History Social Science Standards, Sixth Grade

Standards	Where Standards Are Addressed
6.1 Students describe what is known through archaeological studies of the early physical and cultural development of humankind from the Paleolithic era to the agricultural revolution.	
1. Describe the hunter-gatherer societies, including the development of tools and the use of fire.	pp. 15-23
2. Identify the locations of human communities that populated the major regions of the world and describe how humans adapted to a variety of environments.	pp. 22, 25–31, 33–39 Online Resources: Ch. 3 Enrichment Essay
3. Discuss the climatic changes and human modifications of the physical environment that gave rise to the domestication of plants and animals and new sources of clothing and shelter.	pp. 25–31, 33–39 Online Resources: Ch. 3 Enrichment Essay
6.2 Students analyze the geographic, political, economic, religious, and social structures of the early civilizations of Mesopotamia, Egypt, and Kush.	
1. Locate and describe the major river systems and discuss the physical settings that supported permanent settlement and early civilizations.	pp. 33–36, 71–77
2. Trace the development of agricultural techniques that permitted the production of economic surplus and the emergence of cities as centers of culture and power.	pp. 27–31, 34–39, 46–47, 61
3. Understand the relationship between religion and the social and political order in Mesopotamia and Egypt.	pp. 50–51, 57, 58, 61, 80, 81, 91–97
4. Know the significance of Hammurabi's Code.	pp. 58–59 Online Resources: Ch. 6 Primary Sources
5. Discuss the main features of Egyptian art and architecture.	pp. 80–85, 100–101
6. Describe the role of Egyptian trade in the eastern Mediterranean and Nile valley.	pp. 80, 83, 106 Online Resources: Ch. 8 Enrichment Essay
7. Understand the significance of Queen Hatshepsut and Ramses the Great.	pp. 83, 84–85
8. Identify the location of the Kush civilization and describe its political, commercial, and cultural relations with Egypt.	pp. 105–109
9. Trace the evolution of language and its written forms.	pp. 43, 53, 57, 98–99, 108 Online Resources: Ch. 5 Literature

Correlations **457**

Standards	Where Standards Are Addressed
6.3 Students analyze the geographic, political, economic, religious, and social structures of the Ancient Hebrews.	
1. Describe the origins and significance of Judaism as the first monotheistic religion based on the concept of one God who sets down moral laws for humanity.	pp. 111–115, 117, 122–123
2. Identify the sources of the ethical teachings and central beliefs of Judaism (the Hebrew Bible, the Commentaries): belief in God, observance of law, practice of the concepts of righteousness and justice, and importance of study; and describe how the ideas of the Hebrew traditions are reflected in the moral and ethical traditions of Western civilization.	pp. 111–115, 117, 122–123, 127
3. Explain the significance of Abraham, Moses, Naomi, Ruth, David, and Yohanan ben Zaccai in the development of the Jewish religion.	pp. 111–119, 126–127 Online Resources: Ch. 11 Biographies
4. Discuss the locations of the settlements and movements of Hebrew peoples, including the Exodus and their movement to and from Egypt, and outline the significance of the Exodus to the Jewish and other people.	pp. 112–119, 121, 124–127 Online Resources: Ch. 12 Primary Sources
5. Discuss how Judaism survived and developed despite the continuing dispersion of much of the Jewish population from Jerusalem and the rest of Israel after the destruction of the second Temple in A.D. 70.	pp. 126–127
6.4 Students analyze the geographic, political, economic, religious, and social structures of the early civilizations of Ancient Greece.	
1. Discuss the connections between geography and the development of city-states in the region of the Aegean Sea, including patterns of trade and commerce among Greek city-states and within the wider Mediterranean region.	pp. 271–275, 277, 283–284, 286, 290, 293
2. Trace the transition from tyranny and oligarchy to early democratic forms of government and back to dictatorship in ancient Greece, including the significance of the invention of the idea of citizenship (e.g., from *Pericles' Funeral Oration*).	pp. 277–281 Online Resources: Ch. 29 Biographies (Pericles)
3. State the key differences between Athenian, or direct, democracy and representative democracy.	pp. 280, 285, 322
4. Explain the significance of Greek mythology to the everyday life of people in the region and how Greek literature continues to permeate our literature and language today, drawing from Greek mythology and epics, such as Homer's *Iliad* and *Odyssey,* and from *Aesop's Fables*.	pp. 305–307, 308, 311, 322, 326 Online Resources: Ch. 31 Literature (Aesop); Enrichment Essay
5. Outline the founding, expansion, and political organization of the Persian Empire.	pp. 124, 296–297
6. Compare and contrast life in Athens and Sparta, with emphasis on their roles in the Persian and Peloponnesian wars.	pp. 283–293, 295–301

Standards	Where Standards Are Addressed
7. Trace the rise of Alexander the Great and the spread of Greek culture eastward and into Egypt.	pp. 290–319
8. Describe the enduring contributions of important Greek figures in the arts and sciences (e.g., Hypatia, Socrates, Plato, Aristotle, Euclid, Thucydides).	pp. 309–310, 321–327 Online Resources: Ch. 29 Biographies (Plato); Ch. 31 Literature (Sappho); Enrichment Essay
6.5 Students analyze the geographic, political, economic, religious, and social structures of the early civilizations of India.	
1. Locate and describe the major river system and discuss the physical setting that supported the rise of this civilization.	pp. 136, 138, 141, 142–143, 144
2. Discuss the significance of the Aryan invasions.	p. 160 Online Resources: Ch. 15 Enrichment Essay
3. Explain the major beliefs and practices of Brahmanism in India and how they evolved into early Hinduism.	pp. 160–163
4. Outline the social structure of the caste system.	p. 161
5. Know the life and moral teachings of the Buddha and how Buddhism spread in India, Ceylon, and Central Asia.	pp. 169–175, 179. 180, 181
6. Describe the growth of the Maurya empire and the political and moral achievements of the emperor Asoka.	pp. 177–181
7. Discuss important aesthetic and intellectual traditions (e.g., Sanskrit literature, including the *Bhagavad Gita;* medicine; metallurgy; and mathematics, including Hindu-Arabic numerals and the zero).	pp. 183, 185–191 Online Resources: Ch. 15 Biographies; Literature; Ch. 18 Enrichment Essay
6.6 Students analyze the geographic, political, economic, religious, and social structures of the early civilizations of China.	
1. Locate and describe the origins of Chinese civilization in the Huang-He Valley during the Shang Dynasty.	pp. 209, 213-221
2. Explain the geographic features of China that made governance and the spread of ideas and goods difficult and served to isolate the country from the rest of the world.	pp. 201–211
3. Know about the life of Confucius and the fundamental teachings of Confucianism and Daoism.	pp. 223, 226–227, 228–229 Online Resources: Ch. 21 Primary Sources
4. Identify the political and cultural problems prevalent in the time of Confucius and how he sought to solve them.	pp. 223–227

Standards	Where Standards Are Addressed
5. List the policies and achievements of the emperor Shi Huangdi in unifying northern China under the Qin Dynasty.	pp. 233–239, 240–241
6. Detail the political contributions of the Han Dynasty to the development of the imperial bureaucratic state and the expansion of the empire.	pp. 245–247 Online Resources: Ch. 23 Biographies
7. Cite the significance of the trans-Eurasian "silk roads" in the period of the Han Dynasty and Roman Empire and their locations.	pp. 255–263
8. Describe the diffusion of Buddhism northward to China during the Han Dynasty.	p. 262
6.7 Students analyze the geographic, political, economic, religious, and social structures during the development of Rome.	
1. Identify the location and describe the rise of the Roman Republic, including the importance of such mythical and historical figures as Aeneas, Romulus and Remus, Cincinnatus, Julius Caesar, and Cicero.	pp. 339, 347–351, 353–361 Online Resources: Ch. 34 Primary Sources
2. Describe the government of the Roman Republic and its significance (e.g., written constitution and tripartite government, checks and balances, civic duty).	pp. 348–351
3. Identify the location of and the political and geographic reasons for the growth of Roman territories and expansion of the empire, including how the empire fostered economic growth through the use of currency and trade routes.	pp. 352–363 Online Resources: Ch. 34 Enrichment Essay
4. Discuss the influence of Julius Caesar and Augustus in Rome's transition from republic to empire.	pp. 355, 360–363
5. Trace the migration of Jews around the Mediterranean region and the effects of their conflict with the Romans, including the Romans' restrictions on their right to live in Jerusalem.	pp. 125–127
6. Note the origins of Christianity in the Jewish Messianic prophecies, the life and teachings of Jesus of Nazareth as described in the New Testament, and the contribution of St. Paul the Apostle to the definition and spread of Christian beliefs (e.g., belief in the Trinity, resurrection, salvation).	pp. 377–385, 387–393 Online Resources: Ch. 36 Literature, Ch. 36 Enrichment Essay
7. Describe the circumstances that led to the spread of Christianity in Europe and other Roman territories.	pp. 377, 382–385
8. Discuss the legacies of Roman art and architecture, technology and science, literature, language, and law.	pp. 395, 398–405 Online Resources: Ch. 38 Literature

Historical and Social Science Analysis Skills

Chronological and Spatial Thinking

1. Students explain how major events are related to one another in time.

2. Students construct various time lines of key events, people, and periods of the historical era they are studying.

3. Students use a variety of maps and documents to identify physical and cultural features of neighborhoods, cities, states, and countries and to explain the historical migration of people, expansion and disintegration of empires, and the growth of economic systems.

Historical Research, Evidence, and Point of View

1. Students frame questions that can be answered by historical study and research.

2. Students distinguish fact from opinion in historical narratives and stories.

3. Students distinguish relevant from irrelevant information, essential from incidental information, and verifiable from unverifiable information in historical narratives and stories.

4. Students assess the credibility of primary and secondary sources and draw sound conclusions from them.

5. Students detect the different historical points of view on historical events and determine the context in which the historical statements were made (the questions asked, sources used, author's perspectives).

Historical Interpretation

1. Students explain the central issues and problems from the past, placing people and events in a matrix of time and place.

2. Students understand and distinguish cause, effect, sequence, and correlation in historical events, including the long- and short-term causal relations.

3. Students explain the sources of historical continuity and how the combination of ideas and events explains the emergence of new patterns.

4. Students recognize the role of chance, oversight, and error in history.

5. Students recognize that interpretations of history are subject to change as new information is uncovered.

6. Students interpret basic indicators of economic performance and conduct cost-benefit analyses of economic and political issues.

Notes

Chapter 6
59: Hammurabi, in James Bennett Pritchard, *Ancient Near Eastern Texts Relating to the Old Testament* (Princeton: Princeton University Press, 1950). **63:** Babylonians, in H. W. F. Saggs, *Everyday Life in Babylonia & Assyria* (New York: Putnam, 1965).

Chapter 9
94: Anonymous, in Miriam Lichtheim, *Ancient Egyptian Literature: The New Kingdom,* Vol. 2 (Berkeley: University of California Press, 2006). **98:** Anonymous, in Pierre Montet, *Everyday Life in the Days of Ramesses the Great,* trans. A.R. Maxwell-Hyslop and Margaret S. Drower (Philadelphia: University of Pennsylvania Press, 1981).

Chapter 13
144: Ram Surat Das, in John Chalmers, "India's Ganges, a Holy River of Pollution," *Planet Ark, Jan. 14, 2001, at www.planetark.com.* **146:** Veer Bhadra Mishra, in Mian Ridge, "Holy Man, Secular Plan: Clean Up the River Ganges," *The Christian Science Monitor,* July 23, 2008, at www.csmonitor.com. **147:** Ibid. Ibid.

Chapter 21
227: Confucius, in William Theodore De Bary, et al., eds., in *Sources of Chinese Tradition* (New York: Columbia University Press, 1964). **228:** Laozi, in Herrlee Glessner Creel, *Chinese Thought from Confucius to Mao Tsê-tung* (Chicago: University of Chicago Press, 1953). **229:** Laozi, in Joseph A. Magno, *The Spiritual Philosophy of the Tao Te Ching* (Chicago: Pendragon Pub., 2004). **230:** Han Feizi, in Fei Han, *Han Feizi: Basic Writings, trans. Burton Watson* (New York: Columbia University Press, 2003).

Chapter 31
329: Euripides, in "Gods in Color Opens at Liebieghas Skulpturensammlung," *artdaily.org,* at www.artdaily.com. **330:** *Time,* in Matthew Gurewitsch, *"True Colors," Smithsonian,* July 2008, at www.smithsonianmag.com

Chapter 33
349: Livy, *The History of Rome,* trans. Valerie M. Warrior (Indianapolis, IN: Hackett Pub., 2006). **351:** Cicero, at www.quotationspage.com.

Chapter 34
362: Caesar Augustus, at www.quotationsbooks.com.

Chapter 35
367: Baldus de Ubaldis, in Joseph Canning, *The Political Thought of Baldus de Ubaldis* (New York: Cambridge University Press, 1987).

Photographs

Chapter 36
376: RF/Dreamstime **377:** Corbis/SuperStock **379:** © Lebrecht Music & Arts/Corbis COLLECTION **381:** The Granger Collection, New York **382:** © Scala/Art Resource, NY **383:** © Erich Lessing/Art Resource, NY **384:** Baptism of Constantine I (270-337) (oil on canvas), Puget, Pierre (1620-94)/Musee des Beaux-Arts, Marseille, France/The Bridgeman Art Library

Chapter 37
386: © RF/Michele Falzone/Alamy **387:** © Wally McNamee/CORBIS **388:** All Saints Church, Tarpon Springs, FL **389:** © RF/GFC Collection/Alamy **390:** Blend Images /SuperStock **391L:** fnalphotos From Portugal/123RF **391R:** RF/Marc Dietrich From Germany/123RF **392:** © Douglas Peebles/CORBIS **393:** AP Photo/Oded Balilty

Chapter 38
394: © RF/ Tim Mainiero/Alamy **395:** RF/PHOTOS.COM **396:** © Collection of the New-York Historical Society, USA/The Bridgeman Art Library **398L:**© Bettmann/CORBIS **398R:** Smithsonian American Art Museum, Washington, DC. **399:** © Jim Zuckerman/Corbis **400:** © RF/Karl Risely/Alamy **401TL:** RF/Goran Bogicevic/Shutterstock **401TR:** RF/Zoran Karapancev/Shutterstock **401BR:** © RF/ Stuart Glayzer/Alamy **402:** © Lautaro/Alamy **404:** © RF/TuttItalia/Alamy **406:** Eruption of Vesuvius (gouache on paper) by John Millar Watt (1895-1975) Private Collection/© Look and Learn/The Bridgeman Art Library **407:** RF/Katie Smith Photography/Shutterstock **408T:** RF/Comstock/Fotosearch **408B:** RF/Shutterstock **409:** RF/Jupiter Images/Getty

Resource Opener
412–413: RF/20207851/Shutterstock

Art

Chapter 2
14: Susan Jaekel **16:** Susan Jaekel **18:** Susan Jaekel **20:** Susan Jaekel **22:** Susan Jaekel

Chapter 3
28–29: Renate Lohmann

Chapter 9
92: Len Ebert

Chapter 16
175: Doug Roy

Chapter 20
214: Renate Lohmann
218: Len Ebert

Chapter 21
223–224: Len Ebert

Chapter 26
277: Len Ebert

Chapter 33
351: Len Ebert

Luke Wilson 23

Luke Wilson 23